EVIDENCE-BASED SKILLS IN CRIMINAL JUSTICE

International research on supporting rehabilitation and desistance

Edited by Pamela Ugwudike, Peter Raynor
and Jill Annison

First published in Great Britain in 2019 by

Policy Press
University of Bristol
1-9 Old Park Hill
Bristol
BS2 8BB
UK
t: +44 (0)117 954 5940
pp-info@bristol.ac.uk
www.policypress.co.uk

North America office:
Policy Press
c/o The University of Chicago Press
1427 East 60th Street
Chicago, IL 60637, USA
t: +1 773 702 7700
f: +1 773-702-9756
sales@press.uchicago.edu
www.press.uchicago.edu

© Policy Press 2019

British Library Cataloguing in Publication Data
A catalogue record for this book is available from the British Library

Library of Congress Cataloging-in-Publication Data
A catalog record for this book has been requested

978-1-4473-3301-2 paperback
978-1-4473-3296-1 hardback
978-1-4473-3297-8 ePdf
978-1-4473-3298-5 ePub
978-1-4473-3299-2 Mobi

The rights of Pamela Ugwudike, Peter Raynor and Jill Annison to be identified as editors of this work has been asserted by them in accordance with the Copyright, Designs and Patents Act 1988.

Cover design by Qube Design Associates, Bristol
Front cover image: istock
Printed and bound in Great Britain by CPI Group (UK) Ltd, Croydon, CR0 4YY
Policy Press uses environmentally responsible print partners

Contents

Contents

List of tables and figures

Tables

Figures

Notes on contributors

Jill Annison is associate professor in criminal justice studies at Plymouth University, UK. Her career as a practitioner, in teaching and as a researcher, has focused on women offenders.

Tim Auburn is associate professor in psychology at Plymouth University, UK. His research centres on discursive psychology and social interaction, particularly in relation to institutional contexts such as the criminal justice system.

Ester Blay is a senior lecturer at the University of Girona, Spain. She teaches penology and other criminal justice-related courses both at an undergraduate and master's level. After a PhD dissertation on community service orders, her research has focused on judicial decision making, community sentences and the culture and practices of the professionals involved in their implementation.

James Bonta received his PhD in clinical psychology in 1979. He began his career as the chief psychologist at a maximum security remand centre before joining, in 1990, Public Safety Canada where he was Director of Corrections Research until his retirement in 2015. He is a Fellow of the Canadian Psychological Association, a recipient of the Criminal Justice Section's Career Contribution Award for 2009, the Queen Elizabeth II Diamond Jubilee Medal, 2012, the Maud Booth Correctional Services Award (2015) and the 2015 Community Corrections Award, International Corrections and Prisons Association. His latest publication includes a book co-authored with the late D.A. Andrews entitled *The Psychology of Criminal Conduct*, now in its sixth edition. He is also a co-author of the Level of Service offender risk-need classification instruments that have been translated into six languages and are used by correctional systems throughout the world.

Guy Bourgon is a clinical psychologist specialising in correctional and criminal justice psychology. He has over 25 years of clinical experience in the assessment and treatment of adults and youths involved in the criminal justice system. Dr Bourgon has been dedicated to the development and implementation of empirically validated correctional services. He has published numerous articles on effective correctional treatment services and has extensive international experience in the training and supervision of front-line correctional professionals, helping facilitate the transfer and implementation of empirical knowledge to everyday practice. As co-lead for the Strategic Training Initiative in Community Supervision (STICS), an empirically supported and internationally recognised best-practice model of community supervision, he is recognised for translating Risk–Need–Responsivity principles into useful and practical concepts, skills and techniques that promote client engagement and facilitate prosocial change.

Johan Boxstaens worked as a prison-based social worker before entering into academia in 2006. Since then he has been working as a lecturer and researcher in the Department of Social Work at the Karel de Grote University College, Belgium, and the Department of Sociology, University of Antwerp, Belgium. His research focuses on social work practice in general and on criminal justice social work in particular.

Lol Burke is a reader in criminal justice at Liverpool John Moores University, UK. He has published widely on probation policy and practice and between 2007 and 2016 was editor of *Probation Journal*. His most recent research projects have been on the impact of the Transforming Rehabilitation reforms on the culture of probation and the effectiveness of the new Through the Gate provisions for short-term prisoners in England and Wales. He is co-author (with George Mair) of *Redemption, Rehabilitation and Risk Management* (2012, Routledge) and (with Steve Collett) *Delivering Rehabilitation: The Politics, Governance and Control of Probation* (2015, Routledge).

Ioan Durnescu is a professor in the Faculty of Sociology and Social Work at the University of Bucharest, Romania. He teaches and conducts research in the area of probation and prison. His special interest is comparative probation. Ioan Durnescu is also co-editor of the *European Journal of Probation*. He is also a member of a number of prestigious organisations such as the Confederation of European Probation and the European Society of Criminology.

Pauline Durrance is currently a freelance researcher. Her research career started at UCL working as a research psychologist investigating the long-term psychological impact of HIV infection and AIDS. She joined London Probation in 1996 as an in-house researcher. Since then she has worked extensively on designing and carrying out evaluations of practice. Her particular interests are the needs of BAME and women offenders.

Martine Evans (aka Herzog-Evans) (PhD) teaches law and criminology at Reims University, France. Her majors are criminal law, sentences, probation, prisons and re-entry. Her latest books are *Droit de l'exécution des peines (Sentences' implementation law)* (Dalloz, 2017)), and *Offender release and supervision: The role of courts and the use of discretion* (Wolf Legal Publishers, 2015). She has consulted with the French National Assembly, the Senate, the law commission of the National Assembly, the National Human Rights Commission (Prime Minister's services), and the French Prison Services and worked for the Council of Europe as a co-redactor of the Recommendation CM/Rec(2012)12. She has been an expert for the development of the Bobigny Drug Court, and has been the leading expert for the development of a Paris-based treatment programme for violent extremists.

Andrew Fowler is a senior lecturer in criminology at Sheffield Hallam University and is a former probation officer. He has worked in various roles, from probation service officer, to probation officer and practice tutor assessor. He currently teaches on the Community Justice Learning programme. His background and current role shape his research interest in effective probation practice.

Daniel Gilling is head of the School of Law, Criminology and Government at Plymouth University, UK. His research interests include criminal justice policymaking and implementation, as well as partnership working within the criminal justice system.

Gisella Hanley Santos is a lecturer in criminology and criminal justice studies at Plymouth University, UK. She has conducted research in different countries, being interested in aspects relating to desistance from crime.

Nigel Hosking is a senior probation officer with the London Community Rehabilitation Company (CRC). He qualified as a probation officer in 1983 and has worked in most probation settings. He has a background in offending behaviour programmes as a facilitator, trainer and programme designer. He was seconded to the National Offender Management Service Offender Engagement Programme in 2010 where he contributed to the development of a national skills training programme for practitioners – Skills for Effective Engagement, Development and Supervision (SEEDS). Following the success of SEEDS in England and Wales, he delivered SEEDS training to probation officers in Romania as part of a European Union-funded programme to test the potential for transferring training models to other member states. He is currently responsible for service user involvement for the London CRC. He has received two Butler Trust commendations – one in 2011, and the other in 2016.

Kimberly R. Kras is an assistant professor in the School of Criminology and Justice Studies at the University of Massachusetts Lowell, US. Dr Kras gained her PhD in criminology and criminal justice from the University of Missouri-St. Louis in 2014. Her work centres on the study of community corrections, re-entry and desistance from offending behaviour, and utilises both quantitative and qualitative methodologies. Dr Kras' research considers how desistance occurs from both the offenders' and community corrections agents' perspectives, as well as how these individual-level perceptions influence and are influenced by meso- and macro-level factors. Dr Kras' work has been published in *Criminology & Public Policy*, the *Journal of Criminal Justice* and the *Journal of Drug Issues*.

Shannon Magnuson is a doctoral student in criminology, law and society and a Graduate Research Assistant at the Center for Advancing Correctional Excellence (ACE!) at George Mason University, US. Magnuson earned her master's degree at John Jay College of Criminal Justice. She is an aspiring mixed-methods researcher with current projects using qualitative in-depth interviews and observations as well as survey data with prison and probation/ parole agencies. Currently, her main projects involve translation and implementation of research evidence in practice. Her research interests include organisational change, corrections, process evaluation and translational criminology.

Kimberly S. Meyer is a doctoral student in criminology, law and society and a graduate research assistant at ACE!, George Mason University, US. She gained a master's degree in public administration and studied education before beginning her work in criminology. Her research uses a mix of qualitative (interview and ethnography) and quantitative methods to examine juveniles' experiences as they enter, endure and exit the justice system. She enjoys partnering with agencies to help advance the use of evidence-based practices and promote effective implementation among street-level workers such as probation officers. Agency partnerships to date have examined the disproportionate use of probation violations with Black and

Hispanic juvenile probationers and the effect of probation violations on continued delinquency for teenaged juvenile probationers.

Matthew Millings is a senior lecturer in criminal justice at Liverpool John Moores University, UK. He has published and has project leadership experience of funded research in the fields (among others) of developing evidence-based practice within policing; implementing organisational change within devolved probation services; and exploring innovative community-based and problem-solving orientated criminal justice interventions.

Gemma Morgan is a lecturer in criminology at Swansea University, UK. Her research predominately focuses on evidence-based youth justice policy and practice. She has been involved in research projects that examine how the principles of effective practice are implemented into youth justice practices, as well as the barriers to successful implementation.

Charlene Pereira works as a research assistant with the Monash University Criminal Justice Research Consortium, Australia, and holds the position of clinical supervisor with the Professional Supervision and Coaching Centre in Victoria, Australia. She provides external clinical supervision to practitioners working with adult and young offenders within the Department of Justice and Court Services Victoria. Her research interests include training, staff supervision, evidence-based practice skills, and case management interventions with offenders. She is currently completing her PhD examining the relationship between the style of professional supervision on the development and implementation of core effective practice skills by practitioners working with offenders.

Jake Phillips is a senior lecturer in criminology at Sheffield Hallam University. His research primarily focuses on the relationship between probation policy and practice, explored through an ethnography of probation practice as well as a study of emotional labour in probation. He also conducts research into processes of desistance and deaths in the criminal justice system.

Peter Raynor is a former probation officer and qualified social worker, now emeritus research professor in criminology and criminal justice at Swansea University, UK, where he has worked since 1975. He has published widely on criminal justice and rehabilitation, and much of his research has concerned the effectiveness and impact of probation services. He is a member of the Correctional Services Accreditation and Advisory Panel for England and Wales, the Academy of Social Sciences, the Royal Society of Arts and several criminological societies.

John Rico is the research manager for MTCNovo, the holding company for the London CRC. A former probation officer in the US, he is currently a doctoral student at Middlesex University.

Gwen Robinson is a reader in criminal justice in the School of Law at the University of Sheffield, UK. Her research focuses on community penalties, offender rehabilitation and restorative justice. She is currently co-chair of the European Society of Criminology Working Group on Community Sanctions. She is co-editor (with Fergus McNeill) of *Community Punishment: European Perspectives* (2016, Routledge).

Danielle S. Rudes is an associate professor of criminology, law and society and the deputy director of ACE!, George Mason University, US. She received her PhD from the University of California, Irvine. Dr Rudes is an expert qualitative researcher whose methods include ethnographic observation, interviews and focus groups. She has over 15 years of experience working with corrections agencies at the federal, state and local county levels including prisons, jails, probation/ parole agencies and problem-solving courts. She is recognised for her work examining how social control organisations and their middle management and street-level workers understand, negotiate, and at times, resist change. Dr Rudes' experience includes working with community corrections agencies during adoption, adaptation and implementation of various workplace practices and reforms, including contingency management (incentives/rewards/sanctions), risk-need assessment instruments and motivational interviewing. Dr Rudes serves as associate editor of the journal *Victims & Offenders* and publishes regularly in journals such as *Criminal Justice and Behavior, Federal Probation, Law & Policy* and *Justice Quarterly*. She is also the 2012 winner of the Teaching Excellence Award and the 2015 Mentoring Excellence Award at George Mason University.

Tanya Rugge is a senior research adviser in the Corrections and Criminal Justice Research Unit at Public Safety Canada. Over the years she has interviewed numerous offenders and victims, conducted risk assessments, worked with female offenders in clinical settings, conducted research on recidivism, high-risk offenders, young offenders and Aboriginal corrections, and evaluated several restorative justice programmes as well as community supervision practices. She has been involved with the STICS since its inception in 2006.

Joanna Shapland is the Edward Bramley Professor of Criminal Justice and director of the Centre for Criminological Research at the University of Sheffield, UK. Her research interests span desistance, victimology, restorative justice and probation. She recently brought together experts in desistance worldwide to produce *Global perspectives on desistance: Reviewing what we know, looking to the future* (edited by Joanna Shapland, Stephen Farrall and Anthony Bottoms, 2016, Routledge), and directed the evaluation of the SEED initiative for training experienced probation staff.

Angela Sorsby is a lecturer in criminology in the School of Law at the University of Sheffield, UK. She has researched across a number of areas of criminology, including probation, desistance and restorative justice, with a focus on developing evidence-based criminal justice practices and policies. She played a major role in evaluating the SEED initiative in both England and Romania.

Faye S. Taxman, PhD, is a university professor in the Department of Criminology, Law and Society at George Mason University, where she is also Director of the Center for Advancing Correctional Excellence. She is recognised for her work in the development of systems-of-care models that link the criminal justice system with other service delivery systems, as well as her work in re-engineering probation and parole supervision services and in organisational change models. She has published more than 180 articles and is the co-editor of *Health & Justice*. In 2017 she received the Joan McCord Award from the Division of Experimental Criminology.

Heather Toronjo is a research assistant at ACE! and a graduate student in the Department of Criminology, Law and Society at George Mason University, US. She received her BA in anthropology from Texas A&M University in College Station, Texas and her master's of public policy from George Mason's Schar School of Policy and Government. Her research interests include corrections workforce professional development, desistance and narrative criminology, and social learning theory. Her current work centres around curriculum development for criminal justice workers and partnering with practitioners to implement evidence-based supervision models.

Chris Trotter is professor in social work at Monash University, Australia, and director of the Monash Criminal Justice Research Consortium. He worked for many years as a practitioner and manager in child protection and corrections prior to his appointment to Monash University. He has undertaken many research projects and published widely on the subject of effective practice with involuntary clients. He has an international reputation for his work, particularly in relation to prosocial modelling, and his book *Working with Involuntary Clients*, now in its third edition, has sold widely around the world and is published in German, Japanese and Chinese translation.

Pamela Ugwudike is associate professor in criminology at the University of Southampton, UK. Her research focuses on evidence-based criminal justice policy and practice and she has led research projects that have explored how to embed research evidence in real-world youth justice, probation and prison practice. Her research projects have been funded by the Welsh Government, the Youth Justice Board, the National Probation Service, and the Prison Advice and Care Trust. Dr Ugwudike's publications focus mainly on criminal justice research and her recent texts include: *What Works in Offender Compliance: International Perspectives and Evidence-Based Practice* (2013), co-edited with Professor Peter Raynor published internationally by Palgrave Macmillan, and the *Routledge Companion to Rehabilitation in Criminal Justice* (forthcoming 2018), which is an internationally published text co-edited with Professors Peter Raynor, Fergus McNeill, Faye Taxman and Chris Trotter, and Dr Hannah Graham. Dr Ugwudike sits on several professional and allied committees, for example the British Society of Criminology's Executive Committee, the Offender Health Research Network in Wales, and the Howard League for Penal Reform's Research Advisory Committee.

Maurice Vanstone has been a probation officer, manager, researcher and academic. He is emeritus professor of criminology at Swansea University, UK. His research and writing has focused mainly on probation-related topics, in particular the effectiveness of community sentences and the history of probation practice and theory.

Chalen Westaby is a senior lecturer in law at Sheffield Hallam University whose work centres on the empirical analysis of various aspects of emotional labour. His interest in the concept began when he studied immigration solicitors and the production of emotional labour in their everyday work. He then received funding from the Legal

Education Research Network to complete a study of the impact of law clinics on law students' perceptions of emotional labour. Most recently he has been part of a team studying probation practice through the lens of emotional labour.

Patrick Williams is a senior lecturer in criminology at Manchester Metropolitan University. He is concerned with the enduring nature of racialised disparities within the CJS and is particularly concerned to identity the specific processes and practice that result in unequal outcomes for BAME people. Working with a number of local and national VCS and campaign organisations, he is an independent advisory to the Young review and has made contributions to the recent Lammy review.

Part 1: Contextualising practice: key theoretical, organisational and policy developments

---

ONE

Introduction: Effective practice skills: new directions in research

Pamela Ugwudike, Peter Raynor and Jill Annison

This edited collection brings together international research on evidence-based skills for working with people who are subject to penal supervision or other interventions in the justice system. The text focuses on skills-based practices that are empirically linked to rehabilitation and desistance from crime. The term 'skills' is multidimensional. But broadly conceptualised, the term refers to the proficiencies, capabilities and other attributes that contribute to positive outcomes such as active service-user engagement with supervision objectives, rehabilitation and desistance. We recognise that the term 'desistance' is also multidimensional and as Maruna and LeBel (2010, p 72) rightly note: 'There is no single "desistance theory" any more than there can be said to be a single theory of crime or of poverty.' While some desistance scholars highlight the role of agency in achieving desistance, some emphasise structural factors, and others emphasise the relevance of agential factors constrained by wider structural forces (see generally Giordano et al, 2003; Ugwudike, 2016).

That said, Maruna (2004) offers a useful conceptualisation of desistance as being characterised by primary desistance and secondary desistance. The former refers to a hiatus in a criminal career. According to Maruna (2004), individuals involved in offending inevitably undergo this hiatus at some point, or indeed, at various periods of their offending career. By contrast, secondary desistance is permanent desistance and it involves a transition from primary desistance (a temporary break from offending) to a permanent break from offending that is accompanied by adaptation to a prosocial self-identity – the 'role of identity of a "changed person"' (Maruna, 2004, p 274). This definition very much suggests that desistance is at best viewed as a process. The issue of whether or not criminal justice practitioners who supervise people undertaking court orders can contribute to the process of secondary desistance is perhaps open to question given the widely accepted view that most people involved in offending behaviour eventually desist from offending as they approach maturation and attain turning points in their lives (Thorpe et al, 1980; Sampson and Laub, 1993; Rutherford, 1986).

However, insights from the desistance literature indicate that practitioners can contribute to the process, or as some suggest, facilitate 'assisted desistance' (King, 2014). As Ugwudike (2016) observes, Farrall's (2002a) longitudinal study of the impact of probation supervision on desistance found that probation practitioners can sow 'seeds' of desistance that germinate or are 'fully realised' long after the end of an order (see also Farrall et al, 2014, p 290). Furthermore, it has been suggested that practitioners can contribute to the maturation process by working with service users to help them improve their social networks and personal competencies (McNeill, 2014). Maruna and LeBel (2010, p 76) also argue quite persuasively that practitioners can encourage secondary desistance by deploying delabelling strategies such as positive reinforcements in the form of praise and rewards. They note that 'desistance may be best facilitated when the desisting person's change in behaviour is recognised by others and reflected back to him in a "delabeling process"'. In their view, a Pygmalion effect occurs whereby desisters adapt their self-identity and behaviour to the expectations of others, performing highly if others expect them to do so, and vice versa. Importantly, Maruna (2004) observes that the role of practitioners is crucial because delabelling strategies that are initiated by family members and informal sources of social control are perhaps not as valued or appreciated as those that originate from the formal sources of control that initiated the labelling process. He notes that 'delabeling might be most potent when coming from "on high", particularly official sources like treatment professionals ... rather than from family members or friends' (Maruna, 2004, p 275). He also acknowledges that the Risk-Need-Responsivity (RNR) literature provides guides on how this might be achieved, remarking that 'the "what works" principles for evidence-based correctional practice suggests that positive reinforcement should outweigh punishments by a 4:1 ratio' (Maruna, 2004, p 274).

The past few years have seen the emergence of a growing corpus of international research on one-to-one skills (including delabelling skills). These skills are theoretically informed *and* empirically linked to positive outcomes such as enhanced engagement during supervision and reductions in rates of reconviction (see for example, Sorsby et al, 2013; Raynor et al, 2014; Taxman, 2014; Ugwudike et al, 2014; Trotter et al, 2015; Bonta and Andrews, 2017). The skills incorporate key elements that can support rehabilitation and the processes desistance scholars identify as vital for secondary desistance. Examples of these elements include delabelling using positive reinforcements (Maruna, 2004), building good working relationships (Burnett and McNeill, 2005), improving service users' human capital by equipping them will problem social skills and competencies (McNeill, 2014), offering advocacy and brokerage services that put service users in touch with relevant social welfare services (Farrall, 2004; McNeill, 2014) and employing a client-centred approach that respects service users' autonomy and agency while improving their self-efficacy (see generally McNeill and Whyte, 2007).

It appears that what is needed is a text that brings together the emerging research literature on these skills in one volume, which is what this text achieves. As such, the text is broad in scope; it provides theoretical and empirical insights derived from different models of rehabilitation (such as the RNR and desistance models), from diverse jurisdictions, and from a range of criminal justice settings including probation supervision settings and youth justice practice contexts. The text also comprises chapters on approaches to working with diverse groups such as ethnic minority service users and women to effect long-term positive change. Much of the existing research on supervision practice focuses on practices involving adult male service users. By incorporating chapters that explore evidence-based skills for working with diverse groups, this text addresses a key gap in knowledge. To ensure that it provides a contextualised account of effective supervision skills and practices, the edited collection also explores the organisational and wider policy contexts that might affect the implementation of effective skills and practices. As such, the text offers a good balance of theoretical and empirical insights alongside organisational and policy-related issues.

Reflecting the text's international character, there are contributions from a strong international team of scholars based in jurisdictions such as Australia, Canada, the United States, England, Wales, Romania, Belgium and Spain. Some of the contributors have led recent scholarship in the field of effective skills for working with service users in prison, probation and youth justice settings. Some are also renowned for their contributions to criminal justice research, policy and practice across the world. Contributions from these and other respected scholars from diverse jurisdictions demonstrate the book's wide-ranging coverage and relevance.

Indeed, this book grows out of the work of an international network of researchers, practitioners, policymakers and others interested in evidence-based supervision practice. The network is known as the

Collaboration of Researchers for the Effective Development of Offender Supervision (CREDOS). Members of CREDOS have, over the years, worked hard to promote international knowledge transfer and the network was founded in 2007 after discussions at the European Society of Criminology conference in Tübingen in 2006. The initial suggestion came from Chris Trotter after a presentation on his research in Australia (Trotter and Evans, 2012) and one from Peter Raynor about the skills research that was planned in Jersey, which later became the Jersey Supervision Skills Study (Raynor et al, 2014; Ugwudike et al, 2014). Further discussion with Fergus McNeill led to contacts with other interested researchers and a plan to launch a research network.

The initial organisers of CREDOS were Fergus McNeill, Peter Raynor and Chris Trotter, and the first conference was organised in Prato in Italy, where Chris Trotter was able to arrange use of Monash University's European Centre. This first conference was attended by a mixture of academics and practitioners from several different countries, and this has been a continuing feature of the network's activity. Regular conferences have taken place in locations as diverse as Australia, Lithuania and the US, and the research done by members has appeared in several books and a large number of articles. The original Prato conference of 2007, as well as deciding the name of the organisation, produced a statement of aims about the kind of research we intended to carry out and encourage.

At that time, research on the effectiveness of work with offenders was dominated by evaluations of programmes and by meta-analyses that aimed to draw out broader principles of effective practice. Although most work with people under supervision was in fact carried out through one-to-one contact rather than in groups, less research had been done on such individual work, and CREDOS members were interested in filling this gap.

Some were mainly interested in how relationships with supervisors such as probation staff might help to promote desistance, while others were more focused on the detail of what practitioners were actually doing and what impact it might have. The statement of aims approved at the first conference is worth quoting in full, to see how far it has stood the test of time and how far the current volume still reflects it:

> CREDOS is an international network of researchers, and policy and practice partners in research, who share a common interest in the effective development of offender

supervision. We believe that this interest requires us to engage in high quality, collaborative and comparative research and scholarship exploring:

- How best to measure effectiveness in offender supervision.
- The nature and features of effective offender supervision.
- The characteristics, styles and practices of effective offender supervisors.
- The qualities and features of effective relationships between offenders and those that work with them.
- The social, political, cultural, organisational and professional contexts of effective offender supervision and how these contexts impact upon it.

In pursuing this agenda, CREDOS is committed to:

- Pursuing our research agenda through a diverse range of research methods, recognising that methodological pluralism is necessary to yield the insights required to move policy and practice forward.
- Undertaking collaborative and comparative research wherever possible, so that lessons can be learned about what works in specific national and local contexts and about whether and to what extent there are practices in and approaches to offender supervision that work across diverse contexts.
- Exploring issues of diversity amongst offenders in relation to effective supervision.
- Working to engage offenders and their families in the research process, recognizing the value and importance of their insights into effective practice and what works for them. (McNeill et al, 2010, pp 2–3)

Papers based on work discussed at the early CREDOS conferences were published in the edited collection *Offender Supervision: New Directions in Theory, Research and Practice* (McNeill et al, 2010), which contains a mixture of theoretical work, policy discussion and empirical studies. Chapter Three of the current volume discusses some of these differences in approaches to research. The next book to be explicitly identified with CREDOS was *Understanding Penal Practice* (Durnescu and McNeill, 2014), which contains reports on several studies, including the Jersey supervision skills research discussed at the European conference in 2006. The work of CREDOS has also benefited from close contact and overlapping membership with other organisations, particularly the European Society of Criminology's working group on community sanctions and measures, and the network of European researchers brought together in a research group on offender supervision in Europe funded by the European Community's Cooperation in Science and Technology programme. Books produced from these groups (for example, McNeill and Beyens, 2013; Robinson and McNeill, 2016) have contributed a great deal to our understanding of the topics addressed by CREDOS, and other publications have involved its members and methods (for example, Ugwudike and Raynor, 2013). CREDOS is distinguished from the European organisations by its pattern of membership, which is worldwide but almost entirely from Anglophone countries.

The idea of the current book grew out of discussion at the CREDOS meeting in Porto in 2015. That meeting also marked a change in the leadership of the network, Fergus McNeill and Peter Raynor having passed their organising roles on to Pamela Ugwudike and Jill Annison, with Chris Trotter continuing to organise CREDOS activities in Australia and the wider Pacific region, and Faye Taxman overseeing the network's agenda in North America. The editorial team for this book reflects the energy and enthusiasm of the new organisers, plus some continuity from the original team.

One issue first noted in the introduction to *Offender Supervision*, and still unresolved, is the use of the term 'offender', which implies a continuing offending identity, when the activities we are describing and studying are explicitly intended to promote the opposite, namely desistance and the development of non-offending identities. We are very conscious of this problem of labelling; on the other hand, there is still no generally recognised alternative that is readily understood. 'Service user' will work in some contexts, but is often inaccurate, and also applies to other users of public services; 'people under criminal justice supervision' and similar formulations are cumbersome and do not necessarily avoid labelling.

We are very pleased that we have been successful in attracting a distinguished international group of contributors to this book. The contributors are a mixture of academics and practitioners, including some who have moved between these roles. The variety and vigour of research represented in this volume allow us to continue to be optimistic about the future of this kind of work. Our intention is to provide an up-to-date and comprehensive guide to the current state of research on effective supervision skills in criminal justice contexts around the world. We seek to assemble theoretical and empirical evidence that should support principled policymaking.

The 'new criminology' of the late 1960s was dismissive of so-called 'administrative criminologists' (Young, 1988). These were researchers who were concerned with how to improve policy and make services more effective. They were seen as uncritical, and as accepting the official view of crimes and criminals without question. This criticism was always oversimplified: for example, the development of diversion in the youth justice system by applied criminologists and practitioners depended clearly on a critical understanding that labelling and processing behaviour as a crime was a social process that could be modified (Thorpe et al, 1980; Rutherford, 1986). It now seems that roles have changed. In a post-truth world where policies can be developed and implemented on the basis of no evidence at all, driven by ideology and by perceptions of political advantage, systematic empirical evaluation has acquired critical force and is part of the rational opposition to irrational policies. In other words, 'administrative criminology' now has a critical edge, and better evaluation can inform better practice. We hope that readers will find plenty of examples in this book, and that research in this field will continue to grow and to deliver results that are useful to service providers and service users alike.

The book comprises three sections. Part 1 sets the scene and focuses mainly on the key issues affecting the development of skills research. This section begins with the current chapter, which describes the developments that provided the impetus for this text. A key development is the dearth of empirical insights into evidence-based skills despite the importance of these skills to effective practice and outcomes. Maurice Vanstone extends the discussion in Chapter Two, which focuses on probation practice and locates the paucity of research on evidence-based skills within the historical and contemporary developments that have transformed probation practice. The chapter describes the ways in which probation services in England and Wales, currently swamped with a deluge of policy upheavals, could develop, sustain and apply evidence-based skills.

In Chapter Three, Peter Raynor extends these themes by mapping the trajectory of evaluation research in Britain, from the focus on identifying the outcomes or impacts of probation to the more recent emphasis on studying the previously ignored contents of one-to-one supervision or uncovering what has been described elsewhere as the 'black box' of supervision (Bonta et al, 2008). This shift from studying impact to illuminating process reflects the evolution of the 'what works' or RNR model. It could be argued that the shift is also in part attributable to insights from other models of rehabilitation, namely the desistance and good lives models (see, Maruna, 2001, 2004; Maruna and LeBel, 2010; Ward and Maruna, 2007; Ward and Fortune, 2013). Together, these models suggest that processual dimensions of supervision such as the quality of supervision relationships and interactions can affect outcomes for adult service users (see for example, Burnett and McNeill, 2005) and young people (Barry, 2009, 2010; Gray, 2013). In the chapter, Peter Raynor emphasises the importance of evaluating services to identify and promote evidence-based skills, but argues that policy developments in England and Wales have triggered a retrograde step towards 'evidence-free' policymaking. The latter, he argues, is in turn reflective of regrettable international developments that have culminated in the emergence of a post-truth world.

In Chapter Four, Lol Burke and colleagues maintain the focus on policy developments that impair evidence-based practice. They draw attention to the difficulty of achieving constructive practice within an unfavourable policy climate. Chapter Five also focuses on the nexus of organisational contexts and effective practice. Drawing on research conducted within probation settings in the United States, the authors focus on organisational issues and examine the impact of managerial culture on the effective implementation of evidence-based practice.

Part 2 comprises eight chapters and focuses on the international research literature on evidence-based supervision skills. Empirical accounts of the ways in which supervision skills affect practice and outcomes are covered extensively and the chapters present the findings of studies conducted in different jurisdictions including Australia, North America (Canada and the United States) and Europe (England and Wales, Spain, Belgium and Romania).

In the first chapter of this section, Martine Herzog-Evans provides a theoretical account of several models of evidence-based supervision skills and practices, including the RNR, desistance and Good Lives models. The chapter explores the models' principles by engaging extensively with the key conflicts, debates, attacks and counter-attacks that have characterised exchanges between key proponents of the models. The chapter's objective is to explore how the unifying themes that underpin the models (and other legal models) can be integrated into an overarching theoretical model of effective practice.

The next chapter by Ester Blay and Johan Boxstaens moves away from the focus on theoretical issues and presents the findings of a comparative study that observed probation practitioners in Belgium and Spain, to assess the skills they use to build relationships with service users during the first interview. Issues and complexities that explain some of the differences observed in the jurisdictions are also highlighted, alongside an insightful analysis of the nature of good working relationships. Ioan Durnescu continues the discussion about the importance of relationship skills and other evidence-based skills, in Chapter Eight. The chapter presents the findings of a research study which, similar to that described in the previous chapter, observed probation practitioners (this time in Romania) to assess the use of evidence-based practices identified by the desistance literature as crucial for engaging service users and encouraging secondary desistance. Chapters Six to Eight draw attention to areas of good practice but also identify gaps in the implementation of evidence-based supervision skills.

In Chapter Nine, which focuses on the processes of training staff on how to deploy evidence-based skills effectively, Jim Bonta and colleagues provide a detailed analysis of the Strategic Training Initiative in Community Supervision (STICS) model. The latter is an innovative model and indeed the first model that was created to train probation practitioners on how to apply the evidence-based RNR principles of rehabilitation during one-to-one supervision. The authors describe the initial evaluation of STICS, further international research on the model, and complexities that could accompany efforts to generalise the model.

Angela Sorsby and colleagues also focus on the importance of staff development and training, in Chapter Ten. They present the findings of the Skills for Effective Engagement and Development (SEED)[1] programme, which drew on the STICS model (described in Chapter Nine) and was introduced in England and piloted in 2011–12. The programme was designed to train probation staff on how to deploy evidence-based, one-to-one supervision skills associated with service-user engagement. In their study, Sorsby and colleagues explored the programme's impact by assessing differences in outcomes achieved by SEED-trained practitioners and a control group of other practitioners in England and Romania. The objective was to assess links between staff training on evidence-based skills and outcomes such as service-user engagement. In Chapter Eleven, which also addresses the nexus of staff training and the application of evidence-based supervision skills, Heather Toronjo and Faye S. Taxman provide a comprehensive account of the range of staff training models that have emerged across the United States and Canada. They also critically evaluate the different models.

Chapter Twelve also addresses the issue of effective supervision skills, but deviates from the focus on core correctional practices and staff training models. It explores, instead, emotional skills, and in the chapter, Andrew Fowler and colleagues discuss a study of the emotional labour practitioners invest in supervision relationships. The authors describe emotional labour as an effective practice skill that deserves more organisational attention and support than it currently receives. They call for staff development policies that recognise the important role of emotional labour in enhancing the application of evidence-based skills and the quality of supervision practice.

Continuing the discussion about staff development and the application of evidence-based practice skills in Chapter Thirteen, which is the final chapter in Part 2, Charlene Pereira and Chris Trotter present the findings of a systematic review of the literature on supervisory practices for supporting criminal justice staff. Their findings indicate that supervisory practices motivated by a performance management agenda could undermine reflective practice, skills development and service-user engagement.

The final section of the text brings to the fore typically under-researched aspects of front-line practice, particularly the nature and content of practice involving women, black and minority ethnic (BME) groups and young people. Opening the section, Pamela Ugwudike and Gemma Morgan provide an empirical account of front-line supervision skills in Welsh youth justice settings. They identify gaps between practice and research evidence, and conclude with a discussion of how best to bridge the gaps. In Chapter Fifteen, Chris Trotter continues the discussion about skills and practices within youth justice settings. The chapter adds an international dimension by focusing on practices in Australia. In this chapter, Chris Trotter highlights the benefits of training youth justice staff on evidence-based skills and the challenges of implementing the skills in an adverse organisational context.

The next chapter, by Nigel Hosking and John Rico, brings to the fore the potential contributions of a previously marginalised group in criminal justice practice and research, namely ex-service users. The chapter describes an evaluation project that examined the benefits and pitfalls of recruiting ex-service-users to work with people undertaking probation orders. Several benefits were identified and a key finding was that the ex-service users communicated and interacted effectively with the service users they were supervising and were, as such, able to contribute to service-user engagement and long-term desistance. In Chapter Seventeen, Chris Trotter assesses useful strategies for involving yet another overlooked group in the work that is done to encourage rehabilitation and desistance. Focusing on the role of young people's families in youth justice settings, the chapter explores the importance of engaging this group as part of a holistic effort to reduce youth offending.

Chapter Eighteen, by Patrick Williams and Pauline Durrance, follows the theme set by the previous chapters in this section; it identifies practices that are useful for working with other typically marginalised groups, namely Black and Minority Ethnic Groups. Still on the theme of highlighting effective practices with groups that have long been marginalised from effective practice debates and research, Chapter Nineteen, by Jill Annison and colleagues, explores the experiences of women. The chapter presents the findings of a research study that assessed the operation of a community justice court which was established to enhance the responsivity of sentencing decisions. The court was expected to pursue a gender-responsive agenda based on women's needs, and uphold therapeutic justice principles by diverting women accused of low-level offences to relevant services. In this chapter, the authors describe the practical, procedural, operational and other issues that undermined the court's therapeutic orientation and gender-responsiveness.

In the final chapter, the editors draw on the key themes covered by the preceding chapters to summarise the international research on evidence-based skills in criminal justice. The chapter also locates the key themes within the contexts of the organisational factors, policy conditions, and other issues that affect the deployment of evidence-based skills. Finally, the chapter demonstrates the broad significance of evidence-based skills in criminal justice settings.

Note

[1] The pilot project, which ran between spring 2011 and spring 2012, was named SEED (Skills for Effective Engagement and Development). SEED subsequently became known as SEEDS (Skills for Effective Engagement, Development and Supervision) when it was later offered to other probation trusts, which had not formed part of the original pilot. The change of name was made with the aim of emphasising the link between SEED and the Reflective Supervision Model (RSM) which, like SEED, formed part of the Offender Engagement Programme (OEP).

References

Barry, M. (2009) 'Promoting desistance among young people', in W. Taylor, R. Earle and R. Hester (eds) *Youth Justice Handbook: Theory, Policy and Practice*, Cullompton: Willan, pp 15–16.

Barry, M. (2010) 'Youth transitions: from offending to desistance', *Journal of Youth Studies*, 13(1): 121–136.

Bonta, J. and Andrews, D.A. (2017) *The Psychology of Criminal Conduct* (6th edn), New York, NY: Routledge.

Bonta J., Rugge T., Scott T.-L., Bourgon, G. and Yessine, A.K. (2008) 'Exploring the black box of community supervision', *Journal of Offender Rehabilitation*, 47(3): 248–270.

Burnett, R. and McNeill, F. (2005) 'The place of officer-offender relationship in assisting offenders to desist from crime', *Probation Journal*, 52(3): 221–242.

Durnescu, I. and McNeill, F. (eds) (2014) *Understanding Penal Practice*, Abingdon: Routledge.

Farrall, S. (2002a) *Rethinking What Works with Offenders: Probation, Social Context and Desistance From Crime*, Cullompton: Willan.

Farrall, S. (2002b) 'Long-term absence from probation: officers' and probationers' accounts', *Howard Journal of Criminal Justice*, 41(3): 263–278.

Farrall, S. (2004) 'Supervision, motivation and social context: what matters most when probationers desist?', in G. Mair (ed) *What Matters in Probation*, Cullompton: Willan, pp 187–209.

Farrall, S., Hunter, B., Sharpe, G. and Calverley, A. (2014) *Criminal Careers in Transition: The Social Context of Desistance from Crime*, Oxford: Oxford University Press.

Giordano, P.C., Cernkovich, S.A. and Holland, D.D. (2003) 'Changes in friendship relations over the life course: implications for desistance from crime', *Criminology*, 41(2): 293–328.

Gray, P. (2013) *Report of Research on Youth Offending Team Partnerships and Social Context of Youth Crime*, Plymouth: Plymouth University.

King, S. (2014) *Desistance Transitions and the Impact of Probation*, Abingdon: Routledge.

Maruna, S. (2001) *Making Good: How Ex-Convicts Reform and Rebuild their Lives*, Washington, DC: American Psychological Association Books.

Maruna, S. (2004) 'Pygmalion in the reintegration process: desistance from crime through the looking flass,' *Psychology, Crime and Law*, 10(3): 271–281.

Maruna, S. and LeBel, T.P. (2010) 'The desistance paradigm in correctional practice: from programmes to lives', in F. McNeill, P. Raynor and C. Trotter (eds) *Offender Supervision: New Directions in Theory, Research and Practice*, Cullompton: Willan.

McNeill, F. (2014) 'Changing lives, changing work: social work and criminal justice,' in I. Durnescu and F. McNeill (eds) *Understanding Penal Practice*, Abingdon: Routledge, pp 167–178.

McNeill, F. and Beyens, K. (eds) (2013) *Offender Supervision in Europe*, Basingstoke: Palgrave Macmillan.

McNeill, F. and Whyte, B. (2007) *Reducing Reoffending: Social Work and Community Justice in Scotland*, Cullompton: Willan.

McNeill, F., Raynor, P. and Trotter, C. (eds) (2010) *Offender Supervision: New Directions in Theory, Research and Practice*, Cullompton: Willan.

Raynor, P., Ugwudike, P. and Vanstone, M. (2014) 'The impact of skills in probation work: a reconviction study', *Criminology and Criminal Justice*, 14(2): 235–249.

Robinson, G. and McNeill, F. (eds) (2016) *Community Punishment: European Perspectives*, Abingdon: Routledge.

Rutherford, A. (1986) *Growing Out of Crime*, Harmondsworth: Penguin.

Sampson, R. and Laub, J. (1993) *Crime in the Making: Pathways and Turning Points Through Life*, Cambridge, MA: Harvard University Press.

Sorsby, A., Shapland, J., Farrall, S., McNeill, F., Priede, C. and Robinson, G. (2013) *Probation Staff Views of the Skills for Effective Engagement Development (SEED) Project*, Sheffield: Centre for Criminological Research, available at http://shef.ac.uk/polopoly_fs/1.293093!/file/probation-staff-views-seed.pdf (accessed April 2014).

Taxman, F.S. (2014) 'Second generation of RNR: the importance of systemic responsivity in expanding core principles of responsivity', *Federal Probation*, 78(2): 32–40.

Thorpe, D.H., Smith, D., Green, C.J. and Paley, J. (1980) *Out of Care*, London: Allen & Unwin.

Trotter, C. and Evans, P. (2012) 'Analysis of supervision skills in youth probation', *Australian and New Zealand Journal of Criminology*, 45(2): 255–273.

Trotter, C., Evans, P. and Baidawi, S. (2015) 'Effectiveness of challenging skills in work with young offenders', *International Journal of Offender Therapy and Comparative Criminal Justice*, 61(4): 397–412.

Ugwudike, P. (2016) 'The dynamics of service user participation and compliance in community justice settings', *Howard Journal of Crime and Justice*, 55(4): 455–477.

Ugwudike, P. and Raynor, P. (2013) *What Works in Offender Compliance: International Perspectives and Evidence-Based Practice*, Basingstoke: Palgrave.

Ugwudike, P., Raynor, P. and Vanstone, M. (2014) 'Supervision skills and practices: the Jersey study', in I. Durnescu and F. McNeill (eds) *Understanding Penal Practice*, Routledge.

Ward, T. and Fortune, C. (2013) 'The Good Lives model: aligning risk reduction with promoting offenders' personal goals', *European Journal of Probation*, 5(2): 29–46.

Ward, T. and Maruna, S. (2007) *Rehabilitation: Key Ideas in Criminology*, Abingdon: Routledge.

Young, J. (1988) 'Radical criminology in Britain: the emergence of a competing paradigm', *British Journal of Criminology*, 28(2): 159–183.

TWO

The effective practice of staff development in England and Wales: learning from history and contemporary research

Maurice Vanstone

Introduction

At the time of writing this chapter, the probation service in England and Wales is much reduced, a substantial amount of its traditional work now transferred to private sector community rehabilitation companies. It may not survive (Mair, 2016) but now, part of the civil service and confined to the oversight of people classified as being at high risk of reoffending, more than ever it needs innovative and effective practice in order to continue its unique contribution to the rehabilitation of people who have offended. Current evidence-based theory indicates that cessation of offending, whether classified as primary or secondary desistance (Maruna and Farrall, 2004), is a process involving a complex array of factors that include the strengthening of social bonds through changes in identity and motivation at significant junctures in life (Farrall and Calverley, 2006). Professional interventions designed to contribute effectively to that process need to be founded on skills, knowledge and qualities pertinent to helping the individual through change and transitions; these include elements such as resilience, engagement, commitment, motivation, assessment and relationship building, as well as awareness of issues around diversity and knowledge of resources. This chapter, therefore, explores how those skills might be best developed, sustained and applied. In so doing, it will describe and critically assess various models of staff development in probation's past and recent history. It comes with two important riders: first, the past is not viewed through the easy critical prism of hindsight, but rather seen as part of a contribution to more recent developments; and second, skills are recognised as just one facet of effective practice to be placed alongside what might be described as first-level requirements, namely, relevant human qualities and life experience. It is with some reflection on the latter that the chapter begins.

Canned laughter

Truax and Carkhuff's (1967) much-referenced validation of the role of non-possessive warmth (unconditional caring and respect), empathy, genuineness and concreteness in effective helping, important and accepted as it is, has almost become a cliché. More interesting and relevant to the particular focus of this chapter is what these authors have to say about training people to communicate these qualities. Persuasively, they argue that 'making the communication of these ingredients a genuine communication of real aspects of the therapist himself requires an equally important experiential development' (Truax and Carkhuff, 1967, p 221), which, they might have added, can derive not only from the process of training but also life experience itself. The logic flowing from their insight is that by itself the theoretical teaching of the skill of communicating empathy (for example) is likely to lead to what they describe as 'canned' empathy, as bogus as the superimposed laughter in television sitcoms. Hence, teaching and supervision need to encompass a fusion of theory and personal growth and development. While acknowledging that in the early 1960s evidence of effective training was non-existent, these scholars underscore their proposition with reference to research findings that confirm that experiential and didactic training, as opposed to 'mechanical technique', can engender increases in empathic skill (p 239). In a similar but more idealistic vein, Bruce Hugman (1977, p 2) declared that the:

> ... business of being a good helper is essentially bound up with being a good person, that is to say, thoughtful, generous, sensitive, relatively unselfish, relatively accepting of self, liberated in spirit, tolerant, reliable, acquainted with weakness and inconsistency, caring, committed, purposeful, capable of joy and sadness, and faithful to a belief in the creative humanity of all people.

With some prescience, he covered many of the characteristics of what several years later Chris Trotter (1993) would term prosocial modelling.

Compelling though these arguments are, it is Jimmy Boyle's view from the other side that brings them to life. When considering

Boyle's perspective, it is important to remember that his trajectory from violent criminal to non-offending citizen was linked strongly to, among other things, his love of his mother and his mortification at her funeral about having let her down, education, an acceptance of his own agenda for self-reform, and the realisation of a new sense of masculine identity. However, amid these aspects of his story there is a critical turning point in his perception of Barlinnie Unit staff 'helpers', best told in his words:

> It was strange during this period because there was a great amount of hatred in me for all screws, yet some of the unit staff would approach me in a way that was so natural and innocent it made it difficult for me to tell them to fuck off. Something inside of me, despite all the pent up hatred, would tell me there was something genuine within them. (Boyle, 1977, p 237)

It seems reasonable to infer that without those qualities a probation officer becomes what Whitehead (2010, p 89) terms 'a functioning bureaucratic technician', and that professional work interventions in change efforts, however skilled, are likely to fail. Many years ago, Herschel Prins (1975, p 48) asked whether it is necessary to 'produce skilled technicians [or] informed, responsible practitioners': a current and equally important question for the future of staff development strategies of both the probation service and community rehabilitation companies is whether they are mutually exclusive.

All I gotta do is act naturally

Although evidence of specific in-service training and supervision in early approaches to learning and development in the probation service in England and Wales is elusive, interest and desire for improvement of knowledge and the increase in skills (which it was presumed would follow) are obvious, even from a cursory glance at the literature (see, for example, Helmsley, 1930, 1934: Tuckwell, 1931). In fact, two of the first authoritative texts on police court missionary and probation work, by Gamon (1907) and Leeson (1914) respectively, lay great emphasis on the importance of education and training. Clear though commitment to professional improvement was in both, Leeson in particular placed personality and temperament ahead of education and training. Two subsequent probation historians confirm this desire for knowledge, but also track the progress of in-service training and staff development ideas. Bochel (1976) cites a probation officer expressing the general need for post-appointment guidance as early as 1919 and locates a proposal for supervision of staff in the Probation Rules of 1926. It took another 10 years, but the report of the Departmental Committee on the Social Services in the Courts of Summary Jurisdiction recommended first, the appointment of principal probation officers to supplement the supervisory work of the Probation Committee and second, in areas where numbers were small, the provision of an extra allowance for senior probation officers to carry out supervisory duties. The point at which official impetus was given to what was to become casework supervision seems to be when the Morison Committee (Home Office, 1962) recommended that those officers appointed to principal and senior officer roles should have the necessary skills to undertake the task.

Without doubt, the improvement of knowledge to enhance the quality of practice featured prominently in probation service discourse from the 1920s onwards. However, as King (1969) observed, it was not until the 1950s and 1960s that in-service training expanded, pioneered by the Home Office, the National Association of Probation Officers (NAPO), extra-mural studies departments in universities and the Tavistock clinic, who led refresher courses, local discussion groups, seminars and case conferences. Despite this shared desire for a professional knowledge base, it is difficult to escape the conclusion that it was premised on an assumption that all a well-educated, rounded person who kept up with latest trends in psychology had to do was act naturally in order to help people to stop offending. Of course, skill helped too, but it remained an esoteric notion wrapped in the theoretical framework of casework with its underlying (and generally untested) psychological theory. Admittedly, as the century wore on, probation work became more 'scientific', but for most of it practitioners operated within a bubble of acceptance that the application of social and human sciences was, *ipso facto*, effective. The pinprick of research evidence came relatively late.

Method champions and the foundations of evidence-based practice

The Morison Committee's reminder, in the early 1960s, that probation officers, casework-oriented helpers though they might be, were employed by the state to protect the public was, perhaps, a portend of the probation service's later shift from social work help to law enforcement and its inexorable drift towards 'modernisation and cultural transformation' (Whitehead, 2010, 4). Yet, at that point, probation officers were still quite independent and autonomous, accountable largely to the courts and their caseloads, practice was usually unseen, the medical model still predominated, and caseloads were high and soft-loaded (Vanstone and Seymour, 1986). It was not until the later part of that decade and the beginning of the next that there was an expansion of the service, a growth in hierarchy, a larger and more distant higher management, a lessening of autonomy and a greater imposition of organisational constraints on, and scrutiny of, the individual officer, and more complexity of task. Vanstone and Seymour contended that the search for effectiveness through a diverse range of methods was hindered by Schon's (1973) concept of 'dynamic conservatism' and a lack of a critical culture. Whatever the truth of that is, the service did face some acute problems: its philosophy was unclear, its methodology was haphazard, variable and based on eclecticism and random borrowing, and management and practitioners alike had to grapple with rapid change. Practice was conducted largely in private, perhaps with the result that little attention was paid to skill levels and it was 'relatively easy to project an image of professional expertise [with] little grounding in reality' (Vanstone and Seymour, 1986, p 44). According to Vanstone and Seymour, because there was a lingering but persistent assumption that if a probation officer had self-awareness, an accurate understanding of the probationer, and relevant objectives and tasks, effective practice would follow, there was a need for a coherent practice framework, reflective practice and a learning organisation geared to produce 'predictable and desired results' (1986, p 45).

On reflection, Vanstone and Seymour's view of the state of the probation service seems a polemical generalisation, albeit with grains of truth. Even a light cleaning of the canvas reveals a much more complicated picture of innovative practice and practitioners eager for change and experimentation (and for things to work), and much of it linked to the regional staff development units established in 1969. This addition to the service's staff development resources resulted from a recommendation in a Home Office working party report of the mid-1960s on the work of the probation service (Bochel, 1976), and in the early 1970s the established units began to build their repertoire of residential courses. The late Bruce Seymour, the Regional Staff Development Officer (RSDO) for South Wales and the West, informed me that he and his colleague RSDOs were concerned about the lack of influence of research findings and the low level of concern about effectiveness at that time.[1] In his area, discussions led to the setting up of an assistant chief probation officer advisory group, the members of which had the task of assessing needs in their respective areas that were fed back into the process of constructing a programme of in-service training. Some courses focused on specialisms within the service such as hostel work and prison liaison, some on the new developments of community service and day training centres, and others on methods including groupwork, family therapy, Heimler's Scale of Human Functioning, transactional analysis, behaviour modification, psycho-drama, system intervention, social skills, offending behaviour, one-to-one work, and, later on, reasoning and rehabilitation. (In addition, the units played a role in the induction and confirmation year of newly appointed probation officers.) This influx of what officers saw as less esoteric and more tangible methods stimulated a new enthusiasm and, in particular, spawned method champions, believers who took the newly acquired knowledge back into their local areas and spread the word. For example, Bob Anderson (Anderson, 1985) became an advanced trainer and consultant to other practitioners in Neuro-Linguistic Programming, while also using the approach in his day-to-day practice. Often staff development would coalesce around the new methods with the setting up of internal seminars, training events and support groups, and through this the refinement of in-service training, staff development and support systems gathered momentum.

Priestley and colleagues (1978), drawing on their adaption of Canadian life skills work within a Home Office-funded project in Ashwell and Ranby prisons and the Sheffield Day Training Centre, ran social skills and personal problem-solving courses, many of which were under the auspices of the RSDOs. Some of these incorporated social skills development projects, the aim of which was to provide an opportunity for probation officers to create programmes in a variety of settings and to test them out, thus encouraging skills not only in the practice of the approach but also in evaluation (McGuire and Priestley, 1981). This is an interesting example of staff development encompassing basic qualitative research and data recording furthered by cooperative working. This idea that collective resources of the team had more potency to meet the varied and complex needs of probationers led several services to experiment with team approaches in which the probation office itself became a centre for resources (Preston West Team, 1977; Stanley, 1982; Millard, 1989; Sutton, no date). Though not mentioned specifically in the written reports of these projects, staff development is implicit in the sharing and self-reflective ethos of the teams. As Stanley (1982, p 504) explained, the level of trust between members was crucial to the team approach, and regular team reviews in the form of away days played 'an important part in establishing a sense of sense of purpose and direction' and, more relevant to the issue here, 'helped to reveal weaknesses and strengths and helped to highlight training and other resource needs [and identify] unused skills'.

Other team-based innovations – in approaches such as brief and task-centred casework (Dobson, 1976; Vaisey, 1976) and crisis intervention (Harman, 1978) – flourished during this period, alongside experimentation in supervision and staff development. Some were using live supervision in which practice was observed by colleagues via video link (Liddell and Schwartz, 1983), while others put together staff development packs on subjects such as anti-racist practice, groupwork and interviewing skills to be used (according to assessed need) in team-based staff development training sessions (Vanstone, 1987). When he read the *Probation Journal* article describing the latter project, one colleague commented with well-placed irony that he wished he worked in a service like that. That said, however glossy the written representation and patchy the implementation was, it represented an attempt to instil the idea of staff development as integral to a critical, self-reflective, mutually supportive organisational culture. Workers other than probation officers were an integral part of these developments too, and in places like day centres they were more intensely involved in the work and as a result their needs were being given more attention. For example, the Association of Chief Officers of Probation (ACOP) in a review of the service's training requirements acknowledged the fact and recommended 'regular training provisions' both internal and external (ACOP, 1983).

Meanwhile, the more traditional method of staff development – casework supervision by a senior probation officer – continued. Its history is of interest in itself. Dawtry (1958) refers to the 'recent' introduction of supervised casework and the implications of this for the role of the probation case committees and Macrae (1958) to the fact that principal and senior probation officers underwent 10-day courses in the principles and purpose of casework supervision. In another review of training at that time, Newton (1956, p 134) explained that in casework supervision the 'officer is helped to achieve skilled and conscious use of himself and his knowledge' to help probationers change. Facilitative one to one supervision of this kind survived for most of the twentieth century but McWilliams (1987, pp 107–8) argued that the change from a 'professional-supervisory-administrative' to a 'bureaucratic-managerial' model was enabled by the use of supervision to exercise 'control in the pursuit of policy objectives'. Prescient though he was, he may have overestimated the degree of change. Research carried out between 1987 and 1988 with a sample of 457 probation officers focused primarily on qualifying training tells a different story, certainly in relation to what it revealed about the experience of supervision during the first year (when it would be reasonable to assume that it would be given high priority). Supervision varied in style, some structured, some not, but for the majority it was irregular and most senior probation officers 'seemed to be feeding into the idea of probation officers being autonomous professional creatures from an earlier stage of their career' (Boswell et al, 1993, p 65).

Ironically, as is well known now, all of this took place after emerging evidence that should have undermined faith in rehabilitative effort: most things, it seemed, did not work (Lipton et al, 1975; Folkard et al, 1976). As Brody (1976, p 37) put it, probation intervention, however intense or methodologically varied, had 'no predictably beneficial effects'. So why did officers continue to embrace new approaches and methods with enthusiasm, and why did staff development and in-service training encourage and feed that keenness? Perhaps unavoidably, the answer is speculative. First, individual officers had enough anecdotal evidence of probationers who had turned their lives around to inure themselves against negative research findings. For example, an informant in my PhD research recalled the story of a probationer from a very troubled background whom he steered through to the completion of the probation order who called in to see him some years later to inform him that he had done well and settled down, adding:

> You always looked so calm and you were always the same
> and you were always there ... I was bloody fed up of going
> to see people and finding they weren't in ... they had gone
> off on some interview or were away on a course.

He never came before the courts again. Second, the new methods, with greater or lesser justification, came packaged with an effectiveness guarantee so officers may not have fully accepted negative research results. Finally, they were receptive to more tangible ways of helping probationers: they may have grown tired of the esoteric nature of casework – the magic may have worn off – and in contrast staff development focused on new exciting, stimulating and understandable methods to be applied in cooperation with colleagues and in more intense realistic situations with probationers.

So *that's* why you are on probation

The changes to staff development alluded to by McWilliams, including supervision and in-service training, accelerated with the apparent rediscovery of the offence and the growth of evidence-based experimentation; moreover, they triggered an intriguing dichotomy best characterised by, on the one hand, Porporino's (2010) plea for 'sense and sensitivity' and on the other, the political focus on the 'offender' through the prism of punishment in the community – the difference between facilitating as opposed to imposing change (Home Office, 1984, 1988a, 1988b). This may be putting it rather crudely, but it is important, not least because the politically imposed direction probation was to follow would have crucial implications for the shape and nature of staff development in the 21st century.

In practical terms, the kind of staff development in keeping with Porporino's vision is aptly illustrated by reference to an offending behaviour project undertaken in the South East of England (McGuire and Priestley, 1982). In attempting to explore whether officers could focus specifically on offence-related behaviour, they established a staff development exercise, the prime concern of which was to advance the skills and knowledge of the officers (although the whole project was monitored also for the response of the probationer participants). It consisted of a one-week residential introductory course to familiarise the officers with the methods; a six-month period in which the programmes were implemented; data gathering and report writing by the officers; and collating of data and reports combined with a long-term follow-up. Later in the decade, probation services took on the notion of localised research-based work, as, for example, in Somerset where an alcohol education group was evaluated over a three-year period (Singer, 1991), in the West Midlands where offending behaviour groups were run and evaluated between 1983 and 1990 (Davies and Lister, 1992), and in Bristol where the Berkeley sex offenders group was run and evaluated for seven years (Weaver and Fox, 1984). All involved enhancement of staff skills, but two of the larger experiments involving staff development occurred in Mid Glamorgan with the Straight Thinking on Probation (STOP) experiment, in which almost three quarters of those employed in the area were trained in the reasoning and rehabilitation approach (Raynor and Vanstone, 1996; Ross et al, 1988), and more recently in the phased Pathfinder Project, in which prison and probation staff were trained to implement the FOR a change programme with short-term prisoners (Fabiano and Porporino, 2002; Clancy et al, 2006; Lewis et al, 2007).

25

The detail of both does not need repeating here, but these experiments are relevant to this chapter because they offer a template, constructed around focused training, tutor support, audio/video recordings and playback, programme integrity checklists, performance rating and feedback, destined to feature in future exemplars of staff development.

Contemporary models of staff development

The argument that the refinement of staff skills, whether applied in group programmes or individual supervision, should be framed within what is known about effective practice is incontrovertible. However, as reflection on the history described in this chapter confirms, progression of skills should consist of factors both old and new. Until recently, little attention had been paid to the 'characteristics of effective staff or the best staff practices' (Dowden and Andrews, 2004, p 204), nor has there been much of a focus on models of staff development per se. Hence, in order to elicit an outline of what appropriate staff development might look like, it is necessary to draw on aspects of the methodology of effective practice research.

For this purpose, a summary of the main constituents of effectiveness suggested by research so far will suffice. They include the principles of risk, needs and responsivity (Andrews et al, 1990); prosocial factors such as reliability, punctuality, consistency, respect, and acknowledgement and rectification of mistakes (Trotter, 1993); use of legitimate authority, the modelling and reinforcement of crime free attitudes, imparting of problem-solving skills, effective use of community resources, and mutual respectful relationships based on openness, warmth and optimism (Dowden and Andrews, 2004); and the ingredients of motivational interviewing (Fabiano and Porporino, 2002). Their influence is evident in the United Kingdom government's strategy for the unfortunately and atavistically named treatment managers (Home Office, 2002). Among their prescribed responsibilities are monitoring programmes via video recordings, supervision of staff and oversight of the work of tutors. In an update of the original strategy, video monitoring was re-emphasised as a means of ensuring the maintenance of programme integrity and skill enhancement (Home Office, 2005). The practice continues in the National Probation Service and the community rehabilitation companies, using 'dip samples' and (in the language of accountancy) programme auditing. However, it is in a number of studies focused on assessing the work of practitioners and adherence to programmes that a more enticing model of staff development emerges.

Lowenkamp and colleagues (2006), who examined community-based programmes in the state of Ohio involving 3237 people, offer a reminder of the relationship between programme adherence and the effectiveness of programmes in reducing reoffending. They concluded that programme integrity is pivotal to success and, crucially, that it depends on skilled staff applying effectiveness-related skills. What is more, the Staff Training Aimed at Reducing Re-arrest (STARR) programme 'indicated that training can significantly impact strategies used by officers during supervision and that these strategies lead to lower failure rates' (Robinson et al, 2012, p 183). Building on evidence relating to one-to-one work on risk and recidivism, it measured (through an examination of 665 audio tapes) the performance of 88 officers who volunteered from eight districts and were randomly assigned to experimental and control groups (see also Barnoski, 2004).

In drawing on these findings, Clodfelter and colleagues (2016) stress that the change of emphasis from effective programmes to effective practitioners arose from awareness of practitioners' failure to adhere to success principles and the importance of not just teaching skills but reinforcing them. They report on the effort of one district to implement STARR with a particular interest in competency of staff, organisational support and leadership, and the key skills of supervision, namely role clarification, effective reinforcement, problem solving and understanding and teaching the cognitive model. In that district, volunteers were trained in evidence-based practice and some were further trained as tutors. Successful efforts were made to engender a sense of community and trust among officers, who were given booster sessions involving role play and feedback. Audio recordings with tutor feedback were used (two a month until proficiency was reached) and tutors were mentored by an expert trainer. The overall conclusion to the study was that the 'use of STARR skills have become essential to successful supervision' (Clodfelter et al, 2016, p 37) but equally interesting is its depiction of an organisational culture in which there were high levels of trust among staff and strong support and commitment from top management.

Training staff in this way is one thing, but ensuring that learned skills become ingrained and maintained in everyday practice – a problem identified by Raynor and Vanstone (1996) in the STOP experiment in the UK – is another, and this is exactly the challenge that Bourgon and colleagues (2010) addressed in their controlled study of the Strategic Training Initiative in Community Supervision (STICS) in three Canadian provinces. In order to explore how technology is transferred, used and enhanced, 80 volunteer officers were randomly allocated (eventually 33 to STICS and 19 to the control). The STICS programmes consisted of a three-day residential course, monthly clinical supervision meetings, a refresher course and feedback on audio tapes. The general conclusions were that technological transfer processes were associated with improvement in skills and an increased focus on criminogenic needs, and the more that people were involved in technology transfer processes the more skills were increased.

In the Jersey skills study, video recordings of probation officers' one-to-one supervision sessions were scored using a checklist covering seven skill sets (Vanstone [with Raynor], 2012; Raynor et al, 2014). In preparation for the study, care was taken to separate the process of assessment from management and staff development, while nevertheless creating an accurate, user-friendly checklist, informed by the relevant theoretical and empirical literature, which, post-study, could be applied to observation of practice for staff development purposes. If successful, it was thought that this would result in both the process of observing and identifying what have been described as the 'core correctional practice' (CCP) skills and the kind of practice relationships shown to reduce recidivism being applied during routine supervision and the delivery of accredited programmes. The checklist itself is applicable to visual recordings or live situations and to the supervision and assessment of people, so that in staff development activity observers should be able to feedback on practices, methods and skills used, as well as check for consistency with known effectiveness principles. This use of recorded interviews followed by peer discussion and feedback was also central to the training in problem solving, pro-social modelling, empathy, and the risk principle in Chris Trotter's (1993) influential study. His study is best known, perhaps, for the positive effect of prosocial modelling on reconviction rates, but it is also important for its demonstration that officers could be taught to use CCP skills in a short period of time even with a low level of organisational incentives, and for Trotter's conclusion that greater use of the approach would stem from it being seen as 'an integral and expected part' of daily routine (1993, p 58).

Conclusion

It is a contention of this chapter that effectiveness research studies combined with lessons from history provide not just evidence of how to contribute to desistance from crime, but also valuable ideas about staff development policies and strategies both in the public and private sector. Those ideas coalesce around specific training, rehearsal, observation and feedback on either live or recorded performance, refresher training and expert tutoring, but the conversion of these ideas into practice reality is not straightforward and raises a number of challenging issues.

To begin with the obvious, staff development should not be a substitute for qualifying training, but, rather like the meaning of the original French word développer, it should be a case of unfurling and enhancing skills. Put another way, qualifying training should be predicated on skills and qualities that evidence confirms help people to change their lives and resolve their problems. In addition, it should produce self-reflective, critical practitioners who will contribute positively to the learning culture of the organisation they join. That culture is crucial to effective staff development and, as Taxman and Sachwald (2010, p 189) explain, should be underpinned by leadership that proffers a clear, shared vision and mission, positive role models, useable information on professional progress, and a team-oriented approach to tasks involving 'learning, practice, reinforcement, coaching and mentoring with feedback'. This, of course, is the opposite of what Bailey and colleagues (2007, p 124) characterise as 'an instrumental and technocratic rather than educational approach'. It is the difference between what McWilliams (1980, p 4) classified as the mechanistic organisation with its 'impersonality, ascribed roles and rules, rational efficiency, rigid hierarchical structure' and the organic organisation with its 'personal involvement, achievement orientation, adaptive efficiency' lateral as well as top-down communication, and consultation. This kind of organisation needs to eschew formal responsibility and preoccupation with rules and instead promote substantive accountability with an emphasis on personal responsibility. In effect, the choice is between a formalised managerial approach to staff development and a more organic approach that relates performance to evidence but draws on mutual, less hierarchical support systems. The latter has the best chance of facilitating three cornerstone characteristics of an effective probation officer – resilience, commitment and engagement (Argyris and Schon, 1978).

In their examination of the Netherlands' Strengthen Probation Officers Resilience in Europe project, Vogelvang and colleagues (2014) provide useful insights into the process of empowering officers so that they become more resilient in the face of increasing stress levels and role complexity. According to their analysis, the prerequisites of organisational success in this respect are a professional climate encompassing an appropriate management style, clear communication, manageable workloads and assessment of strengths and areas of vulnerability, bolstered by specialist guidance for tutors, personal wellbeing assessments and peer mentoring training. Similar themes can be discerned in Collins' (2016, p 43) examination of the first two years of employment: they include the generation and sustaining of commitment and an emphasis on supervision targeted at 'the practical and emotional needs of officers'. As far as the third characteristic is concerned, Butler and Hermanns (2011) studied the relationship between engagement and experienced professionalism of a sample of Dutch probation officers and identified a high professional ethos based on humanistic values and the nurturing of competency as the most important contributors to high engagement.

No less important is the role of staff development in keeping staff up to date with legislative and policy development, and understanding about the context of people's lives, including diversity, the effects of discrimination and the factors that evidence increasingly links to desistance from crime. As Whitehead (2010, p 41) puts it, agencies and helpers should be pro-humanistic 'and concerned to understand the reality of clients' lives not from the standpoint of the expert practitioner but clients themselves in all their complexity'. In the populist and punitive climate in which criminal justice currently exists, it is easy to forget that effective use of community resources on behalf of people being supervised is an element of effective practice (Dowden and Andrews, 2004), an observation given credence by a survey of 300 intervention plans in the Dutch probation service (Bosker et al, 2013, p 81). The survey reports that 'basic needs such as education and work, finance and accommodation are often not included in the intervention plan, even when they are assessed to be a dynamic criminogenic need'. Findings like this elevate the importance of the traditional advocacy role of the probation officer in attempting to help and encourage probationers to increase their social capital. Indeed, maybe a current challenge for effectiveness research is to make less opaque the link between effective practice theory and overlapping desistance theory.

Finally, most of the effectiveness research summarised in this chapter raises concerns about the transfer of skills honed in experiment-related training and staff development to the daily routine of organisational life. For example, Bourgon and colleagues (2010) found that even with support some target skills diminished and there was a need for more practice, more follow-up and reinforcement. In a similar vein, Clodfelter and colleagues (2016) in their study of STARR highlighted the need to enhance ways of addressing the strain on coaches trying to transfer experimental work to their day-to-day work, especially because a skill such as empathy is more abstract and difficult to give feedback on. Traction is lost, it seems, unless those key components of staff development, training, monitoring and supervision are embedded in the organisational culture and this is dependent more than anything else on the skills, qualities and philosophy of management. Perhaps, that is where staff development should begin.

Note

[1]   In an interview conducted during research for my PhD.

References

ACOP (Association of Chief Officers of Probation) (1983) *Probation Service Training Needs Now*, Unpublished ACOP Training Committee Discussion Document.

Anderson, B. (1985) *The Application of Neuro-Linguistic Programming to the Work of the Probation Service*, Personal Social Services Fellowship, University of Bristol.

Andrews, D,A., Bonta, J. and Hoge, R.D. (1990) 'Classification for effective rehabilitation: rediscovering psychology', *Criminal Justice and Behaviour*, 17(1): 19–52.

Argyris, C. and Schon, D. (1978) *Organizational Learning: A Theory of Action Perspective*, Reading, MA: Addison Wesley.

Bailey, R., Knight, C. and Williams, B. (2007) 'The Probation Service as part of NOMS in England and Wales', in L. Gelsthorpe and R. Morgan (eds) *Handbook of Probation*, Cullompton: Willan, pp 114–130.

Barnoski, R. (2004) *Outcome Evaluation of Washington State's Research-Based Programs for Juvenile Offenders: Appendix*, Olympia, WA: Washington State Institute for Public Policy.

Bochel, D. (1976) *Probation and After-Care: Its Development in England and Wales*, Edinburgh: Scottish Academic Press.

Bosker, J., Witteman, C. and Hermanns, J. (2013) 'Do intervention plans meet criteria for effective practice to reduce recidivism? How probation officers forgot about social capital', *European Journal of Probation*, 5(1): 65–85.

Boswell, G., Davies, M. and Wright, A. (1993) *Contemporary Probation Practice*, Aldershot: Avebury.

Bourgon, G., Bonita, J., Rugge, T. and Gutierrez, L. (2010) 'Technology transfer: the importance of ongoing clinical supervision in translating "what works" to everyday community supervision', in F. McNeill, P. Raynor and C. Trotter (eds) *Offender Supervision: New Directions in Theory, Research and Practice*, Cullompton: Willan, pp 91–112.

Boyle, J. (1977) *A Sense of Freedom*, Basingstoke: Macmillan Pan Books.

Brody, S.R. (1976) *The Effectiveness of Sentencing*, London: HMSO.

Butler, R. and Hermanns, J. (2011) 'Impact of experienced professionalism on professional culture in probation', *European Journal of Probation*, 3(3): 31–42.

Clancy, A., Hudson, K., Maguire, M., Peake, R., Raynor, P., Vanstone, M. and Kynch, J. (2006) *Getting Out and Staying Out: Results of the Prisoner Resettlement Pathfinders*, Bristol: Policy Press.

Clodfelter, T.A., Holcomb, J.E., Alexander, M.A., Marcum, C.D. and Richards, T.N. (2016) 'A case study of the implementation of Staff Training Aimed at Reducing Re-arrest (STARR)', *Federal Probation* (June): 30–38.

Collins, S. (2016) 'Commitment and probation work in England and Wales', *European Journal of Probation*, 8(1): 30–48.

Davies, H. and Lister, M. (1992) *Evaluation of Offending Behaviour Groups*, Birmingham: West Midlands Probation Service.

Dawtry, F. (1958) 'Whither probation', *British Journal of Delinquency*, 111(3): 180–187.

Dobson, G. (1976) 'The differential treatment unit: part one', *Probation Journal*, 23(4): 105–108.

Dowden, C. and Andrews, D.A. (2004) 'The importance of staff practice in delivering effective correctional treatment: a meta-analytical review of core correctional practice', *International Journal of Offender Therapy and Comparative Criminology*, 48(2): 203–214.

Fabiano, E.A. and Porporino, F.J. (2002) *Focus on Resettlement = A Change*, Canada: T 3 Associates.

Farrall, S. and Calverley, A. (2006) *Understanding Desistance from Crime*, Cullompton: Willan.

Folkard, M.S., Smith, D.E. and Smith, D.D. (1976) *IMPACT. Intensive Matched Probation and After-Care Treatment. Volume 11. The Results of the Experiment*, Home Office Research Study 36, London: HMSO.

Gamon, H.R.P. (1907) *The London Police Court: Today and Tomorrow*, London: J.M. Dent.

Harman, J. (1978) 'Crisis intervention (a form of diversion)', *Probation Journal*, 25(4): 115–121.

Hemsley, N. (1930) 'Training facilities for probation officers', *Probation*, 1(5): 77.

Hemsley, N. (1934) 'Probation officers' summer school', *Probation*, 1(21): 328.

Home Office (1962) *Report of the Departmental Committee on the Probation Service (The Morison Report)*, London: Home Office.

Home Office (1984) *Probation Service in England and Wales: Statement of National Objectives and Priorities*, London: Home Office.

Home Office (1988a) *Punishment, Custody and the Community*, London: HMSO.

Home Office (1988b) *Tackling Offending: An Action Plan*, London: Home Office.

Home Office (2002) *Treatment Manager Strategy*, Probation Circular 57/2002, London: Home Office.

Home Office (2005) *Treatment Manager's Video Monitoring Form, Session Review Form and Guidance Notes*, Probation Circular 30/2005, London: Home Office.

Hugman, B. (1977) *Act Natural. A New Sensibility for the Professional Helper*, London: Bedford Square Press.

King, J. (1969) *The Probation and After-Care Service* (3rd edn), London: Butterworth.

Leeson, C. (1914) *The Probation System*, London: P.S. King and Son.

Lewis, S., Maguire, M., Raynor, P., Vanstone, M. and Vennard, J. (2007) 'What works in resettlement? Findings from seven Pathfinders for short-term prisoners in England and Wales', *Criminology and Criminal Justice*, 7(1): 33–53.

Liddell, H.A. and Schwartz, R.C. (1983) 'Live supervision/consultation: conceptual and pragmatic guidelines for family therapy trainers', *Family Process*, 22(4): 477–490.

Lipton, D., Martinson, R. and Wilks, J. (1975) *The Effectiveness of Correctional Treatment*, New York, NY: Praeger.

Lowenkamp, C.T., Latessa, E.J. and Smith, P. (2006) 'Does correctional program quality really matter? The impact of adhering the principles of effective intervention', *Criminology & Public Policy*, 5(3): 575–94.

Macrae, F.J. (1958) 'The English probation training system', *British Journal of Delinquency*, 111(3): 210–215.

Mair, G. (2016) '"A difficult trip, I think": the end days of probation in England and Wales', *European Journal of Probation*, 8(1): 3–15.

Maruna, S. and Farrell, S. (2004) 'Desistance-focused criminal justice policy research: introduction to a special issue on desistance from crime and public policy', *Howard Journal of Crime and Justice*, 43(4): 358–367.

McGuire, J. and Priestley, P. (1981) *A Social Skills Project*, Bristol: Report for the South West Regional Staff Development Office.

McGuire, J. and Priestley, P. (1982) *An Offending Behaviour Project*, London: Report for the South East Regional Staff Development Office.

McWilliams, W. (1980) 'Management models and the bases of management structures', Unpublished notes.

McWilliams, W. (1987) 'Probation, pragmatism and policy', *Howard Journal of Crime and Justice*, 26(2): 97–121.

Millard, D. (1989) 'Looking backwards to the future', *Probation Journal*, 36(1): 18–21.

Newton, G. (1956) 'Trends in probation training', *British Journal of Delinquency*, 11(2), 123–135.

Porporino, F.J. (2010) 'Bringing sense and sensitivity to corrections: from programmes to 'fix' offenders to services to support desistance', in J. Brayford, F. Cowe, and J. Deering (eds) *What Else Works? Creative Work with Offenders*, Cullompton: Willan, pp 61–85.

Preston West Team (1977) 'Putting the sacred cows out to grass', *Probation Journal*, 24(3): 92–96.

Priestley, P., McGuire, J., Flegg, D., Hemsley, V. and Welham, D. (1978) *Social Skills and Personal Problem Solving: A Handbook of Methods*, London: Tavistock.

Prins, H.A. (1975) 'All things to all people', *Probation Journal*, 22(2): 45–9.

Raynor, P. and Vanstone, M. (1996) 'Reasoning and rehabilitation in Britain: the results of the Straight Thinking On Probation programme', *International Journal of Offender Therapy and Comparative Criminology*, 40(4): 279–291.

Raynor, P., Ugwudike, P. and Vanstone, M. (2014) 'The impact of skills in probation work: a reconviction study', *Criminology and Criminal Justice*, 14(2): 235–249.

Robinson, C.R., Lowenkamp, C.T., Holsinger, A.M., VanBenschoten, S., Alexander, M. and Oleson, J.C. (2012) 'A random study of Staff Training Aimed at Reducing Rearrest (STARR): using core correctional practices in probation', *Journal of Crime and Justice*, 35(2): 167–188.

Ross, R.R., Fabiano, E.A. and Ewles, C.D. (1988) 'Reasoning and rehabilitation', *International Journal of Offender Therapy and Comparative Criminology*, 32(1): 29–35.

Schon, D. (1973) *Beyond the Stable State: Public and Private Learning in a Changing Society*, Harmondsworth: Penguin.

Singer, L.R. (1991) 'A non-punitive paradigm for probation practice: some sobering thoughts', *British Journal of Social Work*, 21(6), 611–626.

Stanley, A.R. (1982) 'A new structure for intake and allocation in a field probation unit', *British Journal of Social Work*, 12(5): 487–506.

Sutton, D. (undated) *A New Approach to Probation Supervision*, Unpublished paper.

Taxman, F.S. and Sachwald, J. (2010) 'Managing chaos: implementing evidence-based practice in correctional agencies', in F. McNeill, P. Raynor and C. Trotter (eds) *Offender Supervision: New Directions in Theory, Research and Practice*, Cullompton: Willan, pp 172–192.

Trotter, C. (1993) *The Supervision of Offenders – What Works. A study undertaken in Community Based Corrections, Victoria*, Report to the Australian Criminology Research Council, Melbourne: Monash University and the Victoria Department of Justice.

Truax, C.B. and Carkhuff, R.R. (1967) *Towards Effective Counseling and Psychotherapy: Training and Practice*, New York, NY: Aldine Publishing Company.

Tuckwell, G. (1931) 'The need for a probation library', *Probation*, 1(7): 97–98.

Vaisey, R. (1976) 'The differential treatment unit: part two', *Probation Journal*, 23(4): 108–112.

Vanstone, M. (1987) 'Keeping in professional shape: a collaborative strategy for skill development', *Probation Journal*, 34(4): 132–134.

Vanstone. M. (with Raynor, P). (2012) *Observing Interviewing Skills: A Manual for Users of the Jersey Supervision Interview Checklist*, St Helier: Jersey Probation and After-Care Service.

Vanstone, M. and Seymour, B. (1986) 'Probation service objectives and the neglected ingredients', *Probation Journal*, 33(2): 43–48.

Vogelvang, B., Clarke, J., Weiland, A,S., Vosters, N. and Button, L. (2014) 'Resilience of Dutch probation officers: a critical need for a critical profession', *European Journal of Probation*, 6(2): 126–146.

Weaver, C. and Fox, C. (1984) 'Berkeley sex offenders group: a seven-year follow-up', *Probation Journal*, 31(4): 143–146.

Whitehead, P. (2010) *Exploring Modern Probation: Social Theory and Organisation*, Bristol: Policy Press.

THREE

The search for impact in British probation: from programmes to skills and implementation

Peter Raynor

Introduction: social science as understanding, measurement and comparison

Evaluating the effectiveness of probation has always been a knotty problem for social science. Like most (perhaps all) social science, it depends on achieving the right combination of different sources of knowledge. This chapter reviews key stages in the development of evaluation research on probation services, with a major but not exclusive focus on England and Wales, and ends with some suggestions about the future. Research on the skills used by probation staff marks a particular and important step in this development.

Social science, as used in evaluative research, is a three-legged enterprise supported by three sources of knowledge or forms of investigation: understanding, measurement and comparison. (Three is usually the minimum number of legs required to support a stable structure.) We need understanding, usually acquired by qualitative research methods, to bring into focus the aims of social actors, their beliefs about the processes they are involved in, and the meanings they attach to what they do and to what happens to them. The criminologist David Matza called this 'appreciation' (Matza, 1969), meaning the attempt to understand social situations from the point of view of those involved. Human action is socially constructed and our social environments are structured by our actions and by those of others (particularly those more powerful than ourselves). Understanding also requires awareness of our own assumptions and our ways of interpreting and shaping experience, because what we learn will be the product of an interaction between our own perceptions and those of our research subjects. This is why qualitative researchers have to try hard to be guided by what they actually find rather than what they expect or hope or prefer to find. However, it is not clear how social science can be *social* without an attempt to understand the meanings of social experience for the people involved. Some notable recent examples of probation research have relied on qualitative methods: for example, research on the occupational culture of probation staff (Mawby and Worrall, 2013) and on their beliefs about the quality of probation work and the nature of good practice (Robinson et al, 2014). However, evaluation research in probation needs to go beyond practitioners' beliefs to develop more independent and objective ways to measure the impact of probation practice: what does it change? What difference does it make?

Here we need to depend more on the quantitative procedures of measurement and comparison. Can we actually identify and measure a difference in outcome? Can we reliably estimate whether it is likely to recur? Can we show that the difference is likely to be due to some probation practice or process, not something that would have happened anyway or that occurs simply by chance? These are the scientific procedures that allow us to claim social investigation as a *science*, capable of generating reliable knowledge and building a cumulative knowledge base. Evaluation research, being centrally concerned with whether professional intervention makes a difference, depends on getting these procedures right so that we can learn what works, how it works and in what circumstances, and how we might make it work better. Without understanding, we cannot get far, but without measurement and comparison, it is difficult to turn understanding into evidence-based statements about the effectiveness of probation practice. It is this effectiveness that has historically, and repeatedly, been called into question. It is, of course, important to make the right comparison: that is, the comparison that is relevant to testing your hypothesis or answering your research question. Much methodological writing has tried to establish a hierarchy of research strategies ranked according to the degree of certainty they offer about the validity of findings. Many argue that controlled trials based on random allocation and a strict experimental model are required, (for example, Harper and Chitty, 2004), while others point out that well-designed quasi-experimental studies offer an almost comparable degree of certainty and are much more feasible in the criminal justice environment (for example, Hollin, 2008). This chapter contains examples of both, and both have made contributions to probation research.

Early days: optimistic practice and sceptical research

Official aspirations to develop an evidence-based or at least evidence-informed probation service in Britain date back at least to the period of ground-breaking and comprehensive social policy reform that followed the end of the Second World War. This delivered a National Health Service and most of the structure of our current welfare state, still recognisable in spite of the damage done by more recent hostile governments. There had been earlier attempts to articulate a scientific basis for probation (described in detail by Vanstone, 2004), but official awareness of probation's potential contribution as an integral part of the state's criminal justice and welfare policies emerged strongly during the late 1940s and 1950s. The White Paper *Penal Practice in a Changing Society* (Home Office, 1959), which set out new aspirations for the prison system, gives a clear insight into official thinking: custody, particularly for the growing number of young offenders, was to lose its punitive emphasis and concentrate on finding the appropriate 'treatment' for offenders who were to be allocated to suitable regimes through a process of assessment and classification, led by psychologists: 'methods of training have been progressively extended and improved, notably in the application of psychiatry and psychology' (Home Office, 1959, p 46). Their effectiveness was to be evaluated by the recently established Home Office Research Unit ('The Research Unit is at present studying the effectiveness of different forms of treatment when applied to different types of offender' [p 5]) and the methodology for the evaluations was to be pragmatically eclectic, but quantitative where possible ('The Research Unit will apply the basic principles of scientific method and attempt to produce its results in quantitative terms. It will not cling to the methods of any particular discipline or school of thought, but will seek to provide answers to specific questions by whatever means appear most appropriate' [p 6]). The overall ambition was to achieve a step change towards an evidence-based and rehabilitative system:

> A fundamental re-examination of penal methods, based on studies of the causes of crime, or rather of the factors which foster or inhibit crime, and supported by a reliable assessment of the results achieved by existing methods, could be a landmark in penal history and illumine the course ahead for a generation. (p 7)

The whole document, from nearly six decades ago, breathes modernity and optimism, faith in new human sciences, and an enlightened rejection of purely punitive approaches. As often happened then and more recently, new thinking about prisons had consequences for probation: for example, new post-custodial after-care responsibilities were acquired, but more fundamentally the new approach set out in the 1959 White Paper was clearly meant to encompass probation. A significant part of the work of the Home Office Research Unit and of the Cambridge Institute of Criminology (supported largely by Home Office funds) was to focus on probation over the next 17 years.

In spite of the confidence about scientific and progressive criminal justice expressed in the 1959 White Paper, doubts about the evidence base and effectiveness of probation were already being expressed in parts of the social science and social policy community. The authors of the White Paper had few doubts: they saw the probation service as a 'nation-wide network of qualified social case-workers' (Home Office, 1959, p 20) fit to assume demanding new tasks in the after-care of prisoners. Others, however, had doubts about the claims of the young social work profession, with which probation was largely identified at that time (and still should be, though that is another story: see, among others, Raynor and Vanstone, 2015). As early as 1943, the sociologist C. Wright Mills argued that attributing social problems to individual malfunctions distracted attention from the need for wider policy reforms (Mills, 1943). Even earlier, in 1931, Dr Richard Cabot's presidential address to the American Association of Social Workers called for more evaluation research, resulting eventually in the Cambridge Somerville Youth Study (Powers and Witmer, 1951). This substantial and methodologically sophisticated experiment was based on a sample of adolescent boys of whom half were randomly allocated to supervision by social workers, and their subsequent level of offending was compared with that of the control group of boys, who were not allocated to social workers. This design was strong on measurement and comparison, but involved little understanding or control of what the social workers were actually doing. As was widely reported at the time (though not much discussed within British social work), the experimental group did no better than the controls; in fact, they were reported to have offended slightly but not significantly more. Thirty years later, in a remarkable follow-up study (McCord, 1978), it was found that the experimental group had continued to do worse, this time significantly and on a range of indicators including crime, unemployment, alcohol abuse, mental illness, stress-related illness and early death.

In 1959, in the same year as the White Paper, came the publication of Barbara Wootton's *Social Science and Social Pathology* (Wootton, 1959), which contained a pointed critique of social casework theory. Other American studies such as the Vocational High experiment (Meyer et al, 1965) and the Chemung County study of family services (Wallace, 1967) showed no clear benefits from social casework. By the 1970s, there were enough of these studies to lead to significant anxiety in American social work (Grey and Dermody, 1972; Fischer, 1973, 1976). Joel Fischer, who undertook a comprehensive review of social work evaluations up to the 1970s, famously summed up his findings like this:

> The bulk of practitioners in an entire profession appear to be practicing in ways which are not helpful or even detrimental to their clients, and, at best, operating without a shred of empirical evidence validating their efforts. (Fischer, 1976, p 140)

What stands out about the American social work evaluations of that era, when tested against the three-legged model of social science, is that they tended to be relatively well executed with regard to measurement and comparison, but they did not really examine, unpack and understand what social workers were actually doing. 'Casework' was evaluated as if it were one uniform activity, stable and consistent like a standardised 'treatment'. This was a weakness in the area of understanding, which left open the possibility (recognised by Fischer) that outcomes that showed no overall benefit might be concealing the fact that some practitioners were doing beneficial work, but that their effect was cancelled out by the poorer work of others so that aggregated effects showed no significant differences from control groups that received no service. (An interesting study in Britain around the same time showed almost the opposite design: clients of a family service agency were interviewed to find out what they thought of the service, using a careful qualitative approach but with little attempt at measurement or comparison [Mayer and Timms, 1970]. The clients, who tended to see their problems in a practical way, often did not understand what the caseworkers were trying to do: why so many questions about early childhood?)

Some similar problems were emerging in research on probation services. For example, an early study of the results of probation by Radzinowicz (1958), who was a strong advocate of probation, found that reconviction rates looked promising but included no comparison with similar offenders receiving different sentences. When Wilkins (1958) published a similar study but included relevant comparisons, people sentenced to probation had outcomes no better than those receiving other sentences. There are clear parallels in this respect with American social work research. The Home Office Research Unit also carried out, throughout the 1960s and early 1970s, a series of carefully designed and methodologically resourceful descriptive studies of probation, aimed largely at developing empirical classifications of probationers and their problems. A very detailed study by Martin Davies (1974) attempted to describe the impact of probation on the social environment of probationers, and argued that only a properly controlled comparative study could show conclusively whether probation was having a positive impact. Such a study was in fact under way, known as IMPACT (Intensive Matched Probation and After-Care Treatment [Folkard et al, 1976]): probationers were randomly assigned to normal or 'intensive' caseloads, and subsequent reconviction rates compared.

The result was a slight but non-significant difference in favour of the control cases: more probation input did not seem to lead to better results. The only group that appeared to benefit from smaller caseloads was a fairly small number of offenders with high self-reported problems and low 'criminal tendencies', who were not very representative of offenders in general. The greater responsiveness of this group might tell us something about the methods officers were using in the extra time made available by lower caseloads: perhaps they were offering a form of counselling, which might help this group more than it helped others. Unfortunately, we know little about what the officers were actually doing; understanding of the process is missing, so that measurement and comparison can only give us the results of an input about which all we know is that some people received more of it than others. We cannot tell what methods were in use or how well they were being implemented. This also represented a missed opportunity to start a fuller investigation of the impact of caseload size on effectiveness: if lower caseloads did not necessarily improve results, there might still be threshold effects leading to poorer results when caseloads are simply too high to allow adequate individual attention, but this common-sense expectation, which most practitioners would support, has never been fully tested.

As in broader social work research, findings of 'no difference' were the norm at this time. There were occasional exceptions, such as Margaret Shaw's study of pre-release help to prisoners (Shaw, 1974), in which those who were randomly allocated to receive more attention from prison welfare officers were reconvicted less, but there was little practical follow-up of this finding until the development of 'resettlement' services some decades later. The general picture, in the US as well as Britain, seemed to be one of failure, and this was summed up by Robert Martinson in his unauthorised, over-simplified but highly influential summary (Martinson, 1974) of the large research review of the effectiveness of rehabilitation carried out for the New York State government (Lipton et al, 1975). Martinson's conclusion that 'the rehabilitative efforts that have been reported so far have had no appreciable effect on recidivism' (Martinson, 1974, 25), although not a fully accurate summary of the review, was widely reported as meaning 'nothing works'. Although not all criminologists accepted this, it had a political impact, particularly in the Anglophone world where many politicians were looking for justifications for reductions in public spending. In Britain, the director of research in the Home Office summed up as follows:

> Penal 'treatments', as we significantly describe them, do not have any reformative effect…. The dilemma is that a considerable investment has been made in various measures and services…. Are these services simply to be abandoned on the basis of the accumulated research evidence? Will this challenge evoke a response … by the invention of new approaches and new methods? (Croft, 1978)

'New approaches and new methods'

After IMPACT, official research on the effectiveness of probation virtually ceased in England and Wales for about 20 years. The 'new approaches and new methods' did gradually appear (Vanstone, 2004), but were mostly not systematically evaluated until much later. In the meantime, rehabilitative criminal justice was overshadowed for a while by the 'justice model' of desert-based proportional sentencing (Hood, 1974; von Hirsch, 1976), and the work of probation and youth justice was increasingly concentrated on creating opportunities for diversion, or 'alternatives to custody'. If their methods could not reliably change people's behaviour, at least they could use their role in court to influence decisions and to encourage the use of sentences that were seen as less harmful (and usually cheaper). Such approaches attracted support from criminologists (for example, Bottoms and McWilliams, 1979) and eventually from government, which articulated a role for the probation service in encouraging the use of non-custodial penalties instead of prison (Home Office, 1984). This strategy worked particularly well in juvenile justice (Rutherford, 1986). However, too much weight was given during this period to the 'nothing works' research, which was actually quite limited in one main respect. Although often strong on measurement and comparison, it tended to be weak in its understanding of inputs: 'probation' or 'prison' were seen as treatments in their own right, rather than needing to be unpacked to see what different inputs were actually being offered by a range of practitioners, and how well they were being delivered.

Although some research on probation's effectiveness continued outside government in England and Wales (for example, Raynor, 1988; Roberts, 1989), the next major steps in research on rehabilitation did not come until research began to benefit from better understanding and control of inputs. Correctional researchers who had never accepted Martinson's verdict began to carry out meta-analyses looking at the characteristics of different programmes and regimes for offenders to see which were more often associated with positive outcomes. The most influential of these (Andrews et al, 1990) combined understanding of inputs with a strong focus on measurement and comparison, and proposed what became the most influential recent approach to rehabilitation, the Risk-Need-Responsivity or RNR model (Bonta and Andrews, 2017). Other meta-analyses reached broadly similar conclusions (for example, Lipsey, 1992; Lösel, 1995; McGuire, 2002; Redondo et al, 2002) and a Scottish research review (McIvor, 1990) helped to raise awareness of this kind of work in Britain, as did a series of 'what works' conferences (McGuire, 1995). The new focus on understanding and describing the service that was actually provided, and the explicit aim of distinguishing between effective and ineffective practice in order to encourage the former, led to a number of innovations and in particular to the development of structured group programmes using cognitive-behavioural methods. These aimed to ensure the right inputs from staff by providing detailed manuals and training, and they emphasised programme integrity, that is, delivery as designed.

One of the first programmes of this kind to be tried in probation in Britain, and the first to be thoroughly evaluated, was the Reasoning and Rehabilitation programme developed in Canada (Ross et al, 1988) and introduced in a Welsh probation area (Raynor and Vanstone, 1996, 1997; Raynor 1998). Unlike some later, larger evaluations (for example, Hollin et al, 2004), the research on this programme used not only measurement and comparison, with modestly positive findings from a two-year reconviction follow-up, but also qualitative approaches, interviewing all programme graduates and a number of staff, and documenting the implementation process through participant observation. Some of the lessons learned from this study about, for example, listening to probationers, taking time to do implementation properly, and involving staff through thorough consultation, seemed later to be forgotten: there was a centrally driven rush to roll out programmes on a massive scale to take advantage of the short-term funding available in the government's Crime Reduction Programme from 1999 to 2002 (Maguire, 2004; Raynor, 2004). The early results of this huge effort were not as good as had been hoped or expected, with many problems of implementation, including poor selection and poor retention of programme participants (Hollin et al, 2004). Thus, the overall message so far seems to be that group programmes, if properly designed, targeted and delivered, and supported where necessary by appropriate individual supervision, can make a useful contribution to the effectiveness of probation services. It is, however, very unfortunate that rushed implementation during the Crime Reduction Programme caused some front-line staff to be suspicious and resentful of 'what works' (Raynor, 2004). The associated research, showing some positive results and leading to many ideas about possible improvements, shows the benefits of a three-legged approach combining measurement and comparison of outcomes with a degree of clarity about inputs, which were defined by the programme designs and manuals at least to the extent of knowing what staff were *meant* to be doing. Many programmes also benefited from analysis of video recording of programme sessions to check integrity of delivery. For the first time, this gave researchers a clearer grasp of what inputs were likely to be producing the measured outputs.

From programmes to skills

In reality, probation has always depended more on individual supervision than on group programmes, and it continues to do so. The next step in understanding the inputs from practice dates mainly from the early years of the current century. Important precursors were the work of Chris Trotter in Australia in the 1990s (Trotter, 1993, 1996) and the recognition of 'core correctional practices' in Canada (Andrews and Kiessling, 1980; Dowden and Andrews, 2004; see also Chapter Nine of this volume). Researchers interested in skills and mostly associated with the Collaboration of Researchers for the Effective Development of Offender Supervision (see the Introduction to this volume) carried out a number of studies that, in spite of some differences of method and focus, were all concerned with studying the impact of better practice skills. Among the best known of these have been Bonta's Strategic Training Initiative in Community Supervision (STICS) study in Canada, which used a random allocation design to compare reconviction rates after supervision by officers who had received additional training in evidence-based practice skills with reconvictions after supervision by officers who had not received the training (Bonta et al, 2011; see also Chapter Nine of this volume); Trotter's continuing series of studies of the impact of particular practice skills (for example, Trotter 2013; Trotter et al, 2015; see also Chapter 15 this volume); Taxman's study of the effects of training in 'proactive community supervision' (Taxman, 2008), and the Staff Training Aimed at Reducing Re-arrest (STARR) study (Robinson et al, 2012), which looked at the impact of skills on re-arrest rates. The quasi-experimental Jersey Supervision Skills Study (JS3), in which two of the editors of this volume were involved, identified a range of skills used by probation staff in videotaped interviews and found significantly lower reconviction rates among people supervised by more skilled staff (Raynor et al, 2014). The differences in reconviction rates found in these studies are substantial, comparable with or greater than those typically reported in programme evaluations: for example, 21 percentage points in STICS, 14 in STARR, 32 in JS3.

A meta-analysis of skills-based research (Chadwick et al, 2015) reports on a number of studies comparing different levels of skill in supervision that consistently show that more skilled supervision is more effective. In addition, other recent work suggests that successful implementation of initiatives for improvement in skills may depend on good management and appropriate agency culture (Bonta et al, 2013). In England and Wales, the Skills for Effective Engagement, Development and Supervision (SEEDS) programme (Rex and Hosking, 2014) aimed at a similar effect through staff training, and although the eventual outcomes are unclear, supervision by SEEDS-trained officers has been shown to result in slightly higher levels of compliance (Sorsby et al, 2017; see also Chapter Ten of this volume). The initiative seems to have been welcomed by staff and managers and SEEDS-based practices are still continuing in some places. Similarly, in Jersey, the probation staff have themselves developed a process of staff development using the research instruments from the JS3 study to assess and discuss each other's interviews, which they record on video. It appears that this kind of research, combining measurement and comparison with an informed understanding of what practitioners are actually doing, has begun to illuminate a significant part of the probation service's input into supervision and is readily translatable into training initiatives that have the potential to improve practice. There is much more work to be done in this area, and it appears likely that the most productive approaches to future probation research will combine measurement and comparison with a detailed understanding of what practitioners are doing, and why. In the meantime, we have come a very long way from 'nothing works', and the three-legged approach to research methods holds plenty of promise for the future.

Next steps?

Although in principle practitioners have much to gain from applying the rationale and methods of evaluative research, these are not always welcomed. Ideally, practice is embedded in a 'culture of curiosity' (Raynor and Vanstone, 2001), in which practitioners want to know if what they are doing is getting results and how they might improve such results. Evaluation is part of evidence-based practice, and evidence-based practice works best when practitioners understand it as something that can help them to achieve the outcomes they look for in their work. When evaluation is seen as a management tool to increase control, or as something done by researchers for their own purposes or careers, or simply as lacking relevance to day-to-day work, it tends to be resisted. In England and Wales, there is currently a high level of insecurity, anxiety and unpredictable organisational change in probation services, which sometimes leads to anxiety about how research might be used. However, it should be clear from the examples outlined earlier in this chapter that in favourable circumstances such obstacles can be overcome if evaluation is rooted in an understanding of practice and a shared goal of effective service. As we have seen, successful evaluations tend to combine qualitative and quantitative approaches: qualitative, to understand the processes and perceptions and goals that point the way to what is worth measuring, and quantitative because without measurement there is no basis for comparison, and comparison is fundamental to the question of what works better or worse than something else.

Finally, it is clear that we are not yet looking productively at everything that matters. We have learned to measure some aspects of service quality, but others remain to be developed. Until recently, it was unusual to include the quality and behaviour of organisations in evaluations of practice, and the approaches needed to begin to do this depend heavily, so far, on evaluation instruments developed in Canada, such as the Correctional Programs Assessment Inventory (see

Chapter Fourteen), that may not be a perfect fit in other organisational cultures (though experience so far suggests that the fit is mostly quite good). Experience also suggests that the attempt to identify good services could make more use of two fields of enquiry that are not yet integrated into evaluation research. First, and perhaps more immediately accessible, is the understanding gained from service users themselves and articulated within studies of desistance that draw on people's own accounts and narratives of how they came to desist from offending.

Studies of desistance in Britain have tended to rely heavily on qualitative methods, mostly interviews, unlike some American studies (for example, Laub and Sampson, 2003) that also use statistical analysis. (An exception is the Sheffield Desistance Study [Bottoms and Shapland, 2011], which produced a large amount of quantitative data, but this has been unusual in British writing about desistance.) Qualitative studies contribute to understanding the desistance process and restoring service users to their rightful place at the centre of that process. This has undoubtedly helped some practitioners to think about the nature and aims of their work. The strengths of British desistance research have been in the area of understanding rather than measurement or comparison, and this has so far tended to limit its contribution to the evaluation of probation work (which, to be fair, was not its main aim). In the decade since McNeill suggested a 'desistance paradigm' for probation practice (McNeill, 2006), desistance scholars have produced little in the way of specific guidance for probation practice; this has not been their role, and it is one they have explicitly resisted (Weaver and McNeill, 2010). Sometimes their work has been presented as an alternative to 'what works' (Farrall et al, 2014; see also McNeill et al, 2015) rather than as a complementary perspective (Ward and Maruna, 2007).

One presumably unintended consequence has been that some practitioners have seen the desistance perspective as an ally against managerialist attempts to impose 'what works' models, and therefore as an endorsement of existing practice. This limits its potential influence on practice: for example, consistent and supportive relationships between service users and supervisors are seen as a useful aid to desistance, and suggest an obvious overlap with thinking about 'core correctional practices' that seek to address the same issues, but little work has yet been done to link these two bodies of work because they belong to different research traditions (see also Chapters Six, Seven and Fifteen of this volume). (Some recent work by Kirkwood [2015] on an interactional approach to desistance is an exception to this rule, and it is hoped that further analysis of recorded interviews from Jersey and Australia will help to show more detail of how interaction and communication with probation staff can support beliefs and behaviour consistent with desistance.) Overall, however, most scholars of desistance have preferred not to engage in quantitative procedures such as measurement and comparison, and this has limited the capacity of this body of work to accumulate reliable knowledge of the kind that is most useful in evaluation research. This is not because evaluation researchers are not interested in qualitative methods: early 'what works' studies made extensive use of qualitative interviewing to elicit service users' perspectives (Raynor and Vanstone, 1997). However, such attempts have not yet been much influenced by desistance research, and there is an agenda for future work here.

The second set of issues that arguably should be taken more into account in evaluation research concerns the influence of the policy context on practice. Briefly, the dramatic policy shifts of recent years have included the nationalisation of formerly local services in 2001, the establishment of the National Offender Management Service (NOMS) in 2004 and the privatisation of most of the probation service's work in 2015. NOMS itself is shortly to be replaced by a new agency, Her Majesty's Prison and Probation Service; is this because NOMS was a failure, or a success, or neither? These changes cannot have failed to affect the quality of practice in a variety of ways, and little research has so far been done to assess the actual impacts on quality. However, this also brings the role and consequences of politics into question.

Evaluating criminal justice in post-truth Britain

As suggested in the preceding section, evaluation researchers who study probation may need to pay more attention to the wide social policy contexts in which their work is located. This can touch on politically sensitive issues: for example, desistance studies point clearly to difficulty in finding employment as an obstacle to desistance (Bottoms and Shapland, 2011), and levels of unemployment reflect wider social structures and, in part, political decisions. More broadly, comparative research on penal systems shows that some societies are consistently more punitive than others (Cavadino and Dignan, 2006) and that variations in the use of imprisonment can be linked to social inequality (Wilkinson and Pickett, 2009): societies with greater inequality of income tend to make proportionately more use of imprisonment than more equal societies. Britain has been becoming more unequal during recent decades, when the prison population has also been rising. This context has an impact on what penal policy can achieve and on the opportunities for service development, and needs to be taken into account in thinking about the actual and potential effectiveness of services.

Social and political context also affect the value attached to evaluative research and the extent of its influence on policy. A clear recent example has been the privatisation of most of the work of the former probation service in 2015, the creation of community rehabilitation companies and the attempt to incentivise better performance through 'Payment by Results' (PbR) (Ministry of Justice, 2013). Originally a thorough programme of piloting was planned to precede the implementation of the new policies, in line with the original plans set out in *Transforming Rehabilitation* (Ministry of Justice, 2013). However, a new justice secretary, Christopher Grayling, decided to accelerate the process by abandoning the pilots that were intended to provide guidance on feasibility and implementation. Instead, two small pilots of after-care for short-term prisoners, which actually measured the impact of providing an after-care service rather than the impact of PbR (Pearce et al, 2015; Disley et al, 2015), were wrongly claimed by politicians as evidence of the success of PbR. As Grayling explained to a Policy Exchange meeting in March 2014, "I don't believe you need to pilot professional and operational freedom" (Grayling, 2014). Evidence was unnecessary to support a policy guided simply by ideology and political conviction. Since the privatisation, almost all the evidence collected by auditors and independent inspectors (for example, National Audit Office, 2016; HMIP, 2016a, 2016b, 2016c) shows that it has made community sentences less reliable and less safe, and has done little to create the new resettlement services for short-term prisoners that were part of the rationale for the policy.

Grayling's evidence-free privatisation was an early example of what, during 2016, would become known in Britain and the US as 'post-truth' politics. A tendency to shape the evidence to support a pre-existing policy line was not new: for example, it was a feature of Tony Blair's foreign policy leading up to the invasion of Iraq in 2003, and the dangers of this approach were thoroughly exposed by the Chilcot Inquiry into the invasion and its aftermath (Chilcot, 2016). However, recent developments have gone beyond simply shaping the evidence to managing without it altogether, or to a complete disregard for facts. In 2016, a plot by a group of 'Eurosceptic' Conservative politicians in England to unseat their party leader led to a referendum on continued membership of the European Union, in which the successful campaign for a 'leave' vote was based on deliberately misleading propaganda, taking full advantage of modern means of mass communication. Inconvenient facts were ignored, and one senior 'leave' campaigner, Michael Gove (for a short while Christopher Grayling's successor as justice secretary) claimed that 'The British people have had enough of experts' (reported in the *Financial Times*, 3 June 2016).

In the US, a similar populist rhetoric was a feature of Donald Trump's successful election campaign, and commentators drew parallels with the disastrous populist movements of the 1930s that used similar appeals to popular prejudice based on widely disseminated and emotive falsehoods. The modern equivalents include 'fake news' and so-called 'alternative facts' (as proposed by Kellyanne Conway, a senior aide to President Trump, in a hilarious press briefing reported in *The Guardian*, 22 January 2017, and all other reputable media). This emerging style of politics (perhaps not so much post-truth as post-Enlightenment) does not provide a promising environment for evaluation research or evidence-based policy in those countries where it is prevalent. However, it is not prevalent everywhere: probation research is flourishing in Europe, and in some of the devolved jurisdictions within the British Isles such as Scotland, Northern Ireland and the Channel Islands. Even within England and Wales there are examples of local research that engages directly with service providers (see Chapter Fourteen). When post-truth policies fail, factual research on how to make probation more effective will be needed to support the necessary evidence-based reform.

References

Andrews, D. and Kiessling, J. (1980) 'Program structure and effective correctional practices: a summary of the CaVIC research', in R. Ross and P. Gendreau (eds) *Effective Correctional Treament*, Toronto: Butterworth, pp 441–463.

Andrews, D.A., Zinger, I., Hoge, R.D., Bonta, J., Gendreau, P. and Cullen, F.T. (1990) 'Does correctional treatment work? A clinically relevant and psychologically informed meta-analysis', *Criminology*, 28(3): 369–404.

Bonta, J. and Andrews, D. (2017) *The Psychology of Criminal Conduct* (6th edn), Abingdon: Routledge.

Bonta, J., Bourgon, G., Rugge, T., Gress, C. and Gutierrez, L. (2013) 'Taking the leap: from pilot project to wide-scale implementation of the Strategic Training Initiative in Community Supervision (STICS)', *Justice Research and Policy*, 15(1): 17–35.

Bonta, J., Bourgon, G., Rugge, T., Scott, T., Yessine, A.K., Gutierrez, L. and Li, J. (2011) 'An experimental demonstration of training probation officers in evidence-based community supervision', *Criminal Justice and Behavior*, 38(11): 1127–1148.

Bottoms, A. and McWilliams, W. (1979) 'A non-treatment paradigm for probation practice', *British Journal of Social Work*, 9(2): 159–202.

Bottoms, A. and Shapland, J. (2011) 'Steps towards desistance among male young adult recidivists', in S. Farrall, M. Hough, S. Maruna and R. Sparks (eds) *Escape Routes: Contemporary Perspectives on Life After Punishment*, Abingdon: Routledge, pp 43–80.

Cavadino, M. and Dignan, J. (2006) *Penal Systems: A Comparative Approach*, London: Sage Publications.

Chadwick, N., Dewolf, A. and Serin, R. (2015) 'Effectively training community supervision officers: a meta-analytic review of the impact on offender outcome', *Criminal Justice and Behavior*, 42(10): 977–989.

Chilcot, J. (Chair) (2016) *The Report of the Iraq Inquiry*, London: HMSO.

Croft, J. (1978) *Research in Criminal Justice*, Home Office Research Study 44, London: HMSO.

Davies, M. (1974) *Social Work in the Environment*, Home Office Research Study 21, London: HMSO.

Disley, E., Giacomantonio, C., Kruithof, K. and Sim, M. (2015) *The Payment by Results Social Impact Bond Pilot at HMP Peterborough: Final Process Evaluation Report*, London: Ministry of Justice.

Dowden, C. and Andrews, D. (2004) 'The importance of staff practice in delivering effective correctional treatment: a meta-analysis', *International Journal of Offender Therapy and Comparative Criminology*, 48(2): 203–214.

Farrall, S., Hunter, B., Sharpe, G. and Calverley, A. (2014) *Criminal Careers in Transition*, Oxford: Oxford University Press.

Fischer, J. (1973) 'Is casework effective? A review', *Social Work*, 18(1): 5–20.

Fischer, J. (1976) *The Effectiveness of Social Casework*, Springfield, IL: Charles C. Thomas.

Folkard, M.S., Smith, D.E. and Smith, D.D. (1976) *IMPACT Volume II: The Results of the Experiment*, Home Office Research Study 36, London: HMSO.

Grayling, C. (2014) Speech to Policy Exchange, March.

Grey, A. and Dermody, H. (1972) 'Reports of casework failure', *Social Casework*, November, 534–543.

Harper, G. and Chitty, C. (2004) *The Impact of Corrections on Re-offending: A Review of 'What Works'*, Home Office Research Study 291, London: Home Office.

HMIP (Her Majesty's Inspectorate of Probation) (2016a) *Transforming Rehabilitation: Early Implementation 5*, Manchester: HMIP.

HMIP (2016b) *An Inspection of Through-the-Gate Resettlement Services for Short-Term Prisoners*, Manchester: HMIP.

HMIP (2016c) *The Effectiveness of Probation Work in the North of London*, Manchester: HMIP.

Hollin, C. (2008) 'Evaluating offending behaviour programmes: does only randomization glister?', *Criminology and Criminal Justice*, 8(1): 89–106.

Hollin, C., Palmer, E., McGuire, J., Hounsome, J., Hatcher, R., Bilby, C. and Clark, C. (2004) *Pathfinder Programmes in the Probation Service: A Retrospective Analysis*, Home Office Online Report 66/04, London: Home Office.

Home Office (1959) *Penal Practice in a Changing Society*, Cmnd 645, London: HMSO.

Home Office (1984) *Probation Service in England and Wales: Statement of National Objectives and Priorities*, London: Home Office.

Hood, R. (1974) *Tolerance and the Tariff*, London: NACRO.

Kirkwood, S. (2015) 'Desistance in action: an interactional approach to criminal justice practice and desistance from offending', *Theoretical Criminology*, online advance access.

Laub, J. and Sampson, R. (2003) *Shared Beginnings, Divergent Lives: Delinquent Boys to Age 70*, Cambridge, MA: Harvard University Press.

Lipsey, M. (1992) 'Juvenile delinquency treatment: a meta-analytic enquiry into the variability of effects', in T. Cook, H. Cooper, D.S. Cordray, H. Hartmann, L.V. Hedges, R.L. Light, T.A. Louis and F. Mosteller (eds) *Meta-Analysis for Explanation: A Case-Book*, New York, NY: Russell Sage, pp 83–127.

Lipton, D., Martinson, R. and Wilks, J. (1975) *The Effectiveness of Correctional Treatment*, New York, NY: Praeger.

Lösel, F. (1995) 'The efficacy of correctional treatment: a review and synthesis of meta-evaluations', in J. McGuire (ed) *What Works: Reducing Reoffending*, Chichester: Wiley, pp 79–111.

Maguire, M. (2004) 'The Crime Reduction Programme in England and Wales: reflections on the vision and the reality', *Criminal Justice*, 4(3): 213–37.

Martinson, J. (1974) 'What works? Questions and answers about prison reform', *The Public Interest*, 35: 22–54.

Matza, D. (1969) *Becoming Deviant*, Englewood Cliffs, NJ: Prentice-Hall.

Mawby, R. and Worrall, A. (2013) *Doing Probation Work*, Abingdon: Routledge.

Mayer, J. and Timms, N. (1970) *The Client Speaks*, London: Routledge.

McCord, J. (1978) 'A thirty-year follow-up of treatment effects', *American Psychologist*, 33(3): 284–289.

McGuire, J. (2002) 'Integrating findings from research reviews', in J. McGuire (ed) *Offender Rehabilitation and Treatment*, Chichester, Wiley, pp 3–38.

McGuire, J. (ed) (1995) *What Works: Reducing Reoffending*, Chichester: Wiley.

McIvor, G. (1990) *Sanctions for Serious or Persistent Offenders*, Stirling: Social Work Research Centre, University of Stirling.

McNeill, F. (2006) 'A desistance paradigm for offender management', *Criminology and Criminal Justice*, 6(1), 39–62.

McNeill, F., Raynor, P., Herzog-Evans, M., and Durnescu, I. (2015) 'Rethinking what helps? Beyond probation and desistance', *Howard Journal of Crime and Justice*, 54(3): 311–317.

Meyer, H., Borgatta, E. and Jones, W. (1965) *Girls at Vocational High*, New York, NY: Russell Sage Foundation.

Mills, C.W. (1943) 'The professional ideology of social pathologists', *American Journal of Sociology*, 49(2): 165–180.

Ministry of Justice (2013) *Transforming Rehabilitation: A Strategy for Reform*, Cm 8619, London: Ministry of Justice.

National Audit Office (2016) *Transforming Rehabilitation*, London: National Audit Office.

Pearce, S., Murray, D. and Lane, M. (2015) *HMP Doncaster Payment by Results Pilot: Final Progress Evaluation Report*, London: Ministry of Justice.

Powers, E. and Witmer, H. (1951) *An Experiment in the Prevention of Delinquency*, New York, NY: Columbia University Press.

Radzinowicz, L. (ed) (1958) *The Results of Probation. A Report of the Cambridge Department of Criminal Science*, London: Macmillan.

Raynor, P. (1988) *Probation as an Alternative to Custody*, Aldershot: Avebury.

Raynor, P. (1998) 'Attitudes, social problems and reconvictions in the STOP probation experiment', *Howard Journal of Crime and Justice*, 37(1): 1–15.

Raynor, P. (2004) 'The probation service 'Pathfinders': finding the path and losing the way?', *Criminal Justice*, 4(3): 309–25.

Raynor, P. and Vanstone, M. (1996) 'Reasoning and Rehabilitation in Britain: the results of the Straight Thinking On Probation (STOP) programme', *International Journal of Offender Therapy and Comparative Criminology*, 40(4): 272–284.

Raynor, P. and Vanstone, M. (1997) *Straight Thinking On Probation (STOP): The Mid Glamorgan Experiment*, Probation Studies Unit Report 4, Oxford: Centre for Criminological Research, University of Oxford.

Raynor, P. and Vanstone, M. (2001) 'Straight Thinking On Probation: evidence-based practice and the culture of curiosity', in G. Bernfeld, D. Farrington and A. Leschied (eds) *Offender Rehabilitation in Practice*, Chichester: Wiley, pp 189–203.

Raynor, P. and Vanstone, M. (2015) 'Moving away from social work and half way back again: new research on skills in probation', *British Journal of Social Work*, 46(4): 1131–1147.

Raynor, P., Ugwudike, P. and Vanstone, M. (2014) 'The impact of skills in probation work: a reconviction study', *Criminology and Criminal Justice*, 14(2): 235–249.

Redondo, S., Sanchez-Meca, J. and Garrido, V. (2002) 'Crime treatment in Europe: a review of outcome studies', in J. McGuire (ed) *Offender Rehabilitation and Treatment*, Chichester: Wiley, pp 113–141.

Rex, S. and Hosking, N. (2014) 'Supporting practitioners to engage offenders', in I. Durnescu and F. McNeill (eds) *Understanding Penal Practice*, Abingdon: Routledge, pp 271–280.

Roberts, C. (1989) *Hereford and Worcester Probation Service Young Offender Project: First Evaluation Report*, Oxford: Department of Social and Administrative Studies, University of Oxford.

Robinson, G., Priede, C., Farrall, S., Shapland, J. and McNeill, F. (2014) 'Understanding quality in probation practice: frontline perspectives in England and Wales', *Criminology and Criminal Justice*, 14(2): 123–142.

Robinson, C.R., Lowenkamp, C.T., Holsinger, A.M., VanBenschoten, S., Alexander, M. and Oleson, J.C. (2012) 'A random study of Staff Training Aimed at Reducing Re-arrest (STARR): using core correctional practices in probation interactions', *Journal of Crime and Justice*, 35(2): 167–188.

Ross, R.R., Fabiano, E.A. and Ewles, C.D. (1988) 'Reasoning and rehabilitation', *International Journal of Offender Therapy and Comparative Criminology*, 32(1): 29–35.

Rutherford, A. (1986) *Growing Out of Crime*, Harmondsworth: Penguin.

Shaw, M. (1974) *Social Work in Prisons*, Home Office Research Study 22, London: HMSO.

Sorsby, A., Shapland, J. and Robinson, G. (2017) 'Using compliance with probation supervision as an interim outcome measure in evaluating a probation initiative', *Criminology and Criminal Justice*, 17(1): 40–61.

Taxman, F.S. (2008) 'No illusions: offender and organizational change in Maryland's proactive community supervision efforts', *Criminology and Public Policy*, 7(2): 275–302.

Trotter, C. (1993) *The Supervision of Offenders – What Works? A Study Undertaken in Community Based Corrections, Victoria*, Melbourne: Social Work Department, Monash University and Victoria Department of Justice.

Trotter, C. (1996) 'The impact of different supervision practices in community corrections', *Australian and New Zealand Journal of Criminology*, 28(2): 29–46.

Trotter, C. (2013) 'Effective supervision of young offenders', in P. Ugwudike and P. Raynor (eds) *What Works in Offender Compliance: International Perspectives and Evidence-Based Practices*, Basingstoke: Palgrave Macmillan, pp 227–241.

Trotter, C., Evans, P. and Baidawi, S. (2015) 'The effectiveness of challenging skills in work with young offenders', *International Journal of Offender Therapy and Comparative Criminology*, online advance access.

Vanstone, M. (2004) *Supervising Offenders in the Community: A History of Probation Theory and Practice*, Aldershot: Ashgate.

von Hirsch, A. (1976) *Doing Justice: The Choice of Punishments. Report of the Committee for the Study of Incarceration*, New York, NY: Hill and Wang.

Wallace, D. (1967) 'The Chemung County evaluation of casework service to dependent multiproblem families: another problem outcome', *Social Service Review*, 41(4): 379–89.

Ward, T. and Maruna, S. (2007) *Rehabilitation*, Abingdon: Routledge.

Weaver, B. and McNeill, F. (2010) 'Travelling hopefully: desistance theory and probation practice', in J. Brayford, F. Cowe and J. Deering (eds) *What Else Works? Creative Work with Offenders*, Cullompton: Willan, pp 36–60.

Wilkins, L.T. (1958) 'A small comparative study of the results of probation', *British Journal of Delinquency*, 8(3): 201–209.

Wilkinson, R. and Pickett, K. (2009) *The Spirit Level*, London: Allen Lane.

Wootton, B. (1959) *Social Science and Social Pathology*, London: Allen & Unwin.

FOUR

Is constructive practice still possible in a competitive environment? Findings from a case study of a community rehabilitation company in England and Wales

Lol Burke, Matthew Millings and Gwen Robinson

Introduction

Gorman and colleagues (2006, p 21) define constructive practice as 'a complex and dynamic process of intervention which is more artistic than technical, more creative than procedural, more collaborative than instrumental'. It certainly seems that in England and Wales, in policy terms at least, contemporary probation practice has in recent years predominantly resembled the latter rather than the former. Increasingly bureaucratic demands on front-line probation practitioners have reduced the availability of face-to-face contact with those under their supervision and displaced 'the centrality of practitioners as agents of change with tools and procedures that are not sensitive enough to the multi-faceted nature of the cultures, practices and practitioners that they seek to change' (Graham, 2016, p 164). Indeed, the official rationale for the wide-ranging restructuring of the probation service[1] resulting from the recent Transforming Rehabilitation reforms (Ministry of Justice, 2013a) would, on the face of it at least, seem to recognise this through an intention to restore professional discretion and reduce bureaucracy with a view to enhancing innovation in front-line delivery. Our concern in this chapter then is to explore whether the changes brought about by the reforms will further serve to consolidate these dominant policy trends and, in Gorman et al's terms, continue to give primacy to the 'technical, procedural and instrumental'.

The study

According to Graham (2016, p 67, emphasis added): 'There is no point in conceptualising and analysing rehabilitation work merely as a *technical* and *instrumental* exercise if the workers involved make sense of it as a normative experience, incorporating affective labour and ideological dimensions'. As such, we were keen to focus on the impact of Transforming Rehabilitation on those front-line practitioners in our study in terms of their working environment and practices and how they mediated such wide-ranging changes to their working practices. Focusing specifically on the role of the newly created community rehabilitation companies (CRCs) in England and Wales, we will explore the potential impact of the shift 'from the logic of the public good to the logic of the market' (White, 2014, p 1002) with specific reference to the supervisory relationship, the scope for innovation, and partnership work.

Methodology

To assist us in this endeavour, we draw on research undertaken by the authors in one CRC case-study area between March 2014 and June 2015.[2] During most of this period, the CRC was still under public ownership and managed by staff from the former Probation Trust while the outcome of the tendering process for the contracts to run the newly formed companies was completed. This meant that at the time that the research was undertaken it was not clear what the service delivery models of the eventual owners would be and therefore too early to evaluate how Transforming Rehabilitation would ultimately play out in the long term. However, we would contend that exploring the hopes, fears and expectations of probation workers during this period of profound change as they moved towards the transition into new ownership provides significant insights into the opportunities and challenges ahead.

There are, of course, a number of other caveats here. First, we are not suggesting that prior to the part-privatisation of the probation service, practice was always 'artistic', 'technical' or 'collaborative', and indeed, as Worrall (2015) has reminded us, the notion of a 'golden age' of probation practice is something of a fallacy. As such, and related to this point, we do not contend that constructive practice is the preserve of a particular organisation or is sectorally specific. Second, we acknowledge that achieving constructive outcomes is challenging, regardless of the commitment, innovation and entrepreneurial skills of front-line practitioners, and is inevitably bounded by wider structural constraints. Finally, it is acknowledged that notions of what constitutes 'constructive' practice are in themselves ultimately highly contested and implicitly linked to individual perceptions of the 'purpose' of probation work which, as Shapland and colleagues (2012) point out, are equally disputed (see also Robinson and McNeill, 2004).

Findings

'More artistic than technical'

> I don't want to process things. I want to engage with people. I want to be inspired by how they can change. I want to feel like I've made a difference. (Probation officer)

As Rob Mawby and Anne Worrall's research (2013) into probation occupational cultures has highlighted, probation staff often achieve best outcomes in their work when practising 'on the edge', that is when they are able to utilise their professional skills and judgement in the interests of individuals and the wider communities in which they are located. The authors contend that probation work 'inevitably involves a willingness to work holistically and optimistically, though not naively, with uncertainty, ambivalence and (to a degree) failure' (Mawby and Worrall, 2013, p 154). Although in this particular context the authors are referring to working with individuals, their description of the challenges facing practitioners could equally be applied to the broader contemporary policy context in which their work is located. Prior to Transforming Rehabilitation, many practitioners were already experiencing 'initiative confusion' and 'change fatigue' in endeavouring to meet an increasing range of demands (Robinson and Burnett, 2007, p 318). Unsurprisingly then, the scale and speed of the changes that the Transforming Rehabilitation agenda has ushered in was an ongoing and constant source of anxiety and unease for staff at all levels within the CRC. Throughout the course of the research, an overwhelming sense of struggling to maintain business as usual (or rather business in the unusual) while also contemplating a long-term future under new ownership was a constant feature among those staff interviewed. The belief that the changes had been rushed through and perceived to have failed to take account of recent improvements in performance understandably tended to shape the individual views of those interviewed.

Robinson and colleagues (2014, p 133) in their study of quality in probation practice found that quality work was seen by front-line staff as 'something delivered by people with the right values, virtues, qualities and experiences, rather than something delivered by a highly trained and technically proficient workforce with specific techniques at their disposal'. This would suggest that for probation practitioners what matters most in their work is the relational aspects of supervision. In recent years, promoted by insights provided by the literature on desistance, there has been a greater awareness of the processes of change involved in moving towards a non-offending lifestyle and how practitioners working alongside others can support this process. More recently there has been a growing appreciation of the 'emotions' involved in probation work that emphasise the human qualities of such interventions (Knight, 2014). In policy terms, though, while the importance of the relationship has continued to be acknowledged through developments such as the Offender Engagement Programme (Sorsby et al, 2013) and SEED,[3] it has mainly been seen as an instrumental means of achieving the wider policy goals of reducing reoffending.

It was evident, particularly in the early stages of the research, that implementing Transforming Rehabilitation had fractured long-standing relationships through the dispersal of individuals between the two newly created entities. As we have discussed elsewhere (Robinson et al, 2016), the pains of this separation were experienced by staff on a number of levels, some of whom expressed concerns about how the organisational turmoil brought about by Transforming Rehabilitation was affecting service users:

> Certainly through the transition there's been a lot [of service users] saying, 'I've never even met my probation officer. I don't know who they are. I've seen a different person every week.' (Probation officer)

This would appear to concur with concerns raised by Kay (2016), who, in researching the experiences of a group of individuals subject to an intensive supervision programme, found that the upheaval caused by the reforms was having a detrimental impact. Many of those subject to supervision were not only having to develop new supervisory relationships but also having to commute considerable distances to attend appointments with their supervisors.

Yet despite concerns about the nature, pace and scale of the changes, many of those practitioners interviewed in our study continued to derive considerable satisfaction from the relational aspects of their work and were keen to maintain what they saw as a 'probation ethos'. Several explicitly stated that they continued to feel motivated by their underlying values and/or reasons for joining the service in the first instance and what emerged for some was the hope (and belief) that this 'ethos' would endure despite the organisational bifurcation engendered by the Transforming Rehabilitation reforms. This would appear consistent with previous research (Annison et al, 2008; Deering, 2011; Grant, 2016) that has suggested that the dominant practice culture within probation, based on penal welfarist values, has remained remarkably resilient, even though inevitably it has had to change and adapt to wider policy narratives. As a result, those practitioners observed in our research employed a range of strategies as they adapted to the changes brought about by Transforming Rehabilitation (see Burke et al, 2016 and Robinson et al, 2016, for a discussion of the strategies employed), which is unsurprising given the insights provided by Pierre Bourdieu that locates the workplace as a 'site of struggle' in which external changes to the field are mediated through the actions, professional ideologies and dispositions of individual workers.

However, we would contend that despite what seemed to be the maintenance of a probation 'habitus',[4] the impact of the perceived cultural shift brought about by Transforming Rehabilitation among probation staff cannot be underestimated (Burke et al, 2016). Some of those interviewed voiced fears and concerns centred on what they perceived to be a (further) fragmentation of 'probation values' and the maintenance of a positive working culture:

> There is a vocational aspect to this work, isn't there, that people really believe in? That I think stands people in good stead, but also can be very difficult, because people feel that there are a lot of principles that are being compromised here. (Middle manager)

The roots of these concerns among those we interviewed appeared to lie in the original splitting of the Probation Trust and the nature of interviewees' relationships with former colleagues who were now working in the National Probation Service (NPS). Reports by Her Majesty's Inspectorate of Probation (HMIP, 2014, 2015a, 2015b, 2016) have highlighted some of the operational issues arising from the early implementation of the reforms; however, our research indicated that a deeper change was occurring in the relationship between these two nascent organisations (see Burke et al, 2016; Robinson et al, 2016).

As our research progressed, it appeared that relations between the two organisations became increasingly instrumental and business-like.

> I think we should say, 'Tesco doesn't give free food or cheap food to Morrisons to sell does it?' You have created separate companies and they have to compete or run alongside each other, but have their eyes on their own budgets. (Probation officer)

Many of those workers interviewed in our study expressed a fear that key facets of the human capital of the CRC (routinely identified as its greatest strength by participants) were being threatened and tested to the point of being broken. Despite this, many participants drew great pride from what they viewed as the collective strength of the organisation. They alluded to the notion of a 'probation ethos' that reflected both the legacy of knowledge and skills, and the resilience of staff to continue to deliver service(s) in the face of external challenges:

> It's still one entity. It's just been broken in two. The values remain on either side, and that's what you take heart from. That's a positive thing. There are so many good people on both sides who are committed to doing the right thing, whomever we work for. (Probation officer)

Continuing professional commitment, though, did not necessarily mean that workers felt the same about their work as they had pre-Transforming Rehabilitation. As one probation officer in our study put it, the reforms had 'taken the shine off' their work. It was clear though that a significant number of the staff group, particularly those who were long-serving (a group described by Mawby and Worrall [2013] as 'lifers') and who had worked for the former Probation Trust, continued to harbour feelings of anger and resentment towards what they viewed as an ideologically driven and somewhat unnecessary change to their working structures and practices. As one experienced probation officer noted: "We had a service that worked and did well and now it's all broken". In this respect, some staff still appeared to be struggling to understand the rationale for such wide-ranging reform. The opening up of the market of probation services was something many of the respondents were anxious about: anxious because they felt they did not fully understand what opening up the market meant in real/practical terms, and anxious because it represented a new, more corporate, era of delivering probation services in which individuals were uncertain about where they and their working practice would fit. For some interviewees, their concerns were more explicitly about wanting the CRC to remain in public ownership. In several interviews, it was clear that these expressed wishes were underpinned by concerns or fears about a creeping 'corporatism' in the identity of the fledgling company, and/or the slightly longer-term prospect of being bought by a company driven solely by a profit motive:

> Fundamentally, I don't like the idea of the private companies running it. I think that the private companies that are in the frame to run it haven't got any innovation in terms of working with people. Their innovation's around structure and saving money, so they can make money for people. So I think it's actually a bit counter-intuitive, really. (Middle manager)

Despite their ideological opposition to the part privatisation of probation, some staff hoped that that the need for the new companies to make a financial return on their investments might increase efficiency and in doing so provide better services:

> On one hand, I think you can't make business and profits out of people and then on the other side I think, well actually, that pushes the bar up. If that improves services, if that gets lazy staff off their arses, well that's what's required then. (Probation officer)

As our research progressed, though, it was clear that the relational aspects of probation work (and the values underpinning them) faced considerable, and at times unprecedented, challenges both in terms of *quantity* (workload pressures) and *quality* (the nature of the work undertaken). The majority of those interviewed reported changes to their role or remit as a result of the restructuring and a belief that their caseloads had increased,[5] which they perceived as undermining their ability to undertake constructive work with those under their supervision:

> This is an opportunity to do some really exciting new ground breaking, cutting edge, innovative work, but then you'll have caseloads of 80 each. People are actually thinking, 'Well, how do I do that?', 'This is an opportunity for new thinking you can't do it the old way', 'Yes, but what is the new way?' (Probation service officer)

Workload pressures are of course not a new phenomenon to probation workers. Robinson and colleagues (2014) identified resource constraints, particularly in terms of the time available, as a significant impediment to the production of quality work. But it appeared that Transforming Rehabilitation had compounded the situation as practitioner colleagues departed the organisation (particularly probation officers who left for jobs in the NPS) and the implementation of the Offender Rehabilitation Act[6] was beginning to generate numbers of short licences. Clearly, then, for many staff, the implementation of the Transforming Rehabilitation reforms marked the start of another prolonged period of organisational turmoil as opposed to the culmination of a sustained period of change. As one respondent remarked: "The work that's coming in is relentless, and I think we're all now beginning to realise this is going to be a very, very long, bitter haul" (probation service officer).

'More creative than procedural'

> I struggle with any notions that it will bring innovation and decent practice because innovation and decent practice come from practitioners getting together and working together. You've split a whole bunch of practitioners away from each other so what was that about? (Middle manager)

As Maurice Vanstone has noted, much of the creativity in probation work has been the result of front-line practitioners who 'have never lacked imagination or the enthusiasm for innovatory ways of endeavoring to achieve their goals' (Vanstone, 2010, p 19). Ironically, though, increased centralisation and standardisation of contemporary probation practice has to some extent stifled innovation as quantitative outcome measures have been prioritised over qualitative processes (Knight et al, 2016). Reflecting this, some of those in our study expressed their frustration at how the probation service had been restricted from operating in ways that allowed it greater autonomy to respond to local issues. The vast majority of staff identified at least some ongoing changes as necessary and as providing a much-needed stimulus in the reorientation of the measures and mechanisms used to gauge the performance and impact of probation. One community service officer talked of the need to "re-boot" an organisation that had "got lost into this tranche of missives and directives". In this sense, there was a feeling of liberation from what they saw as the overly 'command and control' approach characteristic of the Ministry of Justice and National Offender Management Service. The apparent freedoms from nationally determined priorities and working practices was seen as a positive in helping the CRCs to empower themselves to apply their expertise and define their principles and working culture(s):

> It's an opportunity to think outside the box and think very creatively and think business-like and get rid of hierarchies. Get rid of the constraints that a public service, by virtue of its nature, puts on you. (Middle manager)

The CRC management team promoted the period prior to the share sale as a chance to streamline operations, redesignate roles to achieve a better fit with staff skill sets, and explore opportunities for income generation. This form of 'intrapreneurship' whereby workers embrace change, engage in creative work, develop new initiatives using entrepreneurship and innovation (Graham and White, 2015; Graham, 2016) could be seen as an attempt to regain a level of control over externally imposed changes they felt they had little control over. Being a smaller organisation with a 'flatter' management structure than the former Probation Trust was seen as having the potential for the new company to become a more responsive and less bureaucratic organisation that could function within less formalised and leaner systems of governance. It also meant, in theory at least, that the senior management team was able to respond much more quickly to emerging operational and practice issues and also be more accessible to staff. The leaner and more dynamic structure was seen as positively helping the organisation develop through an increased input from the "staff group about how to do things" (senior manager) and being able to better "press down the responsibility and decision-making process" (senior manager). However, the sustainability of this tactic was somewhat precarious, given that this was a temporary arrangement and responsibility would eventually be transferred to the new owners following the completion of the tendering process. Indeed, the former Probation Trust's enthusiastic development of non-programmatic, desistance-based practices had to be abandoned in the context of the turmoil generated by the organisational restructuring, leaving staff to hope that the new owners would ultimately reinstate these (Robinson et al, forthcoming). As such, despite the innovative zeal adopted by the management team, there was an acceptance that innovations developed during this period would in reality only be supported in the long term if they were compatible with the operational models on which the successful bids were based. The fact that ultimately the contract to run the CRC was awarded to a company that was also the preferred bidder to manage other CRC package areas heightened existing apprehensions that this could result in a standardisation of operations to secure economies of scale. This naturally heightened fears of potential job losses if roles were streamlined across contract areas.

Among the wider staff group there also appeared to be an increasing acknowledgement that practice would (or could) be fundamentally different under the new organisational arrangements and some of those interviewed began to see the changes as an opportunity to innovate and provide more focused interventions. It appeared that for a good number of participants the obvious uncertainty and inconvenience created by the speed and scope of organisational change was offset by the perceived promise of reshaping probation working practice made possible through a new sense of freedom:

> I came into probation to work with people, that was what I wanted to do. I think over the last few years, things have become far too much office based and computer based and assessment based. At your desk, rather than with people. I am seeing the CRC as an opportunity to change that way, I suppose. (Probation officer)

The promise of investment in improved IT systems and the opportunity to work more flexibly in the local community was appealing for many of those interviewed. The following contribution captures the pragmatic optimism that characterised a number of the responses:

> The reason I find this change exciting is because that system that I loved, and always wanted to be a part of, I found stifling. I've always felt like I'm working with shackles on; that it's so rigid and it's so prescribed.... I'm an ideas kind of person; creative ideas and creative ways of working, which the probation system didn't allow for. Basically, TR [Transforming Rehabilitation] goes, 'Let's just cut those chains off you', and I take them off, and already I'm being creative. (Operational staff member)

As mentioned earlier, as part of the government's 'rehabilitation revolution', the relaxation of National Standards[7] was promoted as a means of enabling practitioners to exercise greater personal discretion in their work, and backed up by incentivised commissioning systems, enabling them to focus on achieving positive rehabilitative outcomes for those under their supervision as opposed to striving to meet targets based on measurable outputs. In Robinson and colleagues' (2014) study, staff viewed good quality practice as being flexible and adaptable to the individual's circumstances, and, as such, compliance with National Standards was regarded as the most irrelevant factor in delivering quality practice. Despite this, many of those interviewed in our study welcomed what they hoped would be an opportunity to exercise greater discretion and flexibility in their work.

> The best part of it for me is that relaxation, and also because I'm not dealing with a whole caseload of high risk cases. The idea that you could have a whole caseload of really high-risk people is quite terrifying. (Probation officer)

However, the sense of freedom – and the apparent optimism that derived from it – was less palpable among some other operational staff. While several interviewees did identify gains through what they saw as a relaxation of National Standards, these were on occasion tempered by their unease at drifting too far from settled and structured working practices, and at its worst these fears were seen to compromise perceived thresholds of professionalism. Nowhere were people's fears of the threats to the profession more sharply expressed than those voicing concern around the positioning of the probation officer and the uncertainty surrounding the role of the probation officer grade in the CRC and the numbers of qualified staff. For the probation officers in our sample, the most salient aspects of role changes were formal ones, that is the loss of 'high risk of harm' cases now deemed to be the responsibility of the NPS, along with report writing, multi-agency work with high-risk offenders and other duties that were also no longer the responsibility of CRC staff:

> Now, I have to remind myself: I am qualified as a probation officer. That's what I am. The fact that I work for a company that doesn't deal with the things I used to deal with doesn't mean I'm not capable of doing that, because I am. (Probation officer)

According to Fitzgibbon (2016, p 169, original emphasis), privatisation has put the final 'nail in the coffin of practitioner autonomy by reducing practitioners to the status of a *precariat* of lightly trained, insecure employees'. As one of the middle managers in our research remarked:

> I think there's going to be a lot of shedding of staff. I think there's going to be a lot more onus on business and business plans and hitting targets. We've always been, in the years that I've been in probation, very target driven. I think this target, this is going to be much more cash linked. Whilst it's been cash linked in the past, supposedly, there have never been any consequences. Now there are real consequences in terms of those major targets not being hit. (Middle manager)

As the fieldwork wore on, growing numbers of probation staff reported what they considered to be an increased emphasis on the newly formed CRC working to deliver on the expectations and conditions of the contract. For some pockets of staff, this was a source of anxiety, as they expressed concerns about displaying weakness or an inability to meet targets for fear of reprimand. Beyond this, though, was a growing acceptance among practitioners that a contractual culture was leading to increasingly technical approaches to service delivery with, for example, significant attention being paid to the timely completion of initial supervision plans:

> They do say all that, but the minute anyone says, 'Oh, let's be innovative', it's like, 'Well, that's okay, providing you make sure that there is an ISP, a review and a termination or there's a breach file.' Innovative? We're just seeing the same people, only more of them with less constraints. In one sense, that is.… We're being told that we can see people much less often. Is that innovative? (Probation officer)

Robinson (2003) notes that it would be a mistake to dismiss advancing technicality as in itself 'anti-professional'. Technicality can lead to positive professional outcomes providing there is a space where clinical judgements and discretion can be appropriately sustained. Ultimately, though, the Ministry of Justice will retain governance of the CRCs through the highly prescribed contractual arrangements. This is likely not only to restrict the amount of opportunities for innovation (discussed in the next section) that the CRCs are able to operate, but also to ensure that a culture of performance measurement is sustained and the type of edgework identified by Mawby and Worrall severely constrained. The pressure to perform against their contractual obligations may well limit the level of discretion and innovation permitted and as the demands for their services increase, exacerbated by the extension of statutory supervision to short-term prisoners, this could lead to routine practices and processing of individuals. Allied to this, Fitzgibbon (2016) argues that competition in the form envisaged within Transforming Rehabilitation might actually be counterproductive in stimulating innovation because as CRCs will ultimately be in competition with each other when the contracts are retendered they will be reluctant to share or promote innovative approaches for fear of surrendering their competitive advantage in subsequent tendering processes. Fitzgibbon also warns that more labour-intensive interventions will be competing with technology-based surveillance systems (such as electronic monitoring and biometric reporting) that are potentially cheaper and do not require a skilled and highly trained workforce. The danger is that ultimately the need to reduce costs will always be seen as more important than the secondary aim of innovation in the current political climate. It was generally accepted by the workers interviewed in our study that large numbers of individuals would be seen less frequently and that they may then be engaged through new, different and evolving mediums – like supervision centres or partners from the 'prime' owner supply chain – as a means of reducing costs rather than stimulating innovation:

> I guess one of my real concerns, is innovation costs; innovation isn't neutral, I think there's this odd belief that somehow everything is free … innovation costs you; you have to set time aside, you have to staff it. Some of my frustrations in probation have been about not being able to carry through what I see as decent innovations because your day job gets in the way of it…. That's what we seem to be lacking, we seem to have a resistance to newness, and we're just ploughing the same field. That's why if something had come in, from externally, and gone, 'Pow! It's going to be different, we're going to try and do something a little bit sparky.' (Middle manager)

The danger, as Dominey (2016, p 141) notes, is that if reporting arrangements are reduced to merely cursory interactions, 'it is unlikely that supervision will offer anything that supervisees perceive as helpful or engaging'. Suggestions that providers will be able to increase their market share through efficiency savings while at the same time investing in the training and employment of skilled practitioners seem somewhat optimistic to say the least. Unlike the NPS, contracted providers will not be required to adopt the Probation Qualification Framework but 'will be contractually required to have and to maintain a workforce with appropriate levels of training and competence' (Ministry of Justice, 2013b, p 41). What will constitute appropriate levels of training and competence in this context is unclear. However, what is clear is that if such training is not responsive to the changing demands of practice, it will stifle rather than promote the innovation that the designers of the Transforming Rehabilitation agenda were hoping to achieve.

'More collaborative than instrumental'

In recent years, there has been a growing awareness that collaborative relationships in the form of partnership working are central to probation practice. This is because working constructively with individuals with complex needs requires a range of support provided by a range of agencies. Robinson and colleagues' (2014, p 137) observation that collaborative working has become 'part of the cultural fabric of probation practice in England and Wales' was reiterated by those interviewed in our study as they recounted the positive role that partnership work contributed to their work. Among those interviewed in our research there was broad support for encouraging and developing innovative partnerships and approaches and building stronger links with organisations based in the local community. However, concerns were raised that introducing competition into service delivery was undermining established partnerships:

> We very much started to think over the last year that our partners have suddenly – I think in a way we've noticed the difference in some of the partner agencies that we've worked with, because obviously, they're going to be competing for some of the work that we do. I know that there's going to be some organisations that are going to be competing for what we do and probably think that they could do it better, cheaper than us. (Middle manager)

While there was a growing realisation that the CRC was 'not the only game in town anymore' and no longer held a near-monopoly position in the delivery of community-based rehabilitative interventions, there were real fears raised that the Transforming Rehabilitation agenda would struggle to deliver on the objectives of opening up the market to a raft of new third sector providers and the innovative practice that it was hoped would transform probation interventions. Staff expressed doubts as to whether or not the new arrangements would encourage a more diverse range of new rehabilitation partners or bring about significant reductions in reoffending levels hoped for. Their concerns regarded the credibility of the service being offered and the feasibility of being able to deliver services within the newly configured operational structures. For others, the focus of concern was around accountability and the threat to the consistency (and quality) of service that may arise as responsibility for delivering services is spread throughout the partnership chain. Others developed these concerns further and were sceptical that in responding to the new groups of service users – outlined in the Transforming Rehabilitation agenda – the CRC would be able to first find, and then second stimulate, relationships with external agencies. Certainly, there was a feeling that in the period leading up to the split there did not appear to be much evidence of the development of new external partnerships:

> It's not like overnight 100 new third sector organisations have been knocking on our door saying, 'Now you're doing this we want to help more.' It's the same organisations we've always used with one or two faces may be changing. There hasn't been a vast change of the way we work day to day at all. I still link into the same organisations that I ever did. If a new one comes on the market I would have done that the old way and this way. (Probation officer)

An underpinning ambition of the Transforming Rehabilitation reforms was the emphasis placed on integrating third sector and voluntary organisations within a more holistic network of service providers. However, this bringing together of large, often multinational, 'prime' companies with the small often local organisations that constituted their supply chain of services presents very real challenges in constructing logistically effective and representatively fair models of operation. Of the 700 organisations from across the private, public and voluntary sectors that had originally registered an interest in providing services, just eight preferred bidders were awarded the contracts. This bought into sharp focus the need to understand how the financial capacity, resources and ambitions of large private enterprises could be reconciled with the working practices and values of those from the charitable sector. To add to the complexity, half of the contracts were awarded to just two companies – Purple Futures (an Interserve-led partnership) and Sodexo – neither of which had an established record of delivering rehabilitative services. For smaller charitable organisations, it appears that the best of hope for securing funding is through becoming a subcontractor to one of the prime private sector providers, thereby extending the web of privatisation (Corcoran, 2014, p 67; Clinks, 2015).

As Martin and colleagues (2016, p 23) note, 'Contracts bring with them both the promise of stable income and a more formalised strategic relationship with the authority contracting out the service', but there is an obvious tension in the government's plans. On the one hand, they seek to utilise the innovative capital of voluntary organisations, while at the same time subjecting them to contractual requirements, with the attendant bureaucracy that might result in them becoming themselves more bureaucratic and ultimately less flexible. So, although charities are described as full 'partners' in CRCs, in reality their status, influence and income will be vastly outweighed by for-profit contractors (Hucklesby and Corcoran, 2016). The market is further skewed by the fact that monopolisation is also a feature of the charitable sector, with a few 'big players' dominating the landscape. In England and Wales, two thirds of the value of service contracts issued by the central government between 2011 and 2012 went to three charities (Centre for Crime and Justice Studies, 2014, p 20). The owners of the CRCs will inevitably aim to consolidate and increase their market share, and as Martin et al (2016, p 38) caution, as the sector becomes more divided between small locally based charities and large quasi-corporate structures, the danger is that tighter contracts might exclude some of the most significant needs and aspirations of the most marginalised individuals and communities. Moreover, there are already indications that Transforming Rehabilitation has not generated the volume of cases hoped for in the CRCs' business plans (NAO, 2016). While this might be good news for society, it is less so for shareholders of the companies involved. As Burke and Collett (2016, p 130) have noted: 'It remains to be seen if in the face of further planned budgetary cuts, the CRCs will generate enough income to sustain the interests of the business corporations behind them or whether it might lead to consolidation, merger or even retrenchment.'

There are also concerns that commissioning contracts through a Payment by Results (PbR) mechanism might be counterproductive in that it can negatively shape provider behaviour, leading providers to focus on a narrow range of outcomes rather than working holistically. Hough (2016, p 74) claims that: 'The eclipsing of the traditional partnership between probation and TSOs [Third Sector Organisations] by a quantitative, target-driven approach to rehabilitation is inevitable under the new Payment by Results (PbR) system.' A report by Rees and colleagues (2013) analysing the voluntary sectors experience of the Work Programme found that agencies were unwilling to work with individuals who were unlikely to find employment without the input of extensive and expensive resources because there was not the financial incentives to do so. Similarly, in an evaluation of a PbR scheme in HMP Doncaster, Pearce and colleagues (2015) found that providers withdrew services, regardless of need, as soon as the released prisoner was known to have reoffended as they received no income for continuing to work with them. Hudson et al (2010) also found that the support provided by organisations as part of the Work Programme tended to be shaped by the nature of the contractual obligations. Moreover, given that the majority of revenues achieved by the CRCs will be 'fee for service', providers could be encouraged to concentrate their efforts towards those individuals where there is a guaranteed return for their investment rather than on more complex cases with entrenched criminal behaviours where outcomes are less certain. The salutary lessons from the research into PbR suggests that models work best on much smaller scales than the ambitions of Transforming Rehabilitation (see Community Links, 2015) and that specific service-user groups have found their engagement with services disproportionately compromised (see Gelsthorpe and Hedderman's [2012] work on female offenders). The example of the failure to accommodate a programme specifically developed to address the needs of black and minority ethic and Muslim offenders into the CRC delivery model as outlined by Hough (2016) does not bode well in this respect.

Conclusion

When asked about the future legacy of Transforming Rehabilitation, the response from one of the middle managers in our study was that: "It will either go one way or the other. It will either be the worst catastrophe in the history of probation or it will be the best thing that's ever happened." A year after our research was completed, it is still unclear to what extent the practice cultures of the newly reconfigured landscape of probation will reflect either the former or the latter. Despite this, our research in one CRC case-study area suggests that probation workers remain highly committed to working *constructively* with those individuals under their supervision in terms of supporting them towards making positive changes in their lives. Our observations over the course of the research would seem to chime with Hannah Graham's (2016) finding that in most cases criminal justice practitioners pragmatically respond to externally imposed changes utilising their professional agency. Nevertheless, it was also painfully evident that implementing Transforming Rehabilitation had been extremely testing for all involved and in some cases had fractured existing relationships and destabilised established working practices.

Ultimately, though, the space for working constructively will be dictated by the operating models adopted by the CRCs. By its very nature, Transforming Rehabilitation has introduced a potentially wider and more diverse range of providers with the obvious risks of fragmentation and inconsistent delivery. This could have a positive effect in terms of developing new innovations and building relationships with new stakeholders that are more responsive to local needs, but as we have indicated in this chapter there are significant challenges involved. Over time, 'best practice' might emerge from the range of operating models being developed by the current owners, but the danger is that concerns with increasing market shares and issues of commercial confidentiality might in reality hinder this. Much will depend on the ability of the CRCs to recruit those individuals into their organisations that have the right skills and aptitudes as identified by Robinson et al (2014) and Grant and McNeill (2015). It will also involve enabling existing employees to build meaningful relationships with those under their supervision, encourage creative thinking and intellectual curiosity, and build collaborative relationships with other stakeholders. This will require appropriate training and opportunities for specialism and career progression. The omens do not look promising, though. Faced with the prospects of reduced budgets, some CRC owners are planning significant staffing reductions, and the introduction of biometric reporting kiosks by at least one of the current owners as part of its cost-cutting plans could, as Burke and Collett (2016, p 131) argue, suggest 'a potentially dystopian future in which the complexities of human interactions are reducible to a series of impersonal processes'. Second, it will depend on the capacity/willingness of the CRC owners to look beyond profit considerations. This might be akin to expecting sharks to be vegetarians (Brady, 2016), but the owners of the CRCs will need to demonstrate the 'added value' they bring to service delivery as they move towards retendering in the hope of retaining, and hopefully expanding, their market share. As Knight et al (2016, p 55) point out, if CRCs want to push the boundaries of current practice, they 'may need to be persuaded to see the development of emotional skills in the workforce as leading to improved results, better engagement with offenders, and a more fruitful way to achieve the results they are contracted to achieve'.

Notes

[1] Under the Transforming Rehabilitation reforms, the 35 local Probation Trusts were replaced with a new National Probation Service and 21 Community Rehabilitation Companies. The former remains a part of the public sector and has responsibility for supervising high risk of serious harm cases and those subject to Multi-Agency Public Protection Arrangements. The latter manage most medium and low risk of serious harm cases.

[2] This ethnographic study involved over 100 individual and focus group interviews and approximately 120 hours of observations, engaging staff at every level within the new organisation.

[3] The SEED (Skills for Effective Engagement and Development) pilots were conducted between spring 2011 and spring 2012. Their purpose was to develop and test out a practice skills model based on the best evidence about the impact of effective engagement with offenders on reducing reoffending.

[4] Habitus is a system of dispositions, tendencies that organise the ways in which individuals perceive the social world around them and react to it. These dispositions are usually shared by people with similar background and reflects the lived reality to which individuals are socialised, their individual experience and objective opportunities.

[5] On a national level, the CRC business volumes were between 6%–35% less than the Ministry of Justice had anticipated during the procurement process. However, in the CRC studied, the reduction in the number of staff employed had in reality increased the numbers supervised within individual caseloads.

[6] The Offender Rehabilitation Act 2014 extended supervision to all individuals released from prison sentences of under 12 months.

[7] National Standards were introduced in 1992 specifying the core probation tasks and when they must be carried out. Over time they became increasingly prescriptive but in 2011 the Ministry of Justice published revised standards that were less rigid in determining some aspects of offender supervision.

References

Annison, J., Eadie, T and Knight, C (2008) 'People first: probation officer perspectives on probation work', *Probation Journal*, 55(3): 259–27.

Brady, D. (2016) 'Book reviews', *Probation Journal*, 8(2): 102–110.

Burke, L. and Collett, S. (2016) 'Organisational bifurcation and the end of probation as we knew it?' *Probation Journal*, 63(2): 120–135.

Burke, L., Millings, M. and Robinson, G. (2016) 'Probation migration(s): examining occupational culture in a turbulent field', *Criminology and Criminal Justice*, DOI: 10.1177/1748895816656905.

Centre for Crime and Justice Studies (2014) *UK Justice Policy Review, Vol. 3*, London: Centre for Crime and Justice Studies.

Clinks (2015) *Early Doors: The Voluntary Sector's Role in Transforming Rehabilitation*, London: Clinks.

Community Links (2015) *Payment by Results: Issues that Matter, No. 5*, London: Community Links.

Corcoran, M. (2014) The trajectory of penal markets in a period of austerity: the case of England and Wales', Punishment and Incarceration: A Global Perspective, *Sociology of Crime, Law and Deviance*, 19: 53–74.

Deering, J. (2011) *Probation Practice and the New Penology: Practitioner Reflections*, Aldershot: Ashgate.

Dominey, J. (2016) 'Fragmenting probation: recommendations from research', *Probation Journal*, 63(2): 136–144.

Fitzgibbon, W. (2016) 'Probation, privatisation and perceptions of risk', in M. Vanstone and P. Priestley (eds) *Probation and Politics: Academic Reflections from Former Practitioners*, London: Palgrave Macmillan, pp 159–177.

Gelsthorpe, L. and Hedderman, C. (2012) 'Providing for women offenders: the risks of adopting a payment by results approach', *Probation Journal*, 59(4): 374–390.

Gorman, K., Gregory, M., Hayles, M. and Parton, N. (2006) *Constructive Work with Offenders*, London: Jessica Kingsley.

Graham, H. (2016) *Rehabilitation Work: Supporting Desistance and Recovery*, London: Routledge.

Graham, H. and White, R. (2015) *Innovative Justice*, London: Routledge.

Grant, S. (2016) 'Constructing the durable penal agent: tracing the development of habitus within English probation officers and Scottish criminal justice social workers', *British Journal of Criminology*, 56(4): 750–768.

Grant, S. and McNeill, F. (2015) 'What matters in practice? Understanding "quality" in the routine supervision of offenders in Scotland', *British Journal of Social Work*, 45(7): 1985–2002.

HMI Probation (2014) *Transforming Rehabilitation: Early Implementation April 2014–September 2014*, Manchester: HMIP.

HMIP (Her Majesty's Inspectorate of Probation) (2015a) *Transforming Rehabilitation: Early Implementation 2, May 2015*, Manchester: HMIP.

HMI Probation (2015b) *Transforming Rehabilitation: Early Implementation 3, November 2015*, Manchester: HMIP.

HMI Probation (2016) *Transforming Rehabilitation: Early Implementation 4, January 2016*, Manchester: HMIP.

Hough, C.V. (2016) 'Transforming Rehabilitation and its impact on a locally-based rehabilitation programme for black and minority ethnic and Muslim offenders', *European Journal of Probation*, 8(2): 68–81.

Hucklesby, A. and Corcoran, M. (2016) *The Voluntary Sector and Criminal Justice*, London: Palgrave Macmillan.

Hudson, M., Phillips, J., Ray, K., Vegeris, S. and Davidson, R. (2010) *The influence of outcome-based contracting on Provider-led Pathways to Work*, Department for Work and Pensions Research Report No. 638, Norwich: Her Majesty's Stationery Office.

Knight, C. (2014) *Emotional Literacy in Criminal Justice: Professional Practice with Offenders*, London: Palgrave Macmillan.

Knight, C., Phillips, J., Chapman, T. (2016) 'Bringing the feelings back. Returning emotions to criminal justice practice', *British Journal of Community Justice*, 14(1): 45–58.

Martin, C., Frazer, L., Cumbo, E., Hayes, C. and O'Donoghue, K. (2016) 'Paved with good intentions: the way ahead for voluntary, community and social enterprise sector organisations', in A. Hucklesby and M. Corcoran (eds) *The Voluntary Sector and Criminal Justice*, London: Palgrave Macmillan.

Mawby, R.C. and Worrall, A. (2013) *Doing Probation Work: Identity in a Criminal Justice Occupation*, London: Routledge.

Ministry of Justice (2013a) *Transforming Rehabilitation: A Revolution in the Way We Manage Offenders*, London: Ministry of Justice.

Ministry of Justice (2013b) *Target Operating System: The Rehabilitation Programme*, Ministry of Justice: London.

NAO (National Audit Office) (2016) *Transforming Rehabilitation: Report by the Comptroller and Auditor General*, London: NAO.

Pearce, S., Murray, D., Lane, M., GVA and Green, C. [two independent consultants providing objective advice] (2015) *HMP Doncaster Payment by Results Pilot: Final Process Evaluation Report*, London: Ministry of Justice.

Rees, J., Taylor, R. and Damm, C. (2013) *Does Sector matter? Understanding the Experiences of Providers in the Work Programme*, Birmingham: Third Sector Research Centre, University of Birmingham.

Robinson, G. (2003) 'Technicality and indeterminacy in probation practice: a case study', *British Journal of Social Work*, 33(5): 593–610.

Robinson, G. and Burnett, R. (2007) 'Experiencing modernization: frontline probation perspectives on the transition to a National Offender Management Service', *Probation Journal*, 54(4): 318–337.

Robinson, G. and McNeill, F. (2004) 'Purposes matter: examining the "ends" of probation practice', in G. Mair (ed) *What Matters in Probation*, Cullompton: Willan, pp 227–305.

Robinson, G., Burke, L. and Millings, M. (2016) 'Criminal justice identities in transition: the case of devolved probation services in England and Wales', *British Journal of Criminology*, 56(1): 161–178.

Robinson, G., Burke, L. and Millings, M. (forthcoming) 'Probation, privatisation and legitimacy', *The Howard Journal of Crime and Justice*.

Robinson, G., Priede, C., Farrall, S., Shapland, J. and McNeill, F. (2014) 'Understanding "quality" in probation practice: frontline perspectives in England and Wales', *Criminology and Criminal Justice*, 14(2): 123–142.

Shapland, J., Bottoms, A., Farrall, S., McNeill, F., Priede, C. and Robinson, G. (2012) *The quality of probation supervision – a literature review*, Sheffield: Centre for Criminological Research, University of Sheffield.

Sorsby, A., Shapland, J., Farrall, S., McNeill, F., Priede, C. and Robinson, G. (2013) *Probation Staff Views of the Skills for Effective Engagement Development (SEED) Project*, Sheffield: Centre for Criminological Research, University of Sheffield.

Vanstone, M. (2010) 'Creative work: an historical perspective', in J. Brayford., F. Cowie and J. Deering (eds) *What Else Works?*, Cullompton: Willan, pp 19–35.

White, A. (2014) 'Post-crisis policing and public-private partnerships: the case of Lincolnshire Police and G4S', *British Journal of Criminology*, 54(6): 1002–1022.

Worrall, A. (2015) 'Grace under pressure: the role of courage in the future of probation work', *The Howard Journal of Crime and Justice*, 54(5): 508–520.

FIVE

Implementation uptake: organisational factors affecting evidence-based reform in community corrections in the United States

Danielle S. Rudes, Kimberly R. Kras, Kimberly S. Meyer and Shannon Magnuson

Introduction

As many community corrections agencies (for example, probation and parole agencies) undergo organisational change and evidence-based practice (EBP) implementation, most face a complex web of inter- and intra-organisational dynamics and contexts that make implementing reform challenging and sustaining reforms nearly impossible. Some of the demands come from external stakeholders such as judges, police departments, community groups and attorneys, but many reform challenges percolate from *within* the agency. These include barriers to change originating within existing organisational culture/ climate and related to staff cynicism and organisational commitment. Some forward-thinking organisations undergoing change rely on organisational assessments to determine readiness or evaluate whether a culture supports the initiation and sustainment of EBPs. Despite the validity and reliability of organisational readiness surveys for gauging staff perceptions of their organisation pre-change, these assessments may not fully capture the rich contextual nuance encompassing an agency's multifaceted milieu.

Most organisational assessments include some measure of culture/ climate, cynicism and commitment. These characteristics are widely studied in organisational scholarship, and more recently in corrections research. Each concept reflects aspects of the agency, where culture/ climate reflect umbrella constructs and commitment and cynicism serve as proxy measures of organisational functioning and work-related impacts such as job satisfaction or burnout. Although culture and climate are different constructs, scholars use them synonymously in the literature. In fact, climate refers to perceptions of norms and values dictating observable formal and informal practices and procedures within the workplace (Guion, 1973) and culture refers to the evolution and impact of those shared meanings and organisational structures on groups and individuals (Kunda, 1992). While scholars typically discuss culture/climate at the agency level, it also exists at the local level within smaller departments or units. Organisational culture, particularly at local levels, is plainly 'the way things get done' (Deal and Kennedy, 1982; Rudes and Viglione, 2014, p 623). Local culture may contribute to the broader agency culture, but also may compete with it. As a result, culture acts as both a barrier and facilitator to organisational change where the ease of change is largely contingent on how the change is introduced to the organisation and its degree of suggested and actual alignment with local norms and values. For example, findings from Portillo and colleagues (2016), during their work with justice practitioners implementing EBP contingency management (CM) in various problem-solving courts, suggest the highest alignment of CM practice to core CM principles occurred in the courts that discussed the philosophy behind the approach and how to use CM in practice with their staff before and during implementation. Further, Rudes and colleagues (2011), in a study of a work-release facility undergoing transformation to a reentry center, suggest that in the absence of change explanations from upper management, staff attitudes and behaviors undermine reform efforts, suggesting a low readiness or unwillingness to change. Together, these studies suggest culture/climate may impede or facilitate change; however, they also contribute to the ambiguous nature of defining 'culture' specifically. For the remainder of this chapter, we will use the term 'culture' as it best represents a more holistic and dynamic concept. However, prior studies suggest aspects of culture – such as cynicism and commitment – are also influential in the change process, but remain underexplored in community corrections.

Cynicism refers to 'varying degrees of hostile, suspicious, and disparaging attitudes toward work situations and social interactions' (Ulmer, 1992, p 424). Cynicism may surround one's job, organisation, or even specific change efforts (Condrey et al, 2005). Although individual employees can be cynical, DeCelles and colleagues (2013) define cynicism as a multi-level reality, affecting individuals as well as overall organisational climate. Thus, a cynical environment might affect otherwise non-cynical individuals. Common origins of cynicism lie in perceived lack of power (Hepburn, 1987) and conflicts between personal and institutional values, such as punishment versus rehabilitation (Melnick et al, 2009). For example, in one study of juvenile probation officers and their supervisors, Farrell and colleagues (2011) assessed the degree to which individual staff members felt pessimistic about the organisation's ability to change or improve procedures. They report increased cynicism about change, which contributed to staff not using EBPs. Scholars suggest organisational leaders can combat cynicism by involving staff throughout the change process (Farrell et al, 2011), articulating agency goals/vison (Bommer et al, 2005), and communicating reasons for reform (Condrey et al, 2005). However, more information is needed to understand whether strategies combating initial cynicism toward change can also sustain change. Exploring how these strategies affect long-term outcomes may also help improve other aspects of the organisation, such as cultivating organisational commitment.

Organisational commitment is a central occupational attitude defined as 'a bond to the whole organization, and not to the job, work group, or belief in the importance of work itself' (Lambert et al, 1999, p 100). Commitment is multidimensional (Reichers, 1985) and typically measured using attitudinal scales (Lambert et al, 1999). Scholars note that increased role ambiguity (Lambert et al, 2005a) and job stress are related to decreased organisational commitment, while job satisfaction predicts increases in organisational commitment (Lambert and Paoline, 2008). Further, in corrections agencies, studies suggest these factors leading to organisational commitment are related to workplace outputs such as job performance (Culliver et al, 1991), organisational citizenship behavior (Lambert et al, 2008), absenteeism (Lambert et al, 2005b) and turnover (Camp, 1994). Therefore, it is critical to consider staff commitment or evaluate predictors of commitment, particularly when considering the implications of these outputs on organisations undergoing change. Despite this growing body of literature, most research focuses on prison staff rather than community corrections, and none examines the relationship between commitment and EBP implementation.

In this chapter, we examine how organisational features such as cynicism, commitment and broad discussions of culture reflect a continuum of implementing planned change. Specifically, we consider how traditional measures of these organisational features reflect the challenges of reform uptake. Using data collected via mixed methods (surveys, interviews and observations), we provide comparative examples from three types of community corrections agencies (adult probation in two states and juvenile probation in one state) at various stages of the implementation process to consider the ways organisational culture, cynicism and commitment affect the experience of change.

The study

The data for this analysis come from comparable projects investigating EBP implementation using organisational surveys, ethnographic fieldwork and informal interviewing methods in three community corrections agencies – two adult and one juvenile. A total of 899 hours were spent in the field across these three agencies and researchers collected 1,209 surveys from staff at all levels. Specific to this analysis, researchers spent a total of 178 hours in the field to conduct observations and interviews with agency managers/supervisors. This chapter presents a subsample of surveys (n=188) and field visits from these projects to produce comparable datasets, both quantitatively and qualitatively, of managers' perceptions about organisational culture, cynicism, commitment and the EBP implementation process. We focus on managers since they work at the 'nexus between policy creators and policy implementers' and provide important insights connecting the ideas of street-level bureaucrats to those of upper level administrators (Rudes, 2012, p 4).

Methodology

Study sites and data collection

Across all sites, researchers used observational and informal interview methods to collect qualitative data, relying on a grounded theory approach to data analysis (Charmaz, 2006). Primary focal areas across all sites included observing staff engaging with clients, though secondary focal areas pertinent to each organisation varied across each study site. On completion of each day's observations, researchers recorded field-note data. This standard practice of ethnographic methods (where researchers only make small jottings and limit note taking while in the field) preserves participant rapport while also maximising researchers' data recall (Emerson et al, 1995; Emerson, 2001). We present demographic information for each study site in Table 5.1.

Administration of the organisational survey varied per site, involving email and paper distribution depending on the agency. Each survey contained the same measures for organisational climate/culture, organisational commitment and cynicism. The organisational culture/climate measure (Taxman et al, 2007) consists of 20 items, such as 'Ideas and suggestions from employees get fair consideration by unit supervisors' and 'Most staff here believe that they can have open discussions with supervisors and administration about work-related difficulties.' The organisational commitment measure (Caldwell et al, 1990) contains 12 items, such as 'I talk up this organisation to my friends as a great place to work.' Finally, the cynicism measure (Tesluk et al, 1995) contains five items, including 'I've pretty much given up trying to make suggestions for improvements around here.' The cynicism measure is reverse-coded so that lower scores reflect lower cynicism.

Northern State Probation & Parole (NSPP)

NSPP is a state agency supervising nearly 45,000 probationers and parolees in the community and employing approximately 650 supervising staff. In the early 2000s, following a change in political leadership and merging of community corrections with prisons, the state's justice platform and the agency's agenda shifted from an emphasis on evidence-based practices to a containment and risk management focus. Although these strict policies were initially designed for a subset of the overall probation population, targeting violent behaviour, they prevailed over the department, facilitating a flood of unintended consequences for both the organisation's culture and its capacity to answer field-level and legislative demands for reform.

Field-note data from this site came from ethnographic fieldwork in eight probation offices and during training sessions across the state, for a total of 144 hours. The ethnographic fieldwork aimed to understand dissemination of policy and practice, and adoption and use of practices at the office level by front-line officers and managers. Training sessions emerged as an outgrowth of this fieldwork and focused on informing managers about quality improvement models in preparation for implementation of new EBPs. A total of 36 managers participated in the qualitative data collection. Participants were mostly female (69%) and black (75%), with an average age range of 50 to 59 years (42%).

Survey data include a subset of 51 managers from the agency (41% of total managers) who were selected to participate in the training sessions. Administered during the first of three training sessions, the organisational survey garnered a response rate of 100%.

East Coast Probation & Parole (ECPP)

ECPP is a state agency supervising over 60,000 probationers and parolees in the community and employing nearly 800 supervising staff. In 2006, ECPP began implementing numerous EBPs across the state, including risk-need instruments, motivational interviewing and case planning practices. To facilitate implementation and sustainability of these initiatives, the state created a new class of managers tasked with overseeing roll-out of the new practices, measuring quality and improving fidelity of implementation, training line staff and providing on-site coaching. These staff trained line officers in EBP use extensively throughout the late 2000s and during the study period.

Qualitative data for this analysis came from a study on the pilot and subsequent implementation of a client-driven case management initiative in two jurisdictions in the state. Researchers spent nearly 355 hours of fieldwork in two adult probation offices, observing 10 managers over about 14 hours. Managers were primarily female (60%), white (90%) and were most often in their 50s (30%). We administered the organisational survey statewide via email using the web-based survey software QuestionPro. Here, we focus on the survey responses of the 93 managers who participated in the organisational survey.

County Juvenile Probation (CJP)

CJP supervises approximately 575 probationers who entered the justice system while under the age of 18 in one county. CJP employs approximately 300 staff, many of whom work in residential facilities or administrative roles. Beginning in 2006, CJP began using EBPs including risk-need assessments, graduated sanctions matrices and motivational interviewing. After each EBP training, managers were tasked with supporting their subordinates' skills and offering additional training as needed.

Qualitative data for this analysis came from an ethnographic project aimed at understanding EBP implementation in CJP. These data emerged from one year of fieldwork in probation offices, during which researchers spent over 20 hours observing and interviewing five probation managers who supervise 33 juvenile probation officers. The majority of managers were female (80%), white (80%), and had an average age range of 40 to 49 years (60%). Researchers administered the organisational survey via paper and pencil in CJP, visiting each unit and allowing staff to take the survey during work hours. The survey garnered an overall response rate of 73%. Survey responses from 44 managers in the agency are presented in Table 5.1.

Analysis

Analysis of the organisational survey data includes descriptive comparisons of the mean results of the subsamples on scales measuring organisational culture, organisational commitment and cynicism. Independent of the quantitative analyses, researchers coded and analysed qualitative data using Atlas.ti, a commonly used data management tool. Researchers deductively analysed the field-note data for characteristics of the intra-/inter-organisational dynamics focusing on culture, commitment, cynicism and EBP uptake, while also allowing additional themes and descriptions to emerge inductively. Researchers prepared memos on each study site for comparison of the qualitative data, then compared the qualitative results to the quantitative results.

Table 5.1: Qualitative data sample descriptive information for middle managers

Demographic variables	NSPP		ECPP		CJP	
	Freq	%	Freq	%	Freq	%
Number of managers	36	–	10	–	5	–
Gender						
Male	11	31	4	38	1	20
Female	25	69	6	62	4	80
Race						
White	9	25	9	67	4	80
Black	27	75	1	29	1	20
Other	0	0	0	5	0	0
Age*						
20–29	0	0	2	20	0	0
30–39	5	14	2	20	2	40
40–49	14	39	2	20	3	60
50–59	15	42	3	30	0	0
60–69	2	6	1	10	0	0

*During fieldwork, we did not ask staff for their age; rather, researchers estimated their age range and report it here.

Findings

Table 5.2 presents survey subsample mean responses on organisational culture, commitment and cynicism from the organisational survey in each agency. Survey results reveal that managers at each of the three agencies report similar levels of cynicism, commitment and culture within their respective agencies. Survey findings suggest that managers in each of the agencies perceive relatively good organisational culture and report relatively low cynicism and fairly strong organisational commitment.

Despite the similarities regarding climate, cynicism and commitment, the qualitative analyses demonstrate marked differences in the lived experience of organisational change and these measures. While the survey results may indicate a shared narrative by managers that they are 'ready and willing' to implement change efforts, the contextual differences suggested by the qualitative analysis may explain how their narratives of willingness to change often compete with the inability to *actually* change as a result of organisational culture, cynicism and commitment.

Culture

While office culture is difficult to fully disentangle from related concepts like cynicism and commitment, managers in all three agencies share similar perspectives about how culture stifles implementation. Managers regularly discuss what they refer to as stagnant or stale learning cultures within their agencies, wherein managers and staff perceive current training as inadequate, infrequent and/or not advancing the growth and development necessary for successful implementation of policy/practice change.

Table 5.2: Organisational survey results for middle managers

	NSPP (Mean/SD)	ECPP (Mean/SD)	CJP (Mean/SD)
Survey subsample (n)	51	93	44
Gender (male)	42%	50%	50%
Race (white)	35%	76%	73%
Age	50.4 (9.27)	48.5 (9.84)	46.8 (8.84)
Climate	2.93 (0.576)	3.67 (0.719)	3.90 (0.550)
Commitment	3.18 (0.455)	3.24 (0.430)	3.90 (0.541)
Cynicism	2.52 (0.871)	2.01 (0.727)	1.89 (0.814)

Note: SD = standard deviation.

In adult probation (NSPP), one manager notes that the greatest impact of the agency's merger with the prison division (and other related policy/practice changes) includes a plateaued learning culture characterised by a poorly run training academy and stagnation of training topics. He also notes that staff feel they do not possess adequate knowledge about current practices, which contributes to a sense of distrust. Similarly, another NSPP probation manager mentions she believes the agency makes staff feel they are 'not worth good training'. This perceived lack of value creates a workforce that recognises that staff members do not have the technical expertise to understand and/or implement new practices, compounded with a workplace perception that staff members are not worth professionalising at the pace of peers in other states. The disillusioned culture is intensified by a constant flow of policy changes that are often introduced to staff as 'do what you're told'. These messages come via ambiguous language and through channels (such as e-mail) that limit staff dialogue about the policy itself, implementation concerns and unintended consequences of practice.

In juvenile probation (CJP), managers express similar views about a troublesome agency culture. Managers regularly report that they do not possess the knowledge to train their staff on how to use EBPs at the ground level. Managers describe this in relation to the agency's focus on one particular EBP, motivational interviewing (MI). Although managers are principally responsible for EBP implementation, they attribute their hesitation to coach line staff on the practice to not regularly using MI themselves. As such, they frequently cite the need for the agency to include supervisory staff in initial training to cultivate a climate of learning between and among roles and sustain use as intended.

Additionally, facilitating a learning culture and a climate that allows for change demands continued content development for new training topics and involvement of multiple agency positions during training. It also requires introducing the change and the related training in a non-oppositional way. The following field-note excerpt from adult probation (ECPP) demonstrates how an agency's introduction to change can undermine staff willingness to change, even if they might otherwise remain open to it:

> Probation Officer (PO) Dawkins explained that there was a required supervisor training planned for three days in September. They received an e-mail asking them to pick which set of three days they wanted to attend. Both

PO Dawkins and their colleague, PO Cederic, e-mailed the days they wanted, but then the officers received an e-mail from another manager stating that everyone was going to be assigned to a session and they would not be able to switch. If they did not attend, they would have to go to a required two-week training. If they asked to switch sessions, their regional administrator would be notified. Both PO Dawkins and PO Cedric were noticeably upset about this and said that of course they would be assigned to the time that they did not request. PO Dawkins said this is not a good way to start off training – it creates resistance from the beginning and people would get to the training and be pissed off already.

In this example, the rigidity of communication, conflicting instructions for signing up for training and the agency's unwillingness to consider employee scheduling conflicts foster a negative culture during change efforts. Situations like this one often contribute to organisational cultures wherein managers feel mistreated, disconnected or often frustrated with their organisation, making further change implementation especially challenging.

Cynicism

Although survey results indicate relatively low cynicism across the three agencies, the narrative about cynicism found in the qualitative data runs counter to the quantitative finding. Qualitative analysis reveals cynical attitudes about implementation that are virtually identical in all three agencies, suggesting a deeper tone of cynicism within each agency than survey results reveal. As previously discussed, managers from NSPP regularly report feeling undervalued and underappreciated by the agency, with poor training or limited opportunities for continued professional education. Their awareness that the agency has moved away from EBPs reinforces these beliefs. Across the jurisdictions, perceptions of staff being ignored or underdeveloped amplify instances where the organisation does not provide clear assistance for interpretation and implementation of new practices. Managers overwhelmingly suggest that one of the largest contributing factors to cynicism is having many ways of doing the same thing as a result of inconsistent messages of *how* to implement a practice. Managers report feeling frustrated with communication chains regarding protocols for particular practices. For example, in NSPP, managers describe an environment wherein 'everything is done differently [at varying units] throughout the state'. They regularly discuss relying on their peers as a way of interpreting change/reform-related communication. The lack of assistance regarding implementation, coupled with perceptions that they do not receive appropriate training or explanations of how the new practice contributes to organisational goals, leaves managers less likely to hold the agency in esteem and promotes scepticism about the practices themselves.

This scepticism or cynicism manifests as distrust and misuse of specific EBPs. For example, in the following field-note excerpt, one ECPP PO describes her cynicism via the numerous ways she uses the agency's risk/needs assessment tool.

> PO Willis does not think the risk/need assessment tool works properly. She does not like or believe in probationers at Level 3 (minimum supervision). Instead, she notes that the tool frequently puts people at Level 3 and she disagrees. With Level 3, they are on call-in supervision and she says they are felons so this is not a good idea. She believes to achieve community safety they need more supervision than Level 3 provides. Thus, she either: 1) adjusts their tool to put them in Level 2 (moderate) supervision [and does so whenever she sees someone in Level 3, with very few exceptions] or 2) she puts them on minimum (so her supervisor doesn't question why she doesn't have any Level 3s) and requires that they report to the office monthly (even though this is not required for Level 3s). She says probationers are dangerous to themselves and the community and need supervision, regardless of what the tool says.

PO Willis' way of using (or overriding) the risk-needs assessment tool is common in ECPP but is not the only way staff demonstrate their distrust of EBPs. Other POs use various techniques when scoring, assessing and supervising probationers using information contained in the tool. These include having probationers fill out the tool without PO assistance (a violation of tool training protocols), not sharing the tool results with probationers or not using the results in any discernable way for case planning and supervision (for more on this, see Viglione et al, 2015).

These findings suggest that when agencies implement practices quickly and fail to assess organisational capacity to change, as is the case in many correctional agencies responding to rising populations and legislative demands, they create a culture of change that invites cynicism.

Commitment

Evidence of managerial and staff commitment come through in the data in a variety of forms: commitment to self, commitment to specific policies/practices/tools, commitment to clients, commitment to agency and/or commitment to community. Within the three agencies, the type of commitment staff articulate reflects the variations in cynicism and in their descriptions of their agency's change culture.

CJP (juvenile probation) managers report strong commitment to the agency and clients, and feel inconsistences between staff are a result of interpretation, not necessarily a lack of commitment. Overall, there is strong adherence to agency philosophy that describes a desire to provide effective services within a collaborative, research-based and culturally competent environment to promote behavior change and reduction of illegal conduct among clients. This clear mission, especially among unit managers and higher-level administrators, contributes to a strong sense of pride in the organisation, where managers and staff frequently describe their agency as the best in the state and, perhaps, a leader in the country. Deviation from the organisational objective of evidence-based effectiveness occurs at the individual level. The manager of one probation office in CJP described implementation efforts related to commitment as follows:

> In terms of organisational objectives, I believe in them, I consider them to be evidence-based and we take pride in the fact that we deploy EBPs. I do know, however, that each office takes their own spin on the objectives. In addition, each probation officer interprets these organisational goals differently and therefore also puts their own unique spin on them when they deal with clients.

Thus, while each office within CJP works to implement EBPs, there are inconsistencies in how connected they feel to the process. This sentiment is echoed in ECPP, where managers feel committed to their agency but are overwhelmed with numerous reforms, leading them to be only partially committed to any one reform. As an example of non-uniform commitment, in CJP, some managers hold booster sessions within their units to reinforce and improve POs' MI skills, while other managers take more of a hands-off approach, letting staff use MI as they deem necessary. While these differences relate to the overall culture and cynicism present within the organisations, they also pay specific heed to managerial commitment to assuring sound implementation and their desire/attempt to sustain implementation.

By contrast, NSPP managers feel commitment to their profession but not their agency – in part because they feel the agency poorly introduced too many new practices while ignoring problems associated with existing policy/practice. Despite feelings of 'being dumped on' and other organisational challenges, managers and staff remain impassioned by their choice to work for the agency. They often speak about their commitment to their profession and the people they serve. However, they also admit a waning sense of commitment to the agency in its current form. Their desire to be better and work better is echoed in one manager's commentary: "We need to raise our standards." She discusses the need for better communication and collaboration, fostering the ability to have greater expectations of staff, resulting in positive implications for both the organisation and the offenders it supervises.

Despite variations in the levels and types of commitment described by the managers across these three jurisdictions, all express a lack of commitment to implementation when there are too many reforms occurring at the same time or too many barriers for reform to exist. These data also suggest the importance of front-line managerial support of reforms when discussing on-the-ground implementation.

Conclusion

Unsurprising to many, organisational actors diverge from reform, causing the actual implementation processes and outcomes to become disjointed or misaligned from the original intent of the reform or the ways agency leaders 'sell' the change. However, when those actors are managers, rather than street-level staff, faulty implementation creates a potentially larger wrinkle in change/reform efforts than previously explored in most criminal justice research. While prior scholarship views managers as purveyors of and mechanisms for implementing organisational policy and practice, our research suggests that despite relatively positive/non-effectual survey responses about culture commitment and cynicism, they may, in fact, possess feelings in these three areas that hinder or halt policy/practice change. Specifically, they must interpret confusing change, translate this interpretation to line staff and then monitor adherence to the change. While seemingly invisible to upper administration because they are facilitating change similar to what was asked of them, day-to-day narratives suggest the change they are championing may be misaligned from the intent of the reform because they are infusing their own perceptions of and values regarding the ways things should be done. Our analysis suggests managers regularly implement EBPs *begrudgingly*, with little attention to detail, short-sightedness and without discernable connections between EBPs and overall or even specific individual or organisational goals/mission. While standard survey questions ask a holistic index of questions that yield (at least in our studies) what managers feel are acceptable answers given their organisational role and position, observations of and interviews with organisational managers during change often presents a different story of frustration and inattention, and reveals a more complex overall implementation picture.

Second, a common theme in our interviews suggests that many managers do not feel the EBPs their agency implements help them work more *efficiently*. This is particularly challenging in public bureaucracies like corrections or community corrections wherein scarce resources and limited training create a tense and overly burdensome workplace environment. Our research finds that numerous managerial complaints focus on the day-to-day interruption of routine or the extra time and resource expenditure that EBPs cause (as a whole), rather than on a particular EBP. To this end, third, we find managers regularly employ a minimalist approach, wherein they do the minimum necessary for each EBP to claim use, but they do so without any real commitment to the practice. They often pay lip-service to the implementation – "yes, we are doing it" – but without any real link to implementation or sustainability with fidelity.

Organisational theory provides a useful framework for evaluating why and how managers report lower perceptions of culture cynicism and commitment than one might expect, given positive survey results on these three topic areas. Borrowed from population ecology theory, the concept of structural inertia suggests that once an organisation (or set of organisations) is set in motion, it is difficult, yet not impossible, to change (Hannan and Freeman, 1984). The inertial concept of perpetual organisational motion along a particular pathway offers a potential explanation for how and why organisational managers find change difficult, sometimes even despite their best intentions. This is complicated by the intricate relationship managers in these organisations have with their front-line workers, whereby scarce resources, vast discretion and autonomy and limited training creates a relatively unyielding environment for change (Lipsky, 1980). It is also akin to Lindblom's (1959) idea of 'muddling through' work with feelings of 'being dumped on' and juggling a rising workload with strict policies running counter to the agency's previous way of doing business.

In sum, managers play a crucial role during organisational change processes because they fall at the nexus of EBP implementation and uptake. Whereas prior scholarship largely considers managers as loyal followers or 'organizational men' (Whyte, 1956), findings from these comparative case studies within community corrections paint a much more contextualised and dynamic portrait of the managerial role during reform. While street-level workers may provide a window into the black box of organisational culture, managerial perceptions of and contributions to sister concepts like cynicism and commitment yield a richer, more finely tuned magnifying glass for uncovering organisational nuance at the micro-level often overlooked by broader, one-shot methods (such as surveys). Unpacking culture cynicism and commitment within community corrections agencies represents a first, but not final, step toward improving EBP uptake and implementation processes, and ultimately changing outcomes.

References

Bommer, W.H., Rich, G.A. and Rubin, R.S. (2005) 'Changing attitudes about change: longitudinal effects of transformational leader behavior on employee cynicism about organizational change', *Journal of Organizational Behavior*, 26(7): 733–753.

Camp, S.D. (1994) 'Assessing the effects of organizational commitment and job satisfaction on turnover: an event history approach' *The Prison Journal*, 74(3): 279–305.

Caldwell, D.F., Chatman, J.A. and O'Reilly III, C.A. (1990) 'Building organizational commitment: a multi-firm study', *Journal of Occupational and Organizational Psychology*, 63(3): 245–261.

Charmaz, K. (2006) *Constructing Grounded Theory: A Practical Guide through Qualitative Research*, London: Sage Publications.

Condrey, S.E., Facer II, R.L. and Hamilton, Jr., J.A. (2005) 'Employees amidst welfare reform: TANF employees overall job- and organizational-role satisfaction', *Journal of Human Behavior in the Social Environment*, 12(2): 221–242.

Culliver, C., Sigler, R., and McNeely, B. (1991) 'Examining prosocial organizational behavior among correctional officers', *International Journal of Comparative and Applied Criminal Justice*, 15(1–2): 277–284.

Deal, T.E. and Kennedy, A.A. (1982) *Corporate Cultures: The Rites and Rituals of Organizational Life*, Boston, MA: Addison-Wesley.

DeCelles, K.A., Tesluk, P.E. and Taxman, F.S. (2013) 'A field investigation of multilevel cynicism toward change', *Organization Science*, 24(1): 154–171.

Emerson, R.M. (ed) (2001) *Contemporary Field Research: Perspectives and Formulation* (2nd edn), Prospect Heights, IL: Waveland Press.

Emerson, R.M., Fretz, R.I. and Shaw, L.L. (1995) *Writing Ethnographic Fieldnotes* (2nd edn), Chicago, IL: University of Chicago Press.

Farrell, J.L., Young, D.W. and Taxman, F.S. (2011), 'Effects of organizational factors on use of juvenile supervision practices', *Criminal Justice and Behavior*, 38(6): 565–583.

Guion, R. (1973) 'A note on organizational climate', *Organizational Behavior and Human Performance*, 9: 120–125.

Hannan, M.T. and Freeman, J. (1984) 'Structural inertia and organizational change', *American Sociological Review*, 49(2): 149–164.

Hepburn, J.R. (1987) 'The prison control structure and its effects on work attitudes: the perceptions and attitudes of prison guards', *Journal of Criminal Justice*, 15: 29–64.

Kunda, G. (1992) 'Culture and control', in G. Kunda (ed) *Engineering Culture: Control and Commitment in a High Tech Corporation*, Philadelphia, PA: Temple University Press, pp 1–26.

Lambert, E.G. and Paoline, E.A. (2008) 'The influence of individual, job, and organizational characteristics on correctional staff job stress, job satisfaction, and organizational commitment', *Criminal Justice Review*, 33(4): 541–564.

Lambert, E.G., Barton, S.M. and Hogan, N.L. (1999) 'The missing link between job satisfaction and correctional staff behavior: the issue of organizational commitment', *American Journal of Criminal Justice*, 24(1): 95–116.

Lambert, E.G., Hogan, N.L. and Griffin, M.L. (2008) 'Being the good soldier: organizational citizenship behavior and commitment among correctional staff', *Criminal Justice and Behavior*, 35(1): 56–68.

Lambert, E.G., Hogan, N.L., Paoline III, E.A. and Clarke, A. (2005a) 'The impact of role stressors on job stress, job satisfaction, and organizational commitment among private prison staff', *Security Journal*, 18(4): 33–50.

Lambert, E.G., Edwards, C., Camp, S.D. and Saylor, W.G. (2005b) 'Here today, gone tomorrow, back again the next day: Antecedents of correctional absenteeism', *Journal of Criminal Justice*, 33(2): 165–175.

Lindblom, C.E. (1959) 'The science of 'muddling through', *Public Administration Review*, 19(2): 79–88.

Lipsky, M., (1980) *Street Level Bureaucrats*, New York, NY: Russell Sage Foundation.

Melnick, G., Ulaszek, W.R., Lin, H. and Wexler, H.K. (2009) 'When goals diverge: staff consensus and the organizational climate', *Drug and Alcohol Dependence*, 103(S1): 17–22.

Portillo, S., Rudes, D.S. and Taxman, F.S. (2016) 'The transportability of contingency management in problem-solving courts', *Justice Quarterly*, 33(2): 267–290.

Reichers, A.E. (1985) 'A review and reconceptualization of organizational commitment', *Academy of Management Review*, 10(3): 465–476.

Rudes, D.S. (2012) 'Framing organizational reform: misalignments and disputes among parole and union middle managers', *Law & Policy*, 34(1): 1–31.

Rudes, D.S. and Viglione, J. (2014) 'Correctional workers in the organizational change process', in G. Bruinsma and D. Weisburd (eds) *Encyclopedia of Criminology and Criminal Justice*, New York, NY: Springer, pp 617–630.

Rudes, D.S., Lerch, J. and Taxman, F.S. (2011) 'Implementing a reentry framework at a correctional facility: challenges to the culture', *Journal of Offender Rehabilitation*, 50(8): 467–491.

Taxman, F.S., Young, D.W., Wiersema, B., Rhodes, A. and Mitchell, S. (2007) 'The National Criminal Justice Treatment Practices survey: multilevel survey methods and procedures', *Journal of Substance Abuse Treatment*, 32(3): 225–238.

Tesluk, P.E., Farr, J.L., Mathieu, J.E. and Vance, R.J. (1995) 'Generalization of employee involvement training to the job setting: individual and situational effects', *Personnel Psychology*, 48: 607–632.

Ulmer, J.T. (1992) 'Occupational socialization and cynicism toward prison administration', *Social Science Journal*, 29(4): 423–443.

Viglione, J., Rudes, D.S. and Taxman, F.S. (2015) 'Misalignment in supervision: implementing risk/needs assessment instruments in probation', *Criminal Justice and Behavior*, 42(3): 263–285.

Whyte, W.H. (1956) *The Organizational Man*, New York, NY: Simon & Schuster.

Part 2:
International research
on evidence-based skills

SIX

The Risk-Need-Responsivity model: evidence diversity and integrative theory

Martine Herzog-Evans

Introduction

It is to some extent thanks to the considerable volume of evidence harnessed by the Risk-Need-Responsivity (RNR) model that rehabilitation has returned to the forefront. RNR is a structured offender treatment model that relies on a series of **core principles**, including the RNR principles, but also the use of human services, and professional discretion, along with **overreaching principles** such as respect for the person and evidence-based practices (EBPs), and, lastly, **organisational principles** that pertain to staff and management (Bonta and Andrews, 2017). This model is, however, frequently criticised by its opponents or competitors, whom the RNR authors then counter-attack, often with transparent gusto (Andrews et al, 2011; Gendreau et al, 2009). In spite of recent theoretical and practical rapprochement or polite acknowledgement that other approaches are worthy of respect, the academic feud has sadly persisted.

This chapter's aim is to explore the disagreements between proponents of key models of supervision and to suggest an integrative RNR model that draws on a broader theoretical and empirical base. It therefore proposes an integrative model that could innovate current understandings of effective supervision skills and practices.

For indeed, in reality, most RNR opponents have essential qualities in common. Most of them believe in rehabilitation-reintegration, and most of them reject deterrence and punitive policies. It is also patent that most of them truly want to support probationers out of the cycle of offending. Most of them also want offender supervision to be delivered ethically, and none would condone abusive practices. This appears to offer a very favourable foundation for the development of an integrative theory.

Since, moreover, opponents usually have mono-specialty backgrounds and approaches, this leads the majority of them to focus mainly on one dimension or another (for example, desistance: social work), it follows that most of them miss important components, under-theorise others, or become entangled in conceptual contradictions, whereas should they draw on one another, they would, to a degree, be able to complement their respective models. Thus, for instance, RNR typically ignores the wider societal or institutional realities (except for its tentative focus on management in its aforementioned organisational principles (Bonta and Andrews, 2017, p 177, principle no 15) and offender reintegration (Porporino, 2010). Moreover, to a great extent, it does not pay sufficient attention to gender-responsive approaches, although it admits that gender is a responsivity issue. It also leaves a series of unrelated issues outside its core model (see Andrews and Bonta, 2010) in the largely under-theorised concept of 'non-programmatic factors' (Palmer, 1995; Andrews, 2011). If, conversely, desistance theory does draw attention to wider societal circumstances at the point of re-entry into society after supervision, or during offender supervision, and to the considerable time that offenders actually take to desist from crime, it cannot claim to offer a treatment method, other than a list of overreaching principles (see, for example, Farrall et al, 2014) for which there is no evidence base or clarity on their potential effect size. The Good Lives model, for its part, can be credited as being, like RNR, under permanent reconstruction in light of new evidence, and is probably the model that has reached out to the broadest range of empirical and theoretical domains, and, for instance, evolutionary psychology and developmental research (Durrant and Ward, 2015). However, it often emerges as confusingly complex, is, in reality, rather close to RNR, has essentially been built in light of sex offending particularities, and has yet to be empirically validated to the same level as RNR.

Parallel to this, other than unanimously claiming that practices should be ethical, the treatment models cited above – RNR, the desistance model and the Good Lives model – have done little to conceptualise and develop what ethical practice could entail from a dual systemic (law/treatment) viewpoint, and none of them has integrated a model of legal and societal controls over these institutions and staff in order for them to truly behave ethically. Also under-theorised and not satisfactorily woven into the fabric of any model are management and innovation theories, except for a partial translation into the Correctional Program Assessment Inventory instrument (see Lowenkamp et al, 2006). Similarly, if RNR endorses the techniques of motivational interviewing, still singularly missing from most theories is an empirically validated theoretical model of motivation. Tentative typologies made in the emerging compliance studies (Bottoms, 2001; Braithwaite, 2003; Robinson and McNeill, 2008) have yet to include an empirically validated model, such as self-determination theory (SDT) (Deci and Ryan, 1985, 2002).

Clearly, since none of these models can claim to be a 'grand theory' (Cullen, 2012) of offender treatment, it is 'a fruitless enterprise' for respective proponents to attack each other (p 104). In spite of its limitations, RNR is undoubtedly the most empirically validated treatment method that is currently available. Like chemotherapy with cancer, until a radically different approach can revolutionise treatment, it is unreasonable to opt for homeopathy or witchcraft, and it is preferable to try to gain additional effect by adding or adjusting components and by borrowing from other approaches and fields in order to improve fidelity with RNR-based structured treatment and offender compliance.

This chapter first presents the arguments and reasons for the academic feud between the dominant OS models or theories; it then proposes a renewed integrative model that draws on a variety of domains, including legal theory and the legitimacy of justice (Tyler, 2006, 2012).

War

Since its development in the Western world, RNR has been critically assessed in a number of publications (for example, Mair, 2004), and its proponents have responded to some of the critiques (Wormith et al, 2012, p. 111). A common criticism that has been levelled against RNR (from both the Good Lives model and the desistance camp) is that it is a 'punitive', 'non-ethical' model. This argument is raised against both its actuarial tools (Harcourt, 2006; in France, for example, Dubourg and Gautron, 2015) and against its treatment methods, which are alleged to have an exclusive focus on public protection, rather than on rehabilitation (Canton, 2012; McNeill, 2009). In this case, its opponents mistake the theory (which, as its proponents emphasise, is not in the least punitive [Andrews and Bonta, 2010]) for the policies, although it has been acknowledged by some that RNR proponents cannot be blamed for punitive policies (see, for example, McNeill, 2012).

With respect to the criticisms it has received for its emphasis on the use of actuarial assessment tools, it could be argued that the use of non-evidence-based assessment methods may actually be deemed just as unethical, because assessment nevertheless takes place every time, for instance, that a probation officer writes a report, and reliance on a protocol is, so far, the most efficient way, albeit not entirely bias-proof, of limiting errors and discrimination.

Some of the arguments made against RNR's treatment methods can be attributed to the consideration that any attempt at making a difference is a belief in 'the production of technological knowledge' (Harcourt, 2007, p 32), a criticism often made in France (for example, Dubourg and Gautron, 2015) that refutes the idea that science can tell us anything about offender treatment. In many cases, there also is a problem with the critics' logic, such as when one complains about base rates or overriding risks (Gottfredson and Moriarty, 2006) or having too many false positives and negatives (Casey, 2016), but neglects to see that the alternative (Harris, 2003) is, as is frequently the case in France, a clinical judgement, which includes prejudices and other biases and is therefore more likely to generate a far greater number of false positives or negatives (Baratta et al, 2012).

Cognitive behavioural treatment

In many cases, it is cognitive behavioural treatment (CBT) that is criticised as being a universal one-size-fits-all approach and as putting traditional one-to-one supervision in danger (for example, Burnett, 2004; Looman and Abracen, 2013), although it happens to be the best validated psychological treatment known today (Epp and Dobson, 2010; Tafrate and Mitchell, 2014; Bonta and Andrews, 2017), the alternatives being 'nothing works' classic social work (Fischer, 1973), offender supervision (Martinson, 1974), or ineffective long-term psychoanalysis (Smit et al, 2012). It is also important to remember that CBT comes in all shapes and sizes (Dobson, 2010), that it is theoretically and practically diverse in nature (Young et al, 2003).

Indeed, if, when RNR programmes are widely implemented, the one-size-fits-all accusation appears to be pertinent, the model was certainly not developed as such. Its insistence on responsivity is in total contradiction to this criticism. RNR developers have, moreover, long insisted on the utmost importance of individual differences (Andrews et al, 1990; Andrews and Bonta, 2010; Bonta and Andrews, 2007).

An important point has been made by Gannon and Ward (2014): CBT must be delivered by well-trained psychologists with significant experience. This argument rings particularly true in view of the important number of probationers presenting (in France) with personality disorders

(Hemphill et al, 1998; Singleton et al, 1988; Fazel & Danesh, 2002) who require extremely skilled professionals, using refined and specific CBT methods (for example, schema therapy – see Keulen de Vos et al, 2010; Young et al, 2003). It could be argued that in reality, the evidence base for successfully making significant progress with people with personality disorders – particularly antisocial personal disorder (ASPD), bearing in mind that ASPD is one of the 'big four' of RNR theory – is weak at the very best (Matusiewicz et al, 2010); this might incidentally explain the relatively modest results of RNR and its lack of impact on domestic violent offenders (Feder et al, 2008; Smedslund et al, 2011), who often present with personality disorders (Holtzworth-Munroe and Stuart, 1994; Holtzworth-Munroe et al, 2000).

Offender agency and motivation

Another criticism raised by both the desistance model and the Good Lives model, which is a variant of the desistance model (see, for example, Ward et al, 2012; Ward and Fortune, 2013), against RNR concerns the latter's lack of consideration for offender agency. Although RNR has recently added 'respect for personal autonomy' to its model as an overreaching principle (Andrews and Bonta, 2010, p 46), it has no theory of motivation. The Good Lives model, for its part, claims to have included SDT (Deci and Ryan, 1985, 2002), but the theory has not been solidly woven into its treatment method. Self-determination theory offers one of the best validated theories of motivation. In particular, it distinguishes between intrinsic and extrinsic forms of motivation that are particularly relevant in the domain of offender supervision and has, *inter alia*, showed that controlling forms of supervision generates, at best, instrumental and short-term compliance, whereas extrinsically motivated collaborative work yields long-term compliance and improvements (Deci and Ryan, 2002). Self-determination theory also offers a series of clinical principles about supporting people making long-term changes, and are not incompatible, but complementary to a CBT approach, since both models are collaborative. It has not yet been tested on offenders, but its empirical validity as a treatment method for a wide range of behaviours (Sheldon et al, 2013), including addiction (Ryan et al, 1995; Zeldman et al, 2004), is well known, and for this reason, it should be part of an integrated and agentic model, as it could potentially improve substantive compliance and reduce attrition rates.

This should be noteworthy for desistance researchers, who correctly argue that most evaluation studies only assess short-term – official –

results, and that, in fact, moving out of a delinquent life is, in reality, a very long process (Farrall et al, 2014) (requiring intrinsic motivation), and that in the meantime, the criminal justice system, at the very best, achieves short-term instrumental compliance (see, for example, Robinson and McNeill, 2008).

Indeed, many desistance theorists operate in the UK (for example, McNeill, 2012; Farrall et al, 2014), where some evaluations reveal that RNR offender behaviour programmes have not been a success (Cann et al, 2003; Falshaw et al, 2003). These programmes have generated monumental attrition rates (Martin et al, 2009; Olver et al, 2011) and non-compliance (Kemshall and Canton, 2002). On the upside, they have drawn attention to the issue of programme integrity, which relates to the degree to which real-world programmes adhere to RNR principles, and this is now a booming research domain (see, for example, Lowenkamp et al, 2006). This issue would, however, have benefited from drawing on diffusion theories (see the section 'First step: rearranging the theoretical cards' on p 109) and management theories (Lee et al, 2010). Indeed, institutional factors shape practitioners' professional culture, and in particular determine whether staff will be able to collaborate with offenders and draw on their intrinsic motivation. One might thus question hyper-centralised state 'prisonbation' (Herzog-Evans, 2015a), along with the related 'monopolistic institutional research' (Raynor, 2008).

As already noted, the Good Lives model and its proponents have attacked the very theoretical foundations of RNR. To sum up a rather complex line of arguments, they claim that, first, RNR is mostly atheoretical, as it in essence draws on principles from empirical data (a data-driven approach), rather than from theory (abductive method ; see Cording et al, 2016; Polaschek, 2016), and that it has, in particular, no theory of crime (Casey et al, 2013). Second, the Good Lives model authors and other opponents argue that the 'needs' set out by RNR proponents as criminogenic needs (which, as already noted, are mainly dynamic risk factors that are said to be linked to offending behaviour) lack construct validity and fail to establish the existence of a causal link between such factors and reoffending (Cording et al, 2016). In some instances, it might also be illogical to say that dynamic risk factors cause the offence, because the offence itself may have contributed to the dynamic risk factors. Additionally, although RNR makes a strong case for solid evidence, most of the research is, in fact, not truly experimental – and in most cases cannot be for ethical and legal reasons: randomised controlled trials may for instance, violate due process principles – so it could be argued that researchers should avoid 'using causal language' (Serin et al, 2016, p 153). Authors also dispute the pertinence of protective dynamic factors – that is, 'personal, social and institutional resources that foster competence and promote successful development, subsequently decreasing the likelihood of engagement in problematic behaviour' (Walsh, 2013), which are little more than inverted (Polaschek, 2016; Serin et al, 2016) or 'obverse' (Baird, 2009, cited in Serin et al, 2016, p 157; Harris and Rice, 2015) dynamic risk factors. At the very least, however, when identified and addressed, protective factors may be useful in terms of establishing a working alliance since they facilitate prosocial pursuits (Woldgabreal et al, 2014) and the focus on goals that are important to the supervised person.

Diversity issues

Another line or argument has come from some feminists, who dispute that gender is a responsivity issue and consider that women have different needs (Hannah-Moffat, 2016) or variations that are not integrated in the need principle of the RNR model (Taylor and Blanchette, 2009). Critics who argue that ethnicity is presented as being a risk factor (for example, Hannah-Moffat, 2016) may be right in saying that since RNR is blind to politics and social issues, it does not point to the obvious fact that the higher levels of risk generally found around the world in minorities are, to a great extent, the result of ignorance, discrimination and sheer racism, along with poverty. Indeed, one might contend that since RNR aims at being a generalist treatment method, it minimises the existence of specificities, be they for certain categories of people (women, other cultures) or for specific offenders (such as violent offenders, for whom to a degree, specific DRFs [Dynamic Risk Factors] are at stake). Indeed, even if RNR suggests that one should pay attention to individual responsivity, it does little to explain how one should go about it or to uncover the theories that one might draw on in doing so.

The RNR perspective: responding to critics

For its part, RNR proponents have also criticised both Good Lives model and desistance theories, with a stronger emphasis on the latter (for example, Andrews, 2011; Cullen, 2012). RNR has depicted these models as 'knowledge destruction' enterprises (see, in particular, Bonta and Andrews, 2017, pp 537–8). It has also described desistance theories as being essentially qualitative or essayist in nature (Andrews,

2011), thereby neglecting the considerable empirical evidence derived from desistance longitudinal studies. RNR has further insisted that the validity of the targets for treatment that are suggested in both Good Lives model (that is, the pursuit of 'goods' and meeting essential human needs) and desistance (developing human and social capital in domains such as employment, housing, networks, skills and so on) has not been proven in terms of reoffending outcomes (Andrews, 2011; Andrews et al, 2011). On this point, however, the Good Lives model has answered that both targets are pertinent (Ward et al, 2012): Addressing social capital and other human needs is, in fact, vital for establishing a working alliance for several reasons. First, it is pointless to try to change cognitions and skills if one does not address basic needs such as housing and employment. Second, when practitioners respond to social needs they become more credible in the eyes of their clients (see, for example, Kadushin and Kadushin, 2013) as they help meet 'intermediate' human needs such as economic and 'adequate protective housing' (Doyal and Gough, 1991, pp 191–273). In other words, addressing social capital and other human needs is, first and foremost, a human – and in some cases, a legal – duty.

RNR's opponents have concluded that, at the present time, there is nothing unique about the Good Lives model (Wormith et al, 2012). RNR has further accused the Good Lives model of being too simplistic and potentially dangerous by endeavouring to make offenders happy (Bonta and Andrews, 2003), an argument that can be easily debunked, since the Good Lives model is also concerned with public protection (Chu et al, 2014). More importantly, while wishing 'all the best' to the Good Lives model (Andrews and Bonta, 2010, p 512), RNR theorists have argued that the empirical support for this model is 'still in its infancy' (Wormith et al, 2012, p 116).

The debate between RNR and Good Lives models has had some positive consequences: it has revealed that the two models are actually quite close to each other, and that, in fact, there is apparent respect between the two camps (see, for example, Andrews et al, 2011).

In addition, and for its part, desistance is not per se the enemy of RNR theory. In fact, Andrews (2011, p 17) stated that viewing the two models as opposing is a misconstruction. Conversely, he credited Shadd Maruna's *Making Good* (2001) as 'a classic piece of cognitive social psychology' and as being 'utterly consistent with RNR' (Andrews, 2011, p 17). He similarly supported Trotter's own presentation of 'core correctional practices' (CCPs) as being likewise compatible with RNR (Andrews, 2011, p 17). For his part, Cullen (2012, p 95) stated that he was 'sceptical, but not dismissive' of desistance becoming a new paradigm, and that he thought that the Good Lives model 'was 'the most systematic and promising of the creative corrections approaches' (p 101).

Additionally, RNR theory has, with each edition of Andrew and Bonta's *The Psychology of Criminal Conduct* (2003, 2006, 2010; Bonta and Andrews, 2017) very open-mindedly taken stock of some of the criticisms that have been made previously and has included other principles or treatment suggestions. This has unfortunately mostly been done by creating a series of satellite 'tote bags': 'overreaching principles' (Andrews and Bonta, 2010, p 46), 'non-programmatic factors' (see the section on integrative theory) and CCPs, the latter having clumsily been included in RNR as 'organisational principles' (Andrews and Bonta 2010, p 47). To add to the confusion, there are not one, but two CCP models, one linked to RNR and the other created by Chris Trotter (2015). As can be seen in Table 6.1, they share a great number of components, but others are missing from each model.

Table 6.1: CCP models

CCPs	Dowden and Andrews (2004) Adaptation of Andrews and Kiessling (1980)	Trotter (2015)
Effective use of authority	Yes	No
Appropriate modelling and reinforcement	Yes	Yes (called prosocial modelling)
Problem-solving	Yes	Yes
Motivational interviewing	Yes. 'Organisational principle' no 14 (Andrews and Bonta 2010, p 47); not in the original list of CCPs.	Included as an added tool, in order to achieve better treatment adherence and to move offenders to a maintenance stage.
Effective use of community resources	Yes	No
Quality of interpersonal relationships	Yes	Yes
Role clarification	No	Yes
Working with families	Not in CCP, but a treatment for Central Eight (Bonta and Andrews, 2017, p 45, Central Eight no 5).	Yes (Trotter 2013)

Moreover, as we have seen, although they share some practice principles in common, the different models of offender supervision have strikingly different goals. An integrative reframing would thus have to take these differences into account. Second, although it makes sense that legal theories cannot be used to test programmes and that this is not their function, they can incorporate some treatment methods that should be highlighted. Moreover, it is impossible to eliminate the legal system from the equation when a treatment plan is drafted (Herzog-Evans, 2015b). In a democracy, prosecutors, judges or courts also provide the judicial mandate that allows the restriction of offenders' liberties by imposing (treatment) obligations on them.

Likewise, if all psycho-criminological models, along with that of the criminal justice system, aim to solve problems, their understanding of problem solving appears to be different. RNR broadly defines problem solving as the resolution of criminogenic needs; desistance theory defines it as dealing with human and social capital needs; while the Good Lives model sees it as dealing with basic human needs. Problem-solving courts try to solve all sorts of problems, whether criminogenic or not. As for the legal system, it attempts to provide a framework for offenders' legal obligations to try to sort out their various needs and problems. In spite of these divergences, there is enough convergence to develop a common theoretical approach.

A similar conclusion pertains to motivation. Virtually all of the theories acknowledge the relevance of motivation and agency. A practical approach to offender agency actually exists in legal theory. In a judicialised environment (Herzog-Evans, 2015b), such as in the French system or in the problem-solving court movement, due process prevails in issues such as release, important supervision decisions, recall and sanctions. Here issues are analysed as being the fifth phase of the 'penal continuum', after arrest, investigation, deferment (where the case is referred to the prosecutor) and sentencing (Herzog-Evans, 2016). In such a model, probationers and prisoners are 'justiciables', that is parties to a judicial process, who present a release or supervision plan that is theirs, since they are treated as agents of their own lives. It is also noteworthy that only legal theory and practice include various, albeit insufficient (Herzog-Evans, 2016) – levels of control over practitioners and their decisions. Similarly, it is only the legal system that provides a detailed understanding of, and framework for, human rights, although, again, not sufficiently binding (Herzog-Evans, 2016). Only legal theory, particularly with due process and contractual consent (Herzog-Evans, 2015c) in classic legal theory ameliorated with therapeutic jurisprudence (Wexler and Winick, 1996) and practice in problem-solving courts, has a clear understanding of what practitioners' respect and even care for offenders actually means and how it can be enforced. Only the legal system preoccupies itself the issue of fact finding; psycho-criminological models somewhat assume that it is 'the truth' that is being decided and acted on. Conversely, the legal system is oblivious to issues of efficiency and outcome – but for problem-solving courts.

A rather clear-cut conclusion can be reached at this point: proponents of the different approaches agree on some issues and disagree on others, and the treatment methods are, to some extent, quite similar. Indeed, the differences that persist often boil down to the proponents' different professional backgrounds. For this very reason, their collaboration could be more fruitful and could bridge the gaps in each other's approach.

Having set out the key areas of disagreement among proponents of the key models, I now move on to a discussion of the merits of an integrative model that unites key aspects of these models and incorporates law-related elements, particularly the legitimacy-procedural justice model (Tyler, 2006, 2012) and its legal translation, 'therapeutic jurisprudence' (Wexler and Winick, 1996) and ethics.[1] My objective in the section that follows is to highlight skills that are based on a broader range of theories. These skills could usefully inform real-world supervision practice.

Integrative theory

In order to propose an integrative model, it is first necessary to reshuffle the theoretical cards.

First step: rearranging the theoretical cards

In this chapter, I have argued that until a radically revolutionary approach can claim superiority, RNR must constitute the model on which basis any inclusive reframing must be built. For the core theory to include other models and other sources of empirical evidence, it is my view that one must first remove the theoretical clutter.

One such clutter is non-programmatic factors, first mentioned by Palmer (1995) and later incorporated by Andrews (2011) with little change. Palmer and Andrews have essentially provided a list of non-programmatic factors: staff characteristics; offender characteristics; the interaction of staff and client characteristics; size of caseload, frequency of contact, individualised/flexible programming and explicitness of intervention strategies; and setting; they have not, however, defined or theorised them. Reading between the lines, one nonetheless deciphers that non-programmatic factors are factors that, on the one hand, have not been empirically tested, and on the other hand, are out of the reach of programme developers. *A minima*, there is a clear call for more research and theoretical development.

Second, the analysis of non-programmatic factors reveals that the second category (offender characteristics) refers to a responsivity factor and the third (the interaction of staff and client characteristics) would similarly better be included in responsivity and CCP's working alliance. Other non-programmatic factors (staff characteristics, size of caseload, frequency of contact, individualised/flexible programming, explicitness of intervention strategies and setting) are actually institutional in nature and are thus not entirely outside the reach of programmers.

In my view, non-programmatic factors should be included in a renewed definition of responsivity. Currently, Andrews and Bonta (2010, p 46) distinguish between two different forms of responsivity. The first is general responsivity, which is the use of CBT, social-learning methods and skills building; however, in reality, it is not a responsivity issue, but a treatment principle. The second and only true form of responsivity is specific responsivity, that is, offenders' characteristics. However, a host of other factors that are equally responsive in nature, in the sense that they condition implementation, are missing from Andrews and Bonta's model, as we shall see below.

Some might argue that whereas a non-programmatic factors' tote bag may have been acceptable due to its lack of empirical grounds, incorporating its components, along with other factors, into responsivity is another matter entirely, since responsivity is, like risk and needs, data-driven. Nevertheless, what is being proposed here is a more integrated redistribution of the RNR cards, which would need to be substantiated empirically. I contend that non-programmatic factors, augmented by a host of other factors, need to be included in the central RNR model and evaluated, giving rise to a renewed model.

This renewed model redefines responsivity as comprising two sets of components: intrinsic responsivity and extrinsic responsivity. Intrinsic responsivity refers, by and large, to what Bonta and Andrews (2017) called 'specific responsivity', namely the responsivity of the person subjected to supervision. It could also benefit from the inclusion of other factors borrowed from other research domains. As such, it would comprise: mental health, intelligence, personality, gender, ethnicity, culture and identity stages (Helms, 1984, 1990;

Cross, 1991; Robinson, 1998, 2009); personal goals (as suggested by the Good Lives model); personal priorities (as suggested by Trotter); and type and levels of agency and autonomy (as measured by SDT instruments, and along the cycles of change of motivational interviewing).

Extrinsic responsivity necessitates more explanation, since it is presented as an added subcategory to the original RNR model. Extrinsic responsivity refers to the responsivity of the institutions and the practitioners in charge of faithfully implementing the programme; it also refers to the legal system in as much as it facilitates, or conversely, hinders, fidelity (Andrews and Bonta, 2010, p 47). Thus defined, it includes a series of factors, the first of which pertains to 'responsive institutions'. Clearly, a theory of responsive institutions would necessitate considerable empirical research. Fortunately, one of its dimensions, implementation and innovation diffusion, has already been thoroughly researched, and its utility in offender supervision has been presented elsewhere (Taxman and Belenko, 2012). These studies derive from a wide range of domains. For instance, as in probation real-world studies, medicine evidence-based practice (EBP) implementation studies have shown that the actual implementation of medical EBP is extremely disappointing (Grimshaw et al, 2006). As in real-world probation studies (Bonta et al, 2008), medical research has thus found that traditional forms of training are far from efficient, yielding around 10% of behavioural changes (Georgenson, 1982; Saks, 2002). As Taxman and Belenko (2012) aptly stated, in the offender supervision domain, the 'nothing works' findings were essentially a 'nothing is implemented' story (p 85).

Responsive institutions and their staff are not hyper-centralised, hierarchical, autocratic, or corporatist. A good model is that of the problem-solving court (Lee et al, 2010); a negative model is that of the French 'prisonbation' service (Herzog-Evans, 2015a). Good institutions have recruitment and training policies that ensure that the right people, with the right skills (Raynor et al, 2015), are in place. They thus recruit ideal managers and front-line staff who support rehabilitation, while making good use of authority. They also include middle managers who can be appropriate clinical coaches (Smith et al, 2012; Bonta and Andrews, 2017, p 47, principle no 15), while offering probation officers or treatment providers with a safe haven where they can get support (Clarke, 2013), along with emotional awareness coaching (Knight, 2014). Responsive institutions also respect their staff's autonomy, take stock of their networks, and ensure that they are not submerged with clutter-like tasks. A good institution is also organised in such a way that it hires managers, middle managers, and front-line staff who are willing and able to collaborate in an egalitarian and integrative fashion (Sullivan and Skelcher, 2002; Sloper, 2004; Gough, 2010). It further has ties with independent researchers in the field.

Responsive institutions, managers and staff are also ethical, notably in the sense that they also operate within a normative and judicial mandate framework, act along the lines of the legitimacy of justice-procedural-justice-therapeutic jurisprudence paradigm, and are subjected to external control (Herzog-Evans, 2016).

Communities should also be included within the extrinsic responsivity ensemble. This would imply the existence of available, accessible, flexible, innovative, collaborative, adequately funded, and evidence-based friendly community agencies.

Furthermore, an extrinsic responsive legal system would be one in which the substantive laws sustain rehabilitation, for instance by expunging criminal records and tailoring obligations on the basis of criminogenic needs, adjust for the length of time and intensity required to fully address such needs, instead of being based on deterrence, be democratically and externally drafted, abide by the legality principle, and support agency and consent, as well as quasi-contractual reciprocity (Herzog-Evans, 2015c). An extrinsic responsive legal system would favour legitimacy within the criminal justice system by abiding by legitimacy of justice-procedural-justice-therapeutic principles, including in the execution and supervision phase of the 'penal continuum' (Herzog-Evans, 2016). On the basis of this inclusive classification, it is thus an integrated theory that I am advocating.

Second step: building an integrated treatment theory

In Tables 6.2 to 6.4, I outline, without getting too much into the details for fear of being too long-winded, a series of integrated treatment principles based on the complimentary integration into RNR of currently opposing models, and add to this mix legal theory, legitimacy of justice-procedural-justice-therapeutic and SDT, along with innovation diffusion and implementation theories. For clarification purposes, each RNR component is presented in a separate table.

Table 6.2: Integrated treatment principles: risk principle

Risk assessment (structured principle no 11 in Andrews and Bonta, 2010, p 46)	EBP treatment (overreaching principle no 2 in Andrews and Bonta, 2010, p 46)
Risk-level assessment with: static tool or dynamic tool Generalist or specialised (for example, sex offenders)	Adapt the intensity of treatment, supervision and judicial review of the case to the level of risk (Legal: ensure that the measure and the length, nature, and intensity of the obligations are adapted to the level of risk)
Acute assessment (level of imminence/level of risk of harm) with 'acute tools', particularly with sex offenders or high-risk domestic violence offenders (Hanson et al, 2007)	Multiagency risk prevention and victim protection (both in treatment and legal provisions)

Table 6.3: Integrated treatment principles: need principle

Needs principle Treatment (structured principle no 6 in Andrews and Bonta, 2010, p 46)	Needs principle EBP treatment (overreaching principle no 2 in Andrews and Bonta, 2010, p 46)
Assess all criminogenic needs with generalist actuarial tools or specialised tools (for example, for violent or sex offenders)	Attend to every single criminogenic need (breadth principle no 9 in Andrews and Bonta, 2010, p 46) (Legal: ensure that the measure and the nature of its obligations and its duration allow for the treatment of all criminogenic needs)
When relevant, assess for antisocial personality disorder (also NPD or BPD [Borderline Personality Disorder]) and psychopathy with a validated tool (e.g. PCL-R [Psychopathy Checklist-Revised])	Structure treatment (principle no 11 in Andrews and Bonta, 2010, p 46)
For higher risks or highly complex cases, use PICTS (Psychological Inventory of Criminal Thinking Styles) to assess criminal thinking patterns or forensic case formulation	Use accredited and validated treatment (EBP principle no 2 in Andrews and Bonta, 2010, p 46)
For substance abuse cases, use a severity of addiction index	Use CBT (EBP principle no 2 in Andrews and Bonta, 2010, p 46): classic CBT targeting criminogenic thoughts, attitudes and behaviour; specialised (particularly PD [Personality Disorder], for example, Schema therapy; see Young et al [2003])

(continued)

Table 6.3: Integrated treatment principles: need principle (continued)

Needs principle Treatment (structured principle no 6 in Andrews and Bonta, 2010, p 46)	Needs principle EBP treatment (overreaching principle no 2 in Andrews and Bonta, 2010, p 46)
For mental health cases, use EBP diagnosis/refer assessment to forensic psychologists	Use all models of CCPs (see Table 6.1) (principle no 14 in Andrews and Bonta, 2010, p 47)
	Brokerage and advocacy (a CCP: principle no 14 in Andrews and Bonta, 2010, p 47)
	EBP addiction (for example, therapeutic communities; AA [Alcoholics Anonymous]; substitution; CBT; drug courts) and mental health treatment (Miller, 2009)
	Integrated collaboration with community agencies
	(Legal: 'good laws' that allow EBP to be used; rehabilitation oriented [goals and obligations setting]; supporting collaboration)

Table 6.4: Integrated treatment principles: responsivity principle

Type of responsivity	Specificity	EBP treatment or approach
Intrinsic	Age	EBP juvenile treatment, including **family therapy** and **attachment** approaches
	Gender	Gender-responsive programmes and approaches (**feminist** studies)
	Ethnicity-culture-language	Institutional diversity policies (Lewis et al, 2006)/culturally aware staff (Ponterotto et al, 1995)/allocation of compatible **identity stages** staff and probationers (Robinson, 1998, 2009)/available translators
	Mental health and intelligence (assess) – illiteracy/communication deficits	Specialised staff/staff versed in **communication** problems (see for example, La Vigne and Van Rybroek, 2014)/collaborate with a speech pathologist/use non-written material
	Motivation (stage) (assess with validated tool)	Use **motivational interviewing** (Miller and Rollnick, 2012)
	Autonomy – nature and level (assess with an SDT tool) – or agency (**desistance**)	Use autonomy supportive treatment (**SDT**) and a collaborative approach – use a quasi-contractual approach

(continued)

Table 6.4: Integrated treatment principles: responsivity principle (continued)

Type of responsivity	Specificity	EBP treatment or approach
	Personal goals (assess)	**GLM** approach
	Personal priorities (assess)	**Trotter's** (2015) approach to needs
	Geography (for example, rural, urban) and distance (travel and mode of transportation)	One-stop-shop (**PSC** [Problem-Solving Courts] model); support with transportation; delocalise (nomadic) probation and human services; in extreme cases, use videoconference, phone and texts
	Material difficulties: housing; employment; debts	Social work support (**desistance**)
		Problem-solving approach (also in **PSC** and in CCP – Principle no 14 in Andrews and Bonta, 2010, p 47)
Extrinsic	Good institutions	Rehabilitative/not hyper-centralised/not prison or probation/locally embedded/able and willing to collaborate with other agencies/innovative and **innovation diffusion**-friendly/EBP culture/ recruits staff with the right skills and approach/ participative human resource approach/ open to research and evaluation/solid ties with universities/adequate resources/ respect and operate within judicial mandate and laws
	Good partners	Locally embedded/**collaborative**/innovative and EBP culture/funded
	Good managers and middle managers (principle no 15 in Andrews and Bonta, 2010, p 47)	**Leaders** rather than managers (Lee et al, 2010)
		EBP enthusiasts and **innovation** implementers/good clinical coaches/ provide **stress** support system and **emotional literacy** havens/open to research/respect and operate within judicial mandate and laws/respectful and caring (**legitimate working environment**)
	Good frontline probation officers and other staff	Able to use all CCPs and RNR/able to create a good working or therapeutic alliance/well trained and experienced in CBT/open to innovation and professional growth/collaborative/respect and operate within judicial mandate and laws/ respectful and caring (**legitimacy of justice**)

(continued)

Table 6.4: Integrated treatment principles: responsivity principle (continued)

Type of responsivity	Specificity	EBP treatment or approach
	Good courts	LJ-PJ-TJ [Legitimacy of Justice-Procedural Justice-Therapeutic Jurisprudence] judges and courts (**PSC**-like) (respect, care, due process)/collaborative/EBP-trained / therapeutic alliance/adequate use of authority/operant conditioning/use of graduated sanctions/welcoming, courts
	Good laws (**normative legitimacy**)	**Human rights** and subjective rights/ **legality** principle/prohibition of retrospective punitive laws/rehabilitative norms/democratically and externally drafted norms/clear framework and good balance between information sharing and confidentiality
	Good procedures	**Due process** (notably for release/ adding to the intensity of treatment or obligations/sanctions and recall) (= voice/ neutrality/fact finding in **LJ-PJ**)

Conclusion

It is time for the feud between academics and fields to turn into a constructive debate. I have argued that each domain and each theory brings very important ingredients to the offender supervision pot. Each background and each approach also inevitably presents important theoretical gaps, which can be partially filled by weaving the theories together. Other fields, which have been neglected by sociological or psychological criminology likewise, need to be included, and I have particularly underlined the utmost importance of drawing from SDT and innovation diffusion theories. We have also seen that sociological or psychological criminology lacks a theoretical, empirical and practical view of ethics, and it has usually set aside the legal framework, because the legal framework is traditionally deemed out of the reach of programme developers, and less acceptably, because criminology has never considered that probation institutions, staff or decisions require external and legal oversight.

In this chapter, I have tried to weave all the threads together and have chosen to include them in a renewed presentation of RNR theory. It is indeed my understanding that RNR is to probation what chemotherapy is to cancer treatment: extremely perfectible, certainly not efficient in all populations, not without its nocebo consequences, but currently the strongest treatment model. I also hope that a comprehensive model, one that would include all the components – sociological, psychological, criminological and legal – that have been presented in this chapter, can be built, one that can be tested in terms of outcomes. As Kaiser and Holtfreter (2015) have pointed out, legal theory – in this case 'therapeutic jurisprudence' – does not offer a testable model; nor do, at this point, ethical components in psychological or sociological criminology. Only an integrated model would offer such a testable model; it would allow in particular, for the development of augmented 'probation in the real world' checklists.

It is, with undeniable and probably shameful nerve, that I, the lawyer turned criminologist, have ventured far out of my comfort zone, to call on all academics to hold hands and to see the half-full glass that is before them; most are ethical people who want to improve offender supervision and to rehabilitate offenders, while protecting potential victims and making the world a better place. We know much more than we did in 1974, but we can only 'cure' a minority of offenders; thankfully, most of them eventually walk out of crime on their own. Before a radically new type of treatment becomes available, our best option is to take what is out there and think about how we can best generate optimum treatment conditions; this can happen only if we humbly collaborate and draw from each other. Far from a threat, this should be seen as an exciting perspective, one that could produce new research avenues for scientists and new experimentation opportunities for practitioners.

This treatment- and solution-focused perspective should naturally not blind us to the real risks of mass offender supervision (Phelps, 2013; Aebi et al, 2015). One should thus welcome the critical eye of sociologist–criminologists (for example, McNeill et al, 2013). A political and critical look at offender supervision and at wider societal circumstances is crucial. It should not, however, be the enemy of treatment: as these critics typically point out, offenders are humans and individuals, and they deserve to be supported through the desistance process; so do victims, who certainly deserve more care and protection than the criminal justice system typically delivers.

Note

[1] See also (Herzog-Evans, 2016) for more detailed information on how to weave the law into RNR.

References

Aebi, M., Delgrande, N. and Marguet, Y. (2015) 'Have community sanctions and measures widened the net of the European criminal justice systems?', *Punishment & Society*, 17(5): 575–597.

Andrews, D. (2011) 'The impact of nonprogrammatic factors on criminal-justice interventions', *Legal and Criminological Psychology*, 16(1): 1–23.

Andrews, D.A. and Bonta, J. (2003) *The Psychology of Criminal Conduct* (3rd edn), Cincinnati, OH: Anderson Publishing.

Andrews, D.A. and Bonta, J. (2006) *The Psychology of Criminal Conduct* (4th edn), Newark: NJ: LexisNexis.

Andrews, D. and Bonta, J. (2010) *The Psychology of Criminal Conduct* (5th edn), Boston: Anderson Publishing.

Andrews, D.A. and Kiessling, J.J. (1980) 'Program structure and effective correctional practices: a summary of the CaVIC research', in R.R. Ross and P. Gendreau (eds) *Effective Correctional Treatment*, Toronto: Butterworth, pp 441–463.

Andrews, D.A., Bonta, J., and Wormith, J.S. (2011) 'The risk-need-responsivity (RNR) model: does adding the good lives model contribute to effective crime prevention?', *Criminal Justice and Behavior*, 38(7): 735–755.

Andrews, D.A., Zinger, I., Hoge, R.D., Bonta, J., Gendreau, P. and Cullen, F.T. (1990) 'Does correctional treatment work? A psychologically informed meta-analysis', *Criminology*, 28(3), 369–404.

Baird, C. (2009) *A Question of Evidence: A Critique of Risk Assessment Models used in the Justice System*, Report prepared for the National Council on Crime and Delinquency, Madison, WI: NCCD.

Baratta, A., Morali A. and Halleguen, O. (2012) 'La vérité sur l'expertise post-sentencielle' ['The truth about post-sentencing expert risk assessment'], *Annales Médico-Psychologiques*, 170: 96–98.

Bonta, J. and Andrews, D.A. (2003) 'A commentary on Ward and Stewart's model of human needs', *Psychology, Crime & Law*, 9: 215–218.

Bonta J. and Andrews, D.A. (2007) 'Risk-Need-Responsivity model for offender assessment and rehabilitation', available at www.publicsafety.gc.ca/cnt/rsrcs/pblctns/rsk-nd-rspnsvty/rsk-nd-rspnsvty-eng.pdf.

Bonta, J. and Andrews, D.A. (2017) *The Psychology of Criminal Conduct*, 6th edn, New York: Routledge.

Bonta, J., Rugge, T., Scott, T.-L., Bourgon, G. and Yessine, A.K. (2008) 'Exploring the black box of community supervision', *Journal of Offender Rehabilitation*, 47(3): 248–270.

Bottoms, A. (2001) 'Compliance and community penalties', in A. Bottoms, L. Gelsthorpe and S. Rex (eds) *Community Penalties. Change and Challenges*, Cullompton: Willan, pp 87–116.

Braithwaite, V. (2003) 'Dancing with tax authorities: motivational postures and non-compliant actions', in V. Braithwaite (ed) *Taxing Democracy: Understanding Tax Avoidance and Evasion*, Aldershot: Ashgate, pp 15–39.

Burnett, R. (2004) 'To reoffend or not to reoffend? The ambivalence of convicted property offenders', in S. Maruna and R. Immarigeon (eds) *After Crime and Punishment. Pathways to Offender Reintegration*, Collumpton: Willan, pp 152–180.

Cann, J., Falshaw, L., Nugent, F. and Friendship, C. (2003) *Understanding What Works: Accredited Cognitive Skills Programmes for Adult Men and Young Offenders*, Home Office Research Findings 226, London: Home Office.

Canton, R. (2012) 'The point of probation: on effectiveness, human rights, and the virtues of obliquity', *Criminology & Criminal Justice*, 13(5): 577–593.

Casey, S. (2016) 'Dynamic risk and sexual offending: the conundrum of assessment', *Psychology, Crime & Law*, 22(1): 104–123.

Casey, S., Day, A., Vess, J. and Ward, T. (2013) *Foundations of Offender Rehabilitation*, Abingdon: Routledge.

Chu, C.M., Ward, T. and Willis, G. (2014) 'Practising the Good Lives model', in I. Durnescu and F. McNeill (eds) (2014) *Understanding Penal Practice*, Abingdon: Routledge, pp 206–222.

Clarke, J. (2013) *Sustaining Probation Officer Resilience in Europe (SPORE). A Transnational Study*, SPORE and European Union.

Cording, J.R., Beggs Christofferson, S.M. and Grace, R.C. (2016) 'Challenges for the theory and application of dynamic risk factors', *Psychology, Crime & Law*, 22(1/2): 84–103.

Cross, W.E. Jr (1991) *Shades of Black. Diversity in African-American identity*, Philadelphia, PA: Temple University Press.

Cullen, F.T. (2012) 'Taking rehabilitation seriously: creativity, science, and the challenge of offender change', *Punishment & Society*, 14(1): 94–114.

Deci, E.L. and Ryan, R.M. (1985) *Intrinsic Motivation and Self-Determination in Human Behaviour*, New York, NY: Plenum.

Deci, E. and Ryan, R. (eds) (2002) *Handbook of Self-Determination Research*, Rochester, NY: University of Rochester Press.

Dobson, K.S. (ed) (2010) *Handbook of Cognitive Behavioral Therapies*, New York, NY: Guilford Press.

Dowden, C. and Andrews, D.A. (2004) 'The importance of staff practice in delivering effective correctional treatment: a meta-analysis', *International Journal of Offender Therapy and Comparative Criminology*, 48(2): 203–214.

Doyal, L. and Gough, I. (1991) *A Theory of Human Needs*, Basingstoke: Macmillan.

Dubourg, V. and Gautron, V. (2015) 'La rationalisation des méthodes d'évaluation des risques de récidive. Entre promotion institutionnelle, réticences professionnelles et prudence interpretative' ['Rationalising risk assessment methods. Between its institional promotion, professional resistance, and interpretative caution'], *Champ pénal/ Penal field*, XI, available at http://champpenal.revues.org/8947; doi: 10.4000/champpenal.8947.

Durrant, R., and Ward, T. (2015). *Evolutionary criminology: Towards a comprehensive explanation of crime*. London: Elsevier.

Epp, A.M. and Dobson, K.S. (2010) 'The evidence base for cognitive-behavioral therapy', in K.S. Dobson (ed) *Handbook of Cognitive Behavioral Therapies* (3rd edn), New York, NY: Guilford Press, pp 39–73.

Falshaw, L., Friendship, C., Travers, R. and Nugent, F. (2003) *Searching for 'What Works': An Evaluation of Cognitive Skills Programmes*, Home Office Research Findings 206, London: Home Office.

Farrall, S., Hunter, B., Sharpe, G. and Calverley, A. (2014) *Criminal Careers in Transition: The Social Context of Desistance from Crime*, Oxford: Oxford University Press.

Fazel, S. and Danesh, J. (2002) 'Serious mental disorder in 23,000 prisoners: a systematic review of 62 surveys', *Lancet* (359): 545–550.

Feder, L., Wilson, D.B. and Austin, S. (2008) *Court-Mandated Intervention for Individuals Convicted of Domestic Violence*, Campbell Systematic Reviews 2008:12, The Campbell Collaboration.

Fischer, J. (1973) 'Is casework effective? A review', *Social Work*, 18(1), 5–20.

Gannon, T.A. and Ward, T. (2014) 'Where has all the psychology gone? A critical review of evidence-based psychological practice in correctional settings', *Aggression and Violent Behavior*, 19(4), 435–446.

Gendreau, P., Smith, P. and Thériault, Y.L. (2009) 'Chaos theory and correctional treatment. Common sense, correctional quackery, and the law of fartcatchers', *Journal of Contemporary Criminal Justice*, 25(4): 384–396.

Georgenson, D.L. (1982) 'The problem of transfer calls for partnership', *Training and Development Journal*, 36(10): 75–78.

Gottfredson, S.D. and Moriarty, L.J. (2006) 'Statistical risk assessment: old problem and new applications', *Crime & Delinquency*, 52(1): 178–200.

Gough, D. (2010) 'Multi-agency working in corrections: cooperation and competition in probation practice', in A. Pycroft and D. Gough (eds) *Multi-Agency Working in Criminal Justice: Control and Care in Contemporary Correctional Practice*, Bristol: Policy Press, pp 21–33.

Grimshaw, J., Eccles, M., Thomas, R., Maclennan, G., Ramsay, C., Fraser, C. and Vale, C. (2006) 'Toward evidence-based quality improvement. Evidence (and its limitations) of the effectiveness of guideline dissemination and implementation strategies 1966–1998', *Journal of General Internal Medicine*, 21(Suppl. 2): S14-S2.

Hannah-Moffat, K. (2016) 'A conceptual kaleidoscope: contemplating "dynamic structural risk" and an uncoupling of risk from need', *Psychology, Crime & Law*, 22(1/2): 33–46.

Hanson, R.K., Harris, A J.R., Scott, T L. and Helmus, L. (2007) *Assessing the Risk of Sexual Offenders on Community Supervision: The Dynamic Supervision Project, 2007*, Ottawa: Public Survey, Canada.

Harcourt, B.E. (2006) *Against Prediction. Profiling, Policing, and Punishing in an Actuarial Age*, Chicago, IL: University of Chicago Press.

Harris, G. (2003) 'Men in his category have a 50% likelihood, but which half is he in? Comments on Berlin, Galbraith, Geary, and McGlone', *Sexual Abuse: A Journal of Research and Treatment*, 15(4): 389–392.

Harris, G.T. and Rice, M.E. (2015) 'Progress in violence risk assessment and communication: hypothesis versus evidence', *Behavioral Sciences & the Law*, 33(1): 128–145.

Helms, J.E. (1984) 'Towards a theoretical explanation of the effects of race on counselling: a black and white model', *The Counseling Psychologist*, 12(4): 153–165.

Helms, J.E. (1990) 'Development of the white racial identity attitude inventory', in J.E. Helms (ed) *Black and White Racial Identity: Theory, Research and Practice*, New York, NY: Greenwood Press.

Hemphill, J.F., Hare, R.D. and Wong, S. (1998) 'Psychopathy and recidivism: A review', *Legal and Criminological Psychology*, 3: 141–117.

Herzog-Evans, M. (2015a) 'France: legal architecture, political posturing, "prisonbation" and adieu social work', in G. Robinson and F. McNeill (eds) *Community Punishment: European Perspectives*, Abingdon: Routledge and COST EU, pp 51–71.

Herzog-Evans, M. (ed) (2015b) *Offender Release and Supervision: The Role of Courts and the Use of Discretion*, Nijmegen: Wolf Legal Publishers.

Herzog-Evans, M. (2015c) 'Consent and probation: an analogy with contract law', *European Journal of Probation*, 7(2): 143–16.

Herzog-Evans, M. (2016) 'Law as an extrinsic-responsivity factor: what's just is what works!', *European Journal of Probation*, 8(3): 146–169.

Holtzworth-Munroe, A. and Stuart, G.L. (1994) 'Typologies of male batterers: three subtypes and the differences among them', *Psychological Bulletin*, 116: 476–497.

Holtzworth-Munroe, A., Meehan, J.C., Herron, K., Rehman, U. and Stuart, G.L. (2000) 'Testing the Holtzworth-Munroe and Stuart typology', *Journal of Clinical and Consulting Psychology*, 68, 1000–1019.

Kadushin, A. and Kadushin, G. (2013) *The Social Work Interview* (5th edn), New York, NY: Columbia University Press.

Kaiser K.A. and Holtfreter, K. (2015) 'An integrated theory of specialized court programs. Using procedural justice and therapeutic jurisprudence to promote offender compliance and rehabilitation', *Criminal Justice and Behavior*, DOI 10.1177/0093854815609642.

Kemshall, H. and Canton, R. (2002) *The Effective Management of Programme Attrition. A Report for the National Probation Service*, Leicester: de Montfort University.

Keulen de Vos, D.G., Bernstein, D.P. and Arntz, A. (2010) 'Schema therapy for aggressive offenders with personality disorders', in R.C. Tafrate and D. Mitchell (eds) *Forensic CBT: A Handbook for Clinical Practice*, Chichester: Wiley, pp 66–84.

Knight, C. (2014) *Emotional Literacy in Criminal Justice: Professional Practice with Offenders*, Basingstoke: Palgrave Macmillan.

La Vigne, M. and Van Rybroek, G. (2014) '"He got in my face so I shot him": how defendants' language impairments impair attorney-client relationship', *CUNY Law Review*, 17: 69–121.

Lee, W.J., Koenigsberg, M.R., Davidson, C. and Beto, D.R. (2010) 'Leadership style and leadership success among probation director in the US', *Federal Probation*, 74(3): 34–42.

Lewis, S., Raynor, P., Smith, D. and Wardak, A. (2006) *Race and Probation*, Cullompton: Willan.

Looman, J. and Abracen, J. (2013) 'The risk need responsivity model of offender rehabilitation: is there really a need for a paradign shift?', *International Journal of Behavioural Consultation and Therapy*, 8(3–4): 30–36.

Lowenkamp, C.T., Latessa, A.J. and Smith, P. (2006) 'Does correctional program quality really matter? The impact of adhering to the principles of effective intervention', *Criminology & Public Policy*, 5(3): 575–594.

Mair, G. (ed) (2004) *What Matters in Probation*, Cullompton: Willan Publishing.

Martin, J., Kautt, P. and Gelsthorpe, L. (2009) 'What works for women? A comparison of community-based General Offending Programme completion', *British Journal of Criminology*, 49(6): 879–899.

Martinson, R. (1974) 'What works? Questions and answers about prison reform', *The Public Interest*, 35: 22–34.

Maruna, S. (2001) *Making Good. How Ex-Convicts Reform and Rebuild their Lives*, Washington, DC: American Psychology Association.

Matusiewicz, A.K., Hopwood, C.J., Banducci, A.N. and Leuez, C.W. (2010) 'The effectiveness of cognitive behavioural therapy for personality disorders', *Psychiatry Clinics of North America*, 33(3): 657–685.

McNeill, F. (2009) 'What works and what's just?' *European Journal of Probation*, 1(1): 21–40.

McNeill, F. (2012) 'Four forms of "offender" rehabilitation: towards an interdisciplinary perspective', *Legal and Criminological Psychology*, 17(1): 18–36.

McNeill, F., Robinson, G. and Maruna, S. (2013) 'Punishment in society: the improbable persistence of probation and other community sanctions and measures', in J. Simon and R. Sparks (eds) *The Sage Handbook of Punishment and Society*, London: Sage Publications, pp 321–355.

Miller, P.M. (ed) (2009) *Evidence-Based Addiction Treatment*, London: Elsevier.

Miller, W.R. and Rollnick, S. (2012) *Motivational Interviewing: Preparing People to Change* (3rd edn), New York, NY: Guilford Press.

Olver, M.E., Stockdale, J.C. and Wormith, J.S. (2011) 'A meta-analysis of predictors of offender treatment attrition and its relationship to recidivism', *Journal of Consulting and Clinical Psychology*, 79(1): 6–21.

Palmer, T. (1995) 'Programmatic and nonprogrammatic aspects of successful intervention: new directions for research', *Crime & Delinquency*, 41(1): 100–131.

Phelps, M.S. (2013) 'The paradox of probation. Community supervision in the age of mass incarceration', *Law & Policy*, 35(12): 51–80.

Polaschek, D.L.L. (2016) 'Desistance and dynamic-risk factors belong together', *Psychology, Crime & Law*, 22(1/2): 171–189.

Ponterotto, J.G., Casas, J.M., Suzuki, L.A. and Alexander, C.M. (1995) *Handbook of Multicultural Counseling*, London: Sage Publications.

Porporino, F.J. (2010) 'Bringing sense and sensitivity to corrections: from programmes to "fix" offenders to services to support desistance', in J. Brayford, F. Cowe, and J. Deering (eds) *What Else Works? Creative Work with Offenders*, Cullompton: Willan, pp 61–85.

Raynor, P. (2008) 'Community penalties and home office research: on the way back to "nothing works"?', *Criminology & Criminal Justice*, 8(1): 73–87.

Raynor, P., Ugwudike, P. and Vanstone, M. (2015) 'The impact of skills in probation work: a reconviction study', *Criminology & Criminal Justice*, 14(2): 235–249.

Robinson, L. (1998) *Race, Communication and the Caring Professions*, Buckingham: Open University Press.

Robinson, L. (2009) *Psychology for Social Workers. Black Perspectives on Human Development and Behaviour* (2nd edn), Abingdon: Routledge.

Robinson, G. and McNeill, F. (2008) 'Exploring the dynamics of compliance with community penalties', *Theoretical Criminology*, 12(4): 431–449.

Rogers, E. (2003) *Diffusion of Innovations* (5th edn), New York, NY: Free Press.

Ryan, R.M., Plant, R.W. and O'Malley, S. (1995) 'Initial motivations for alcohol treatment: relations with patient characteristics, treatment involvement, and dropout', *Addictive Behavior*, 20(3): 279–297.

Saks, A.M. (2002) 'So what is a good transfer of training estimate? A reply to Fitzpatrick', *Industrial-Organizational Psychologist*, 39: 29–30.

Serin, R.C., Chadwick, N. and Lloyd, C.D. (2016) 'Dynamic risk and protective factors', *Psychology, Crime & Law*, 22(1/2): 151–170.

Sheldon K.M., William, G. and Joiner, T. (2013) *Self-Determination Theory in the Clinic: Motivating Physical and Mental Health*, New Haven, CT: Yale University Press.

Singleton, N., Meltzer, H. and Gatward, R. (1998) *Psychiatric morbidity among prisoners in England and Wales*, London,UK: Stationery Office.

Sloper, P. (2004) 'Facilitators and barriers for co-ordinated multi-agency services', *Child: Care, Health and Development*, 30(6): 571–580.

Smedslund, G., Dalsbø, T.K., Steiro, A.K., Winsvold, A. and Clench-Aas, J. (2011) *Cognitive Behavioural Therapy for Men who Physically Abuse their Female Partner*, Campbell Systematic Reviews 2007:4, The Campbell Collaboration.

Smit, Y., Huibers, M.J., Ioannidis, J.P., van Dyck, R., van Tilburg, W. and Arntz, A. (2012) 'The effectiveness of long-term psychoanalytic psychotherapy: a meta-analysis of randomized controlled trials', *Clinical Psychology Review*, 32(2): 81–92.

Smith, P., Schweizte, M., Labrecque, R.M. and Latesssa, E.J. (2012) 'Improving probation officers' supervision skills: an evaluation of the EPICS model', *Journal of Crime and Justice*, 35(2): 189–199.

Sullivan, H. and Skelcher, C. (2002) *Working Across Boundaries: Collaboration in Public Services*, Basingtoke: Palgrave Macmillan.

Tafrate, R.C. and Mitchell, D. (eds) (2014) *Forensic CBT: A Handbook for Clinical Practice*, Chichester: Wiley.

Taylor, K.N. and Blanchette, K. (2009) 'The women are not wrong: it is the approach that is debatable', *Criminology & Public Policy*, 8(1): 221–229.

Taxman, F.S. and Belenko, S. (2012) *Implementing Evidence-Based Practices in Community Corrections and Addiction Treatment*, New York: Springer.

Trotter, C. (2013) *Collaborative Family Work: A Practical Guide to Working with Families in the Human Services*, Crows Nest: Allen & Unwin.

Trotter, C. (2015) *Working with Involuntary Clients: A Guide to Practice* (3rd edn), Abingdon: Routledge.

Tyler, T.R. (2006) *Why People Obey the Law* (2nd edn), New Haven, CT: Yale University Press.

Tyler, T.R. (2012) 'The virtues of self-regulation', in A. Crawford and A. Hucklesby (eds) *Legitimacy and Compliance in Criminal Justice*, London: Routledge, pp 8–28.

Walsh, J. (2013) *Theories for Direct Social Work Practice* (3rd edn), Stamford: Cengage Learning.

Ward, T. and Fortune, C.A. (2013) 'The Good Lives model: Aligning risk reduction with promoting offenders personal goals', *European Journal of Probation*, 5, 29–46.

Ward, T., Yates, P.M. and Willis, G.M. (2012) 'The Good Lives model and the risk need responsivity model. A critical response to Andrews, Bonta, and Wormith (2011)', *Criminal Justice and Behavior*, 39(1): 94–110.

Wexler, D. and Winick, B. (1996) *Law in a Therapeutic Key: Developments in Therapeutic Jurisprudence*, Durham, NC: Carolina Academic Press.

Wilsford, D. (1994) 'Path dependency, or why history makes it difficult but not impossible to reform health care systems in a big way', *Journal of Public Policy*, 14(3): 251–283.

Woldgabreal, Y., Day, A. and Ward, T. (2014) 'The community-based supervision of offenders from a positive psychology perspective', *Aggression and Violent Behavior*, 19(1): 32–41.

Wormith, J.S., Gendreau, P. and Bonta, J. (2012) 'Deferring to clarity, parsimony, and evidence in reply to Ward, Yates, and Willis', *Criminal Justice and Behavior*, 39(1): 111–120.

Young, J., Klosko, J. and Weishaar, M.E. (2003) *Schema Therapy: A Practitioner's Guide*, New York, NY: Guilford Press.

Zeldman, A., Ryan, R.M. and Fiscella, K. (2004) 'Motivation, autonomy support, and entity belief: their role in methadone maintenance treatment', *Journal of Social and Clinical Psychology*, 23(5): 675–696.

SEVEN

Professional practices and skills in first interviews: a comparative perspective on probation practice in Spain and Belgium

Ester Blay and Johan Boxstaens

Introduction

As this volume reflects, there is a growing body of empirical research on the practice of offender supervision in Europe and some recent work on probation practice using observations (Raynor et al, 2010, 2014; Trotter and Evans, 2012; Durnescu, 2014). As far as we know, however, probation practices have never been addressed *comparatively* using observation as a method.

In this chapter, we address the initial phase of the working relationships practitioners and service users develop in the context of community sentences in Flanders and Catalonia. In particular, we focus on the practices undertaken and the skills used in first interviews; we also reflect on how these practices set the scene for the working relationship between probation officers and probationers.

To do so, we have gathered documentary data (legal information, regulations and mission statements, national standards and practitioners' guidelines) and have drawn on empirical research: previous research by the authors involving in-depth interviews with practitioners and structured observation of first interviews between practitioners and probationers.

The observations were conducted by researchers from various European jurisdictions in the context of a subgroup of the COST Action on Offender Supervision in Europe (Boxstaens et al, 2015).[1] The main aim of this international group of researchers, who were members of the COST Action subgroup on Practising Supervision, was to explore the use of observation as a method for data collection in comparative research on probation practice. Although the aim was methodological and the study necessarily exploratory, the substantive data gathered in the two jurisdictions is rich enough for a comparative exercise.

The relationship between clients and therapists

In the field of psychotherapy and counselling, it is well established that the relationship between clients and therapists or counsellors is a vital component of the therapeutic process (Lambert and Barley, 2002; Binder et al, 2009; Norcross, 2011; DeLude et al, 2012). A very broad, but widespread, definition of a relationship in a therapeutic context was introduced by Gelso and Carter (1994): 'The relationship is the feelings and attitudes that therapist and client have toward one another, and the manner in which they are expressed' (Gelso and Samstag, 2008, p 268). This definition can be linked to the Rogerian tradition in which the relationship is considered to be the vehicle for change that can lead to personal growth (Rogers, 1957). Empirical research has shown that relational factors have an effect on therapeutic outcomes and treatment adherence (Ross et al, 2008). Studies in the field of mental health (for example, Horvath and Greenberg, 1994; Norcross, 2002, 2011) and substance abuse (for example, Connors et al, 1997; Miller and Rollnick, 2002) have shown that the professional relationship between clients and therapists or counsellors can be regarded as a key component in effective behavioural change programmes. Lambert and Barley (2002) argue that the therapist–client relationship accounts for 30% of the variance in client outcome, which exceeds the effect of other variables such as the type of therapy provided. These findings are consistent with the results of other meta-analytic studies (Horvath and Luborsky, 1993; Orlinsky et al, 2004) that also underline the paramount importance of a good client–therapist relationship for positive therapy outcomes.

In this chapter, we argue that in offender supervision the relationship between probation officers (POs) and probationers cannot be considered as being 'therapeutic' in its essence. The PO–probationer relationship is framed by a legal mandate. This mandate, given by a third party (for example, a court) legitimises the interventions of practitioners, which is different from a therapeutic relationship formed on the basis of a client's demand for help and framed by mutual agreement. This does not mean that in offender supervision it is not necessary to build a strong, supportive relationship in order to support the process of desistance from crime (Burnett and McNeill, 2005). However, it seems necessary to differentiate the professional relationship between POs and probationers from the therapeutic relationship as described by Rogers (1957). This might be possible by using the concept of a 'working alliance' (Bordin, 1979).

The working alliance between probation officers and probationers

The working alliance is rooted in Freudian psychoanalyses and was developed to a broader theoretical construct by Bordin (Ross et al, 2008). By doing so, Bordin (1979) introduced the concept of the 'working alliance' as a core element, not only in all forms of therapy and counselling, but in all processes of change in general. In this perspective and unlike the term **therapeutic** alliance, the concept of the **working** alliance can be used in every situation that involves making changes in people's lives, for example in a student–teacher relationship (Ross et al, 2008), hence also in offender supervision. Translated to the field of probation, the working alliance consists of three important dimensions: a **bond** that reflects the nature of the relationship between PO and probationer; an agreement on the **goals** of supervision; and an agreement on the **tasks** that need to be completed to achieve these goals (DeLude et al, 2012).

It can be argued that goals, tasks and bonds are present in every probation process (Hart and Collins, 2014). In the first meetings between POs and probationers, supervision goals are set and both parties come to an agreement on the way these goals will be achieved (tasks). An example of a goal that needs to be achieved in this context is the pursuit of meaningful daily activities (such as a job, volunteer work, an educational or therapeutic programme). Throughout the probation process, different tasks will need to be devised to reach these goals (for example, search for a job online or in newspapers, apply for volunteer work, search for information on appropriate therapeutic programmes).

As argued previously, the relationship between POs and probationers is framed by a legal mandate. This means that an external body (generally a court) often sets the scene for the goals and tasks that need to be achieved in offender supervision. POs and probationers must seek to develop a shared commitment to these goals and actively contribute to their achievement by collaboratively completing different tasks. The bond that develops throughout the supervision process could form an important mediating factor in PO–probationer relationships (Binder et al, 2009). It could constitute a trusting, non-judgemental and respectful relationship that facilitates common task and goal setting (Ross et al, 2008; Hart and Collins, 2014). Cherkos and colleagues

(2008) found a link between the perceived helpfulness of probation and the way probationers reflect on the relationship with their PO. Positive qualities of this relationship (such as patience, trust, open communication and willingness to listen) are highly appreciated by probationers (Cherkos et al, 2008), which supports the idea that a bond between both parties is an important mediating factor within PO–probationer relationships. Indeed, recent research has shown that the working alliance is highly predictive of probationers' views on the success of their probation process (DeLude et al, 2012; Hart and Collins, 2014). Other findings suggest that probationers who score highly on a self-report questionnaire concerning the working alliance demonstrate lower recidivism rates than those who report lower scores (Wild, 2011). Further research is certainly needed, but it seems plausible to conclude that developing a strong working alliance in offender supervision practice can result in significantly positive outcomes.

Although it is argued that training concerning the working alliance could easily be incorporated in PO training programmes (Hart and Collins, 2014), we would like to point out that practitioners in offender supervision are faced with the challenge of developing a good working alliance while balancing the demands of a double professional role: on the one hand, they are charged with protecting community safety (control), while on the other they are assumed to promote offender rehabilitation (care) (Skeem and Manchak, 2008). In this context, we would like to refer to Klockars' (1972) theory of probation supervision.

Klockars' theory of probation supervision

Based on ethnographic research, Klockars (1972) distinguishes between four types of probation officer that can be placed on the continuum between care and control as goals of their interventions (Skeem and Manchak, 2008). The typology is linked to the 'working philosophy' that probation officers develop and Klockars (1972, p 550) defines as 'the role which the officer sets for himself and the logic and rationale he develops to explain what he does or what he ought to do'. On the 'control' end of the continuum, we find the 'law enforcers' and 'time servers'. Both types of probation officer take a surveillance approach to supervision. This means that they are both very focused on monitoring compliance with rules and regulations and enforcing them in a very strict way. However, as opposed to the law enforcers, the practice of time servers is not value-driven. Their only concern seems to be meeting minimum job requirements in a bureaucratic way. At the other end of the control–care continuum, we can situate 'therapeutic agents', who take a treatment approach to offender supervision and conceptualise their professional role as effecting behavioural change in an effort to improve the life of individual offenders. A fourth and last professional type are synthetic officers. In their working philosophy, synthetic officers synthesise (combine) the surveillance and treatment approach. Balancing this dual role is considered to be a difficult, but very important, element of effective supervision (Trotter, 1999).

After the presentation of his typology of probation officers, Klockars (1972) goes on to describe the process that synthetic practitioners go through in an effort to successfully balance surveillance and treatment goals and, in doing so, develop effective supervision practices. He uses the concept of exchange in the officer–probationer–department triad to explain this process which is pictured in Figure 7.1.

According to Klockars (1972), the probation officer has to be very clear about rules and regulations in first meetings with probationers. As depicted in the first triad of Figure 7.1, POs tend to start off by clearly positioning themselves as representatives of the probation department, which articulates their surveillance approach. In follow-up meetings, POs can develop their treatment role by offering social support to probationers (triad 2 in Figure 7.1). In order to successfully combine the treatment and surveillance approach, POs exchange the controlling part of their professional role with the probation department. By introducing the probation department into the relationship with probationers, POs create a triad. They can refer to the probation department as the third party that has the actual authority to make decisions concerning possible violations of imposed conditions. Klockars (1972) claims that the authority of the department is fictional to a large extent: POs can use their professional discretion to

Figure 7.1: The exchange process in the development of effective supervision

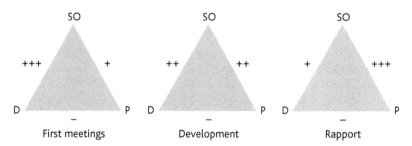

Note: SO = Synthetic Officers; D = Department of Probation; P = probationer.
Source: adapted from Klockars (1972, p 556)

decide what information they give the department and how strictly conditions are imposed. By emphasising that the department and themselves are two different entities, POs can successfully combine the surveillance approach with the treatment approach. Although Klockars' claim still seems valid to a large extent in Belgium and Catalonia, we acknowledge that this may vary across different jurisdictions and through time. For example, since the introduction of National Standards in England and Wales, the authority of the probation service and its impact on probation practice is very significant.

Skeem and Manchak (2008) derive two mechanisms for effective supervision from Klockars' theory. The first mechanism had already been acknowledged by Trotter (1999) and implies the successful reconciliation of a surveillance approach (targeting behavioral monitoring and control) and a therapeutical approach (targeting behavioural change). Klockars (1972) claims that by combining both approaches, so-called synthetic officers might enable probationers to establish a strong rapport. This close professional relationship – equivalent to the concept of the working alliance – should encourage probationers to 'tell all', which allows for POs to closely assess whether conditions are complied with and makes it possible to intervene as soon as necessary. Moreover, Klockars (1972) argues that some probationers will be motivated to be compliant not only to avoid sanctions from the probation department, but also because they want to work together with a probation officer with whom they have established rapport. More recent studies show that probationers might be motivated to comply for several other reasons, for example, because they believe that the costs of non-compliance would be too high or because of the fact that their movements are being monitored electronically (Ugwudike and Raynor, 2013). The second mechanism for effective supervision is related to the good quality of the relationship that might develop between synthetic officers and probationers. This relationship might be therapeutic in itself (Skeem and Manchak, 2008). As argued previously, research has shown that the quality of the working alliance between a service provider and a client can have strong effects on outcomes, not only in the field of psychotherapy and counseling (Lambert and Barley, 2002; Binder et al, 2009; Norcross, 2011; DeLude et al, 2012), but also in the field of offender supervision (Taxman, 2002). Research has shown that in order to enable probationers to establish a strong rapport and co-construct a good-quality working alliance, POs have to develop – among other things – problem-solving skills, strong verbal and non-verbal communication skills, use prosocial modelling techniques and use authority effectively (Andrews and Bonta, 2003; Raynor et al, 2014).

Klockars' theory is useful to clarify that – even in the challenging context of offender supervision where POs have to balance a dual role – it seems plausible to assume that a good working alliance or professional relationship between probationers and POs is vital to the effectiveness of the supervision process. This hypothesis is supported by a growing body of research that points at the importance of a good relationship between probationers and POs in the development of effective supervision (for example, Andrews and Kiessling, 1980; Trotter, 1996, 2006; Dowden and Andrews, 2004; Burnett and McNeill, 2005; Paparozzi and Gendreau, 2005; Skeem et al, 2007; Annison et al, 2008; Kennealy et al, 2012; Labrecque et al, 2013; Raynor and Vanstone, 2015).

In summary, research highlights the paramount importance of the skills that POs need to – as Klockars (1972) puts it – establish rapport or pursue a good professional relationship with probationers (DeLude et al, 2012). The concept of the working alliance seems to have an added value in explaining the nature of this relationship and which elements are important its development: tasks, goals and bond.

In this contribution, we want to focus on the professional practices and skills that are observed in first meetings between POs and probationers. We reflect on how these practices set the scene for establishing the professional relationship or working alliance between POs and probationers in two different jurisdictions, Flanders and Catalonia.

The study

In order to contextualise the comparative method adopted by the current study, we shall briefly address the legal and organisational contexts of probation in both Flanders and Catalonia and describe the role of probation officers as reflected in regulation, policy documents and guidelines in the two jurisdictions.

A brief reference to the legal and organisational frameworks in Catalonia and Flanders

Catalonia

Supervision in the community in Catalonia is currently undertaken within the framework of suspended sentences with requirements and community service orders. Sentences of up to two years can be suspended, and the judge may impose requirements, such as attending a treatment programme, periodically presenting oneself to the probation service or not communicating with the victim (arts. 80 and 83 CC [Criminal Code]). In the case of intimate partner violence, every time a judge suspends a prison sentence, requirements have to be imposed, in particular, a treatment programme and some victim protection requirements (art. 83 CC). Prison sentences of up to five years might be suspended for drug users with the requirement that the person follows a drug treatment programme and does not reoffend. Community service can be used both as a requirement of a suspended sentence and as a stand-alone sentence. In practice, community sentences are mainly used to punish driving offences and, to a lesser extent, intimate partner violence (Blay and Larrauri, 2015).

There is a single Criminal Code and a single judicial power for the whole of Spain; however, there are two administrations with power to implement sentences and supervise offenders: one in Catalonia[2] (set in the Department of Justice of the Catalan government) and one for the rest of the Spanish territory (set in the Home Ministry of the Spanish government). This division has led to diverse practices in the implementation of community sentences and the development of two different administrative settings with diverse ethos (see Blay and Larrauri, 2015). In this chapter, we focus exclusively on practices in Catalonia.

Although there is no probation service as such in Catalonia, the Justice Department has developed a structure for the supervision of offenders in the community. This system involves the supervision of offenders in the community by (mainly) social workers and psychologists. These practitioners are not directly employed by the Justice Department, but since 2001 by non-profit organisations contracted out by the Justice Department. They tend to work in court settings and their work is functionally and territorially distributed between the various organisations.

There are currently 7,302 individuals serving prison sentences in Catalonia and 7,664 under supervision in the community (Department of Justice Statistics, 2016). According to the same source, approximately 70% of those under community supervision are serving community service orders and 30% are on probation.

Flanders

The legal and organisational framework of community supervision in Belgium/Flanders is currently subject to ongoing developments. Up until recently, the implementation of all community penalties in Belgium was the responsibility of the Department of Offender Guidance, which fell under the jurisdiction of the Federal Ministry of Justice (Bauwens and Devos, 2015). This task was carried out in 28 local 'Houses of Justice' (HoJ) that are spread throughout the country. However, in 2011, the formation of a new federal government led to an agreement on the so-called 'sixth state reform', which regulates the transfer of federal competences to the regions and communities. This agreement resulted in the transfer of all tasks concerning offender guidance *extra muros* to the communities. Hence, the Government of Flanders has been officially responsible for the organisation, tasks and functioning of the 13 Flemish HoJ since 1 July 2014. Between 1 July 2014 and 31 December 2014, practical arrangements were made to prepare the actual transfer of financial means and personnel. Since 1 January 2015, the Flemish HoJ have been a part of the Flemish Department of Welfare, Public Health and Family. In several documents, the minister has set the goal to develop a new legal framework that regulates the organisation and tasks of the Flemish HoJ. However, due to the lack of public information, it remains unclear which changes will be anchored in the new framework.

For now, the organisation and tasks of the Flemish HoJ remain regulated by the Act on the organisation of the HoJ of 13 June 1999 (BS,[3] 29 June 1999). In addition, the federal government created a legal framework for electronic monitoring (BS, 15 June 2006). Since 2007, the HoJ are responsible for the supervision of offenders under electronic monitoring (BS, 27 January 2007).

In 2014, Belgian prisons housed 11,769 individuals serving a prison sentence (Belgian Federal Government, 2014). At the same time, the Belgian HoJ had 44,104 individuals serving a community sentence (21,689 in Flanders) (HoJ, 2014).

The role of probation officers in Catalonia and Flanders: law and guidelines

Catalonia

Professionals in charge of implementation are rarely mentioned in the Criminal Code or in any other piece of legislation in Spain. When so, their role is described in terms of 'controlling the implementation' of the obligation to attend treatment programmes in the case of probation or 'facilitating work placements' in the case of community service, and periodically reporting to the judge about the probationers' performance, particularly if there is any violation of the imposed requirements or obligations (arts. 49 and 83 CC).

To sum up, the most important regulations describe the task of POs in terms of managing (undertaking the necessary practical steps to implement) the sentence, controlling probationers' performance and reporting to the judge. Neither the Criminal Code nor the Regulation for Implementation[4] contains any mention of a supporting role.

A more complex role for probation officers is reflected in policy documents and guidelines of the Catalan administration (Department of Justice, n.d.a, n.d.b). At this level, while maintaining the language of control, documents introduce parallel references to support. When the mission statement describes the role of probation officers, it starts by stating that officers should ensure the implementation of sentences, keeping judges informed about compliance and probationers about their obligations and the content of their order (Department of Justice, n.d.c). However, the mission statement states that POs should also 'promote the social integration of the person, through socio-educational follow up and support', aim at avoiding recidivism and link service users to community resources (Department of Justice, n.d.c). Working protocols repeat this language and introduce the idea that POs should encourage offenders 'to take responsibility for the motivation, content and aims of the sentence' and get 'committed' and 'involved' in its implementation (Department of Justice, n.d.a, n.d.b, authors' translation). Documents at an internal administrative level, therefore, clearly reflect the double role POs develop.

Flanders

The HoJ are currently responsible for the following tasks (Bauwens and Devos, 2015):

- supervision, guidance and social enquiry reports on the basis of statutory acts relating to the mentally ill and to habitual offenders, pertaining to suspended sentences, probation, conditional sentences and preventive detention;
- providing information and advice to all clients of the HoJ, and if necessary, the tasks of referral to the appropriate services;
- structuring and promoting collaboration among the key stakeholders, both within and outside the criminal justice system;
- coordination, promotion and disclosure of information with regard to alternatives in the area of the settlement of disputes, and of community sanctions;

- making offices available to support the provision to all citizens of initial legal aid dispensed by barristers, and to facilitate the holding of legal aid and Probation Commissions meetings.

Information on how these tasks are carried out is not integrated in law, but in internal documents. The mission of the HoJ is defined as 'the judicial guidance and supervision of offenders in order to prevent recidivism and promote restorative justice' (HoJ, 2010, p 1; authors' translation). In a vision statement, the HoJ elaborate on what is called their 'basic philosophy'. The text stipulates that it is the purpose of the judicial system to find a balance between offender rights on the one hand and community rights on the other (HoJ, 2013). In this context, 'justice assistants' are defined as one of the groups of actors that can intervene in this regulatory process, which should lead to non-recidivism (HoJ, 2013). To reach this goal, justice assistants have certain means that are defined by a legal mandate. This mandate is constituted by the conditions that are imposed following a sentence or alternative measure. These conditions are described as the means, the tools or the instruments that are of paramount importance within the learning process of the offender towards the development of behaviour that will no longer lead to judicial interference. Additionally, the imposed conditions can be considered as an important framework in which the relationship between justice assistant and offender can be established.

In offender supervision, the HoJ always combine guidance and supervision (HoJ, 2013). This is reflected in the definition of offender supervision as 'social work under judicial mandate', which entails that justice assistants have a double role: reducing the risk of recidivism on the one hand, and fostering social inclusion of offenders and protecting their fundamental rights on the other (Bauwens, 2011, p 18).

In the following section, we go beyond the description of professional roles by regulation and internal documents and focus on observed practices.

Methodology

Comparative professional practices and the building of a working alliance

This section is based on the observation of 30 first interviews between POs and individuals under supervision in the community. In both jurisdictions, a single PO supervises each individual, so the professionals conducting the first interviews work with individuals until the completion of their sentence. Fourteen of these interviews were conducted in Catalonia and 16 in Flanders, and they involved 11 POs (five from Catalonia, six from Flanders) observed an average 3.8 times each. Interviewees had been sentenced to probation or to community service orders.[5] To ensure the gathering of *comparable* data, an observation grid was collaboratively developed to capture both the content and the practices and skills involved in the interviews (see Boxstaens et al, 2015 for a detailed discussion).

Findings

In the following paragraphs, we address the extent to which POs in each jurisdiction adopt the practices and skills involved in the building of an effective working alliance and discuss how these practices play along the care/control tension (Skeem and Manchak, 2008).

The use of working alliance-related skills in Catalonia and Flanders

DeLude and colleagues (2012) tried to measure the link between probationers' perception of their relationship with their PO and the extent to which they found probation helpful overall. In order to do this, they surveyed a sample of probationers using a 'satisfaction survey' based on the work of Cherkos and colleagues (2008). This survey contained various demographic and probation information items and was followed by 15 questions to measure 'probationers' perceptions of their PO …, the professionalism of the office environment and … the overall helpfulness of probation' (DeLude et al, 2012, p 37). We have adapted the concepts used by DeLude and colleagues (2012) in order to analyse the data gathered with our observation grid. We have summed up results in Table 7.1, and address them along the following lines:

- appropriate amount of time spent with probationers;
- collaboration between PO and probationer to complete tasks involved in probation;
- respect;
- listening;
- collaboration between PO and probationer in establishing supervision goals;
- complimenting probationers when appropriate;
- caring and assisting;

- showing understanding;
- creating trust;
- showing optimism about the future of the probationer.

These concepts are explored in detail below.

Appropriate amount of time spent with probationers

Time spent by POs in interviews may convey interest for, and importance granted to, probationers. It should probably be put in relation to the (comparatively little) time spent by other criminal justice system professionals with the probationer (Blay, 2011). This probably makes time spent all the more relevant for probationers, although more research is needed as to how this time is perceived by them and managed by professionals.

Observed interviews lasted from 15 to 91 minutes, with an average of 35.13 minutes. Interviews were considerably longer in Catalonia, where they lasted an average of 43.78 minutes, while in Flanders they lasted 27.56 minutes on average. This difference may be due to the detailed discussion of both personal data and the probationer's attitude towards the offence in Catalonia. These discussions are later used by POs to decide how intensive their supervision should be and how fast probationers should start treatment.

Collaboration between PO and probationer to complete tasks involved in probation

Tasks involved in probation (for example, the completion of a programme or the need to attend interviews) are largely mandated by judicial ruling. Within these limits, however, POs should strive to involve probationers in the various decisions involved, such as in choosing a work placement or a suitable day and time for treatment. This involvement facilitates commitment and compliance (Skeem and Manchak, 2008).

Most POs in our sample encourage probationers' collaboration during decision making (88% of interviews observed), including the timing of the next appointment (75%). This reflects POs wanting to accommodate the needs of probationers, and is likely to help build a balanced and non-authoritarian relationship. Future plans are always discussed in first interviews, and obligations are discussed in detail (in 92% of cases). On the whole, Flemish POs score above average in the use of these skills: they use them to a large extent 94% of the time, whereas Catalan POs use them to a large extent 84% of the time. This might be explained by differences such as Flemish POs requesting probationers to propose a time for the next meeting and Catalan POs proposing a time themselves and then asking for the probationer's input, for example.

Respect

Respect on the part of the PO towards the probationer is reflected both in non-verbal and verbal communication. As argued by Vanstone and Raynor (2012, p 10), non-verbal behaviour can have a direct effect on trust building, levels of intimacy and openness to collaborative problem solving. Looking at the observational data, it seems that POs are very aware of the importance of their non-verbal communication. We used the criteria of the SOLER acronym developed by Egan (2002), which allows for observing POs sitting squarely, holding an open posture, leaning towards the service user, maintaining adequate eye contact and appearing relaxed. Based on the observational data, all POs get an excellent score on non-verbal communication. This means that all of them squarely faced the service user, adopted an open posture, initiated and tried to keep appropriate eye contact, and appeared relaxed.

About half of the observations in both jurisdictions involved probationers with an immigrant background. Qualitative notes on these observations made it clear that communication skills are very culture-sensitive: eye contact, for example, is interpreted differently depending on the cultural context. This means that use of body language is not always as straightforward as theory implies in jurisdictions where individuals under supervision come from different cultural backgrounds. This issue has implications for the training and the recruiting of POs in increasingly diverse societies.

POs show understanding and display warmth and respect in almost all interviews observed in both jurisdictions. This may be reinforced by a handshake after each interview. This conveys the picture of sympathetic POs, trying to establish a bond on which to base the relationship, already in the first interview.

Listening

The willingness of POs to listen to probationers and encourage them to talk is reflected in many ways, and various items in the grid help capture them. Good body language, involving nodding and eye contact, coupled with time given to service users to talk, can convey this attitude. Our observation grid more specifically tried to capture the use of eye contact, which we interpret as conveying interest and focus;[6] this was used habitually by POs in both jurisdictions, albeit more so in Catalonia (97%) than in Flanders (87%).

The willingness of POs to listen to probationers' explanations is also reflected in the use of open-ended and non-leading questions, which show the wish to create a space where the probationer can talk. As is reflected in Table 7.1, these skills are used to a lesser extent, with an average 70% in these two items, and Flemish POs scoring higher than Catalan POs.

When we take into account the scores of all items related to a listening attitude, professionals in both jurisdictions score an average 88%, with only small percentage differences and Catalonia below average (85%) and Flanders slightly above (90%).

These data demonstrate that non-verbal language is perhaps used more effectively than verbal language to convey listening. This might be explained because, as we shall address later, first interviews are very much about gathering personal and practical information needed to enforce a judicial mandate.

Collaboration between PO and probationer in establishing supervision goals

In most first meetings, the general goals of supervision as stated by mission statements or guidelines, such as reducing reoffending or rehabilitation, are not or only very briefly addressed. POs talk about the aims of the order in 50% of the interviews observed; however, they talk about the obligations of the order in 93% of interviews. This shows that first interviews are perhaps more focused on clearly setting specific rules of probation than more general goals. When we look at jurisdictions we see that POs in Catalonia only talk about the aims of orders in 21% of interviews, whereas they do so in 72% of interviews in Flanders. This reinforces the idea that first interviews in Catalonia seem to be more focused on establishing rules and less on making the offender understand why these rules are important (to attain certain goals). Of course, this might change in follow-up interviews (and ongoing research by the authors points in this direction; Blay, forthcoming).

Complimenting probationers when appropriate

Positive comments outweigh negative comments in most interviews (71%), albeit more markedly by Flemish than Catalan professionals (79% versus 62.5%). Individual styles are important here, and attitudes are likely to change as the supervisory process develops.

Caring and assisting

POs' care for probationers and their willingness to assist them may be conveyed in many ways. The 'prelude' of the observed interviews in both jurisdictions, also useful for 'breaking the ice' and facilitating introductions, is one way of doing so. By greeting probationers in the waiting room, walking with them to the interview room making small talk, and expressing interest in probationers at the beginning of the interview ('How are you?', 'How are you feeling?'), POs start to show they care.

Care may also be conveyed through an attentive body language, by POs showing consciousness and focus on the interview by contributing often and at length and by responding to probationers' inquiries with relevant information. Professionals from both jurisdictions score very highly in the use of skills related to communicating care to offenders (96%), with minimal differences between jurisdictions.

Showing understanding

Understanding can be displayed by active listening and adequate responses by professionals to probationers' narration of their stories and feelings (Vanstone and Raynor, 2012). Catalan POs were observed showing less understanding than Flemish professionals (78.57 % versus 96.25%). Since we have only a limited number of observations, it is difficult to ascertain if this is due to individual supervision styles. It might be the case, though, that these data reflect again first interviews in Catalonia being, to a greater extent, about making enforcement rules clear.

Creating trust

Trust was generated both through verbal and non-verbal language, by being open and clear about roles and responsibilities and also by expressly ensuring the confidentiality of the situation and the information exchanged during the interview. Observed POs almost always used these practices (97%), with very small differences between jurisdictions. As we discuss below, in spite of this, architectural and organisational constraints may affect professional practices and probationers' perceptions.

Showing optimism about the future of the probationer

Optimism about the possibility of change on the part of the probationer was not dominant in first interviews: it was observed in 30% of Catalan and 45% of Flemish interviews. This reflects that change in itself was not always an issue in first interviews. This probably changes as the supervision process develops.

To sum up and as Table 7.1 reflects, POs in both jurisdictions tend to use skills and practices related to the effective building of a working alliance with probationers. What is perhaps most outstanding is the excellent use of those skills related to non-verbal language in both jurisdictions (trying to convey care, respect, understanding and willingness to listen). However, POs seem to resort to a lesser extent to verbal skills directed at the creation of a space for dialogue: open questions and non-leading questions. Results regarding optimism about the future and positive comments are also less observed. This trend, slightly more marked in Catalonia, reflects that first interviews are extremely complex acts, where besides efforts made by POs to present themselves as caring professionals, there are also important constraints, such as the need to state the rules of supervision (control) and to gather personal and practical information to manage the implementation of the order. Other fundamental issues, such as change of the offender and goals, seem to be left to future encounters.

In the following paragraphs, we focus on what the skills and practices used by professionals reveal about the dual demands on POs.

The working alliance and probation officers' dual professional role

Earlier semi-structured, interview-based research in nine of the 13 Flemish HoJ shows that POs in Flanders present themselves as being what Klockars (1972) and Skeem and Manchak (2008) would call 'synthetic officers': this corresponds with the theory that is presented in the mission and vision statement (Boxstaens, 2013). POs in Flanders incorporate a double role in which they combine an emancipatory and controlling approach, and when asked to position themselves on the dichotomy between care and control (literally mark their position on a line between both poles), the majority of POs put themselves closer

Table 7.1: Working alliance skills and practices employed by probation officers in Flanders and Catalonia

Working alliance items		Catalonia (%)	Flanders (%)	Average (%)
Time spent together		100	62.79	81.39
Working together to complete probation	PO encourages collaboration during decision-making	94.28	82.5	88.39
	Service user-input in making an appointment for the next meeting	57.14	94.44	75.79
	PO talks about obligations involved in the order	85.7	100	92.85
	Are future plans discussed during the interview	100	100	100
	Average for 'working together'	84.28	94.23	89.25
Respect	PO sits facing servise user	100	100	
	Adequate eye contact	100	100	
	PO is polite and respectful	92.85	100	96.42
	Average 'respect'	97.61	100	
Listening	PO holds an open posture	100	100	100
	PO is attentive	100	100	100
	PO uses mostly open questions	61.42	78.75	70.08
	PO avoids using leading questions	64.28	76.25	70.26
	PO determines the subject/direction of the meeting but leaves space for service user to give input	91.42	100	95.71
	PO shows consciousness by having eye contact with probationer	97.14	87.5	92.32
	Average 'PO listens to me'	85.71	90.41	88.06
Working together on goals	PO talks about the aims of the order	21	72	46.5
Being positive	Positive comments outweigh negative comments	62.5	79.68	71.09

(continued)

Table 7.1: Working alliance skills and practices employed by probation officers in Flanders and Catalonia (continued)

Working alliance items		Catalonia (%)	Flanders (%)	Average (%)
Caring for the probationer	PO sits facing probationer	100	100	100
	PO is attentive to probationer during interview	100	100	100
	Adequate eye contact	100	100	100
	PO shows consciousness by having eye contact with probationer	97.14	87.5	92.32
	PO is focused on the meeting by contributing often and at length in the interview	90	98.75	94.37
	PO responds directly to service user and providfes relevant information	100	87.5	93.75
	Average for 'care'	97.85	95.62	96.74
Showing understanding	Does the PO show understanding towards the probationer?	78.57	96.25	87.41
Generating trust	CCTV outside the building (inverted)	21.5	100	60.75
	CCTV inside the building (inverted)	21.5	100	60.75
	Security control to get into the building (inverted)	21.5	100	60.75
	Privacy of the interview room assured in order to enhance disclosure	21.5	37.5	29.5
	Do distractions occur during the time of the interview? (inverted)	14.29	43.74	29.01
	Is confidentiality of the information and situation assured by the probation officer?	100	100	100
	Average for 'trust'	33.38	80.20	56.79
Being optimistic about the future of the probationer	PO is optimistic about the possibility of change	30	45	37.5
	Average jurisdiction	72.93	86.9	79.91
	Average skills (jurisdiction minus architecture)	83.95	89.12	86.53

to the 'caring' pole. One of the advantages of observational research is that it allows the researcher to capture *practice*, rather than professional discourse on practice.

Earlier in this chapter, we describe how Klockars (1972) proposed a process of exchange during supervision. According to his model, synthetic officers balance their dual professional role during the supervision process by exchanging their controlling role with the Probation Department. During first interviews, POs would assume a role more focused in control than in care. If this is so, we could expect our data to reveal POs displaying more skills related to control than to care. In order to assess this, we have built a 'care scale' and a 'control scale' to try to measure the extent to which professionals in each jurisdiction use skills and practices linked to one role or the other. This is reflected in Table 7.2.

The results in Table 7.2 seem to point at least in the following directions:

1. POs score relatively highly on both scales, habitually using skills and practices that research links to good practice and a reduction of recidivism (Burnett and McNeill, 2005; Skeem et al, 2007; Raynor and Vanstone, 2015).
2. POs in both jurisdictions score higher in control-/enforcement-related skills than in care-related skills (average 85% for control skills versus 76% for care skills).
3. There is a noticeable difference in the use of skills and practices between jurisdictions, with Flemish professionals seeming to use both kinds of skill to a larger extent, scoring between 10 and 11 percentage points higher than Catalan professionals.
4. The distance between scores in each type of skills and practices is the same in both jurisdictions and is not very marked (8.5 percentage points).

These results allow us to qualify Klockars' (1972) model to a certain extent. Observed interviews point at synthetic practices, albeit with only slightly stronger trends towards control, in first meetings: besides setting the scene for offender supervision and presenting themselves as law enforcers, professionals make a considerable effort to put probationers at ease, display openness, warmth and empathy. It is clear that – as described earlier – observed POs possess good relational skills and find it important to use them in an effort to create a bond from the beginning of their task with probationers.

Table 7.2: The 'care scale' and 'control scale'

	Catalonia (%)	Flanders (%)	Average (%)
'Care scale'			
Is privacy of the interview room assured in order to enhance disclosure?	21.5	37.5	29.5
Is confidentiality of the information and situation assured by the PO?	100	100	100
Does the PO talk during the interview about the aims of the order?	21	72	46.5
PO facing the service user during the interview	100	100	100
PO holding an open posture during the interview	100	100	100
PO being attentive to service user during the interview	100	100	100
Adequate eye contact	100	100	100
PO uses mostly open questions	61.42	78.75	70.08
PO avoids using leading questions	64.28	76.25	70.26
PO shows understanding	78.57	96.25	87.41
PO displays warmth	91.42	90	90.71
PO tries to engage in enthusiastic dialogue	54.28	80	67.14
PO polite and respectful	92.85	100	96.42
PO promotes flexible dialogue	62.85	76.25	69.55
PO uses humour to engage	54.28	67.5	60.89
Is the PO optimistic about the possibility of change of the probationer?	30	45	37.5
The PO encourages collaboration during decision-making	94.28	82.5	88.39
Positive comments by the PO outweight negative comments	30	45	37.5
The PO shows consciousness by having eye contact with the probationer	97.14	87.5	92.32
Appointment for next meeting made with input by probationer	57.14	94.44	75.79
PO shakes probatiuoner's hand at the end of the meeting	85.71	100	92.85
Average 'care scale'	**71.27**	**82.33**	**76.80**
'Control scale'			
Interview takes place in law enforcement building	*100*	*62*	*81*
CCTV outside the building	*78.5*	*0*	*39.25*
CCTV inside the building	*78.5*	*0*	*39.25*
Security control at the entrance of the building	*78.5*	*0*	*39.25*
PO explains the content of the judicial order	67.85	85.93	76.89
PO talks during the interview about the obligations involved in the order	85.7	100	92.85
PO talks during the interview about the consequences of non compliance	71.4	81.25	76.325
PO is clear about the roles and responsibilties in relation to the contents of the interview	94.28	96.25	95.26
Average 'control scale'	**81.84**	**53.17**	**67.51**
Average 'control scale' minus architecture	**79.80**	**90.85**	**85.33**

Conclusion

In this chapter, we have addressed the skills and practices POs use in first interviews with probationers in two different European jurisdictions. We have presented the concept of working alliance as the professional relationship that should be developed between POs and probationers to promote desistance. We have also presented Klockars' (1972) model for the evolution of practices and skills used by professionals during the process of supervision and tried to ascertain the extent to which professionals in our sample use them.

The quantitative analysis of data gathered by directly observing interviews and using a common observation grid (Boxstaens et al, 2015), shows that both in Catalonia and Flanders POs display a high level of skills, slightly higher in Flanders. Data also seem to point out that professional practice is balanced in first interviews, but the elements linked to the role of control/enforcement are perhaps more important. Overall, first interviews in both jurisdictions are events in which POs set the scene and present themselves as law enforcers but also strive to establish a relationship with probationers, trying at the same time to gather the practical information they need to enforce the sentence. Follow-up interviews were not included in our study, but we expect to see this balance change and perhaps move from more directive *interviews* (where certain information needs to be gathered for practical reasons) towards more balanced and open *dialogues* focused on support for change.

How can we explain the differences and similarities between jurisdictions? Many factors are at play when trying to explain professional performance, both individual and jurisdictional. Thus, background, years on the job, motivation, culture, legal framework, organisational constraints and the physical setting of interviews might all be relevant. The number of interviews and professionals observed was relatively small, so we cannot be completely sure whether differences are individual or jurisdictional and our explanations here are necessarily tentative.

Similarities can probably be explained by a common mandate for POs in both jurisdictions, with mission statements and guidelines including the enforcement of sentences and social or educational support in the description of their professional role. Tasks developed are similar: supervision through interviews, managing the implementation of sentences, keeping judges informed. They can probably also be explained by common constraints, such as the need to make relevant decisions about the management and implementation of the sentences immediately after the first interview. Backgrounds might also contribute to similarities: all POs observed in Flanders were social workers, and POs in Catalonia were psychologists. Although there are differences in these backgrounds, the importance of *relating* to the person being helped or supervised is stressed in both social work and psychology.

Without aiming at being exhaustive, we would like to put forward some elements possibly bearing on the differences between jurisdictions. Professional practices do not take place in a vacuum: physical and architectural settings can also play important roles at communicating the nature of the interaction to participants (Phillips, 2014). As reflected in Table 7.2 in italics, most interviews in Flanders where held in social services settings, without security control or CCTV, whereas in Catalonia they were mostly held in court settings, with security control at the entrance and CCTV control both outside and inside the building. In post-observation interviews, Catalan professionals revealed that they expected this to help communicate who they were and what their role was. However, more research is needed to explore the communicating role of physical settings and how it bears on professional practices.

Organisational and labour constraints are also likely to play a role in explaining differences between, and also within, jurisdictions. Observed POs had 8.9 years of experience on average, with POs from Flanders accumulating an average 11.6 years and Catalan POs only an average 4.75 years on the job. This probably reflects differences in the system of delivering offender supervision in both jurisdictions. The fact that delivery in Catalonia is based on periodical reviews to externalise the service to non-profit organisations influences hiring practices and involves less job stability for professionals (Blay, 2010). This system might also help explain that the largest variations in ratings happened within Catalonia, with both the highest- and lowest-rating PO being Catalan. Although the number of observations is small, there seems to be a trend whereby POs enforcing probation use more skills related to good practice than those enforcing community service. This cannot be explained by the law, since the Criminal Code states that community service may be complied with either through unpaid work or through a treatment or educational programme (that is, as a probation order), and POs are to make this decision after first interviews. Recent research in Belgium underlines the importance of the organisational settings in professional practices (Bauwens, 2011), an issue to be further explored in Catalonia.

First interviews encapsulate the tensions of the supervision relationship (care/control), and they probably reflect further tensions and constraints. Not only is there a concern to establish a bond and to make sure the order is complied with, but POs are also under pressure to make sure the practical steps to manage the sentence can be taken after the first interview. So, as our observations make clear, POs take on their double role, together with perhaps a third role as managers, with strong similarities in jurisdictions, but also differences that are difficult to fully explain with our current data and that would be worth exploring in the future.

Notes

1. The COST Action is a funded European network that comprises researchers from various European jurisdictions who are involved in research-focused networking (McNeill and Beyens, 2014).

2. Spain is divided into 17 autonomous regions (called communities). Catalonia is the only autonomous region with power to manage the implementation of sentences for adults.

3. *Belgisch Staatsblad* (*Belgian Law Gazette*; authors' translation).

4. Royal Decree 844/2011, which establishes implementation rules for community sentences for the whole of Spain, including Catalonia.

5. The observation of interviews related to community service orders was included in Catalonia because according to the Criminal Code they may be completed through the offender's participation in a treatment or educational program (that is, just as probation) or unpaid work. After the first interview the PO has to make this decision, depending on the needs of the person involved. This means that, at least according to legislation, the role of the PO in these first interviews is very similar in probation and in community service orders.

6. We are aware that eye contact, as much body language, has diverse cultural meanings, so the 'adequateness' of the contact had to be locally interpreted and adapted by each observer.

References

Andrews, D. and Bonta, J. (2003) *The Psychology of Criminal Conduct*, Cincinnati, OH: Anderson.

Andrews, D. and Kiessling, J. (1980) 'Program structure and effective correctional practice: a summary of CaVIC research', in R. Ross and P. Gendreau (eds) *Effective Correctional Treatment*, Toronto: Butterworths, pp 439–463.

Annison, J., Eadie, T. and Knight, C. (2008) '"People first": probation officer perspectives on probation work', *Probation Journal*, 55(3): 259–271.

Bauwens, A. (2011) 'Organisational change, increasing managerialism and social work values in the Belgian Houses of Justice, Department of Offender Guidance', *European Journal of Probation*, 3(3): 15–30.

Bauwens, A. and Devos, A. (2015) 'Belgium', in I. Durnescu and A.M. Kalmthout (eds) *Probation in Europe*, Utrecht: Confederation of European Probation, available at http://cep-probation.org/wp-content/uploads/2015/03/Chapter-Belgium-final.pdf.

Belgian Federal Government (2014) 'Prison population in Belgium', available at http://statbel.fgov.be/nl/statistieken/cijfers/bevolking/andere/gevangenen.

Binder, P., Holgersen, H. and Nielsen, G. (2009) 'Why did I change when I went to therapy? A qualitative analyses of former patients' conceptions of successful psychotherapy', *Counseling and Psychotherapy Research*, 9(4): 250–256.

Blay, E. (2010) '"It could be us": recent changes in the use of community service as a punishment in Spain', *European Journal of Probation*, 2(1): 62–81.

Blay, E. (2011) 'El papel de los jueces en la ejecución de las penas comunitarias' ['The role of judges in the enforcement of community sanctions'], in E. Larrauri and E. Blay (eds) *Penas comunitarias en Europa* [*Community sanctions in Europe*], Madrid: Trotta, pp 60–82.

Blay, E. (forthcoming) 'Prácticas de supervisión de los Delegados de Ejecución de Medidas. Un estudio basado en la observación de entrevistas' ['Supervision practices by probation officers. A study based on interview observation'].

Blay, E. and Larrauri, E. (2015) 'Community punishments in Spain: a tale of two administrations', in G. Robinson and F. McNeill (eds) *Community Punishment: European Perspectives*, Abingdon: Routledge, pp 191–202.

Bordin, E. (1979) 'The generalizability of the psychoanalytic concept of the working alliance', *Psychotherapy: Theory, Research and Practice*, 16(3): 252–260.

Boxstaens, J. (2013) 'Justitieel sociaal werk. Onder druk in Vlaanderen' ('Judicial social work. Under pressure in Flanders'), *Alert*, 39(1): 14–20.

Boxstaens, J., Blay, E., Melendez, A. and Déscarpes, P. (2015) 'Interpreting performance in offender supervision. The use of observation as a data collection method', *European Journal of Probation*, 7(3): 218–240.

Burnett, R. and McNeill, F. (2005) 'The place of the officer-offender relationship in assisting offenders to desist from crime', *Probation Journal*, 52(3): 221–242.

Cherkos R., Ferguson, J. and Cook, A. (2008) 'Do we care what offenders think?', *Perspectives*, 32(3): 53–58.

Connors, G., Carrol, K., DiClemente, C., Longabaugh, R. and Donovan, D. (1997) 'The therapeutic alliance and its relationship to alcoholism treatment participation and outcome', *Journal of Consulting and Clinical Psychology*, 65(4): 588–598.

DeLude, B., Mitchell, D. and Barber, C. (2012) 'From the probationer's perspective: the probation officer-probationer relationship and satisfaction with probation', *Federal Probation*, 76(1): 35–39.

Department of Justice (n.d.a) 'Criteris bàsics d'intervenció' ['Basic intervention criteria'], available at http://justicia.gencat.cat/web/. content/documents/arxius/criteris_intervencio.pdf.

Department of Justice (n.d.b) 'Metodologia de la intervenció. Formes substitutives de l'execució de les penes privatives de llibertat' ['Methodology for intervention. Substitutes of the enforcement of prison sentences'], available at http://justicia.gencat.cat/web/. content/documents/arxius/metodol_intervencio.pdf.

Department of Justice (n.d.c) 'Mesures penals alternatives. Definició i característiques' ['Alternative sanctions and measures. Definition and main traits'], available at http://justicia.gencat.cat/ca/ambits/ mesures_penals_alternativ/que_son.

Department of Justice Statistics (2016) 'Descriptors estadístics de mesures penals alternatives' ['Alternative sanctions and measures descriptive statistics'], available at www.gencat.cat/justicia/estadistiques_mpa.

Dowden, C. and Andrews, D. (2004) 'The importance of staff practice in delivering effective correctional treatment: a meta-analytic review of core correctional practice', *International Journal of Offender Therapy and Comparative Criminology*, 48(2): 203–14.

Durnescu, I. (2014) 'Probation skills between education and professional socialization', *European Journal of Criminology*, 11(4): 429-444.

Egan, G. (2002) *The Skilled Helper*, Pacific Grove, CA: Brooks/Cole Pub. Co.

Gelso, C. and Carter, J.A. (1994) 'Components of the psychotherapy relationship: their interaction and their unfolding during treatment', *Journal of Counseling Psychology*, 41(3): 295–305.

Gelso, C. and Samstag, L.W. (2008) 'A tripartite model of the therapeutic relationship', in S. Brown and R. Lent (eds) *Handbook of Counseling Psychology*, New York, NY: Wiley, pp 267–283.

Hart, J. and Collins, K. (2014) 'A "back to basics" approach to offender supervision: does working alliance contribute towards success of probation?', *European Journal of Probation*, 6(2): 112–125.

Horvath, A. and Greenberg, L. (1994) *The Working Alliance: Theory, Research and Practice*, New York, NY: Wiley & Sons.

Horvath, A. and Luborsky, L. (1993) 'The role of the therapeutic alliance in psychotherapy', *Journal of Consulting and Clinical Psychology*, 61(4): 561–573.

HoJ (Houses of Justice) (2010) *10 years Houses of Justice. Balance and Perspectives. Conference Record Book Colloquium December 2 and 3 2009*, Brussels: Federal Justice Department.

HoJ (2013) *Vision Statement Offender Supervision*, Brussels: Houses of Justice, Federal Justice Department.

HoJ (2014) *Annual Report Flemish Houses of Justice 2014*, Brussels: Department of Welfare, Public Health and Family, Flemish Government.

Kennealy, P.J., Skeem, J.L., Manchak, S.M. and Eno Louden, J. (2012) 'Firm, fair, and caring officer relationships protect against supervision failure', *Law and Human Behavior*, 36(6): 496–505.

Klockars, C. (1972) 'A theory of probation supervision', *Journal of Criminal Law, Criminology and Police Science*, 64(4): 549–557.

Labrecque, R.M., Schweitzer, M. and Smith, P. (2013) 'Probation and parole officer adherence to the core correctional practices: an evaluation of 755 offender-officer interactions', *Advancing Practices*, 3: 20–23.

Lambert, M. and Barley, D. (2002) 'Research summary on the therapeutic relationship and psychotherapy outcome', *Psychotherapy: Theory, Research, Practice, Training*, 38(4): 357–361.

McNeill, F. and Beyens, K. (2014) *Offender Supervision in Europe*, Basingstoke: Palgrave Macmillan.

Miller, W. and Rollnick, S. (2002) *Motivational Interviewing* (2nd edn), New York, NY: Guilford Press.

Norcross, J. (ed) (2002) *Psychotherapy Relationships that Work: Therapist Contributions and Responsiveness to Patient Needs*, New York, NY: Oxford University Press.

Norcross, J. (2011) *Psychotherapy Relationships that Work: Therapist Contributions and Responsiveness to Patient Needs* (2nd edn), New York, NY: Oxford University Press.

Orlinsky, D., Norcross, J., Helge-Ronnestad, M. and Wiseman, H. (2004) 'Outcomes and impacts of the psychotherapist's own psychotherapy. A research review', in J. Geller (ed) *The Psychotherapist's own Psychotherapy: Patient and Clinician Perspectives*, Oxford: Oxford University Press, pp 214–230.

Paparozzi, M.A. and Gendreau, P. (2005) 'An intensive supervision program that worked: service delivery, professional orientation and organizational supportiveness', *The Prison Journal*, 85(4): 445–466.

Phillips, J. (2014) 'The architecture of a probation office. A reflection of policy and an impact on practice', *Probation Journal*, 61(2): 117–131.

Raynor, P. and Vanstone, M. (2015) 'Moving away from social work and half way back again: new research on skills in probation', *British Journal of Social Work*, 46(4): 1131–1147.

Raynor, P., Ugwudike, P. and Vanstone, M. (2010) 'Skills and Strategies in Probation Supervision. The Jersey Study', in F. McNeill, P. Raynor and C. Trotter (eds) *Offender Supervision: New Directions in Theory, Research and Practice*, Cullompton: Willan.

Raynor, P., Ugwudike, P. and Vanstone, M. (2014) 'The impact of skills in probation work: a reconviction study', *Criminology and Criminal Justice*, 4(2): 235–249.

Rogers, C.L. (1957) 'The necessary and sufficient conditions of therapeutic personality change', *Journal of Consulting Psychology*, 21: 95–103.

Ross, E., Polaschek, D. and Ward, T. (2008) 'The therapeutic alliance: a theoretical revision for offender rehabilitation', *Aggression and Violent Behavior*, 13(6): 462–480.

Skeem, J. and Manchak, S. (2008) 'Back to the future: from Klockars' model of effective supervision to evidence-based practice in probation', *International Journal of Offender Rehabilitation*, 47: 220–247.

Skeem, J., Eno Louden, J., Polaschek, D. and Camp, J. (2007) 'Assessing relationship quality in mandated community treatment: blending care with control', *Psychological Assessment*, 19(4): 397–410.

Taxman, F. (2002) 'Supervision: exploring the dimensions of effectiveness', *Federal Probation*, 66(2): 14–27.

Trotter, C. (1996) 'The Impact of Different Supervision Practices in Community Corrections', *Australian and New Zealand Journal of Criminology*, 29(1): 29–46.

Trotter, C. (1999) *Working with Involuntary Clients: A Guide to Practice*, London: Sage Publications.

Trotter, C. (2006) *Working with Involuntary Clients: A Guide to Practice* (2nd edn), London: Sage Publications.

Trotter, C. and Evans, P. (2012) 'An analysis of supervision skills in youth probation', *Australian and New Zealand Journal of Criminology*, 45(2): 255–273.

Ugwudike, P. and Raynor, P. (2013) (eds) *What Works in Offender Compliance: International Perspectives and Evidence-Based Practice*, Basingstoke: Palgrave Macmillan.

Vanstone, M. and Raynor, P. (2012) *Observing Interview Skills: A Manual for Users of the Jersey Supervision Interview Checklist*, St Helier: Jersey Probation and After-Care Services.

Wild, W. (2011) 'Probation officer role orientation, helping alliance and probationer readiness for change: the impact on juvenile offender recidivism', *PCOM Psychology Dissertations*, Paper 197.

EIGHT

Desistance-related skills in Romanian probation contexts

Ioan Durnescu

Introduction

This chapter presents the results of a research study that was conducted between 2012 and 2014 in Romania. More specifically, the chapter analyses the extent to which probation practice in Romania follows the principles of desistance. To do so, the chapter starts with an overview of what the desistance literature suggests is required for effective probation practice. The chapter then goes on to present the findings of a study that was based on external observations of practice using a checklist. In its conclusion, the chapter explores the implications of the study's findings for practice.

Desistance literature

One of the few certainties in criminology is that offending behavior peaks in the teenage years and then starts declining (Glueck and Glueck, 1943; Gottfredson and Hirschi, 1990). This observation led Hoffman and Beck (1984, p 621) to conclude that there is an age-related 'burnout' phenomenon. Research is replete with evidence that offenders change as they age (Shover, 1985; Cusson and Pinsonneault, 1986; Kazemian, 2007). Formal and informal forms of social control become more prominent with age (for example, getting married, changing friends, getting a job and so on). Fear of going back to prison, for example, can be described as a formal form of social control that becomes more acute with age, as shown by Shover (1986). That said, it seems that different factors affect desistance at different ages. For instance, factors associated with desistance before the age of 18 are different from the factors associated to desistance after the age of 30.

This disparity is explained by what Matza (1964) and Glueck and Glueck (1974) describe as the maturation reform. According to Glueck and Glueck (1974, p 149), 'the physical and mental changes which enter into the natural process of maturation offer a chief explanation of improvement of conduct with the passing of years'. They argue that desistance occurs in the late twenties and early thirties. With age, other developments take place, such as attitudes, beliefs and values. Most of these changes are usually consequences of life experiences (Bushway et al, 2001).

If the Gluecks attribute desistance to maturation, Gottfredson and Hirschi (1990, p 141) view desistance as a direct effect of age on crime: offending decreases 'due to the inexorable aging of the organism' (p 141). Therefore, they do not explain how age affects crime but claim that desistance just happens and it is not affected in any way by life events or by situational or institutional influences. In this respect, the influence of supervision is limited. However, as mentioned by McNeill and Whyte (2007), probation services could develop practices that help offenders attain maturity. Examples include practices that enable them to accept responsibility and facilitate positive life change with the development and maintenance of positive social ties, and a belief in their own potential for change.

Desistance can be also explained by the social expectations and lifestyles that change as people get older. Warr (1993), for instance, showed how differential association works with age. He demonstrated how peer association (exposure to peers, time spent with peers, loyalty to peers) changed dramatically with age. When this factor – peer association – is taken out of the analysis, the association between age and crime is weakened and even disappears entirely for some offences.

Other desistance studies have found that gender (Graham and Bowling, 1995; Baskin and Sommers, 1998; Uggen and Kruttschnitt, 1998), ethnicity (Calverley, 2013) and social circumstances such as employment status (Sampson and Laub, 1993) may in some cases, affect desistance and should be taken into account to ensure that supervision practice is desistance-focused. It has also been argued that these factors are not important in themselves, but depend on the meaning they have for the offenders. The importance of meaning and subjectivity was also stressed by Maruna (2001), who interviewed 55 men and 10 women and observed that those who desisted tended to undergo a change in personality and self-concept. Desisters tended to use phrases like 'new person' or 'new outlook of life'. Reformed offenders were more other-oriented, interested in generative behaviour, felt they had more control over their lives and found meaning in life. Thus, desisters seemed to incorporate their past in a meaningful way and looked forward to the future. As he described it, these elements seemed to be a part of the 'reform story'. Maruna's (2001) main contribution is his suggestion that individuals should be seen more as the agents of their own change. In Maruna's opinion (2001), cognitive change is a precursor of behavioural change. 'Identity deconstruction' is necessary to begin the process of desistance.

'Cognitive transformation' and the presence of 'hooks for change' are also seen as essential ingredients of the desistance process by Giordano and colleagues (2002). In their study Giordano et al, 2002), they identified four main components of desistance or types of cognitive transformation: a general openness to change; exposure and reaction to 'hooks of change'; the replacement of self; and the transformation of the ex-offender's views regarding the deviant behaviour. The first type is the most fundamental one and it is 'a shift in the actor's basic openness to change' (Giordano et al, 2002, p 1000). This readiness for change is very well documented, especially in the addiction literature. The second type of cognitive shift is the exposure to a particular hook or set of hooks for change (such as the presence of a wife, the prospects of a job and so on). The hook in itself is not important, as it is its perceived availability, its meaning, salience or importance for the individual that matters. The actor only needs to see the presence of this hook as a positive development. The successful hooks are those that provide the actors with a cognitive blueprint for proceeding as a changed individual. The third type of cognitive transformation occurs when the actor begins to 'fashion an appealing and conventional "replacement self" that can supplant the marginal one that must be left behind' (Giordano et al, 2002, p 1001). This new identity makes certain illegal behaviours not appropriate 'for someone like me'. The fourth transformation involves a change in the way the individual defines deviant behaviour or lifestyle. The desistance process is almost complete when the actor no longer sees the deviant behaviour as positive, viable and personally relevant. As the authors stress, these types of cognitive transformations are linked to each other and have the ability to inspire and direct the behaviour.

Desistance-focused probation practice

Building on the existing desistance literature, McNeill and colleagues (2005) argue that desistance-focused probation practice should take into account the following central themes:

- Desistance is a process which is commonly characterized by ambivalence and vacillation. It is not an event. This suggests the need for motivational work to prompt, support and sustain change efforts.

- Desistance may be provoked by life events, depending on the meaning of those events for the offender.
- Desistance may be provoked by someone 'believing in' the offender.
- Desistance is an active process in which agency (the ability to make choices and govern one's own life) is first discovered and then exercised. Supervision processes should respect this agency by seeking to maximize involvement and participation.
- Desistance requires social capital (opportunities) as well as human capital (capacities). This suggests an advocacy role for practitioners seeking to support change and underlines the need to target systems beyond the individual offender.
- Desistance is about 'redemption' or restoration and often involves finding purpose through 'generative activities'. This implies the need, at an appropriate point in the process, to support the development of a more positive identity by accessing opportunities to make a positive contribution to local communities. (McNeill et al, 2005, pp 3–4)

Taking these observations as a starting point, the research reported here explores the extent to which probation officers in Romania focus their practice on:

- motivating offenders to change – using motivational interviewing techniques (including empathy);
- actively involving offenders in decisions;
- explaining the aims of the assessment;
- identifying offenders' strengths;
- identify community resources and social capital;
- taking into account the gender and the ethnic origin of the offenders.

These themes can be observed independently during the first meetings between the probation officers and their clients.

The study

This study took place between 2012 and 2014 in the probation service in Romania. The service is a relatively new one in the Romanian context – it was established in 2001. At the time of the fieldwork, the service had a double subordination: one towards the Ministry of Justice (a methodological one) and one towards the county courts (an administrative one). However, the service is now independent of the courts and has branches in every county.

The service works with both juveniles and adults and is responsible for drafting pre-sentence reports and supervising offenders in community. In 2012, 16,500 offenders were under probation supervision. Each probation office has between five and 19 probation officers. Out of a total of 292 probation staff in 2012, 107 were law graduates, 85 social workers, 51 psychologists, 14 sociologists and 35 other specialties.

The current research focused on the main professional groups: law, social work and psychology. With respect to the training probation officers receive, in most cases, after recruitment, new probation officers undertake a short-term course of one or two weeks. This training is then followed up by one year of supervised practice under the supervision of a more experienced probation officer.

Methodology

The study involved 20 probation officers from six different probation offices. Although all probation officers from these six probation areas were invited to participate (approximately 60 probation officers in total), only 20 agreed to do so. The main reasons given were: feeling uncomfortable with recording; just returned or preparing to go on maternity leave; or being too busy. The demographic profile of the 20 participating probation officers did not differ much from the national population of probation officers: 16 probation officers were women and four were men. Most of them were between 31 and 40 years old.

Each of the 20 probation officers was invited to submit two videos from the assessment meeting. This study focuses on the assessment meeting because the meeting provides the opportunity for probation officers to make explicit statements regarding the objectives of supervision. Depending on the needs identified during that meeting, probation officers draft their supervision plans while bearing in mind the court's requirements. The assessment meeting is an activity that takes place at the beginning of the supervision process, usually in the first or second meeting between the probation officer and the offender.

The video cameras that were used to capture assessment meetings for subsequent evaluation were provided by the research team and probation officers were instructed on how to use them. All participants in the study – probation officers and their clients – were informed of the aim of the study and they provided written consent to participate in the study.

The video tapes were analysed and rated using a coding manual developed based on similar scales used by Raynor and colleagues (2010, 2014), Bourgon and colleagues (2009) and Trotter (2009). In order to better capture the desistance-related themes, more items were included in the scale, such as the probation officer asks questions about the strengths of the offender and the probation officer enquires about the resources available in the offender's neighborhood. Although the scale had more sections (interview organisation, structuring skills, relationship skills, prosocial modelling), this chapter focuses mainly on relationship skills, 'needs' evaluation skills and motivational interviewing skills used by the officers (for more on this subject, see Durnescu, 2013). This is because the three sections of the coding manual focused mainly on the desistance themes that are highly relevant from the beginning of the supervision process. The relationship skills selected in this section are based mainly on the literature of working with involuntary clients (Trotter, 1999; Rooney, 2009), for example use of self-disclosure, use of summarisation, empathy and role clarification. The items included in the needs assessment section were as follows: the officer explains what evaluation consists of and its purpose; the questions are clear and easy to understand by the beneficiary; the officer patiently clarifies the potential unclear matters; the officer actively involves the beneficiary in formulating the needs and making decisions; the officer identifies the beneficiary's strengths; the officer asks about the community resources and opportunities; and the officer prioritises the needs of the beneficiary. The motivational interviewing section included the following indicators: officers encourage offenders to be confident; officers use reflection; officers identify and amplify discrepancies; officers avoids confrontation; officers identify and use the self-motivating statements.

The video tapes were scored independently by the main researcher and two volunteer students undertaking a master's programme in probation studies. After scoring each interview, the raters had a consensus meeting where scores were discussed and agreed. In most cases, the scores were close between the raters.

Findings

The scoring was based on a 1 to 5 Likert scale, where 1 means the skill is not present and 5 means that there is evidence that the skill is used adequately. Looking at the mean scores in respect of all the skill sets scrutinised, one can observe a reasonably high level of professionalism among the probation officers in Romania. The general mean score is M = 3.5, which is a score between 'skill present occasionally' and 'skill present quite frequently'.

However, the scores attributed to the use of motivational interviewing were lower than average (M = 3.1). This low score was mainly due to the low scores obtained for the use of self-motivating statements (M = 1.4) and the use of discrepancies (M = 2.4). For example, there were many situations where the offenders stated that they were confident they would succeed one day. These statements were not picked up by the probation officers and were not reflected back. The same goes for the use of discrepancies. There were only rare occasions when the officers asked about the offender's general aims in life.

The evaluation stage is a good opportunity for the probation officer to disclose what might be the target of intervention. In this respect, two aspects are important: the content of the evaluation and the process – in other words, what is to be evaluated and how it is evaluated.

As we have seen in the literature review section, as far as desistance is concerned, it is important for correctional staff to pay attention not only to risk factors but also to the strengths (Maruna, 2001; McNeill et al, 2005). Moreover, probation officers should also focus on social capital and opportunities available in the offender's community (Sampson and Laub, 1993; Laub et al, 1998; Farrall et al, 2014).

As far as the evaluation process is concerned, the desistance literature makes a convincing case for the authentic involvement of offenders in defining their own situation. The evaluation stage could be a perfect moment for actively involving offenders in their own perceptions of the problems and solutions.

However, as illustrated in Figure 8.2, this seems to be a missed opportunity for the probation officers in Romania. The scores for actively involving the offender in decision making, identifying relevant

Figure 8.1: General scores

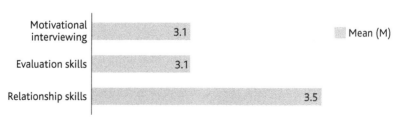

Figure 8.2: Needs assessment and desistance

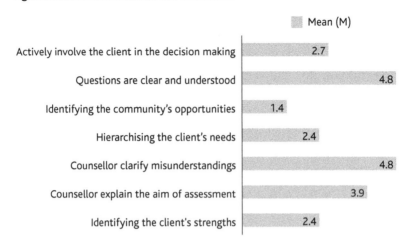

community resources (including jobs) and identifying the offender's strengths speak for themselves.

As noted, during the observations, some of the probation officers used assessment forms that included the main sections to be evaluated. The sections of the forms were set up around the main criminogenic needs as they are known in the 'what works' literature (Andrews and Bonta, 2010) and only retrospectively. This means that most of the current assessment is based on past behaviours and past variables. Future and potential strengths are not introduced in the assessment forms and practice at all. Moreover, community resources and opportunities receive no attention in the current forms. This may be an example of how structures (in this case – the forms) can shape a certain type of probation practice.

The mean score for the relationship skills was also quite high (M = 3.5). By relationship skills, we mean those skills that are needed to engage effectively with involuntary clients such as probationers. However, as shown in Figure 8.3, there is great diversity among the scores attributed to different sub-skills.

For instance, the scores for openness, enthusiasm, displaying understanding, effective use of authority, respect, firm but fair, displaying a positive attitude, use of normal voice and explaining what supervision is were 4 or above, which means a good command of these skills.

On the contrary, use of self-disclosure, reflecting feelings, reflecting thoughts, role clarification, clarifying the client's expectations, explaining confidentiality and explaining what is negotiable received scores of around 2, which indicate poor use of those skills.

Figure 8.3: Scores for relationship skills

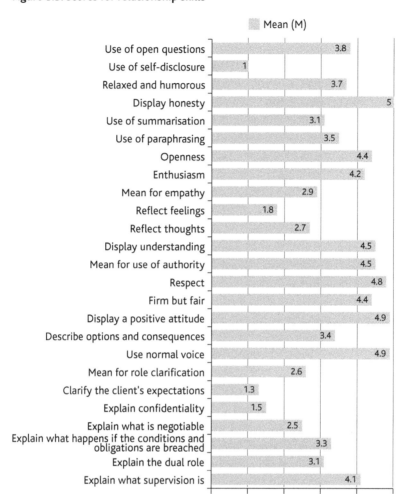

Conclusion

Based on the analysis provided in this chapter, we can conclude that probation practice in Romania is only partly informed by the desistance literature. Of course, this is only a snapshot of probation practice: it captures only one stage of supervision (assessment) and it does not include a large or representative sample of probation officers. However, as there were no large differences in scoring between probation officers from different probation areas and at the demographic level, and as the sample mirrored the main features of all staff practice, we could safely consider these conclusions as indicative of the national level.

More research could be done on a larger sample to explore supervision practices at a later stage. It may be that probation officers start looking at community resources when they reach the point of drafting the supervision plan or when they implement rehabilitative actions. However, in order to be systematic, these should be implemented during assessment as well. One important conclusion of this study is that observational studies such as the one reported here or elsewhere (see also Chapters Seven and Fourteen of this volume) could produce useful knowledge on what happens in the 'black box' of supervision.

While speaking of assessment practice, it should be noted that some probation officers were using a form that is provided by the Probation Department for assessment purposes. The other probation officers who did not use the form followed more or less the same routine but with no paper before them. Therefore, needs assessment is a policy-led activity. By giving probation staff an assessment form, probation managers could shape the objectives and the features of the supervision process. It may be that if this form had included questions regarding opportunities in the community, the scores would look different. Thus, tools are more than tools. They are powerful instruments that shape the direction and the content of supervision. This observation also opens up the debate about the use of discretion in probation practice. It may be that if probation staff were allowed more leeway in the assessment process, more areas would come under scrutiny, including those relating to desistance.

As probation staff display to a certain extent attitudes and values such as respect, openness and honesty, and use, even at a minimum level, empathy and motivational interviewing, it can be concluded that probation practice in Romania could incorporate more desistance-informed practices and therefore become more effective.

One important observation is that probation officers tend to structure evaluation in a way that does not allow sufficient probationer collaboration. What probationers and their community could constructively bring to the supervision process is almost totally neglected. Probation officers may give away some of their 'expert role' in addressing offending behaviour and take a more 'believing in the offender' role (McNeill et al, 2005). By doing so, they would allow the clients to take the driving seat in their own process of change. In this scenario, the probation officer would play the role of a companion rather than the role of a law enforcement officer. This change in approach could lead to a different kind of working alliance that would facilitate offenders to become more confident that an alternative lifestyle is possible. Furthermore, if the offender's role as a 'healer' is recognised, it becomes self-evident that he or she needs to be actively involved in assessment, drafting the supervision plan or in running supervision activities. New forms, training and other ways of professional socialisation could be undertaken by the Probation Department in order to promote these changes. It seems that the right premises are there already.

References

Andrews, D.A. and Bonta, J. (2010) *The Psychology of Criminal Conduct* (5th edn), Boston: Anderson Publishing.

Baskin, D. and Sommers, I.B. (1998) *Casualties of community disorder: Women's careers in violent crime*, Boulder, CO: Westview.

Bourgon, G., Bonta, J., Rugge, T., Scott, T.-L. and Yessine, A. (2009) *Translating 'What Works' into sustainable everyday practice: Program design, implementation and evaluation*, Ottawa: Public Safety Canada.

Bushway, S.D., Piquero, A.R., Broidy, L.M., Cauffman, E. and Mazzerolle P. (2001) 'An empirical framework for studying desistance as a process', *Criminology*, 39(2): 491–515.

Calverley, A. (2013) *Cultures of Desistance: Rehabilitation, Reintegration and Ethnic Minorities*, New York, NY: Routledge.

Cusson, M. and Pinsonneault, P. (1986) 'The decision to give up crime', in D.B. Cornish and R.V. Clarke (eds) *The Reasoning Criminal*, New York, NY: Springer-Verlag, pp 72–82.

Durnescu, I. (2013) 'Probation skills between education and professional socialization', *European Journal of Criminology*, 11(4): 429–444.

Farrall, S., Hunter, B., Sharpe, G. and Calverly, A. (2014) *Criminal Careers in Transition: The Social Context of Desistance from Crime*, Clarendon Series in Criminology, Oxford: Oxford University Press.

Giordano, P., Cernovich, S. and Rudolph, J. (2002) 'Gender, crime and desistance: toward a theory of cognitive transformation', *American Journal of Sociology*, 107(4): 990–1064.

Glueck, S. and Glueck, E. (1943) *Criminal Careers in Retrospect*, New York, NY: Commonwealth Fund.

Glueck, S. and Glueck, E. (1974) *Of Delinquency and Crime*, Springfield, IL: Thomas.

Gottfredson, M.R. and Hirschi, T. (1990) *A General Theory of Crime*, Stanford, CA: Stanford University Press.

Graham, J. and Bowling, B. (1995) *Young people and crime*, Home Office Research Study 145, London: Home Office.

Hoffman, P.B. and Beck, J.L. (1984) 'Burnout-age at release from prison and recidivism', *Journal of Criminal Justice*, 12: 617–23.

Kazemian, L. (2007) 'Desistance from crime: theoretical, empirical, methodological and policy considerations', *Journal of Contemporary Criminal Justice*, 23(1): 5–27.

Laub, J.H., Nagin, D.S. and Sampson, R.J. (1998) 'Trajectories of change in criminal offending: good marriages and the desistance process', *American Sociological Review*, 63: 225–38.

Maruna, S. (2001) *Making Good: How Ex-Convicts Reform and Rebuild Their Lives*, London: American Psychological Association.

Matza, D. (1964) *Delinquency and Drift*, New York, NY: John Wiley.

McNeill, F. and Whyte, B. (2007) *Reducing Reoffending: Social Work and Community Justice in Scotland*, Cullompton: Willan.

McNeill, F., Batchelor, S., Burnett, R. and Knox J. (2005) *21st Century Social Work. Reducing Re-offending: Key Practice Skills*, Edinburgh: Scottish Executive.

Raynor, P., Ugwudike, P. and Vanstone, M. (2010) 'Skills and strategies in probation supervision: the Jersey study', in F. McNeill, P. Raynor and C. Trotter (eds) *Offender Supervision: New Directions in Theory, Research and Practice*, Cullompton: Willan, pp 113–129.

Raynor, P., Ugwudike, P. and Vanstone, M. (2014) 'The impact of skills in probation work: a reconviction study', *Criminology & Criminal Justice*, 14(2): 235–249.

Rooney, R.H. (2009) *Strategies for Working with Involuntary Clients*, New York, NY, Columbia University Press.

Sampson, R. and Laub, J. (1993) *Crime in the Making: Pathways and Turning Points through Life*, Cambridge, MA: Harvard University Press.

Shover, N. (1985) *Aging Criminals*, Beverly Hills, CA: Sage Publications.

Shover, N. (1986) *Great Pretenders: Pursuits and Careers of Persistent Thieves*, Boulder, CO: Westview Press.

Trotter, C. (1999) *Working with Involuntary Clients*, London: Routledge.

Trotter, C. (2009) 'Pro-social modelling', *European Journal of Probation*, 1(2): 124–134.

Uggen, C. and Kruttschnitt, C. (1998) 'Crime in the breaking: Gender differences in desistance', *Law & Society Review*, 32: 339–366.

Warr, M. (1993) 'Parents, peers and delinquency', *Social Forces*, 72(1): 247–264.

NINE

From evidence-informed to evidence-based: the Strategic Training Initiative in Community Supervision

James Bonta, Guy Bourgon and Tanya Rugge

Introduction

The 1970s was marked by a general pessimism in the belief that offender recidivism could be reduced through rehabilitation. This pessimism was triggered by a review of the treatment literature that concluded that there 'little reason to hope that we have ... found a sure way of reducing recidivism through rehabilitation' (Martinson, 1974, p 50). Thus was launched the so-called 'nothing works' era, with its focus on deterrence and getting tough on offenders. Not everyone accepted the nothing works doctrine and the conclusion by Martinson was soon challenged by narrative literature reviews that concluded treatment to be effective (Gendreau and Ross, 1979; Ross and Gendreau, 1980).

Although various reviews of the treatment literature in the 1970s and 1980s reached the same general conclusion that some treatments actually did reduce recidivism, there was little understanding of the circumstances under which treatment was most effective. Then in 1990 Andrews and colleagues published the outline of what is known as the Risk-Need-Responsivity (RNR) model of offender assessment and rehabilitation (Andrews et al, 1990a). The paper was based on a selective review of the treatment literature that found treatment to be most effective if it followed three principles. The first principle, the risk principle, stated that the intensity of treatment should be proportional to the risk level of the offender, with the higher-risk offender receiving the most treatment and the lower-risk offender less treatment. The need principle distinguished between criminogenic needs and non-criminogenic needs. Criminogenic needs are related

169

to offending (for example, procriminal attitudes, criminal companions) and non-criminogenic needs unrelated to criminal behaviour (for example, poor self-esteem, neurotic anxiety). When criminogenic needs are targeted in treatment, recidivism is reduced. Finally, the responsivity principle argued for delivering treatment in a way that is meaningful to the offender, and in general cognitive-behavioural interventions are the best suited for most offenders.

An empirical test of the RNR model followed shortly after with a meta-analysis of offender rehabilitation programmes that found adherence to all three principles was associated with a 35-percentage point reduction in recidivism when delivered in the community and 17 percentage points when delivered in residential/custodial settings (Andrews et al, 1990b). Subsequent meta-analyses have confirmed these results for adults, youth, males and females (Bonta and Andrews, 2017). It is important to note that all of the reviews were of programmes with a particular treatment target (such as anger management, substance abuse, employment), often with a specific offender population (such as youthful offenders), and only a general categorisation of the treatment modality (for example, cognitive-behavioural, psychodynamic). Little attention was paid to the actual behaviours of the staff and therapists.

Correctional staff behaviour in treatment

A meta-analysis of 15 studies published between 1980 and 2006 on the effectiveness of probation and parole was reported by Bonta and colleagues (2008). They found a negligible effect on general recidivism ($r = 0.02$, 95% CI = 0.014 to 0.030, N = 53,930) and no effect on violent recidivism ($r = 0.00$, 95% CI = –0.008 to 0.016, N = 26,523). This raised the question of why community supervision was not effective in reducing recidivism, particularly since knowledge of the RNR model goes back to 1990 and effective staff practices as far back as 1980 when Andrews and Kiessling (1980) first described the five dimensions of effective practice. The five dimensions were: positive relationship with the client; effective use of authority; prosocial modelling and reinforcement; problem solving; and the effective use of community resources. In a meta-analysis of what Dowden and Andrews (2004) called core correctional practice (CCP), all of these dimensions except for the effective use of community resources were significantly related to reductions in offender recidivism. The authors also noted that such practices were very infrequently found in the studies – no more than 16% of cases.

The infrequency of RNR-based staff behaviour was confirmed in a study of 62 probation officers and their clients from the Canadian province of Manitoba (Bonta et al, 2008). Looking into the 'black box' of supervision, the probation officers audio-recorded their supervision sessions. The recordings were then analysed with respect to the presence of behaviours that adhered to the RNR principles and core correctional practices. Although the probation agency had policies to support the RNR model, there was minimal to moderate evidence that the probation officers followed the principles of risk, need and responsivity. The findings, first, that there is little evidence on the effectiveness of community supervision, and second, that observation of probation officers with their clients, show, at best, moderate adherence to effective staff practice suggested a need for training specifically on RNR-based skills.

The first attempt at training correctional staff in effective practice was by Trotter (1996). It was a small study involving 12 probation officers in Australia. The training consisted of a five-day workshop focusing on two CCPs: prosocial modeling and problem solving. Analyses of cases notes found that the 97 clients of the trained officers who continued with ongoing refresher training had a four-year recidivism rate of 54%. The rate for the 273 clients of 18 probation officers who did not continue with refresher trainings (that is, continued in their routine practices) was 64%. The next major initiative in staff training in effective supervision arose in 2011.

The Strategic Training Initiative in Community Supervision

Building on the Manitoba study and the work of Trotter, the Strategic Training Initiative in Community Supervision (STICS) was developed by researchers at Public Safety Canada to enhance adherence to the RNR principles in the everyday supervision of offenders. In its original formulation, STICS began with a structured three-day training programme and continued with ongoing clinical skills development. The initial training consisted of two general components. First, staff needed to understand the importance of criminogenic needs and, in particular, the fundamental role of procriminal attitudes in criminal conduct. Second, staff needed to learn how to facilitate prosocial change in their clients. This required building a positive rapport with clients and using cognitive-behavioural techniques to replace procriminal attitudes with prosocial attitudes.

Recognising that learning complex behavioural interventions cannot be mastered in a three-day training event, continued training was provided. Clinical support was provided through monthly meetings and annual refresher trainings. The monthly meetings were held at the office level coordinated by a 'coach'. Each half-day meeting had a theme (such as building rapport with the client), with exercises and role play led by the coach. Near the end of a meeting, a teleconference was held with one of the STICS trainers when the exercises were reviewed and summarised, and questions answered. A one-day refresher course was provided by a trainer approximately one year after the initial training, with refreshers continuing annually. This ongoing professional skills development required commitment from senior management as staff needed workload relief to participate in the monthly meetings and annual refresher courses.

The STICS model was evaluated in a randomised experiment (Bonta et al, 2011). Eighty volunteer probation officers from three Canadian provinces were randomly assigned to STICS training or a supervision-as-usual condition (in a ratio of 60:40 with 51 in the experimental group and 29 in the control group). As the study progressed, 21 probation officers dropped out of the study, leaving 33 experimental and 19 control probation officers. The probation officers were asked to recruit two medium- and four high-risk clients. Low-risk offenders, except for a few exceptions (for example, sex offenders), were excluded from the study (in adherence with the risk principle). Supervision sessions were recorded at the beginning of supervision, at the three-month mark, and at six months. The 52 probation officers recruited 143 probationers into the study, yielding almost 300 audio recordings.

Analyses of the audio recordings found clear differences between the experimental and control groups. The experimental probation officers spent more time on the criminogenic needs of their clients and less time on non-criminogenic needs. In other words, the STICS officers adhered more closely to the need principle. With respect to the responsivity principle, the trained probation officers were much more likely to apply cognitive-behavioural techniques. Thus, STICS training led to changes in the behaviour of the probation officers towards their clients. More importantly, a two-year follow-up found a reconviction rate of 25% for the clients of the probation officers trained in STICS and a reconviction rate of 39.5% for the control clients. STICS was also developed as an ongoing professional development model. It was expected that with continued clinical support probation officers would become more skilled and more effective. Analysis of the outcomes for the clients of those STICS officers who were most involved with the ongoing clinical supports (that is, high attendance and participation rates in the monthly meetings and refresher courses) found a further reduction in the recidivism rate (19%).

An experimental replication: Edmonton, Alberta

The 2011 evaluation of the STICS model was promising, but replication was necessary to build confidence in the effectiveness of STICS. Shortly after the 2011 study, two experimental replications were initiated. The first study began in November 2012 with probation officers from Edmonton, Alberta who were trained by four of the STICS developers (Bonta, Bourgon, Rugge and Gutierrez). The second study is in Sweden with training provided by the STICS developers, but the evaluation is being conducted by Swedish researchers. Results from the international replication will be reported in 2017. Both studies involve random assignment, the audio recording of supervision sessions over a six-month period and ongoing clinical supervision. At the time of writing (2016), we are able to report only on the analysis of the audio recordings from the Edmonton experiment. Recidivism outcomes are expected in 2017.

Thirty-six probation officers from four Edmonton offices volunteered to participate in the study and were randomly assigned (50:50 ratio) to four days of STICS training or to supervision as usual. There were three additional probation officers who were previously trained in STICS and they were assigned to the experimental group (N = 21). As with the 2011 experiment, some attrition occurred, with 18 (of 21) STICS probation officers and 12 (of 18) control officers submitting 273 audio recordings on 133 clients. Most of the clients were male (88%) and 38% were of Aboriginal heritage. Consistent with the recruitment protocol, almost all the clients were medium and high risk (54% and 42% respectively).

A breakdown of the audio recordings across the three time periods for the experimental and control groups is shown in Table 9.1. It is worth noting that the Edmonton experiment had fewer participating probation officers than the 2011 STICS experiment (30 versus 52) but, they had almost as many clients (133 versus 143) and audio

Table 9.1: Breakdown of audio recordings

Group	Audio recordings over time (N)			
	Intake	3 months	6 months	Total
Experimental	84	56	34	174
Control	43	29	27	99

recordings (273 versus 295) than the original STICS study. The Edmonton replication appears to have had better adherence to the research protocols.

In the RNR model, the effectiveness of intervention depends largely on addressing criminogenic needs using cognitive-behavioural techniques (Bonta and Andrews, 2017; Hollin et al, 2013; Rugge and Bonta, 2014). The STICS model encourages following these two principles. If probation officers are to reduce recidivism, they must recognise the criminogenic needs of their clients and take steps (cognitive-behavioural) to address these needs. STICS also places emphasis on procriminal attitudes, the thoughts, cognitions and sentiments that underlie all criminogenic needs. Therefore, before we can understand whether probation officers can reduce the recidivism of their clients, we must demonstrate that the trained probation officers actually change their own behaviour in a way that could alter the procriminal thinking of probationers. Table 9.2 summarises the differences between the experimental and control group in targeting criminogenic needs, reducing the time spent on the conditions of probation and applying cognitive interventions, as well as the differences in the totality of their STICS skills.

Although both groups discussed the criminogenic needs of the clients in a similar ratio, it does not mean that the probation officers from both groups addressed these needs equally well. For example, the control probation officers may have been engaging in frequent assessment questions (such as 'Are you still taking drugs?') and not doing change work. Evidence from the 2011 STICS study suggests that a critical technique is the use of cognitive techniques. This involves having clients understand that it is their thinking that leads to behaviour and in order to act more prosocially they must change their thoughts (Rugge and Bonta, 2014). The STICS-trained officers were far more likely to attempt cognitive interventions with the control officers showing *no* evidence of cognitive techniques. That is, the STICS officers were much more likely to engage in techniques to help their clients change. In addition, if we consider the totality of STICS skills (for example, structuring a session, establishing rapport effective use of reinforcement

Table 9.2: Edmonton: discussion areas and using cognitive-behavioural skills

Group	Criminogenic needs (% of session)	Probation conditions (% of session)	Cognitive techniques (mean score)	Total STICS (mean score)
Experimental	45	17	0.33	31.1
Control	43	27	0.00	27.1

and disapproval), the experimental probation officers performed at a higher level. Moreover, the experimental officers spent less time on the conditions of probation. Too much time spent discussing probation conditions interferes with relationship building and has been associated with higher recidivism rates (Bonta et al, 2008).

A large-scale implementation of STICS

British Columbia was one of the provinces that participated in the original 2011 STICS experiment. Following the study, the Corrections Branch made the decision to implement STICS across the province with the assistance of the researchers at Public Safety Canada. In September 2011, the first group of probation officers attended training. This started a three-and-a-half-year implementation of STICS that would eventually involve more than 350 probation officers. Not only was this the largest STICS project undertaken to date, but it involved probation officers who did *not* volunteer for training; it was mandatory. Probation staff were well aware that STICS was originally an experimental innovation and there was a risk that some staff would view STICS as a transitory, 'flavour-of-the-month' initiative and therefore not invest in STICS. However, the Corrections Branch intended STICS to become the new way of doing community supervision in the province, and was prepared to meet with some staff resistance, which did happen (discussed in the section 'Doing the unthinkable').

The roll-out of STICS has a very large research component and staff were asked to collect data similar to the previous experiments (Bonta et al, 2013). Probation officers were expected to audio-record their sessions with six randomly selected medium- and high-risk offenders over three different time periods (the random assignment is discussed later). There were two very important differences between the STICS province-wide implementation and the experiments. First, there was a need to integrate features that would give British Columbia the capacity to continue training and monitoring without the help of Public Safety Canada, in order to ensure independence from outside experts and fidelity to the STICS model. Second, the evaluation of the implementation did not include an experimental design but rather a pre- and post-test comparison. To conduct an experimental design with the random assignment of over 350 probation officers and clients across a geographical area exceeding 944,000 square kilometers (or over 364,000 square miles, larger than the United Kingdom and even California and Nevada combined) was unreasonable.

Capacity building and fidelity

Both Public Safety Canada and the Community Corrections Branch of British Columbia were acutely aware that to sustain STICS, the province would need its own staff who could train newly hired probation officers, champion the use of STICS among staff, and monitor the integrity of the model. In other words, the tasks historically assumed by the researchers at Public Safety Canada and their expertise needed to be cloned. Thus, the project's three- to four-year time frame was also an opportunity to develop structures and capabilities within the probation organisation that would sustain STICS.

With the support of senior management in British Columbia, a formal personnel structure was created to facilitate the integration of STICS into community supervision practices. First, each probation office had a coach (in very small offices, there could be one coach serving two locations). Unlike the experiments where coaches volunteered for the duties, these coaches had a reduced caseload so they could better manage their various tasks (such as arranging and chairing monthly meetings, and providing clinical support to their colleagues). Coaches were expected to provide 25–30 hours per month for these STICS-related tasks. The coaches were also provided with enhanced training by the STICS researchers.

The provincial corrections agency also created four full-time positions called STICS coordinators. The coordinators received enhanced training in STICS beyond what the coaches received, including supervised practice in delivering some of the training modules and the refresher courses. A major role of the coordinators was to give detailed, individual feedback to their fellow probation officers on their audio recordings and to provide additional support and consultation to the coaches. This pyramidal model of levels of STICS expertise was expected to provide close monitoring and supervision of individual probation officers as they practised STICS skills. The model was also intended to provide the probation agency with internal capacity to ensure the long-term viability of STICS.

Evaluation strategy for officer behaviour

A three-year training schedule was developed for the probation offices across the province. Prior to the training of a particular office, the probation officers were asked to submit four recordings of supervision sessions with clients. Two of the recordings were to be conducted early in supervision (within three months of the start of supervision) and two later in the supervision period (three to six months). It was expected that as the probation officer became more familiar with his/ her client, the content of a session would change. The clients chosen were to be medium- or high-risk probationers as measured by the agency's risk-need assessment instrument. Data from these recordings represented our baseline measure of officer performance.

After training, the client selection protocol was as follows. Six medium- to high-risk clients were randomly chosen for audio recording. Not all probationers agreed to be recorded. Staff began with the first new client of every month and continued until they had recorded a first tape with each of the six clients (usually by the second to fourth session of supervision). Tape 2 was recorded at approximately the three-month mark (session 8–12), and tape 3 (session 15–20, about six months). Thus, comparing officer behaviour with their client prior to and following training formed the foundation of the evaluation.

Doing the unthinkable

As noted earlier, training began in the autumn of 2011 and by December of 2012, nine trainings had been delivered to 163 probation officers. However, things were not going as well as expected, and in January of 2013 the decision was made to pause all trainings. Halting a roll-out at the mid-point is almost unheard of in criminal justice implementation projects. Yet, it was deemed necessary to ensure the integrity of the project and not to proceed and risk a faulty implementation of STICS. There is abundant research that insufficient quality control threatens the efficacy and viability of new treatment innovations (Andrews, 2006; Goggin and Gendreau, 2006; Bourgon et al, 2010b; Bonta and Andrews, 2017).

The following three factors were influential in bringing a pause to the STICS roll-out: the submission of requested audio recordings was only 64%; the required pre-training baseline recordings were not being completed by the majority of officers coming for training; and a quick look at the early results was needed to ascertain whether training was having an effect in the desired direction. Thus, the 'pause', as it became known, was an opportunity to assess probation officer buy-in to STICS (for example, was the poor submission of research recordings due to poor motivation, difficulties with mastering STICS concepts and skills, or some other factor?). To document and understand what was happening in the field, researchers from Public Safety Canada conducted structured interviews with probation officers, their managers and senior officials at headquarters, administered questionnaires, and undertook an analysis of 92 post-training audio recordings. All of this was done with reassurances from the researchers that what the interviewees reported would be confidential.

The fact-finding mission revealed a number of issues that needed to be addressed. The lower-than-expected number of audio recordings was due to a number of factors ranging from the minor (for example, technical difficulties uploading the audio files) to the more serious (for example, difficulties in persuading clients to have the supervision sessions recorded, poor staff morale in certain offices, and difficulties in understanding some of the training concepts). The knowledge that was gathered directly from staff allowed the researchers and senior managers to develop a plan to try to rectify the difficulties in the field.

Immediately after the results were presented to senior managers, headquarters assumed a more active communication strategy for all staff. This involved clarifying the roles of the various staff (coaches, coordinators, office managers) and the expectations from the staff. For example, it was made clear that an office would not be trained until most staff submitted pre-training recordings and managers were charged with improving staff morale and increasing STICS participation. Another important step was that the STICS researchers made some modifications to the training and research protocols to improve staff cooperation. For example, STICS activities were better integrated with other treatment programmes offered by the probation service, more time was spent discussing the probation officer's role as a change agent, coaches were provided additional training, and probation officers were given added guidance in the electronic submission of audio recordings.

The 92 post-training recordings were compared with the recordings from the original STICS experiment. During the pause, there was insufficient time to code baseline recordings and the data from the British Columbia site were assumed to be representative of untrained officer behaviour in the current situation.

Analysis of the two sets of audio recordings showed positive changes. The trained probation officers scored higher on relationship and cognitive-behavioural skills. The use of cognitive techniques was particularly evident when examining recordings later in supervision (three- and six-month time intervals). At the later intervals, 45.8% of the officers demonstrated the application of a cognitive technique compared with only 4.6% of officers who had not received STICS training. Survey results also found that staff found the STICS skills useful in their supervision of probationers (80% reported that the

STICS model is 'somewhat' to 'very useful'). STICS training resumed in September of 2013 and there was a significant increase in pre-training audio recordings (over 75%). The training continued until the last office was trained in the spring of 2014.

Some preliminary results

At the time of writing, over 1,800 offenders had provided 3,647 recordings. Three hundred and thirty-three of the 340 trained officers submitted audio recordings (a 98% participation rate). The following early results are based on 1,045 recordings that have been coded. This includes 236 pre-training recordings and 773 post-training recordings. As in the Edmonton replication, the majority of probationers recorded were male (88%) and very few were low-risk offenders (4%). Approximately a quarter (28%) were Aboriginal probationers.

Table 9.3 displays some of the preliminary results examining the same variables used in the Edmonton replication study (Table 9.2). With training, improvements are noted in the factors associated with reduced recidivism. The trained officers spent a larger proportion of their time discussing their clients' criminogenic needs and less time on the conditions of probation. They were also far more likely to apply cognitive techniques to influence change and overall, more likely to engage in STICS relevant behaviours. In comparison with the Edmonton results, engagement in STICS skills was generally at a higher performance level in British Columbia. The one exception was that the trained British Columbia probation officers spent more time on probation conditions than the Edmonton experimental group, but they were far more likely to use cognitive interventional skills. This is important since prior research has suggested that cognitive skills use is the single most important technique associated with recidivism reduction (Bourgon and Gutierrez, 2012; Rugge and Bonta, 2014).

Table 9.3: British Columbia: discussion areas and using cognitive-behavioural skills

Group	Criminogenic needs (% of session)	Probation conditions (% of session)	Cognitive techniques (mean score)	Total STICS (mean score)
Post-training	49	27	1.71	40.5
Pre-training	40	36	0.09	30.6

The sincerest form of flattery

It is said that imitation is the sincerest form of flattery, and the STICS model appears to have reached a high level of admiration. There have been two direct spin-offs from STICS and another more minor, indirect variant. These are Staff Training Aimed at Reducing Rearrest (STARR), Effective Practices in Community Supervision (EPICS) and Skills for Effective Engagement, Development and Supervision (SEEDS) (Rex and Hosking, 2013). The first two programs operate in the United States and the third in England. STARR and EPICS have been introduced on a large scale with formal evaluations while the SEEDS programme has yet to be rigorously evaluated, although early findings are promising (Rex and Hosking, 2013). The first two programmes show the closest relationship with STICS. In fact, the developers of STARR and EPICS had meetings with the STICS developers and access to the materials used in STICS (Bonta and Andrews, 2017). Even one of the English programme developers (Nigel Hosking) visited the STICS researchers. With more research on STARR and EPICS, a brief summary of the two programmes is warranted.

Both STARR (Robinson et al, 2011) and EPICS (Smith et al, 2012) consist of a similar length training (three to three-and-a-half days for STARR and four days for EPICS) and the modules in the training cover many of the same topics as STICS (for example, prosocial modeling, role clarification, and the use of effective approval and disapproval). The programmes also include coaching sessions. STARR is particularly similar to STICS in its ongoing clinical support, which includes refreshers and specially trained probation officers to provide feedback and guided practice to probation officers long after the initial training.

Evaluations of STARR have been quite positive, while the results from EPICS have been more equivocal. STARR used an evaluation design identical to the STICS initial research (Robinson et al, 2011, 2012). Most of the volunteer probation officers (N = 88) were randomly assigned to training or to routine supervision (two districts refused to participate in the random assignment). The probation officers recorded their supervision sessions (at the beginning of supervision, and after three and six months). The trained officers (N = 41 after attrition) and control officers (N reduced to 26) provided data on over 500 probationers.

Evidence from the recordings showed the trained probation officers demonstrating more role clarification and more effective use of approval and disapproval compared with the control group. The experimental group also showed more frequent use of a cognitive model of behaviour. One-year recidivism results showed a recidivism rate of 26% compared with 34% for the clients of the control officers. A two-year follow-up (Lowenkamp et al, 2014), although not statistically significant, found lower recidivism rates for the clients of the STARR-trained probation officers (28%) than for the clients of the control officers (41%; reduction in the client numbers reduced the power of the statistical test).

The evaluations of EPICS have been based on small samples. The first study consisted of 10 probation and parole officers supervising adult and juvenile offenders (Smith et al, 2012) and the second study involved 44 officers (Labrecque et al, 2013a). Neither study used an experimental methodology (that is, random assignment), nor did they provide recidivism outcomes. However, in both studies the trained officers demonstrated more of the skills taught in EPICS compared with the control group. There is one experimental evaluation of EPICS that included recidivism outcomes (Latessa et al, 2013). Forty-one probation officers were randomly assigned to training or routine supervision. The behaviour of the trained officers changed in the expected direction, but the experimental probationers actually showed *higher* recidivism rates than the control clients. Additional moderator analysis found risk and actually applying the skills taught were important factors influencing recidivism. High-risk offenders supervised by 'high-fidelity' probation officers (as measured on a 32-item EPICS adherence score sheet of staff proficiency with EPICS) had lower recidivism rates.

STARR and EPICS have been embraced by many jurisdictions in the US and elsewhere. Presently STARR is being rolled out across the US federal probation service, with a plan to train over 4,000 probation officers from 94 districts. This large-scale implementation includes a large cadre of 442 coaches who oversee feedback on officer recordings and monthly booster sessions. With respect to EPICS, the programme has been delivered to 84 state/county correctional agencies in addition to an international agency (Singapore; Labrecque et al, 2014). Indeed, the influence of STICS has been substantial.

Lessons learned and an agenda for the future

The STICS model shows that community corrections staff can be trained in RNR-based supervision practice. Evidence from audio recordings finds behavioural improvements in a range of important interventional skills (such as focusing on criminogenic needs and applying cognitive techniques to change procriminal thinking). Other research on training staff provides further confirmation of the value of the RNR principles in everyday practice (Robinson et al, 2011, 2012; Smith, et al, 2012; Labrecque et al, 2013a,b; Rex and Hosking, 2013; Raynor et al, 2014; Chadwick et al, 2015). However, there is much to be done and much to learn. The STICS model and the way it is implemented continue to develop as the evidence accrues. We close this chapter with a summary of steps being taken and steps to be taken in order to provide a more effective way of helping medium- and high-risk offenders become more prosocial.

Revisiting the delivery of training

The traditional way of providing staff training is to bring staff together for a few days, deliver some didactic teaching and perhaps some participatory exercises and send the participants home. At the outset of STICS, this approach was judged to be insufficient. It is well known that staff may forget much of what was taught without some sort of post-training event(s) (Miller et al, 2004; Bourgon et al, 2010a; Alexander, 2011). When an agency does acknowledge the need to provide something more, it is often in the form of a one- or two-day refresher or booster session. Certainly, STICS and other training programmes include such refreshers.

An important feature of STICS is that it adopts a **continuous professional development** view of training; that is, training is on a regular basis and far after any initial training or refresher. In British Columbia where STICS has become the new way of doing business, probation officers not only attend refresher courses every eight to 12 months, but meet monthly to discuss and practise STICS. The probation officers also submit recordings of supervision sessions for feedback from experienced STICS practitioners. Research has found that those who make the most use of such ongoing clinical support demonstrate better outcomes with their clients (Bourgon et al, 2010a; Bourgon et al, 2013).

Beyond personal professional development there is a need to ensure that the organisation has the capacity to maintain staff skill levels and to train new staff. In British Columbia, STICS included a hierarchy of staff positions intended to support officer skills development and the training of new staff. Coaches and coordinators work together to manage monthly meetings, deliver refresher courses and provide feedback on audio recordings. The original intention was to train coordinators to deliver the initial STICS training independently of the developers at Public Safety Canada. The coordinators attended trainings with the Public Safety Canada researchers and were assigned different modules to present under supervision. This posed some difficulties as some coordinators were very good with some modules while others were not. No one coordinator could deliver all training modules, raising the question as to how new staff would be trained in STICS without the help of Public Safety Canada.

To deal with the challenge of training new staff with only internal agency resources, a new approach was needed. The training approach that was adopted had two important phases. In the first phase, newly hired probation officers would simply work within the office learning what a probation officer does in general (for example, writing presentence reports and monitoring compliance with court imposed conditions) *and* interact with trained probation officers, coaches and coordinators. During the first phase of approximately one year, the new staff member would also complete an online course that gave an introduction to the RNR model and the 'what works' literature. Essentially, the new probation officer would be gradually exposed to the conceptual and research basis for STICS (online learning) and the practice of STICS (observation of fellow officers).

By the second year of employment, the new probation officer is ready for more in-depth exposure to STICS. Exposure came in the form of three workshops that presented the STICS skills and interventions, allowing officers the opportunity to practise while receiving feedback. Each workshop lasted two days and focused on specific techniques. Officers would learn various aspects of the STICS model and then had about six months to practise the techniques back at their office, while partnered with a mentor and receiving feedback on their skills. After this period, officers would attend the next workshop, where they would learn more advanced techniques, and then return to their offices to practise again.

The first workshop focused on soft skills such as relationship building, role clarification, collaborative goal setting, how to talk about attitudes with a client, and so on. The second workshop focused on cognitive-behavioural techniques and the final workshop was advanced cognitive skills and integration. While members of the STICS research team developed the workshops, coordinators and coaches were trained to deliver the material. Communities of practice, one for each workshop as well as the online course, were developed so members could become experts in the specific material. Coordinators and coaches who excelled in certain areas of the model were chosen for the respective communities. This lowered the expectation that any one person would be an expert in all areas of STICS, but could focus on certain areas. This new training model saw the communities also being responsible for further developing exercises for refreshers and evolvement of that specific material. Lastly, this new delivery model addressed the issue of coach and coordinator turnover, leaving British Columbia with a much larger pool of people who could deliver the training moving forward.

Organisational readiness

Not every agency is ready for STICS, or a STICS-like programme such as STARR or EPICS. There are at least five general considerations an organisation needs to undertake before adopting STICS as its model for community supervision. First, and in keeping with the overarching principles of the RNR model, the agency must place great value on the person as an autonomous individual with goals, wants and needs. From this value statement would flow interventions based on an empirically defensible psychological theory. In other words, the mission of the correctional agency is rehabilitation (not punishment) through respectful, ethical, humane, psychologically informed treatment.

Second, the agency must honestly conduct a self-assessment. The authors have seen far too many agencies claim they already follow RNR principles and refuse to admit that there exists room for improvement. For example, the original STICS experiment was only made possible after conducting the Manitoba 'black box' study that found routine community supervision fell short of RNR-based practices (Bonta et al, 2008). Only after this demonstration did other Canadian provinces admit a need for improving supervision practices. An agency does not have to conduct a 'black box' study, as there are other ways of assessing the organisation's level of adherence to best practice. Subject-matter experts can be convened to review programs (Rex and Raynor, 2008) or structured assessment tools such as the Correctional Program Assessment Inventory (Gendreau et al, 2015) can be used. Whichever method is used, the agency must be prepared to accept and to act on the findings.

Third, the agency must be willing to invest resources *over the long term*. STICS assumes a professional development model where learning is continuous and requires well-trained staff to support skill development. In British Columbia, additional resources were secured to train staff and hire new staff with the argument that to adopt STICS was money well spent. We are not sure what arguments were made to justify the huge resources for the implementation of STARR, but in both cases the resource allocations went beyond a year or two. Undoubtedly, there was strong leadership at the most senior levels.

Fourth, the agency should expect that implementation will not progress smoothly and there will be obstacles to overcome; recall the introduction of a pause in training during the roll-out in British Columbia. However, steps can be taken to minimise the risks during implementation. For example, in two sites we are testing the concept of a Living Laboratory to understand what could happen in a STICS roll-out and what needs to change. In a Living Laboratory, STICS is introduced on a small scale, perhaps in one or two probation offices. Not only are officer behaviours observed, but information is collected at an organisational level. Questions are asked about which policies and procedures require changes (for example, recording compliance with probation conditions or documenting progress in addressing criminogenic needs) and which workload adjustments are needed. It is better to know what needs to be changed now when few are affected rather than waiting until after a large-scale implementation has been launched.

Finally, there is a need to take the long view for building capacity. In the province of Ontario, Canada's most populous province, there are over 850 probation officers to be trained. A Living Laboratory study is being conducted to prepare for organisational changes. In addition, probation officers from a few offices volunteered for STICS training and from this group a small cadre of staff was selected for mentoring to become future STICS leaders (that is, coaches, feedback writers, and/or trainers). The plan for the roll-out is to begin in a four offices (the Living Laboratory offices), then move to one of five regions, and continue until all five regions have been trained. Senior managers are well aware that the roll-out will take at least five years. The important lesson is that if you want to do it right, you have to go slowly.

Questions remaining

All of the STICS projects have been mainly research evaluations. Even in the case of the jurisdiction-wide implementations, there is an important research function; that is, the goal is always to learn more about the effectiveness of STICS, its implementation and its limits. One important question is 'What are the effective ingredients of STICS?' By identifying the factors that matter in reducing recidivism, steps can be taken to modify the training and bring about improved outcomes. Already, researchers have identified the importance of using cognitive techniques (Rugge and Bonta, 2014) and building rapport with clients (Bourgon and Gutierrez, 2013) to bring revisions to the training. Results from the other STICS-like programmes can also be informative and influence STICS. For example, research on STARR has found that adding training in motivational interviewing improves outcomes (Lowenkamp et al, 2014) and EPICS researchers have found targeting procriminal attitudes and cognitions to be particularly important (Labrecque et al, 2013b).

As noted earlier, STICS and similar programmes require considerable resources if they are to be implemented with fidelity. Those with the responsibility to manage taxpayers' money need strong arguments to justify spending in an area that is typically not well regarded by the public (that is, corrections). There is a growing literature demonstrating that investing in offender treatment and crime prevention has significant cost savings (Aos, et al, 2011; Taxman et al, 2014; Farrington and Koegl, 2015). Cost-benefit studies are also needed with STICS, STARR, EPICS and similar programmes.

In closing this chapter, we have a few comments to make on the effectiveness of STICS. It is important to bear in mind that there is only one study on the impact of STICS in reducing recidivism (Bonta et al, 2011). There are a number of evaluations in progress that will include recidivism outcomes, but, thus far, the evidence on the effectiveness of STICS rests on officer behaviour as measured by the audio recordings. Clearly, replications with recidivism results are needed before we can transition STICS from an evidence-*informed* intervention to an evidence-*based* programme.

Along with strengthening our confidence on the overall effectiveness of STICS, it will be necessary to explore possible limitations with offender sub-populations. For example, will STICS 'work' with women, minorities or sexual offenders? This work is just beginning. Wanamaker (2016) selected recordings from 710 probationers whose probation officers were trained in STICS and searched for differences in officer behaviour as a function of client age, race and gender. She found no differences in officer behaviour towards younger and older clients or in terms of ethnicity (Caucasian, Aboriginal, other). However, the probation officers behaved differently with women than with male clients. With women clients, the probation officers demonstrated more frequent use of encouragement and reinforcement, but less frequent use of cognitive interventions. Moreover, the supervision sessions were considerably less structured. It may be that because many women who are involved in the criminal justice system have underlying mental health issues, correctional staff focus on these issues at the expense of their criminogenic needs (Cloyes et al, 2010; Wooldredge and Steiner, 2016). Hence, using cognitive techniques could become less of a priority and crisis managing the situation may affect the session structure. One surprising finding reported by Wanamaker (2016) was that there were no gender differences in the use of relationship skills. Probation officers appear to make an equal effort in building rapport with their clients irrespective of gender.

STICS is the first training programme to bring a comprehensive RNR-based approach to community supervision. As the research continues, we will gain a clearer picture on the effectiveness of STICS across client populations, settings and culture. Already, STICS has brought about changes in community supervision in Canada and in Sweden where a nationwide implementation is underway. A Danish version of STICS has been introduced in Denmark and programmes like STARR and EPICS are having an impact in the US. There is still much more to do, but the work has begun.

References

Alexander, M. (2011) 'Applying implementation research to improve community corrections: making sure that "new" thing sticks!', *Federal Probation*, 75(2): 47–51.

Andrews, D.A. (2006) 'Enhancing adherence to risk–need–responsivity: making quality a matter of policy', *Criminology and Public Policy*, 5(3): 595–602.

Andrews, D.A. and Kiessling, J.J. (1980) 'Program structure and effective correctional practices: a summary of the CaVIC research', in R.R. Ross and P. Gendreau (eds) *Effective Correctional Treatment*, Toronto: Butterworth, pp 439–463.

Andrews, D.A., Bonta, J. and Hoge, R.D. (1990a) 'Classification for effective rehabilitation: rediscovering psychology', *Criminal Justice and Behavior*, 17(1): 19–52.

Andrews, D.A., Zinger, I., Hoge, R.D., Bonta, J., Gendreau, P. and Cullen, F.T. (1990b) 'Does correctional treatment work?: a clinically relevant and psychologically informed metaanalysis', *Criminology*, 28(3): 369–404.

Aos, S., Lee, S., Drake, E., Pennucci, A., Klima, T., Miller, M., Anderson, L., Mayfield, J. and Burley, M. (2011) *Return on Investment: Evidence-Based Options to Improve Statewide Outcomes* (Document No 11-07-1201), Olympia, WA: Washington State Institute for Public Policy.

Bonta, J. and Andrews, D.A. (2017) *The Psychology of Criminal Conduct* (6th edn), New York, NY: Routledge.

Bonta, J., Bourgon, G., Rugge, T., Gress, C. and Gutierrez, L. (2013) 'Taking the leap: from pilot project to wide-scale implementation of the Strategic Training Initiative in Community Supervision (STICS)', *Justice Research and Policy*, 15(1): 17–35.

Bonta, J., Bourgon, G., Rugge, T., Scott, T.-L., Yessine, A., Gutierrez, L. and Li, J. (2011) 'An experimental demonstration of training probation officers in evidence based community supervision', *Criminal Justice and Behavior*, 38(11): 1127–1148.

Bonta, J., Rugge, T., Scott, T., Bourgon, G. and Yessine, A. (2008) 'Exploring the black box of community supervision', *Journal of Offender Rehabilitation*, 47(3): 248–270.

Bourgon, G. and Gutierrez, L. (2012) 'The general responsivity principle in community supervision: the importance of probation officers using cognitive intervention techniques and its influence on recidivism', *Journal of Crime and Justice*, 35(2): 149–166.

Bourgon, G. and Gutierrez, L. (2013) 'The importance of building good relationships in community corrections: evidence, theory, and practice of the therapeutic alliance', in P. Ugwudike and P. Raynor (eds) *What Works in Offender Compliance: International Perspectives and Evidence-Based Practice*, Basingstoke: Palgrave Macmillan, pp 256–278.

Bourgon, G., Bonta, J., Rugge, T. and Gutierrez, L. (2010a) 'Technology transfer: the importance of on-going clinical supervision in translating what works to everyday community supervision', in F. McNeill, P. Raynor and C. Trotter (eds) *Offender Supervision: New Directions in Theory, Research, and Practice*, Cullompton: Willan, pp 88–106.

Bourgon, G., Bonta, J., Rugge, T., Scott, T.-L., and Yessine, A.K. (2010b) 'The role of program design, implementation, and evaluation in evidence-based "real world" community supervision', *Federal Probation*, 74(1): 2–15.

Bourgon, G., Gutierrez, L. and Rugge, T. (2013) 'Supporting probation officers' evidence-based professional development in the Strategic Training Initiative in Community Supervision (STICS): ongoing clinical support activities and the individuals who lead the charge' in F. McNeil and I. Durnescu (eds) *Understanding Penal Practices*, London: Routledge, pp 236–254.

Chadwick, N., DeWolf, A. and Serin, R. (2015) 'Effectively training community supervision officers: a meta-analytic review of the impact on offender outcome', *Criminal Justice and Behavior*, 42(10): 977–989.

Cloyes, K.G., Wong, B., Latimer, S. and Abarca, J. (2010) 'Women, serious mental illness and recidivism: a gender-based analysis of recidivism risk for women with SMI released from prison', *Journal of Forensic Nursing*, 6(1): 3–14.

Dowden, C. and Andrews, D.A. (2004) 'The importance of staff practice in delivering effective correctional treatment: a meta-analytic review of core correctional practice', *International Journal of Offender Therapy and Comparative Criminology*, 48(2): 203–214.

Farrington, D.P. and Koegl, C.J. (2015) 'Monetary benefits and costs of the Stop Now and Plan program for boys aged 6–11, based on the prevention of later offending', *Journal of Quantitative Criminology*, 31(4): 263–287.

Gendreau, P., Andrews, D.A. and Thériault, Y. (2015) 'The Correctional Program Assessment Inventory-2010 (CPAI-2010)', available from yvetheri@yahoo.ca.

Gendreau, P. and Ross, R.R. (1979) 'Effective correctional treatment: bibliotherapy for cynics', *Crime & Delinquency*, 25(4): 463–489.

Goggin, C. and Gendreau, P. (2006) 'The implementation and maintenance of quality services in offender rehabilitation programs', in C.R. Hollin and E.J. Palmer (eds) *Offending Behaviour Programs: Development, Application, and Controversies*, Chichester: Wiley, pp 247–268.

Hollin, C.R., Palmer, E.J. and Hatcher, R.M. (2013) 'Efficacy of correctional cognitive skills programmes', in L.A. Craig, L. Dixon and T.A. Gannon (eds) *What Works in Offender Rehabilitation: An Evidence-Based Approach to Assessment and Treatment*, New York, NY: John Wiley & Sons, pp 117–128.

Labrecque, R.M., Schweitzer, M. and Smith, P. (2013a) 'Probation and parole officer adherence to the core correctional practices: an evaluation of 755 offender-officer interactions', *Advancing Practice*, 3: 20–23.

Labrecque, R.M., Smith, P., Schweitzer, M. and Thompson, C. (2013b) 'Targeting antisocial attitudes in community supervision using the EPICS model: an examination of change scores on the Criminal Sentiments Scale', *Federal Probation*, 77(3): 15–20.

Labrecque, R.M., Luther, J.D., Smith, P. and Latessa, E.J. (2014) 'Responding to the needs of probation and parole: the development of the effective practices in a community supervision model with families', *Offender Programs Report*, 18: 1–2, 11–13.

Latessa, E.J., Smith, P., Schweitzer, M. and Labreque, R.M. (2013) *Evaluation of the Effective Practices in Community Supervision Model (EPICS) in Ohio*, available from author, University of Cincinnati.

Lowenkamp, C.T., Holsinger, A., Robinson, C.R. and Alexander, M. (2014) 'Diminishing or durable effects of STARR? A research note on 24-month re-arrest rates', *Journal of Crime and Justice*, 37(2): 275–283.

Martinson, R. (1974) 'What works? Questions and answers about prison reform', *The Public Interest*, 35: 22–54.

Miller, W.R., Yahne, C.E., Moyers, T.B., Martinez, J. and Pirritano, M. (2004) 'A randomized trial of methods to help clinicians learn motivational interviewing', *Journal of Consulting and Clinical Psychology*, 72(6): 1050–1062.

Raynor, P., Ugwudike, P. and Vanstone, M. (2014) 'The impact of skills in probation work: a reconviction study', *Criminology & Criminal Justice*, 14(2): 235–249.

Rex, S. and Hosking, N. (2013) 'A collaborative approach to developing probation practice: Skills for Effective Engagement, Development and Supervision (SEEDS)', *Probation Journal*, 60(3): 332–338.

Rex, S. and Raynor, P. (2008) 'Accreditation', in G. McIvor and P. Raynor (eds) *Development in Social Work with Offenders*, London: Jessica Kingsley, pp 113–127.

Robinson, C.J., VanBenschoten, S., Alexander, M. and Lowenkamp, C.T. (2011) 'A random (almost) study of Staff Training Aimed at Reducing Re-Arrest (STARR): reducing recidivism through intentional design', *Federal Probation*: 75(2): 57–63.

Robinson, C.J., Lowenkamp, C.T., Holsinger, A.M., VanBenschoten, S., Alexander, M. and Oleson, J.C. (2012) 'A random study of staff training aimed at reducing re-arrest (STARR): using core correctional practice in probation interactions', *Journal of Criminal Justice*, 35(2): 167–188.

Ross, R.R. and Gendreau, P. (ed.) (1980) *Effective Correctional Treatment*, Toronto: Butterworth.

Rugge, T. and Bonta, J. (2014) 'Training community corrections officers in cognitive-behavioral intervention strategies', in R.C. Tafrate and D. Mitchell (eds) *Forensic CBT: A Handbook for Clinical Practice*, Chichester: John Wiley & Sons, pp 122–136.

Smith, P., Schweitzer, M., Labreque, R.M. and Latessa, E.J. (2012) 'Improving probation officers' supervision skills: an evaluation of the EPICS model', *Journal of Crime and Justice*, 35(2): 189–199.

Taxman, F.S., Pattavina, A. and Caudy, M. (2014) 'Justice reinvestment in the United States: an empirical assessment of the potential impact of increased correctional programming on recidivism', *Victims and Offenders*, 9(1): 50–75.

Trotter, C. (1996) 'The impact of different supervision practices in community corrections', *Australian and New Zealand Journal of Criminology*, 29: 1–18.

Wanamaker, K. (2016) 'Officer use of effective correctional skills with STICS clients: a comparison across client demographics', Paper presented at the 77th Annual Convention of the Canadian Psychological Association, 11 June, Victoria, British Columbia.

Wooldredge, J. and Steiner, B. (2016) 'Assessing the need for gender-specific explanations of prisoner victimization, *Justice Quarterly*, 33(2): 209–238.

TEN

Promoting quality in probation supervision and policy transfer: evaluating the SEED¹ programme in Romania and England

Angela Sorsby, Joanna Shapland and Ioan Durnescu

Introduction

One-to-one supervision of those on probation or licence is both a core element in probation and also relatively hidden work (Shapland et al, 2013). The supervisor is (usually) alone in a room with the supervisee² and any monitoring or managing tends to be on the basis of perusal of records afterwards. Yet, if the aim is to promote desistance and rehabilitation, or to increase reintegration, it is the interaction with the supervisee that bears the key load in accomplishing this (Dowden and Andrews, 2004; Raynor et al, 2014). A key aspect for promoting quality in one-to-one probation supervision is hence to focus on what practitioners actually do with those they are supervising during supervision sessions.

The Skills for Effective Engagement and Development (SEED) training package was developed in the United Kingdom by the National Offender Management Service (NOMS) for practising probation staff in England and Wales. The package aimed to provide staff with additional training and continuous professional development in skills they could use in supervising offenders, particularly in one-to-one meetings, drawing from research on effective probation delivery and on desistance. This was a new initiative that aimed not to teach individual skills or 'tools', or just to provide refresher courses, but to enable staff to draw on their existing knowledge to provide the most appropriate supervision for the individual supervisee and to plan the course of that supervision. Current knowledge of desistance suggests that an offender-centred, individually tailored approach to supervision is the most beneficial (Sapouna et al, 2015). A pilot of the

SEED package was undertaken by NOMS in England[3] in 2011–12, evaluated by ourselves. The training was subsequently implemented by the Romanian probation service and evaluated in three areas of Romania, again by ourselves. This enabled us to: test whether a model developed and piloted in England would be suitable in a different EU jurisdiction; explore whether the model needed to be adapted for use in this jurisdiction; and test whether the approach developed by the University of Sheffield to evaluate the model, in England, could also be applied in another EU jurisdiction.[4]

In this chapter, as well as providing overall results from the two evaluations, we reflect on the experience of conducting evaluations in the two countries and the process of policy transfer needed given the differences in the history of probation and lengths of orders for probation supervision.

The SEED training package

SEED training is designed for probation practitioners who already have experience of providing probation supervision. The training focuses on what practitioners do with the people they are supervising during supervision sessions. It is a 'training plus' package, building on practitioners' previous training. An important element of SEED is that teams are trained together with their manager.

The SEED model is based on the principle that the relationship between the practitioner and the probation supervisee can be a powerful means of changing behaviour (Rex, 2012). The SEED training package was influenced by training developed in the Strategic Training Initiative in Community Supervision (STICS) project in Canada (Bourgon et al, 2008, 2010; see also Chapter Nine of this volume) and by the Jersey probation project (Raynor et al, 2010), as well as by the aims of the broader NOMS Offender Engagement Programme (Rex, 2012).

SEED training, like STICS, was designed in accordance with Risk-Need-Responsivity (RNR) principles. The training brings together elements from relationship building, prosocial modelling, motivational interviewing, risk–need–responsivity and cognitive-behavioural techniques, within a framework of structuring both individual supervision sessions and the overall order (Rex and Hosking, 2014). The training aims to promote practitioners' use of what have been termed core correctional practices, the use of which has been linked to reduced offending (Dowden and Andrews, 2004). Quality of interpersonal relationships, appropriate modelling and reinforcement, effective use of authority and problem solving are all key elements of SEED. The training provides practice in these skills though exercises and role play. In particular, there is a great deal of emphasis on enabling supervisees to solve their own problems and on developing reflective practice.

The study

In both England and Romania, there was an initial long training session,[5] plus four subsequent shorter sessions at quarterly intervals,[6] to provide continuous professional development over a year's period. At each session, participants reflected on what was useful in practice and anything that had presented difficulties. In between sessions, there were team practitioner meetings to discuss particularly interesting 'live' cases (known as peer group learning in Romania and action learning sets in England) and observation of probation supervision by managers with feedback to practitioners. Further details of the SEED initiative can be found in Sorsby et al (2013). Seventy-three practitioners took part in the training in England and 30 in Romania.

Evaluating SEED

The evaluation was linked closely to the aims of SEED, which are outlined in the previous section. Hence what was important was:

- whether those being trained found the training helpful, intended to bring it into their practice, and, when asked later, reported that they felt they had used it in their practice;
- whether those being supervised noticed any difference between the supervision they received from SEED-trained practitioners as opposed to non-SEED trained practitioners;
- whether there were effects on supervisees' behaviour, comparing SEED-trained practitioners with non-SEED trained practitioners. These effects could be on compliance with the orders or subsequent reconviction.

The second and third elements of the evaluation required the construction of comparison groups, in order to compare SEED-trained practitioners and non-SEED trained practitioners.

Some differences between England and Romania

The probation service in Romania is much younger than that in England and Wales. In Romania, probation supervision started in 2001, following an experimental period of five years (Carbunaru, 2014), whereas the probation service in England and Wales has been in existence for over one hundred years (Teague, 2007). The time periods during which the training was delivered and evaluated were periods of change or imminent change in both countries, although the nature of those changes was different.

In England, SEED training and its evaluation took place at a time when the probation service was moving from highly target-driven National Standards to potentially more flexible National Standards, which had more scope for supervisor discretion. The new National Standards allowed probation trusts to specify how they wished standards to be operationalised locally (House of Commons Justice Committee, 2011) and the trusts in the evaluation had not, at the time of the evaluation, prescribed a new regime. Towards the end of the SEED training year, it became apparent that probation provision was likely to be restructured into an at least partially privatised service (which subsequently came about, with the creation of the community rehabilitation companies for each geographical area, alongside the National Probation Service for court work and high risk cases: Robinson et al, 2016). This was a cause of considerable dismay and apprehension (Robinson et al, 2016).

In Romania, a new Criminal Code and Criminal Procedure Code were enacted during the course of the training. The probation service became a directorate in its own right, responsible for its own budget. It also acquired a considerable range of new tasks, including preparing reports on the execution of penalties, supervising unpaid work for adult offenders, providing more reintegration programmes, and supervising conditionally released prisoners on licence from prison (Romanian Parliament, 2014).

Methodology

In England and Wales, probation trusts volunteered to take part in the SEED initiative. Training was delivered within eight probation trusts in total, three of which were included in our external evaluation: London, Merseyside and Thames Valley. The three trusts to be used for the external evaluation were selected by NOMS on the basis of the size of the trusts. It selected the three largest trusts to ensure a sufficient number of supervisees for the study. Within each of the evaluated trusts, one or two teams (each normally comprising the probation provision for one town or set of London boroughs) were chosen by the trust to receive SEED training and one or two teams, which did not receive SEED training, formed the comparison group(s). The teams chosen all had fairly generic caseloads. There could be no random assignment of supervisors to training and comparison groups, because a key part of SEED training is that teams are trained together; a substantial element of SEED training involves colleagues learning from one another. Random assignment of teams to training and comparison groups would require an excessive number of teams for a pilot study.

In Romania, the National Directorate chose three probation services to take part in the initiative: the capital, Bucharest, and two more rural areas, Dolj and Brasov. These areas were chosen to include both rural and urban areas in the study, while being reasonably accessible in terms of the trainer from England visiting the areas. They cannot, however, necessarily be assumed to be representative of all probation areas in Romania. In England, the probation office was closed while staff undertook training and the entire team of practitioners was trained. In Romania, it was not considered possible to close the offices so that all practitioners could attend the training. The comparison group was therefore formed of those practitioners who were not SEED-trained within the same office. However, this meant that contamination (the comparison group knowing about SEED training methods, tips and so on) was highly likely in Romania. Practitioners who were trained, and comparison practitioners in the same offices, all did the same kinds of work, without particular specialisation.

As the areas to be included in the study, in both England and Romania, were not chosen at random, this could influence the generalisability of the findings, although the findings were very similar in both England and Romania. As random assignment was not possible; underlying differences between trained and comparison groups could create or mask differences between the groups on outcome measures. However, in examining effects on compliance, the statistical technique of propensity score modelling was used to take account of differences between the groups on supervisees' Offender Assessment System (OASys) data. Details of this can be found in Sorsby et al (2016).

The practitioners in England, in both the SEED-trained and comparison groups, supervised those serving community sentences and those released on licence from prison. However, probation supervision in Romania was, at the time of the training, confined to those on community orders. The supervision period for community sentences was much longer in Romania than in England. In England, the average length of supervision was approximately one year, while in Romania it was just over five years. In Romania, as compared with England, there was a higher proportion of supervisees for whom this was their first conviction.

The training package and its evaluation in Romania were designed to be as similar as possible to those in England. In Romania, the training was delivered by a NOMS trainer from England, who had played a key role in developing SEED in England and delivered much of the training there, together with a co-trainer from Romania. It was important to have a trainer from England to facilitate consistency of delivery across countries.

In planning the implementation of SEED training in Romania, it was realised that the training events would need to be somewhat longer than in England, in order to allow time for language translation at the events and to ensure the participants understood the training manual, which had been translated from English in advance of the events. Hence each session was slightly longer in Romania.

The content of the training in Romania was identical to that used in England with the following two exceptions. First, an element of the training dealing with unconscious bias was slightly amended for Romania because this section included information on relevant national legislation and this obviously differed between the two countries. Second, in Romania a session on planning for the future beyond supervision replaced a session on recent desistance research and links with SEED. This change was made because planning for the future was something that the English participants had identified as potentially useful. In addition, the topics covered in the follow-up events were delivered in a slightly different order in Romania. As planning for the future is something the English participants felt would be helpful, this may have slightly improved the training in Romania, which might lead to somewhat more favourable ratings in that country. It seems unlikely the other minor differences would have much impact.

Practitioners' views of SEED in the two countries

In both countries, after each event, practitioners were asked to complete an anonymous feedback questionnaire for the independent evaluators, ourselves. The questionnaires were developed by the evaluators and were as similar as possible in both countries (though there were differences in terminology, such as supervisors being called offender managers in England and probation counsellors in Romania). The questionnaires were then translated directly into Romanian. Participants were asked how they had found each element of the current training event and how useful they felt these would be for their practice. They were also asked about the extent and ease with which they had been able to apply practice material covered at previous training events and about the support they had received from colleagues and managers. Most questions used closed responses or scales, but there was also opportunity for participants to comment through the inclusion of open-ended questions.

Findings

Practitioners from both countries were very positive about the training. Average ratings of the overall usefulness of each training event are provided in Figure 10.1. Ratings from both countries were very favourable for each event and were even more favourable in Romania as compared with England.

At the final review event, probation supervisors were asked a series of questions about the impact of the entire SEED training package on various aspects of their practice. The findings are provided in Table 10.1. Views were very positive in both countries and were again even more favourable in Romania.

What was it about the training that practitioners found helpful?

In both countries, all elements of the training were considered interesting and useful by most participants, both at the time and after

Figure 10.1: How useful did you find the SEED training?

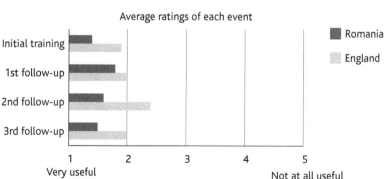

Table 10.1: Looking back over the whole SEED training and your practice, what has been the overall impact on you and your practice? (On all questions, 1 = very positive; 5 = not at all positive)

	Romania mean (SD)	England mean (SD)
On your confidence in doing one-to-one supervision	1.6 (0.67)	1.7 (0.69)
On your ability to deal with different offenders	1.3 (0.46)	1.8 (0.70)
On your knowledge and skills	1.6 (0.75)	1.7 (0.56)
On your ability to plan the course of supervision	1.6 (0.69)	1.9 (0.84)
On your ability to deal with unexpected crises	1.6 (0.50)	2.2 (0.76)
On the extent to which you talk with the offender about the purpose of supervision	1.3 (0.55)	2.0 (0.64)
On the extent to which you talk with colleagues about one-to-one supervision	1.4 (0.50)	2.1 (0.81)
On the extent to which you talk with your line manager about particular cases	1.3 (0.55)	2.1 (0.74)

Note: SD = standard deviation.

using the material in practice. Positive responses to training, that emphasised similar skills to SEED, have also been reported by Canton (2006) in a project where aspiring probation practitioners in Ukraine took part in training which emphasised 'principles of "What Works" (Chapman and Hough, 1998) and approaches informed by cognitive behavioural psychology (McGuire, 2001)' (Canton, 2006, p 506). In the current study, unlike the Ukrainian project, participants were practising probation practitioners, already familiar with much of the content of SEED, but they still appreciated having their skills and knowledge refreshed and having a more structured framework.

Why the positivity?

The positive results seemed to reflect SEED's focus on actual practice and day-to-day work for supervisors – what they were struggling with and making the hidden transparent. The practitioner questionnaires, together with interviews with practitioners in Romania and observation of practitioners' reflections during the training, indicated that training on putting all the skills together was considered the most important aspect of SEED in both countries.

> It was like we had a cupboard full of clothes and now we put some order to the clothes. (Romania)

> Structuring the activity and buying some time. (Romania)

> Using SEED techniques it is easier to adapt to individual needs. I don't feel surprised by situations, by crises. My work is more structured, more focused. (Romania)

> My sessions are better time managed, more focused and more productive. It also promotes thinking about the individual, their learning style and what materials would be most engaging. (England)

> I have thought more about what I want to achieve in my sessions and structured them around this. (England)

Practitioners saw SEED as a set of interventions and techniques that helped them structure their practice, as well as a convenient 'tool box' where one could go and pick up the relevant technique or exercise depending on the supervisee's situation or characteristics.

Interviews with practitioners in Romania indicated that they saw SEED as something different from a 'programme'. A programme, in their opinion, took the form of a rigid set of sessions and exercises that should be implemented in a certain way. SEED, on the other hand, was seen as a framework that helped to structure their work while allowing a certain degree of flexibility and access to a wide range of 'tools'. Practitioners appreciated the interplay between structure, flexibility and tools.

Were there any problems in implementing SEED?

Probation practitioners, from both our SEED evaluation and previous work in England (Robinson et al, 2014), want to produce high-quality probation supervision. However, in both England and Romania, practitioners felt that there were practical obstacles that frustrated quality supervision. Time and caseload were important issues.

> Those sessions that I have the time to plan are more focused. However, very frustrating that I don't have enough time to plan due to very high caseloads and therefore some offenders are getting better supervision than others. (England)

Time and caseload have been found to be issues in studies of other probation initiatives, such as the NOMS Offender Management Model (Turley et al, 2011). In that study, it was reported that a lack of time and caseloads meant practitioners did not have time to work on changing offender behaviour.

Some practitioners, however, felt that SEED enabled them to make better use of their time, through being more focused and structured, and that SEED's emphasis on encouraging the supervisee to take responsibility meant they could transfer some tasks to the supervisee instead of trying to solve all the supervisee's problems themselves.

> Plan work before – decide what resources to use. Structure sessions with aims/goals. Set tasks for client so all focus is not on Offender Manager doing all the work. (England)

> This training has enabled me to spend more time planning sessions, dealing with crises more effectively. (England)

SEED puts the emphasis on planning, over the session and over the course of the order. If practitioners have not previously planned much, it takes time to do this, and reflect afterwards as well as write up notes. However, practitioners found that after a while it could work:

> SEED comes somehow to put some order in all these methods, to show how some different methods, that have nothing in common, can be implemented in practice. (Romania)

Availability of office space was also seen as an issue, though in different ways in the two countries. In England, shortage of interview rooms was a problem in some offices. This meant that practitioners sometimes had to keep people waiting, which hinders prosocial modelling. In Romania, supervision sessions were conducted in shared offices. The lack of privacy and confidentiality was felt by some to impair their confidence in applying SEED. Very similar findings were reported by Turley and colleagues (2011) in the Offender Management Community Cohort Study. In that study, practitioners reported that one-to-one sessions sometimes had to be delayed due to lack of suitable space, or that practitioners sometimes had to meet with supervisees in the corridor. The latter was felt to inhibit offence focused work due to confidentiality issues.

Working together

An important element of the SEED model is that teams train together. Furthermore, the SEED initiative is not just about training days; it also involves working together between training sessions. Practitioners meet in groups to discuss live cases and there is observation of one-to-one supervision sessions by managers. Both these practices were more likely to be novel for practitioners in England than those in Romania. Almost three quarters of the practitioners in England (73%) said that the case discussions were a new practice for their team, compared with less than a fifth (17%) of practitioners in Romania. Ninety percent of the English practitioners said observation by managers was a new practice for their team, compared with less than a third of practitioners (31%) in Romania.

The questionnaire responses indicated that all the aspects of working together were found helpful by practitioners in both countries, as illustrated in Table 10.2. In England, although most practitioners found observation by seniors to be a helpful practice, it was also considered quite a stressful process by many practitioners. Romanian practitioners were less likely to rate this practice as stressful, probably because many were already used to being observed (because of the shared offices).

The opportunity to discuss cases and learn from one another in the peer group learning (action learning sets in England) was commented on very positively in the focus groups that took place at the final SEED event, as well as in interviews with practitioners and in comments on the questionnaires.

> Very useful. Helps to support each other. Opportunity to share knowledge and understanding. (England)

> Very important tool to look at other ways to deal with a tricky situation/offender. (England)

Table 10.2: Questionnaire ratings of working together

	Romania mean (SD)	England mean (SD)
1 = very helpful; 5 = not at all helpful		
How helpful did you find training with your team members?	1.4 (0.60)	1.4 (0.71)
How helpful did you find training with your manager?	1.4 (0.59)	2.2 (1.29)
1 = very helpful; 4 = not at all helpful		
How helpful did you find the sessions where you discussed live cases?	1.5 (0.70)	1.6 (0.57)
How helpful did you find observation by managers?	1.5 (0.64)	1.8 (0.71)

Note: SD = standard deviation.

It was felt that they stimulated reflective practice, provided different perspectives on cases and gave an opportunity to learn from one another. Practitioners felt they provided a safe space to question risk management and techniques. They were felt to be empowering and affirming, and built confidence, as well as helping to alleviate stress through peer support. In addition, they were considered to be helpful in developing team working and cohesion. We found similar results in evaluating restorative justice, where team meetings with reflective learning were found to be key in building confidence and dealing with more unusual cases (Shapland et al, 2011).

There were also positive comments in relation to observation of supervision sessions by managers.

> It offers the probation officer the possibility to develop in a good way by considering the feedback received. (Romania)

> Unique opportunity to gain feedback, increase confidence and identify areas for professional development. (England)

It should be noted that, although practitioners were keen to see both these practices continue beyond the initiative, there were fears in both countries that increasing workload pressures might push both practices out. It was felt that steps should be taken to ensure their survival – and that sufficient time needed to be allocated to do these practices justice.

In our opinion, facilitating group learning and enabling observation, discussion and feedback in relation to supervision practice is important, because supervision tends to be hidden work and can be challenging and lonely work. It is therefore important that practitioners are able to discuss their approach to difficult cases and learn from one another; and that managers are able to observe and understand the nature of supervisory work for those staff.

What did those being supervised think about their supervision? Did SEED training make any difference?

A self-completion questionnaire was designed to capture supervisees' perceptions of their probation practitioner's use of SEED skills. The questionnaire was developed by the evaluation team in England, with the version used in Romania being a direct translation of the English version. Any supervisee commencing supervision with a SEED-trained or comparison group practitioner during the evaluation period was given the opportunity to complete a questionnaire. The questionnaire was administered at the first available opportunity, after three months of supervision in England and after five months of supervision in Romania. These time periods were chosen to ensure the participant had sufficient experience of supervision to make judgements. It was administered further into the order in Romania because supervision in Romania is more spread out, with supervision sessions being less frequent. Completion of the questionnaire was voluntary and its answers confidential to the evaluation team. The questionnaires were given to the supervisee in sealable envelopes by receptionists, administrators, volunteers or any member of the probation staff who was not their own supervisor. Questionnaires were completed by 482 people in England and 495 in Romania.

In both countries, participants in both groups (that is, trained and comparison) were generally positive about their probation supervision. Opinions were generally favourable in both jurisdictions, but the Romanian participants were particularly positive about the supervision they were receiving. In Romania, the views of those in the comparison group were so favourable there was very little scope for improvement in their satisfaction ratings, making it unlikely that we would find additional positive effects of training. This was also true, but to a somewhat lesser extent, in England. In both jurisdictions, there were few significant differences between trained and comparison groups in the perceptions of those being supervised.

There may be a number of reasons for the limited differences between the groups. There are likely to be pre-training differences between practitioners in the extent to which they are already using the skills covered by SEED, and therefore possibly differences between SEED-trained and comparison groups in the extent to which they are already using these skills. It is also likely that there will be differences between practitioners in the impact the training has on them, and the extent to which they are able to apply the training to their practice. There are also methodological reasons why the differences may be limited, including possible contamination of the comparison groups, particularly in Romania, where it seems likely SEED-trained and comparison practitioners may have discussed the SEED model. In addition, in order for us to detect a difference between the groups, not only would the training have to bring about a difference in supervision practice, but this would also have to be noticed by those being supervised.

Romanian supervisees supervised by either trained or comparison practitioners were extremely positive about the supervision they were receiving. The level of satisfaction did cause us to reflect on whether the positivity was real or whether it may be a consequence of linguistic or cultural factors. Could it, for example, be a consequence of suspicion that their responses might have been seen by the authorities or their supervisor, despite confidentiality assurances? We decided that this was unlikely, because the positivity about probation supervision that was expressed in the questionnaire ratings was matched by positivity in the written responses people provided.

> I have only good things to say about my probation counsellor; she is really professional (in my opinion), she has made me open my soul and made me understand that I am not alone. She helped me a lot (even though she didn't realize, she guided me and supported me unconditionally). After the first meeting, over two years ago, I realised that there are people who are really 'human'. She gave me hope, purpose in life; she made me able to walk again with my head held high, she taught me how to say 'no', she made me realise that I can live and raise my children with dignity. She also made me realise that no one can judge me for a mistake. Thank you very much! (Trained group)

> For now I am pleased with the help that was given to me, I expected it to be worse but it is actually very good. (Trained group)

> I want to say that I didn't expect to have this kind of moral support from my probation counsellor. No matter about the offence I've committed, my probation counsellor believes in me and morally he helps me a lot, he challenges me to think, to live optimistically and have perseverance. My probation counsellor gave me the 'drive' I needed to feel reinserted in a community that failed me at some point and which I failed in my turn. (Comparison group)

> It gave me the strength to move on, to find a job and especially to think more positively than I used to do. (Comparison group)

The universally positive comments about the actual supervision can be compared with a greater negativity directed towards other elements of the criminal justice system, particularly the fairness of the sentence and especially the length of the sentence.

> The supervision period is too long considering what happened and that this is the first time I have broken the law. (Trained group)

Furthermore, negative comments about other elements of the criminal justice system indicate that at least not all the participants were unwilling or afraid to express negative sentiments. This distrust of other parts of the criminal justice system may have made experiences of Romanian probation unexpectedly positive.

Did the SEED training have an effect on supervisory practice, as seen by the supervisees?

In England, there was some evidence, from principal component analysis and supervisees' scores across the components, that practitioners in the trained group were perceived as using a fuller range of SEED skills overall, compared with those in the comparison group (Shapland et al, 2017). This finding was not replicated in Romania, but, as stated previously, because in Romania the comparison group's ratings were extremely favourable across all the questions, we were unlikely to find any additional effect of training. In England, those supervised by SEED-trained practitioners were significantly more likely than those in the comparison group to feel there was a plan for what would be achieved by the end of the order. There was no such difference between the trained and comparison groups in Romania; however, supervisees across both groups in Romania were more likely than those in England to feel there was a plan. In England, in cases where it was suggested that supervisees needed to go to another agency (for example, for housing), those with SEED-trained practitioners were significantly more likely than those in the comparison group to suggest that the supervisee should ring the agency themselves while still in the probation office (an approach that encourages the supervisee to take responsibility), rather making the appointment for them or just telling the supervisee to do it.

In both jurisdictions, there were differences between the trained and comparison groups in relation to the content of supervision sessions, but these differences were not the same for the two countries. In Romania, discussions appeared to be more focused in the trained group, with practitioners talking about particular topics in particular sessions, rather than discussing almost everything every session. There was no evidence of more focused discussions in the trained group in England, but there were statistically significant differences between the SEED-trained and comparison groups in the extent to which they indicated that 'attitudes to offending', 'getting work or training' and 'achieving goals' were discussed. These topics, which are relevant to desistance, were each reported to be talked about more regularly by supervisees with SEED-trained practitioners.

In terms of differences between the countries, supervisees in Romania, across both groups, were significantly more likely than those in England to feel there was a plan for what they should do between sessions and that there was an overall plan for the supervision over the order. Romanian practitioners were more likely to tell people where to go when suggesting another agency, while those in England were more likely to 'refer' them by making the appointment for them or assisting them in making their own appointment.

Why were there differences between the countries? In England, SEED was introduced as part of the broader Offender Engagement Programme, one of whose aims was:

> ... to reduce unnecessary prescription through performance targets based on the time taken to complete certain tasks and National Standards for probation practice. The greater freedoms are intended to enable practitioners to use their professional discretion and skills required to reduce re-offending. (Rex, 2012, p 6)

The backdrop in Romania was different. In the period prior to its introduction, there had not been the same emphasis on performance targets, based on outputs, at the potential expense of engagement that there had been in England. Hence, at the outset, practitioners in Romania may have felt more enabled and supported in using engagement skills, compared with those in England. In addition, supervisees in Romania had, on the whole, committed less serious offences than those supervised in England. These factors may, at least in part, explain why Romanian practitioners, in both the SEED-trained and comparison groups, were judged by their supervisees to be using engagement skills to a somewhat greater degree than their counterparts in England.

Compliance

In both countries, we were provided with administrative data on compliance with orders. The only reliable data available to us were whether the order was completed successfully or whether official action was taken. This is what Robinson and McNeill (2008) have referred to as *formal* compliance, as compared with *substantive* compliance, which requires 'the active engagement and cooperation of the offender' (Robinson, 2013, p 28). In England, we found some small but statistically significant positive effects of SEED on formal compliance (Sorsby et al, 2016). SEED training was related to whether supervision terminated successfully or unsuccessfully. It seemed to prevent both reoffending during the supervision period *and* breaches of probation conditions, with a somewhat greater impact on the former than the latter. Although breach decisions are partly determined by the supervising practitioner, taking enforcement action for reoffending is outside the practitioner's control, so it seems unlikely that the effect was due only to more appropriately taken enforcement proceedings. There were no significant differences in relation to other measures of compliance with community sentences, such as the decision to initiate breach proceedings.

The evaluation in Romania was not set up with the intention of evaluating the effects of SEED on compliance in that jurisdiction. The timescale of the evaluation, combined with the length of probation orders in Romania, meant there was not sufficient time to properly assess whether SEED had any impact on compliance. In Romania, only a tiny proportion of cases (3%) were terminated during the evaluation period. Apart from one case, where there was a fresh offence, these were all for administrative reasons. The average length of orders in Romania was just over five years and no case actually reached the natural end of the order during the evaluation period. We did collect data on breach for the very first part of the orders. During the monitoring period, which ranged from one day to 11 months, depending on when the case commenced, breach proceedings were initiated after a first meeting with a practitioner in only 0.4% of cases in the comparison group and 0.3% in the SEED-trained group. This is not a significant difference.

Transferring SEED to Romania: why was it popular among practitioners in both countries?

The focus group sessions[7] and practitioner interviews undertaken at the end of SEED training in Romania concluded that SEED seemed to travel very well from England to Romania and had the potential to travel further: across Romania, and to other types of community sanctions (for example, community service) or other jurisdictions provided there is an interest in offender rehabilitation.

We think that, at a time of change in both countries, featuring increased discretion for staff in England and increased probation responsibilities in criminal justice in Romania, SEED was popular among staff because:

- it was seen as investing in staff training and expertise (that is, caring about the challenges facing staff at a time of change);
- it concentrated on the 'core job' for probation – one-to-one supervision;
- it picked up from initial and previous training that had focused on particular tools/skills, bringing them together within a framework that helped to structure supervision while simultaneously allowing flexibility;
- it brought teams together, enabling them to learn from and support one another;
- although it involved more time and effort initially, it had the potential to enable staff to work more effectively and efficiently.

Are there any lessons for probation policy transfer and its evaluation?

In a similar vein to the Ukrainian project, reported by Canton (2006), the SEED project was more concerned with practice transfer, which may ultimately influence policy, rather than beginning with policy transfer itself. So, was the transfer of training and evaluation a smooth, unproblematic passage? Not entirely. First, language was an important consideration. It was necessary to allow more time for the training events themselves, in order to allow time for language translation. The use of a local co-trainer was important to ensure the training and materials had been understood and made sense within the local context. The use of a local co-trainer was also important for diffusion of knowledge. Durnescu and Haines (2012, p 897) emphasise the importance of 'matching or the equivalence of personnel, roles and knowledge between partners in the exchange process'. They saw this approach as key in establishing probation in Romania and in the development of the Training Plan for Romania with the assistance of Britain. In the current study, commercial translators were used to translate the training and evaluation materials, but it proved essential for these to be checked by a local expert in probation to ensure that technical aspects were translated correctly and current terminology used.

Knowledge of legal and cultural differences and ways of working was essential, in order to ensure that all aspects of the initiative could be accommodated. The need to take account of the local context in policy transfer is highlighted by Durnescu and Haines (2012). Transfers may fail because 'insufficient attention may be paid to the differences between the economic, social, political and ideological contexts in the transferring and the borrowing country' (Dolowitz and Marsh, 2000, p 17). Although, as Canton (2006, p 515) points out, 'This hazard is minimised by developing current practice [as was the case with the current initiative] and institutions rather than importing new ones', the transfer still has to be carried out appropriately. It was essential that the evaluation team included academics who had evaluated the initial initiative in England, but also importantly, a Romanian academic (Ioan Durnescu) with extensive knowledge of the Romanian probation system and cross-cultural comparative research. It was also key for the English evaluators to visit Romania at an early stage, prior to commencement of the initiative, to ascertain what was possible in relation to implementation and evaluation and finalise the details. A further visit was also undertaken further into the project to discuss, among other things, the fine details of record keeping, databases and justice statistics in Romania. Meeting face to face with a representative of the IT department, alongside probation managers and practitioners, was very useful to ascertain how compliance procedures operated and how they, and other elements of supervision, were recorded in databases, as well as what the various database codes meant.

Ongoing liaison and support from senior people within probation were also essential. We had an extremely helpful senior coordinator. The SEED initiative was very strongly supported by senior managers in Romania. Strong support from the top of the organisation was a vital factor in successful transfer. It helped to ensure that the practitioners were motivated in undertaking the initiative and believed they would be supported in doing so. The strong support from the top of the organisation also greatly facilitated the evaluation.

Finally, it is important to be aware of what is happening more generally within the probation service. Here, again, a Romanian evaluator and ongoing liaison was essential. Staff respond in terms of their current view on their work and it is important to be aware of the broader contextual factors that may be influencing their views.

Conclusion

SEED training was appreciated by practitioners in both jurisdictions. Aspects of SEED that were particularly appreciated were that it involved teams training together and also discussing cases together between training, and that it provided a framework for supervision based on empirical evidence while allowing sufficient flexibility to be applied to all cases.

The impact of SEED training on supervisees' views of the supervision they were receiving was limited. In England, there was some evidence that practitioners in the trained group were perceived as using a fuller range of SEED skills overall, compared with those in the comparison group. This finding was not replicated in Romania, but, particularly in Romania, supervisees' ratings were so favourable across all rating scales for both the trained and comparison groups of supervisors that it was unlikely we would find any additional effect of training. It should be remembered that SEED training is for experienced practitioners, and that practitioners will all have had prior training in most of the skills that SEED addresses. The training is about refreshing those skills and bringing them together within a framework. There will be pre-training differences between practitioners in the extent to which they are already using the skills covered by SEED and possibly also pre-training differences between the SEED and comparison practitioners in the extent to which they were already using these skills. Studying videotapes of supervision sessions conducted by probation practitioners in Jersey, Raynor and colleagues (2014) found considerable variation between practitioners in their use of core correctional practices, the skills that are also the focus of SEED training. In addition to pre-training differences in the use of the skills covered by SEED, it is likely that there will also be differences between practitioners in the impact the training has and the extent to which they feel able to implement the skills in practice. In view of these factors, it would be unrealistic to expect SEED training to create a dramatic difference between the trained and comparison groups in supervision practice and for those being supervised to notice this.

In Romania, the timescale of the evaluation and the length of orders meant any impact on compliance could not be properly assessed. There were very few breaches during the evaluation period, and, although the evaluation periods are not equivalent, breaches of supervision seemed to be a less frequent occurrence in Romania than in England.

In England, there was a small but statistically significant impact of SEED training on formal compliance. There may be a number of reasons why the impact was not greater. The quality of probation supervision is, of course, just one of a number of factors that may affect compliance (which is not the same thing as recidivism). Ugwudike (2010) identifies a number of obstacles to compliance, including practical issues such as childcare and transportation costs that have nothing to do with criminality. SEED training, which is principally designed with the aim of promoting desistance, does not specifically target non-criminogenic practical obstacles to compliance, rather prioritising RNR principles in terms of criminogenic needs to reduce recidivism (Andrews et al, 1990; Andrews and Bonta, 2010). SEED training specifically does not prioritise non-criminogenic needs that are only weakly related to recidivism (Andrews and Bonta, 2010). SEED training did appear to have a greater impact on offending during the order than it did on failure to comply with probation conditions.

This chapter has focused on the experience of one-to-one supervision in two very different countries and probation cultures. The potential for policy transfer (in this case, SEED training) was perhaps almost ideal in our situation: there was strong support among policymakers and senior probation staff; it was a time of change and so practitioners were both prepared for change and welcomed the SEED focus on their daily lives; and some of the people involved in mounting the initiative were the same in both countries. There were still some key practical difficulties, centred around language, past criminal justice cultures and distance. Yet the overarching impression with which we were left was the real desire of both supervisors and supervisees in both countries to try to create best practice – and that best practice centred around trying to create the best probation supervision to support desistance, involving creating and developing a relationship over many months that had a plan and that focused on the actual needs of those being supervised.

Notes

[1] The evaluation in England and Wales was of the pilot project, which was named SEED (Skills for Effective Engagement and Development). SEED subsequently became known as SEEDS (Skills for Effective Engagement, Development and Supervision) when it was later offered to other probation trusts that had not formed part of the original pilot.

[2] Supervisees were, at the time of the research, usually called 'service users' in England and 'convicted persons' in Romania. In this chapter, we shall use the term 'supervisee' to refer to those being supervised on a community sentence or on licence after release from prison in England and to those being supervised in the community in Romania.

[3] The jurisdiction in which the initiative was evaluated was England and Wales, which is part of the United Kingdom, but the probation areas included in the external evaluation by the University of Sheffield were all in England.

[4] Funding for the evaluation in England and Wales was from NOMS to the University of Sheffield. Funding for the evaluation in Romania was from the EU as part of the STREAM programme (Strategic Targeting of Recidivism through Evaluation and Monitoring), the partners for which included NOMS and the Universities of Bucharest and Sheffield.

[5] Lasting three days in England and four in Romania. It was longer in Romania to allow for translation.

[6] Three follow-up training events, which lasted one day in England and one-and-a-half days in Romania, and a final review session that lasted half a day in England and one day in Romania.

[7] These sessions included all participants who took part in the training, that is, both supervisors and managers. There were 15 participants at the Dolj and Brasov event and 11 participants at the Bucharest event. In the morning, the participants were split into four groups to discuss the strengths, weaknesses, opportunities and threats of: the SEED model; observation and feedback by managers; peer group learning; and follow-up training. In the afternoon, participants were split into two groups in Bucharest and three groups at the Dolj/Brasov event. One group at each event generated suggestions for the Ministry of Justice to sustain the model and the other group(s) developed local sustainability plans.

References

Andrews, D.A. and Bonta, J. (2010) *The Psychology of Criminal Conduct* (5th edn), Boston: Anderson Publishing.

Andrews, D.A., Bonta, J. and Hoge, R.D. (1990) 'Classification for effective rehabilitation: rediscovering psychology', *Criminal Justice and Behaviour*, 17(1): 19–52.

Bourgon, G., Bonta, J., Rugge, T., Scott, T. and Yessine, A. (2010) 'The role of program design, implementation, and evaluation in evidence-based "real world" community supervision', *Federal Probation*, 74: 2–15.

Bourgon, G., Rugge, T., Guiterrez, L., Simpson, K., Bonta, J., Scott, T., Yessine, A., Li, J. and Helmus, L. (2008) 'Strategic Training Initiative in Community Supervision (STICS)', Paper presented to the Canadian Psychology Association 69th Annual Convention, Halifax, Nova Scotia, 14 June.

Canton, R. (2006) 'Penal policy transfer: a case study from Ukraine', *The Howard Journal of Crime and Justice*, 45(5): 502–520.

Carbunaru, I. (2014) 'Probation in Romania: change, challenge, progress', Paper presented to the final conference of the STREAM project, 'Evaluation in practice', Malta, 22–24 October, available at www.stream-probation.eu/default.asp?page_id=221.

Dolowitz, D.P. and Marsh, D. (2000) 'Learning from abroad: the role of policy transfer in contemporary policy making', *Governance*, 13(1): 5–24.

Dowden, C. and Andrews, D.A. (2004) 'The importance of staff practice in delivering effective correctional treatment: a meta-analytic review of core correctional practice', *International Journal of Offender Therapy and Comparative Criminology*, 48(2): 203–214.

Durnescu, I. and Haines, K. (2012) 'Probation in Romania. archaeology of a partnership', *British Journal of Criminology*, 52(5): 889–907.

House of Commons Justice Committee (2011) *The Role of the Probation Service* (HC 519-1), London: The Stationery Office.

Raynor, P., Ugwudike, P. and Vanstone, M. (2010) 'Skills and strategies in probation supervision: the Jersey study', in F. McNeill, P. Raynor and C. Trotter (eds) *Offender Supervision: New Directions in Theory, Research and Practice*, Cullompton: Willan, pp 113–129.

Raynor, P., Ugwudike, P. and Vanstone, M. (2014) 'The impact of skills in probation work: a reconviction study', *Criminology & Criminal Justice*, 14(2): 235–249.

Rex, S. (2012) 'The Offender Engagement Programme: rationale and objectives', *Eurovista: Probation and Community Justice*, 2(1): 6–9.

Rex, S. and Hosking, N. (2014) 'Supporting practitioners to engage offenders', in I. Durnescu and F. McNeill (eds) *Understanding Penal Practice*, London: Routledge, pp 271–280.

Robinson, G. (2013) 'What counts? Community sanctions and the construction of compliance', in P. Ugwudike and P. Raynor (eds) *What Works in Offender Compliance: International Perspectives and Evidence-Based Practice*, Basingstoke: Palgrave Macmillan, pp 26–43.

Robinson, G. and McNeill, F. (2008) 'Exploring the dynamics of compliance with community penalties', *Theoretical Criminology*, 12(4): 431–449.

Robinson, G., Burke, L. and Millings, M. (2016) 'Criminal justice identities in transition: the case of devolved probation services in England and Wales', *British Journal of Criminology*, 56(1): 161–1789.

Robinson, G., Priede, C., Farrall, S., Shapland, J. and McNeill, F. (2014) 'Understanding "quality" in probation practice: frontline perspectives in England and Wales', *Criminology & Criminal Justice*, 14(2): 123–142.

Romanian Parliament (2014) Romanian Penal Code, available at www.avocatconstanta.com/Noul%20Cod%20Penal%20actualizat.pdf (accessed 27 February 2017).

Sapouna, M., Bisset, C., Conlong, A.-M. and Matthews, B. (2015) *What Works to Reduce Reoffending: A Summary of the Evidence*, Edinburgh: Scottish Government, available at www.gov.scot/Publications/2015/05/2480/0 (accessed 27 February 2017).

Shapland, J., Robinson, G. and Sorsby, A. (2011) *Restorative Justice in Practice*, London: Routledge.

Shapland, J., Sorsby, A., Farrall, S. and Priede, C. (2017) 'Experiencing supervision in England – on licence and on community sentences', in R. Armstrong and I. Durnescu (eds) *Supervised Freedom: International Perspectives of Life on Parole*, London: Routledge.

Shapland, J., Sorsby, A., Robinson, G., Priede, C., Farrall, S. and McNeill, F. (2013) 'What quality means to probation staff in England in relation to one-to-one supervisio', in I. Durnescu and F. McNeill (eds) *Understanding Penal Practice*, London: Routledge, pp 139–152.

Sorsby, A., Shapland, J. and Robinson, G. (2016) 'Using compliance with probation supervision as an interim outcome measure in evaluating a probation initiative', *Criminology and Criminal Justice*, advance online publication, doi: 0.1177/1748895816653992.

Sorsby, A., Shapland, J., Farrall, S., McNeill, F., Priede, C. and Robinson, G. (2013) *Probation Staff Views of the Skills for Effective Engagement Development (SEED) Project*, Centre for Criminological Research Occasional Paper No 4, Sheffield: University of Sheffield, available at www.sheffield.ac.uk/polopoly_fs/1.293093!/file/probation-staff-views-seed.pdf (accessed 27 February 2017).

Teague, M. (2007) 'The history of probation: politics, power and cultural change 1876–2005', *British Journal of Criminology*, 47(3): 523–525.

Turley, C., Ludford, H., Callanan, M. and Barnard, M. (2011) *Delivering the NOMS Offender Management Model: Practitioner Views From the Offender Management Community Cohort Study*, Ministry of Justice Research Series 7/11, London: Ministry of Justice.

Ugwudike, P. (2010) 'Compliance with community penalties: the importance of interactional dynamics', in F. McNeill, P. Raynor and C. Trotter (eds) *Offender Supervision: New Directions in Theory, Research and Practice*, Cullompton: Willan, pp 325–343.

ELEVEN

Supervision face-to-face contacts: the emergence of an intervention

Heather Toronjo and Faye S. Taxman

Introduction

The heart of probation and/or parole supervision is face-to-face contact, which involves the interaction between the individual under supervision and the authorising government official (or in some rare instances, a contractual employee). Face-to-face contacts are an opportunity for the government official to communicate the goals of supervision, review progress, and modify plans to accommodate the status of progress.

Under an enforcement (compliance) model of supervision, such contacts take the form of monitoring adherence with a focus on ensuring that the supervisee is abiding by the rules of supervision. A social work framework focuses on obtaining services depending on court orders, or trying to address behaviours that are causing problems on supervision. A refined model – behavioural management – is postured as an approach that bridges the two polar extremes but focuses on the officer using cognitive restructuring strategies to identify those factors that are drivers of criminal conduct and that identify factors to make progress in reducing the risk of further involvement in criminal conduct (Taxman, 2008).

The behavioural management approach has been reclaimed as the Risk–Need–Responsivity (RNR) model of supervision, which has been found to be the most effective supervision strategy to reduce recidivism in two meta-analyses. Drake (2011) found that this model reduced the risk for recidivism by 16% as compared to no change in recidivism with intensive supervision models (with surveillance only) and a 10% reduction with intensive supervision with treatment. Chadwick and colleagues (2014) also found that clients of officers trained in CCP had a lower recidivism rate as compared to clients of officers not trained in CCP, with the rate of CCP trained officer clients being 13 percentage points lower than that of non-CCP trained officer clients. Collectively, the research appears to confirm that supervision face-to-face contacts can be enhanced by using these strategies. The unanswered question is what are the strategies considered critical in this new model of supervision?

This chapter explores the content of curricula that are considered part of the RNR supervision framework, examining the core components. More importantly, the review will ask the question of whether the revised face-to-face contacts under these frameworks are different from practice in a compliance-driven model. These curricula are used in the US, Canada, and other places around the world to advance practices of supervision agencies. In fact, researchers from the US and Canada are working with supervision agencies across the world on many of these curricula. In other words, are the curricula focusing on risk or behavioural management – risk management refers to public safety, while behavioural management focuses on individual-level tailoring of the contacts – to reduce drivers of criminal behaviour? And how do the curricula advance different supervision practices that can be tied to reductions of recidivism? Finally, this chapter lays out a research agenda for assessing what is important to accomplish in supervision to reduce recidivism.

History of core correctional practices as it relates to supervision

Andrews and Kiessling (1980) developed the five primary dimensions of effective correctional practice, now referred to as core correctional practices (CCPs), in the late 1970s as part of a Canadian programme to train volunteer probation officers (Canadian Volunteers in Corrections). The authors crafted concrete supervision practices rooted in the burgeoning differential association (Burgess and Akers, 1966) and social learning (Bandura, 1969) theories. Burgess and Akers (1966) elaborated on Sutherland's differential association theory by infusing learning behaviours and termed the revised theory 'differential association-reinforcement theory of criminal behaviour'. The theory explains that deviant behaviour is learned in the same way all behaviour is learned, via mechanisms of differential reinforcement and imitation (Akers, 2011). This is consistent with Bandura's (1977) social learning theory, which focuses on 'reciprocal determinism' whereby behaviour, personal factors and environmental factors all operate as 'interlocking determinants of each other' (p 10). The theory explicates the effect of *expectation* of reinforcement on determining behaviour. To be effective, reinforcements must be known ahead of time. Bandura (1977) noted that people decide what to pay attention to, being more likely to pay attention to and seek out models that possess engaging qualities (models lacking pleasant characteristics tend to be ignored or rejected), and that people retain behaviour better when they code modelled activities into words, concise labels, or vivid imagery and then rehearse the modelled responses. Social learning theory notes the value of feedback for refining new behaviours by helping people make self-corrective adjustments.

CCP authors saw the promise of social learning and differential association in guiding community supervision. As Andrews (1979b) notes:

> Social learning theory examines the interpersonal style of the officer as behaviours which might act as discriminative stimuli for certain behaviours by the client, as responses which might act as rewards or punishment of client behaviour, and as behaviours which might be imitated or modeled by the client. (p 5)

Andrews and Kiessling (1980) go on to establish the following three intermediate targets: first, individuals under supervision should have a 'heightened awareness, perceived certainty and perceived validity of the formal legal sanctions associated with rule violations' (p 11); second, officers should note a 'prosocial shifts in attitudes, values and beliefs' in supervision clients (p 12); and third, officers should note an increase in the 'frequency, the quality and the variety' of rewards (or satisfactions) associated with prosocial activity, or 'conventional or non-criminal pursuits with conventional others in conventional settings' (p 12). The authors operationalised mechanisms for achieving these intermediate targets into five core practices, which included a quality relationship distinguished by trust, caring, understanding and interpersonal openness; effective use of authority; modelling and reinforcing anticriminal attitudes and behaviours through the use of positive or negative reinforcement; concrete problem-solving skills; and actively engaging in arranging appropriate services (Andrews, 1979a).

Gendreau and Andrews (1989) expanded the original five CCPs to eight CCPs. The change was not radical, but provided slight changes to the structure and added one additional practice. The new list separated effective reinforcement and disapproval from the umbrella of anticriminal modelling and included a structured learning component. Anticriminal modelling entails officers modelling prosocial behaviours and reinforcing clients' behaviour when they do the same. To effectively reinforce behaviour, officers should use supportive statements and focus on the reasons why this behaviour is desirable. This should be followed by considering the short- and long-term benefits associated with continued behaviour. To effectively disapprove, officers should communicate disapproval for a specific behaviour along with the reasons why this behaviour is undesirable. This must be followed by a consideration of the short- and long-term costs associated with continued use of the behaviour and a clear demonstration of an alternate, prosocial behaviour.

Problem solving is a specific social skill that officers teach clients to address a variety of high-risk situations, and cognitive restructuring requires that officers help clients describe problematic situations and the client's related thoughts and feelings. Officers help clients identify risky thinking and practise more prosocial alternatives. Officers with quality relationship skills are warm, open, non-judgmental, empathetic, flexible, engaging, solution-focused and directive.

The enhancement to CCPs involved structured learning, which is a method of teaching behavioural strategies to assist clients in developing prosocial skills to avoid or manage high-risk situations. Skills are taught in a structured manner that involves defining, modelling and rehearsing the skill followed by constructive feedback, and has the expectation that clients practise the skill in increasingly difficult situations.

Motivational interviewing as a counselling and/or communication tool

CCPs emerged concomitant with a shift in the field of substance abuse treatment toward a focus on client-centered practices aimed at increasing client engagement in treatment. The practice termed motivational interviewing (MI) derived from Dr William Miller's clinical practice working with problem drinkers. In 1983, Miller broke with popular clinical conceptions that a client's poor motivation to change was reflective of some inherent personality trait. Instead, Miller viewed lack of motivation as a dynamic, changeable state. Drawing from Carl Rogers' work on client-centered care (that is, having empathy, optimism and respect for client choice) and social psychological principles of motivation counselling, Miller developed a method by which counsellors could explore clients' own internal motivational struggle and channel those internal motivations toward a specific goal in the direction of change (Miller, 1983; Miller and Rollnick, 2012).

MI focuses on individual strengths and begins with a place of trust – the belief that people have wisdom about themselves and that they have good reasons for doing whatever problem behaviour they are engaging in. MI is a natural fit with CCP given the heavy emphasis on individual responsibility and internal attribution of change.

The four main processes of MI include engaging, focusing, evoking and planning (Miller and Rollnick, 2012). Engagement is a process meant to establish a helpful, positive working relationship. It is the foundation on which everything else rests. Focusing is a process by which counsellors develop and maintain a specific direction for the conversation about change. At the heart of MI is evoking change. This is the process whereby counsellors elicit the client's own internal motivations for change. Planning occurs when the client's motivation reaches a tipping point – when the client starts talking more about when and how to change and less about whether and why to change. Five communication skills cut across all four processes. These are referred to as OARS: asking open-ended questions; affirming; reflective listening; summarising; and informing and advising.

Arguably, the greatest challenge to integrating MI with RNR-based supervision is the process of becoming proficient in the use of MI. While the authors of MI are not prescriptive about the process of developing MI skills, they liken it to learning to fly a plane and emphasise the importance of continuous guided practice (Miller and Rollnick, 2012, p 322). They suggest an initial one- to two-day clinical workshop to familiarise potential users with the general concepts and practices of MI and the development of onsite coaches who become subject-matter experts. They also recommend training several (but not necessarily all) staff members in MI so that they may form work groups to practice and discuss the skills. They recommend that any MI training include 12 specific learning goals: understand the underlying spirit of MI (partnership, acceptance, compassion and evocation); develop skill and comfort with reflective listening and OARS; identify change goals; exchange information and provide advice within an MI style; be able to recognise change talk and sustain talk; evoke change talk; respond to change talk and strengthen it; respond to sustain talk without amplifying it; develop hope and confidence; time and negotiate a change plan; strengthen client commitment; and flexibly integrate MI with other clinical skills and practices.

The intensity of MI training with its need for continuous practice and feedback, its focus on specific clinical practices, and its reliance on high-level clinical abilities constitutes a formidable barrier for community corrections agencies seeking to integrate MI practices into a supervision model. Any effort to integrate MI practices into supervision models must take into account these challenges. MI tends to focus on building strengths instead of merely examining deficits, which is a common criticism of CCP.

Rise of evidence-based supervision models

Several curricula now exist to train probation and parole officers by translating CCPs into actionable, concrete steps that define the supervision intervention. In other words, these curricula operationalise the evidence-based supervision model. Though the models differ in content and implementation methods, the following supervision models all seek to incorporate CCP, RNR and MI (motivational communication) into everyday use. The models compared in this chapter include Proactive Community Supervision (PCS) developed by George Mason University and Maryland Department of Probation and Parole (Taxman et al, 2004; Taxman, 2008), Strategic Training Initiative in Community Supervision (STICS), developed by the Canadian Department of Public Safety (Bonta et al, 2011); Staff Training Aimed at Reducing Rearrest (STARR) developed by the US Federal Probation and Pretrial Services (Robinson et al, 2012); Effective Practices in Community Supervision (EPICS) developed at the University of Cincinnati (Smith et al, 2012); and Skills for Offender Assessment and Responsivity in New Goals (SOARING2) developed at George Mason University (Maass et al, 2013).

To note, all of the curricula aim to incorporate CCPs into everyday use, though they differ in how those practices are operationalised. STICS, STARR and EPICS craft concrete skills steps that operationalise the CCPs, whereas PCS and SOARING2 stick to the spirit of the CCPs with a focus on building quality relationships and modelling and reinforcing prosocial behaviour. These models do not specifically use the language of CCP. Models also differ in their explanation of the RNR principles. While the principles are implicit in all models, only SOARING2 and STICS have learning modules dedicated to explaining the basics of those principles. The modules also differ in the format and content of initial training.

Proactive Community Supervision

PCS in Maryland began in the late 1990s as a means to re-engineer probation supervision from an enforcement model to a behavioural management model. The then director, Judith Sachwald, recognised that officers did not have the skills for CCP given that face-to-face contacts were more of a check-in instead of being behaviourally focused. The transformation of community supervision was built on a process of improving officers' skills through a series of comprehensive trainings and practice sessions over several years. The first one was communication skills and the second was 'sizing up'. Wrapped around the training were organisational reinforcers (now referred to as quality improvement processes) to solidify the agency's commitment to the goals of a behavioural management type of supervision. The model was deployed in all districts in Maryland over a six-year period. During the study's pilot period, which included four offices using the model, researchers found that the offices trained in PCS had reduced recidivism compared with those that were using the standard 'check-in' supervision model (Taxman, 2008).

Tools of the Trade: A Guide to Incorporating Science into Practice (Taxman et al, 2004) outlines the key components of the supervision model, which is focused on officers facilitating behavioural change. The manual includes seven sections: behavioural change; assessment and planning that focuses on prioritisation, case planning and behavioural contracts; communication skills that include deportment, interview structure and principles of motivational communication; information tools that include contact, collateral contacts, monitoring technologies and drug testing; incentives to shape client behaviour; service tools to match clients to services; and typologies of clients that include an example of how to supervise the individual. CCPs were incorporated into these skills. The emphasis was on supervision adopting these seven components with a focus on tailoring supervision goals and components based on the different risk-need profiles of individuals.

The PCS model involved a series of steps. First, officers addressed supervision policies including reporting requirements and identifying risk level. Second, officers identified any needs or crises needing attention (for example, suicidal ideation, homelessness, or active psychosis). Third, officers turned their attention to the client's needs and answered four questions: what intervention should target procriminal attitudes and behaviours?; what intervention should target the client's relationships and associates?; what are the drivers of criminal behaviours?; are there other needs (for example, housing, financial or leisure problems) that require help?

The relationship and communication skills protocol adapted the MI model for community supervision, and provided the first effort to apply this counselling-type technique in supervision settings. This was generally a two-day training with four booster sessions. The adaptation included more about the role of the officer, the use of communication as a way to define goals and objects, the techniques of OARS applied to community supervision, the building of a working relationship, and the ability for the client to have a voice. A number of tools were developed to facilitate these actions. The O-SELF was a checklist for officers to use to help the client identify what they aim to achieve during the period of supervision (voice). Having the client select the areas of their life that they desire to change allows the officer and client to outline common supervision goals. This was accompanied by a management information system – the Maryland Division of Parole and Probation offender case planning software, known as MOSCE – which included the risk-need information, goals and the ability to manage goals.

The 'sizing up' curriculum was devoted to understanding risk needs, using risk-needs information in case plans and identifying different client typologies. This was a two-day training with four booster sessions and had to occur at a minimum of one year after the officer had undertaken the communication training. It was designed to reinforce the communication skills and PCS model, and apply specifics to different client typologies. The emphasis was on learning about different typologies to tailor supervision to address the drivers of criminal behaviour. The typologies were viewed as a method to help officers identify the unique risk-need profiles of their clients, to use this information to build a case plan, to use behavioural contracting techniques (for example, signed contracts outlining expectations that include reinforcers and consequences associated with certain behaviours or goals, all rooted in the CCP skills) to reinforce positive behaviours, to use incentives to reinforce positive and desired behaviours, and to incrementally work through difficult behavioural issues. Unlike the CCP model, which emphasises 'effective disapproval', the PCS model focuses on contingency management (that is, the strategic use of incentives to motivate treatment engagement and behaviour change), motivational engagement, and strengths to address negative behaviours. The MOSCE system had these factors built into the software to reinforce the emphasis on target behaviours. For example, probationers were asked what would incentive their behaviour and these incentives were then built into their case plans, which were tailored to their driving criminogenic factors. Substance abusers tended to have treatment as a major feature of their case plan, where reducing drug testing might be used as an incentive after the person was drug-free for 90 days or more. For those involved in criminal lifestyles, an emphasis on licit work would be reinforced, as well as participation in criminal thinking therapy.

Organisational reinforcers were used to promote the PCS framework. The supervisors in the district offices held learning sessions to reinforce the educational component of the curriculum – recognising that training sessions are merely the beginning of the change process. The learning sessions were geared around the seven chapters of the manuals, which was accompanied by a toolkit referred to as the 'Nuts & Bolts of PCS'. On-site external facilitators also assisted by providing booster sessions, and by developing materials for the officers. Performance measures were used to examine how many clients achieved their goals, and this information was used to highlight the behavioural change requirements of the typologies. The PCS framework was built on a normative-reeducative model to focus on officers readjusting their supervision-related roles and responsibilities to emphasise behavioural change.

Strategic Training Initiative in Community Supervision

The STICS supervision model is based on a General Personality and Cognitive Social Learning (GPCSL) theoretical perspective (Andrews and Bonta, 2010; see also Chapter Nine of this volume). Underlying this perspective are three main assumptions: criminal behaviour is learned via the mechanisms of reinforcement and by vicarious experience; learning results from the interactions of an individual with their environment; and procriminal cognitions and attitudes reinforces behaviours (Bourgon et al, 2010). The authors sought to build on the work of Trotter (1996) by crafting a training for supervision officers that shifted the role of supervision officers from 'case manager', defined by traditional case management techniques, to 'change agent', wherein officers actively engage with the client to directly facilitate change (Bourgon et al, 2011). The authors created STICS with two key interrelated challenges in mind: increasing officer understanding of the fundamentals of cognitive-behavioural interventions, and enhancing officer ability to appropriately incorporate risk-need assessments into intervention plans.

STICS incorporated the risk principle by encouraging officers to focus on high-risk clients for interventions including increasing treatment and programming dosage concomitant with risk level (Andrews and Bonta, 2010). Like PCS, STICS officers were instructed to assess clients' criminogenic needs and focus intervention efforts on these specific needs (Bourgon et al, 2010). The STICS model focused on: a positive officer–client relationship; the use of cognitive-behavioural techniques; simple, understandable and concrete tools and skills with which to teach clients; and the creation of a learning environment through the use of structured sessions. Essentially, the approach is to give a step-wise approach to face-to-face contacts.

The creators recognised four practical steps required to effectively implement cognitive-behavioural techniques. First, officers must identify with the client the link between thoughts and behaviour. STICS officers were taught how to teach clients that behaviour is a direct result of the one's thoughts, and only one's thoughts. The authors note that clients must understand this before officers can engage in any further intervention work. Second, officers must help the client identify personal thinking patters that cause the client's problem behaviours; in other words, officers must work with clients to increase their self-awareness.

To accomplish the first and second tasks, officers use structured activities with clients aimed at teaching clients to understand and practise self-awareness, assisting clients to recognise the consequences of their behaviours, and increasing clients' awareness of personal thinking patterns. Third, officers must teach clients concrete thinking and behavioural skills. Officers teach clients concrete thinking skills via a method referred to as 'countering'. Officers use a variety of behavioural skills including resumé (that is, curriculum vitae) writing, basic communication, negotiation/conflict resolution and problem solving. Finally, officers must facilitate practice and generalisation of these new skills. Practice should include both role play with the supervision officer and practice outside of supervision such as trying communication skills with a partner (Bourgon et al, 2012).

CCPs, as 'techniques of influence', were conceptualised as structuring skills, relationship-building skills, behavioural techniques and cognitive techniques. Structuring techniques focused on how to structure the client sessions. This included a review of the previous session, discussion of previous homework and assigning future homework, focus on intervention targets, and prioritising needs. Homework focused on activities that allowed clients to learn and practise self-awareness skills. Relationship-building skills, aimed at increasing the quality of client relationship, included role clarification, attention to agreement on goals, active listening skills, and effective feedback skills. To incorporate the use of behavioural techniques, officers were instructed on the effective use of reinforcement and disapproval, problem solving, self-management skills, and the use of rehearsal strategies. And finally, to incorporate the use of cognitive-behavioural techniques, officers were instructed on how to identify and address expressions of procriminal attitudes and replace them with prosocial attitudes (Bourgon et al, 2010). At the heart of the STICS model of supervision is an effort to convey to clients, in a concrete and practical manner, that 'the reason they behave as they do is a direct result of their thoughts alone and *for no other reason*' (Bourgon et al, 2012, p 8, original emphasis). The curriculum does not encourage officers to discuss triggers or external events that may be affecting behaviour. The authors note: 'This "external event caused the internal event which caused the behavior" outlook is exactly the kind of thinking we are attempting to change' (Bourgon et al, 2012). This differs from other supervision models that explicitly address triggers.

Implementation of the model included a three-day onsite officer training session covering material in 11 modules. In crafting the training, STICS authors practised what they preached and followed the same principles of learning behaviour underlying CCP. They sought to engage and motivate officers to want to change behaviour, and they modelled the skills and attempted to demonstrate the power of cognitive restructuring, prosocial modelling, and reinforcement. The training focused on the importance of recognising and changing procriminal attitudes and cognitions. The first two modules gave an overview of STICS, provided a rationale for the model, explained the RNR principles, and discussed how to implement them into practice. Module 3 focused on criminogenic needs. Module 4 introduced the concept of procriminal attitudes. Modules 5 through 10 taught the officers skills. Module 5 focused on building a good relationship with clients. Module 6 taught officers how to use a cognitive-behavioural model. Modules 7, 8, and 9 focused on the various techniques of influence targeting cognitive restructuring such as effective reinforcement and disapproval and problem solving. Module 10 consisted of integrating skills into scenarios in which officers practised skills using role play. Finally, Module 11 was an overview of the training and an explanation of upcoming skill maintenance processes. The modules highlight the benefits of using a strategic supervision structure in each client session as well as over the entire supervision period (Bonta et al, 2011). Like PCS, the emphasis is on formal supervision requirements, risk level, needs, targeted interventions and reinforcements.

Skill maintenance was achieved through monthly half-day group meetings, clinical feedback to officers on audiotaped meetings with clients, and a one-day refresher course. STICS probation officers met monthly in groups of three to 12 officers to discuss their use of STICS concepts and skills. Officers participated in discussions around themed audiotaped examples (such as how to teach the behavioural model to a client) provided by trainers prior to the meetings. Trainers provided clinical oversight of the meetings via teleconference, and researchers assessed and tracked officer participation including frequency of attendance and level of participation (for example, engaged in active discussion). Trained officers were encouraged to submit audiotapes for individual clinical feedback. The feedback was provided to officers only when requested and focused on the officer's use of STICS concepts, skills and techniques, with an emphasis on rewarding and encouraging their use. Finally, the one-day refresher course was delivered approximately one year after the initial training (Bonta et al, 2010, 2011). Directors from three Canadian provinces (British Columbia, Saskatchewan and Prince Edward Island) asked for volunteers from staff who supervised adult clients (18 and older) (Bonta et al., 2010; 2011). Eighty out of a possible 710 officers volunteered. Fifty-one were randomised to the treatment group. Of these 51, less than half submitted tapes. Twenty-eight officers did not submit any post-training data.

In an exploratory analysis of the correlates of officer discussion of procriminal attitudes/cognitions and the use of cognitive-behavioural intervention techniques, Bourgon and Gutierrez (2012) found that using relationship skills was independent of using cognitive intervention techniques. However, greater use of cognitive-behavioural intervention techniques was associated with greater use of modelling, behavioural rehearsal and structuring skills, such as having an identified target for change and structuring the session time. The authors propose that this may be due to the increased complexity involved in cognitive intervention techniques, the use of which requires a certain level of familiarly with more fundamental skills such as behavioural and structuring skills, the implication being that officer skill training might benefit from a structure that builds from less to more complex skills.

Staff Training Aimed at Reducing Rearrest

Building on the success of PCS and STICS, researchers with the Administrative Office of US Courts Probation and Pretrial Services crafted and tested a similar supervision model that incorporated RNR principles and CCPs for federal probation. This model, STARR, emphasises improving officers' skills in interactions with clients to align with the principles of RNR and CCPs (Robinson et al, 2011, 2012). The authors of STARR completed analysis on the federal Post Conviction Risk Assessment (PCRA), a third-generation risk-need assessment designed by Administrative Office of the United States (Oleson et al, 2012). The latest version, PCRA 2.0, identifies four major criminogenic needs – cognitions, social networks, alcohol/drug problems and education/employment. The PCRA 2.0 scoring guide includes guidance on intervention concerns for each domain, and that guidance is in line with social learning theory and differential association theory. STARR operationalises CCPs into specific strategies including active listening, role clarification, effective use of authority, effective disapproval, effective reinforcement, effective punishment, problem solving, and teaching, applying and reviewing the cognitive model. The skills fall into one of three categories. Relationship skills include active listening, giving feedback and role clarification. Active listening and feedback are meant to increase client self-efficacy. STARR integrates MI strategies, such as OARS, into many of the skills.

Bridging skills include effective reinforcement, effective disapproval, effective punishment or consequences, and effective use of authority. Effective use of reinforcement binds positive encouragement to prosocial behaviour and encourages client exploration of the current and future benefits of engaging in the desirable behaviour. Effective disapproval entails a swift reprimand, closely tied to a specific problematic behavior, and facilitates client exploration of current and future costs of engaging in the undesirable behaviour; and includes a discussion how to avoid the behaviour in the future. Effective punishment entails delivering punishment followed by a discussion of how to avoid the behaviour in the future. Effective use of authority includes a firm but fair approach to resistant clients wherein officers give clients the option of maintaining undesirable behaviour, outlining the consequences of the continued behaviour, or the option of undertaking desirable behaviour, along with the consequences of that option, and asks the client to choose between the two.

Intervention skills aim to increase client self-awareness of risk factors, develop clients' internal self-control, increase self-efficacy, and, in the vein of STICS, teach clients that thinking controls behaviour. The skills include teaching the cognitive model, applying the cognitive model, reviewing application of the cognitive model, and problem solving. The cognitive model is an exercise that teaches clients to recognise high-risk thoughts and replace them with new thoughts that are likely to lead to a better outcome. At the core of the STARR skills is an effort to have clients internalise the strategies so they can learn and apply them on their own (Robinson et al, 2011). To this end, clients are asked to complete 'thinking reports' – a tool used to examine internal responses to a situation. Thinking reports aspire to help clients more easily work through the cognitive model process.

Somewhat different from the original Andrews and Kiessling (1980) conception of problem solving, in STARR problems are identified by the client and not necessarily related to criminogenic needs. To help the client craft an effective action plan, officers encourage clients to clarify their goal in solving the problem. The client then brainstorms solutions and weighs the costs and benefits of each solution before deciding on a course of action and crafting a reviewable action plan.

Implementation of STARR includes a three-and-a-half-day classroom training that draws on the technology transfer literature. The training examines the model's underlying theory and discusses the curriculum's development. This includes a discussion of the RNR principles and the research on the effectiveness of skill-focused supervision. The training also includes a demonstration of each skill and practice exercises, both via video and in person, in which officers practise skills and receive feedback. Officers also role play the use of skills. Skill cards, which outline the skill steps, serve as a reference for officers. Like STICS, officers send in audiotaped contacts with moderate- or high-risk clients at designated intervals – at the initial meeting, after three months, and after six months. Trained researchers review the tapes and provide feedback to officers. Skill maintenance is enhanced with four booster trainings held over a year, each lasting approximately one hour. Delivered via phone, the sessions focus on specific skill deficits identified on the tapes. The session includes discussion of the specific skills, audiotape examples of the skill, and individual feedback and coaching (Robinson et al, 2011). The classroom training also includes a discussion on the importance of coaching generally, and peer coaching specifically, though it is unclear to what extent peer coaches are trained apart from the standard training and what if any role peer coaches have in implementing the model (see Robinson et al, 2012).

Effective Practices in Community Supervision

The EPICS model, created by researchers at the University of Cincinnati's Corrections Institute (UCCI), builds on the other models with an emphasis on face-to-face interactions with clients (Smith et al, 2012). EPICS includes supervisors and peer coaches to aide in officer skills development and support sustainability. EPICS seamlessly integrates the principles of motivational interviewing into officer skills. The content of EPICS is rooted in RNR principles and the eight service delivery skills identified by the Correctional Program Assessment Inventory (Latessa et al, 2013). Officers learn to increase dosage with high-risk clients, to focus efforts on targeting criminogenic needs (EPICS creators consider antisocial attitudes and beliefs, antisocial peer groups, and certain personality characteristics such as low self-control and lack of problem-solving skills, to be the most appropriate targets for officer–client sessions), and to use interventions rooted in social learning theory and cognitive-behavioural practices (Smith et al, 2012). The EPICS model operationalises the expanded CCPs (anticriminal modelling, effective reinforcement, effective disapproval, effective use of authority, structured learning, problem solving, cognitive restructuring and relationship skills) into concrete skills for officer use. EPICS operationalisation closely aligns with that for STARR. Many skills steps are identical or vary only slightly.

EPICS adds to the three STARR skill categories with the addition of assessment skills. Like STARR, EPICS relationship skills include active listening, giving feedback and role clarification. Active listening and giving feedback, like many of the EPICS skills, incorporate principles of motivational interviewing such as using OARS. Role clarification includes an explanation of the goals of supervision and what clients can expect. It sets the stage for a collaborative supervision process by asking clients what they hope to accomplish during supervision. Assessment skills include risk assessment and behavioural analysis. The behavioural analysis is an information-gathering tool meant to help officers and clients recognise patterns in behaviour. It allows for a deeper understanding of contextual factors associated with criminogenic needs, and the information gathered informs the use of high-level intervention skills. Omitting effective use of punishment, the bridging skills are identical to those for STARR. They include effective use of reinforcement, effective use of disapproval (both of which rely on MI principles to evoke change talk), and effective use of authority. Lastly, the intervention skills include problem solving, the cognitive model, and the so-called RACE skills (Recognize, Avoid, Cope, Evaluate). Problem solving entails working through a client-identified problem and guiding the client to consider options, weigh the costs and benefits of each option, and eventually craft a reviewable action plan. EPICS trains officers to refer clients to community-based treatment providers that use cognitive-behavioural approaches. Where STICS focused narrowly on teaching clients that behaviour was a product of their thoughts alone, like STARR, EPICS also incorporates additional barriers to change and focuses on increasing motivation to change (Latessa et al, 2013).

Implementation of the model includes a three-day, in-person training session for officers that includes opportunities to practise the skills. The first day of training focuses on the rationale, development and structure of the EPICS model. The second day of training focuses on the model's interventions (that is, cognitive restructuring, problem solving and structured learning) and their mechanisms of action. The third day of training focuses on behavioural practices (that is, anticriminal modelling, effective use of reinforcement, effective use of disapproval and effective use of authority), and working with families and other sources of collateral support. Skill maintenance and development is done through monthly coaching sessions for both supervisors and officers that last two years (a total of 24 sessions). Sessions act as refreshers of the EPICS model. Topics include the structure of client contacts (that is, check-in, review, intervention and homework), helping clients recognise the link between thoughts and behaviours, identifying high-risk situations, identifying antisocial thinking and behaviours and alternative prosocial thoughts and behaviours, addressing client motivation, skill building and problem solving, anticriminal modelling, effective reinforcement, effective disapproval, effective use of authority, and officer–client relationships (Latessa et al, 2013). Coaching sessions mirror officer client contact sessions in structure, beginning with a check-in, and questions and concerns, followed by a review of the previous session during which officers ask questions and receive performance feedback on audiotaped contacts. Following the review, external facilitators present on a different EPICS topic from the initial training, which includes demonstrations of the topic via audio, video, or live modelling. Finally, officers practice the skill and get feedback from peers and UCCI presenters (Latessa et al, 2013).

The EPICS implementation model includes infrastructure for fidelity and sustainability. To ensure fidelity, officers are required to submit at least one audio-recorded client contact per month. EPICS-trained researchers evaluate the recording and provide officers with feedback on their use of skills (Latessa, 2012; Smith et al, 2012). To bolster sustainability, supervisors and peer coaches receive additional training for supervising the use of EPICS in practice and providing continuous support to officers in their use of the EPICS skills (Smith et al, 2012). The model also includes supervisor-specific components such as a designated period of time following coaching sessions for external coaches and supervisors to discuss the coaching session, identify possible barriers to implementation and work through possible solutions. Supervisors also participate in running coaching sessions with staff, and to help in this effort, the supervisors meet with external coaches two days prior to review audiotape feedback, and discuss the key skills highlighted in the upcoming session. In this meeting, external coaches outline the framework for the discussion and clarify content, roles and responsibilities. Supervisors are also required to carry a small caseload to practise using EPICS skills. The model highlights the importance of providing individual support to officers in addition to group coaching sessions. To increase officer self-efficacy in using the skills, UCCI encourages sites to have supervisors review audiotapes and written feedback by the external coach with officers (Smith et al, 2012; Latessa et al, 2013; Labrecque and Smith, 2015).

Skills for Offender Assessment and Responsivity in New Goals

SOARING2 diverges from previous supervision models by trading the in-person training that typically starts the implementation of a new model for an eLearning curriculum that users access at their own pace over the course of several weeks. The eLearning component is an interactive system incorporating simulations, real-time feedback, printable resources, audio enhancements and video demonstrations. Similar to the curricula described previously, SOARING2 is based on RNR principles, but unlike other models, focuses more on understanding the knowledge associated with CCPs rather than concrete operationalisation of the CCPs. The SOARING2 model also departs from previous curricula in the inclusion of a focus on desistance. This curriculum grew out of the need to help practitioners understand the core concepts of CCP since the basic knowledge is not available in other curricula and existing trainings. SOARING2 users can choose modules targeting a variety of topic areas. The standard version, however, consists of five modules where each module includes a basic, intermediate and advanced lesson; this moves the individual from building knowledge to applying concepts. These three levels of competency provide opportunity for officers to learn the material. The advanced level requires officers to evaluate case scenarios and answer associated questions. Module 1 instructs users on the RNR principles as well as stabilisers and destabilisers. Module 2 instructs users on the principles and practices of motivational communication, and particularly on supporting and motivating clients through the behaviour change process in the face of resistance to change. Module 3 instructs users on creating individualised case plans, taking into account gender and cultural considers and incorporating graduated sanctions and incentives. Module 4 walks users through the problem-solving skill steps, and is consistent with STICS in that problems should relate to criminogenic needs. Module 5 represents more of a radical departure from other supervision models with its lesson on desistance, a strength-based approach to understanding how and why people desist from criminal behaviour.

SOARING2 differs in the tools provided to officers. Rather than a cognitive model, SOARING2 teaches officers to use a behavioural offence chain. Similar to the cognitive model, the behavioural offence chain asks the client to discuss background factors and thoughts leading up to criminal behaviour; however, the behavioural offense chain focuses on emotions and coping mechanisms, the implication being that clients should learn new coping mechanisms. Rather than detailing the steps to effective use of reinforcement or effective use of disapproval, SOARING2 provides instruction on the use of graduated sanctions and incentives along with a sample sanctions and incentives schedule. Finally, the desistance process map helps users focus on and strengthen existing and possible desistance factors. Key lesson takeaways are operationalised into 20 officer skills in four categories: increasing client engagement; creating a quality working relationship; effectively assessing and managing risk; and problem solving. Many of the SOARING2 skills require the use of motivational interviewing tactics such as OARS. SOARING2 encourages the exploration of triggers and encourages officers to have structured client sessions that include the following: check-in; engage client; identify issue of the day; problem solve the issue of the day; rehearse proposed alternative actions; reinforce effort and strengths; assign homework; and summarise session.

SOARING2 does not include booster sessions for officers as all users have continued access to all course materials and module resources, which include brief refreshers of the material. Users are also tested on the material as they go to ensure a level of understanding before moving on. Imperative to the SOARING2 model is the use of internal coaches. Prior to implementation, agency leaders identify internal coaches. These internal coaches, typically supervisors, complete the eLearning component before SOARING2 is rolled out to the rest of the agency. Coaches also attend a two-day coaches training course with researchers from George Mason University (GMU) that focuses on their role as a coach and the supervision skills which they will coach officers to use. SOARING2 team members from GMU train coaches on giving feedback to officers as they complete the advanced quizzes in the eLearning programme, and on using an observation rating scale to rate officers' use of skills. Once coaches have completed the eLearning programme, they facilitate a kick-off meeting with their team of students to explain the SOARING2 process, including purpose and expectations. Once staff begin the eLearning programme, coaches grade advanced quizzes and provide feedback to officers. Officers complete the eLearning programme by passing all quizzes with a minimum of 80%, after which coaches begin observations. Coaches observe three to five officer–client contacts per officer each quarter. Immediately following the contact, coaches provide officers with feedback using an immediate feedback form.

The process is collaborative in nature, as the form asks clients to discuss strengths and areas for improvement before coaches give their own feedback. The feedback ends with officer and coach crafting the goals for future client contacts. Coaches assess officer use of skills on the 20-skill observation rating form and provide feedback at regular coaching sessions while using positive reinforcement (Maass et al, 2013; Maass, 2017).

Discussion

This chapter set out to explore three questions: what are the new revised face-to-face contacts promoted under the new supervision models, and how do they differ from a compliance driven model?; how do the curricula advance different supervision practices?; and what should a research agenda include for assessing what is important to accomplish in supervision to reduce recidivism? To answer these questions, we have looked at the theoretical foundations of the models and compared their various components and implementation strategies.

The supervision models collectively referred to as 'evidence-based' supervision or 'RNR-based' supervision move beyond the notion of managing risk. While risk-need assessments appear to align with technocratic management in that they do seek to 'sort and classify, to separate the less from the more dangerous, and to deploy control strategies rationally' (Feeley and Simon, 1992, p 452), they also focus on the individual and on rehabilitative measures targeting dynamic risk factors. These new supervision models move beyond a simple focus on compliance to explore ways to engender cooperation with court-required oversight. The emphasis is on tailoring supervision to the drivers of criminal behaviour (risk-need) and the degree to which the client is making progress (problem solving).

Table 11.1 compares the components included in each model. PCS focuses on motivation as a key component through advancing the client's voice by establishing common goals and objectives of supervision. It uses a cognitive-behavioural model to focus on thinking

Table 11.1: Comparison of supervision model components

Skills/themes	PCS	STICS-II	STARR	EPICS-II	SOARING2
Risk assessment	✓	✓	✓	✓	✓
Identifying criminogenic needs	✓	✓	✓	✓	✓
Cognitive restructuring	✓	✓	✓	✓	✓
Effective use of authority	✓	✓	✓	✓	✓
Effective disapproval	✓	✓	✓	✓	✓
Effective reinforcement	✓	✓	✓	✓	✓
Effective problem solving (client defines problem)	✓		✓	✓	
Effective problem solving (risk-related problem)	✓	✓			✓
Active listening	✓	✓	✓	✓	✓
Use of MI	✓		✓	✓	✓
Role clarification	✓	✓	✓	✓	✓
Effective feedback	✓	✓	✓	✓	✓
Application of the cognitive model	✓	✓	✓	✓	✓
Prosocial modeling	✓	✓	✓	✓	✓
Community partnerships	✓	✓			✓
Structured sessions	✓	✓	✓	✓	✓

and behaviour, while emphasising attention to the unique risk needs of individuals and the drivers of their criminal behaviour. STICS is a cognitive–behavioural intervention that focuses on criminal attitudes to the exclusion of other criminogenic needs, the assumption being that attitudes affect all other criminogenic needs (for example, lack of employment as a risk factor should be addressed by addressing a person's belief's about work) (Bourgon et al, 2010). STARR and EPICS have many of the same skills while building on PCS and STICS by incorporating additional tools to help supervision officers better use the skills and to integrate them. STARR uses skill cards to serve as quick guides for officers on the skill steps. EPICS adds 'assessment skills' to the existing categories of skills (relationship, bridging and intervention) in STARR and STICS. SOARING2 breaks from the others with a focus on building and applying knowledge of RNR, motivation and engagement, case planning, problem solving and desistance. SOARING2 skills tie to engaging clients in the supervision process, establishing a good working relationship, managing dynamic risk factors and situations (criminogenic needs, destabilisers and triggers), and problem solving.

All supervision models discussed here are rooted in the CCPs and thus share assumptions about the nature of learning and criminal behaviour in particular. They share the following common goals: applying the principles of RNR within the context of individual case management; improving officer use of relationship and intervention skills related to client behaviour change; developing officer ability to balance the dual supervision goals of care and control; and ensuring treatment fidelity by providing officer feedback. The models do differ in how CCPs are operationalised. PCS focuses attention on different typologies of client drivers that affect criminal behavior, whereas the others techniques focus on the structure of the interaction. SOARING2 includes a focus on desistance to reiterate the emphasis on a strength-based approach (Farrall and Maruna, 2004; McNeill et al, 2012; Ward et al, 2012).

From an implementation perspective, all models recognise that the training session is just a beginning. All use some form of coaching or booster sessions. STICS, STARR, and EPICS all rely on the use of audiotapes and outside evaluators to ensure fidelity. All use coaching sessions run by a trained facilitator (monthly for STICS and EPICS, quarterly for STARR). SOARING2 relies on in-person observations and feedback completed by trained in-house coaches (typically front-line supervisors) and does not include additional coaching sessions facilitated by someone outside of the agency. Table 11.2 compares implementation methods of the various supervision models.

All of the models attempt to overcome practical challenges to implementing evidence in real-world practice. This includes probation officer buy-in and convincing probation officers that their clients' antisocial behaviour is a product of learning. All developers acknowledge the importance of increasing officer buy-in and participation by providing an explanation of the problem. Despite this, questions remain to be answered about the feasibility of supervision

Table 11.2: Comparison of implementation strategy

Implementation strategy	PCS	STICS-II	STARR	EPICS-II	SOARING2
In-person officer training	✓	✓	✓	✓	
eLearning					✓
Internal coaches	✓		✓	✓	✓
External coaches/mentors	✓	✓	✓	✓	✓
In-person coaches training		✓	✓	✓	✓
Officer booster training	✓	✓	✓	✓	✓
Coach booster training	✓			✓	✓
Observations					✓
Tapes reviewed		✓	✓	✓	

models in existing agency frameworks, and efforts to this point have helped refine new avenues for research.

One example of a practical challenge to existing models is the use of high-level working relationship and engagement skills. Many of the models require the use of motivational interviewing skills (or at least some aspect of MI), but taking into account the degree of difficulty in learning MI (even for professional counsellors), we must ask how realistic the expectations of these models are. Other questions of interest focus on what coaching sessions should look like, how often they should occur, and who should be involved. This is an area of future research, since there are few studies that examine the best models of coaching. One study conducted in a juvenile justice setting found that coaching that reinforced a social climate to support the innovation was more important than coaching for skills development (Taxman et al, 2014). This study also illustrates the importance of agency support to the implementation and sustainability of these models. Future research should examine how best to bring this about. A few unanswered questions remain. What does verbal commitment look like, and how can agencies provide the time and resources to support the additional demands placed on officers and coaches? How can agencies best incorporate discussions that are collaborative, reciprocal, and experiential?

Conclusion

Collectively this review has illustrated that the main curricula to advance supervision practices have many similarities and differences. A major question is the degree to which attention is focused on strengths or building the individuals sense of self-efficacy. The typical criminology-focused interventions (namely, STICS, STARR and EPICS) seek to transform behaviour by assisting clients to understand what makes their behaviours and thoughts antisocial (criminal). The style is more deficit-based in that it looks at the client's past behaviour with an emphasis on trying to retrain the individual. PCS and SOARING2 are focused more on incentivising positive behaviours. Until comparative research is available, it is unclear which approach will have an impact on recidivism behaviour. Now that these curricula are available, there is a need to research the efficacy of the curricula, training methods, coaching methods and officer skills development. While Chadwick et al (2014) note that studies find that clients fare better with officers trained in these curricula (about a 13% reduction in recidivism), the research is not clear which techniques officers use, which techniques clients find useful, and which aspects of the new supervision models are effective. In other words, we now have models to test, and there is a need to develop an understanding of the causal mechanisms that bring about officer skills development and client change. Understanding effective supervision practices is still in its infancy.

References

Akers, R.L. (2011) *Social Learning and Social Structure: A General Theory of Crime and Deviance*, New Brunswick, NJ: Transaction Publishers.

Andrews, D.A. (1979a) *The Friendship Model of Voluntary Action and Controlled Evaluations of Correctional Practices: Notes on Relationships with Behaviour Theory and Criminology*, Ottawa: Ministry of Correctional Services.

Andrews, D.A. (1979b) *The Dimensions of Correctional Counselling and of Supervisory Process in Probation and Parole*, Ottawa: Ministry of Correctional Services.

Andrews, D.A. and Bonta, J. (2010) *The Psychology of Criminal Conduct*, New Providence, NJ: Routledge.

Andrews, D.A. and Kiessling, J.J. (1980) 'Program structure and effective correctional practices: a summary of the CaVIC research', in R.R. Ross and P. Gendreau (eds) *Effective Correctional Treatment*, Scarborough, Ontario: Butterworth, pp 439–463.

Bandura, A. (1969) *Principles of Behaviour Modification*, New York, NY: Holt, Rinehart and Winston.

Bandura, A. (1977) *Social Learning Theory*, Upper Saddle River, NJ: Prentice Hall.

Bonta, J., Bourgon, G., Rugge, T., Scott, T.L., Yessine, A.K., Gutierrez, L. and Li, J. (2011) 'An experimental demonstration of training probation officers in evidence-based community supervision', *Criminal Justice and Behavior*, 38(11): 1127–1148.

Bonta, J., Bourgon, G., Rugge, T., Scott, T.L., Yessine, A.K., Gutierrez, L.K. and Public Safety Canada (2010) *The Strategic Training Initiative in Community Supervision: Risk-Need-Responsivity in the Real World 2010–01*, Ottawa: Public Safety Canada.

Bourgon, G. and Gutierrez, L. (2012) 'The general responsivity principle in community supervision: the importance of probation officers using cognitive intervention techniques and its influence on recidivism', *Journal of Crime & Justice*, 35(2): 149–166.

Bourgon, G., Gutierrez, L. and Ashton, J. (2011) 'The evolution of community supervision practice: the transformation from case manager to change agent', *Irish Probation Journal*, 8: 28–48.

Bourgon, G., Gutierrez, L. and Ashton, J. (2012) 'The evolution of community supervision practice: the transformation from case manager to change agent', *Federal Probation*, 76(2): 27–35.

Bourgon, G., Bonta, J., Rugge, T. and Scott, T.L. (2010) 'The role of program design, implementation, and evaluation in evidence-based real world community supervision', *Federal Probation*, 74(1): 2–15.

Burgess, R.L. and Akers, R.L. (1966) 'A differential association-reinforcement theory of criminal behaviour', *Social Problems*, 14(2): 128–147.

Chadwick, N., Dewolf, A. and Serin, R. (2014) 'Effectively training community supervision: a meta-analytic review of the impact on offender outcomes', *Criminal Justice and Behavior*, 42(10): 977–989.

Drake, E.K. (2011) *'What Works' in Community Supervision: Interim Report*, Document No. 11-12-1201, Olympia: Washington State Institute for Public Policy, available at www.wsipp.wa.gov/ReportFile/1094.

Farrall, S. and Maruna, S. (2004) 'Desistance-focused criminal justice policy research: introduction to a special issue on desistance from crime and public policy', *The Howard Journal of Crime and Justice*, 43(4): 358–367.

Feeley, M.M. and Simon, J. (1992) 'The new penology: notes on the emerging strategy of corrections and its implications', *Criminology*, 30(4): 449–474.

Gendreau. P. and Andrews, D.A. (1989) *The Correctional Program Assessment Inventory*, New Brunswick, Canada: University of New Brunswick.

Labrecque, R.M. and Smith, P. (2015) 'Does training and coaching matter? An 18-month evaluation of a community supervision model', *Victims & Offenders*, 12(2): 1–20.

Latessa, E. (2012) 'Effective practices in community supervision (EPICS)', Presentation for the Colorado Alliance for Drug Endangered Children at the Best Practices Meet the Community Conference, 10-12 April, Denver, Colorado.

Latessa, E.J., Smith, P., Schweitzer, M. and Labrecque, R. (2013) *Evaluation of the Effective Practices in Community Supervision Model (EPICS) in Ohio*, Cincinnati, OH: University of Cincinnati, School of Criminal Justice.

Maass, S.A. (2017) *Individual, Organizational, and Training Design Influences on Probation Training Outcomes*, Doctoral dissertation, Virginia: George Mason University.

Maass, S.A., Taxman, F.S., Serin, R., Crites, E., Watson, C.A., and Lloyd, C. (2013) 'SOARING 2: An eLearning training program to improve knowledge of EBPs', Paper presented at the American Society of Criminology Annual Conference, 20–23 November, Atlanta, GA.

McNeill, F., Farrall, S., Lightowler, C. and Maruna, S. (2012) 'Reexamining evidence-based practice in community corrections: beyond "a confined view" of what works', *Justice Research and Policy*, 14(1): 35–60.

Miller, W.R. (1983) 'Motivational interviewing with problem drinkers', *Behavioural and Cognitive Psychotherapy*, 11(2): 147–172.

Miller, W.R. and Rollnick, S. (2012) *Motivational Interviewing: Helping People Change*, New York, NY: Guilford Press.

Oleson, J.C., VanBenschoten, S., Robinson, C., Lowenkamp, C.T. and Holsinger, A.M. (2012) 'Actuarial and clinical assessment of criminogenic needs: identifying supervision priorities among federal probation officers', *Journal of Crime and Justice*, 35(2): 239–248.

Robinson, C.R., VanBenschoten, S., Alexander, M. and Lowenkamp, C.T. (2011) 'A random (almost) study of Staff Training Aimed at Reducing Re-arrest (STARR): reducing recidivism through intentional design', *Federal Probation*, 75(2): 57–63.

Robinson, C.R., Lowenkamp, C.T., Holsinger, A.M., VanBenschoten, S., Alexander, M. and Oleson, J.C. (2012) 'A random study of Staff Training Aimed at Reducing Re-arrest (STARR): using Core Correctional Practices in probation interactions', *Journal of Crime and Justice*, 35(2): 167–188.

Smith, P., Schweitzer, M., Labrecque, R.M. and Latessa, E.J. (2012) 'Improving probation officers' supervision skills: an evaluation of the EPICS model', *Journal of Crime and Justice*, 35(2): 189–199.

Taxman, F.S. (2008) 'No illusions: offender and organizational change in Maryland's proactive community supervision efforts', *Criminology & Public Policy*, 7(2): 275–302.

Taxman, F.S., Shephardson, E. and Byrne, J.M. (2004) *Tools of the Trade: A Guide to Incorporating Science into Practice*, Washington, DC: National Institute of Corrections.

Taxman, F.S., Henderson, C., Young, D.W. and Farrell, J. (2014) 'The impact of training interventions on organizational readiness to support innovations in juvenile justice offices', *Administration of Mental Health Policy and Mental Health Services Research*, 41(2): 177–188, doi: 10.1007/s10488-012-0445-5.

Trotter, C. (1996) 'The impact of different supervision practices in community corrections', *Australian and New Zealand Journal of Criminology*, 29(1), 1–18.

Ward, T., Yates, P.M. and Willis, G.M. (2012) 'The Good Lives model and the Risk Need Responsivity model: a critical response to Andrews, Bonta, and Wormith (2011)', *Criminal Justice and Behavior*, 39(1): 94–110.

TWELVE

Understanding emotions as effective practice in English probation: the performance of emotional labour in building relationships

Andrew Fowler, Jake Phillips and Chalen Westaby

Introduction

In this chapter, we examine the performance of emotional labour by probation practitioners to uncover the complex use of emotion that underpins the development of the officer–offender relationship inherent to effective probation practice. We begin by mapping the way in which the use of emotion has been marginalised from policy over the past 30 years, making links to the rise of managerialism and the 'what works' movement, as well as more recent developments such as the Offender Engagement Programme and the Skills for Effective Engagement and Development (SEED) programme, which sought to pilot a practice-based model based on evidence of what works to reduce reoffending (NOMS, 2011; see also Chapter Ten of this volume). We then use data that were generated through interviews with probation practitioners to analyse one aspect of SEED – the development of the relationship. We do this through the lens of emotional labour. In doing so, we focus on the way in which practitioners engage in both deep and surface acting to get to know and understand their clients as well as create clear boundaries. These are the two elements of practice that are seen to be crucial in the creation of effective professional relationships in the SEED model. We conclude by arguing that the development of the relationship with the client as described in the SEED model requires considerable emotional labour that has, hitherto, been unacknowledged in probation policy, and reflect on what might need to be done, in light of our findings, were probation providers to consider reintroducing SEED following the implementation of the government's Transforming Rehabilitation reforms, which privatised around 60% of probation work.

Emotions as effective practice

It is necessary to offer some context to understand how this research sits in terms of literature on both emotional labour and effective probation practice. The relative importance attached to, or marginalisation of, the use of emotion in one-to-one supervision can be mapped against the 'disappearance and appearance of the relationship' as discussed by Burnett and McNeill (2005, p 222). While this literature review aims to trace the ebb and flow of the prominence attached to the role of emotion in effective practice, Garland (2001, p 22) cautions that 'talk should not be mistaken for action'. The presence or absence of 'emotion work' in academic literature, government policy and criminal justice practice does not account for the continued use of emotion by practitioners in the field – this is what we seek to bring to light. The development of probation policy in the 1980s and 1990s has been well rehearsed (Raynor and Vanstone, 2007). In this chapter, we are interested primarily in the way in which the efficacy of probation coincided with concerns about the perceived 'softness' (Garland, 2001; Robinson and Ugwudike, 2012) of the probation service. These developments, combined with successive governments' belief in the market principles of efficiency, cost effectiveness and economy (the role of competition) (see Ranson and Stewart, 1994; Deering, 2011) resulted in the first National Standards (Home Office, 1992) placing more emphasis on enforcement and the performance of this enforcement. This manifestation of National Standards as targets, performance data and accountability arguably represents the rise of a more technical form of practice that is subject to routine practices (Robinson, 2003). This is in opposition to the 'indeterminacy' of practice based on specialist knowledge, its interpretation and the use of professional judgement. The loss of control over the labour process or 'technical proletarization' (Derber, 1982, cited in Robinson, 2003, p 594) can be analogised to Hochschild's (1983) flight attendants in her seminal work on emotional labour, *The Managed Heart*. Hochschild describes the way in which employees lose autonomy over how they use their feelings in their work. Emotional labour is defined by Hochschild (1983, p 7) as 'the management of a way of feeling to create a publicly observable facial and bodily display ... for a wage'. Therefore, workers are expected to manage their feelings in accordance with display rules as prescribed by the organisation for which they work (Hochschild, 1983; Ashforth and Humphrey, 1993). In order for a worker to engage in emotional labour, Hochschild described three necessary criteria. The worker must first interact either face to face or voice to voice with members of the public. Second, the worker must be expected to manage both the emotional state of those members of the public they interact with as well as their own. Finally, the organisation must have a certain amount of control over the expected emotional labour of the worker. This can be through either training or supervision.

It is argued that with the shift to 'case management' from 'caseworker' (see Burnett, 1996), surveilling relationships discouraged probation staff from forming a relationship in the late 1990s to early 2000s. Burnett and McNeill (2005, p 224) comment that 'current practice, gleaned from websites for probation areas and training consortia and from key documents give little hint of the support, friendliness and warmth that once characterised the supervision of offenders'. Furthermore, the severing of probation work from social work, a 'punitive turn' and the introduction of cognitive-behavioural approaches replacing person-centred work changed the interaction between supervisor and supervisee. This toughening up of the image of probation work, which includes the movement away from associations with the welfare of offenders, labelling court disposals as 'punishments' and introducing measurable standards of change, further marginalised the importance of emotions in practice at the policy level.

The 'what works' approach (Chapman and Hough, 1998) is concerned with the enquiry into effective probation practice. Ugwudike and colleagues (2014) argue that the 'what works' approach is based on three key principles of risk, need and responsivity introduced by Andrews and various colleagues in the 1990s (see Andrews and Kiessling, 1980; Dowden and Andrews, 1999). The subsequent emergence of core correctional practices (Dowden and Andrews, 2004) and the Strategic Training Initiative in Community Supervision (Bonta et al, 2008; Chapter Nine of this volume) represented structured training, mentoring and evaluation of key skills and characteristics required by probation officers for effective practice. This type of research had the potential to bring the study of emotions in from the margins, given its emphasis on interpersonal contact. However, the concept of responsivity, where the use of emotion is likely to be most relevant, was neglected (Porporino, 2010). For example, consistency in practice was favoured over relationship building (Mair, 2004). While emotion is inherent in descriptions of these approaches to best practice, how emotions are used in the process is never made explicit.

The emergence of the Offender Management Model (NOMS, 2005, p 13) was underpinned by the argument that practice should be about 'forming and working through warm, open and enthusiastic relationships'. Again, such a development could have represented the re-emergence of the significance of emotion through the emphasis placed on the officer– offender relationship. To some degree, this can be seen in the SEED training (NOMS, 2011). However, within this training the use of emotions still remains implicit and unexplored. The aim of SEED was to 'reduce unnecessary prescription through process-based performance targets and National Standards to enable practitioners to use their professional discretion and skills to reduce reoffending' (Rex and Hosking, 2013, p 333). Rex and Hosking recognised that 'organisational culture could enable or inhibit effective engagement with service users' (2013, p 336) and sought to introduce training to reinforce evidence-led best practice to support purposeful and focused engagement with people on probation. Unfortunately, the implementation of SEED coincided with Transforming Rehabilitation (MoJ, 2013; see also Chapter Four of this volume), a major reform package that has led to the privatisation of probation services for low- and medium-risk offenders and the creation of the National Probation Service (NPS), which supervises high-risk offenders. This meant that this project was not a priority for the fragmented and emerging organisations. Arguably, then, the opportunity to explore in greater detail the use of emotion in relation to effective practice was lost.

We would argue that the use of emotion in effective probation practice has not been ignored, but rather marginalised. This is not to say that no studies have been conducted showing the importance of emotion in effective practice. For example, in her interviews with people on probation, Rex (1999) found that for probationers to feel committed and positively engaged, the probation officer needed to demonstrate empathy and a capacity to listen, to show interest and understanding, and to enable them to talk. Moreover, Trotter (1996, 2012) found that empathy was linked to lower levels of recidivism, and desistance literature recommends creating 'hope and optimism' (McNeill and Weaver, 2010). The quality of the relationship between supervisor and supervisee is significant to the goals of reducing reoffending and working towards change. In addition, the use of emotion is implicit in the description of what is found to be effective practice. Knight (2014, p 34) highlights the fact that no specific reference is made in the core correctional practice skills model (a model of practice that is informed by the principles of risk, need and responsivity as well as underpinned by evidence around staff skills and characteristics) 'to the significance of self-awareness of emotions, or of the effective management and regulation of emotion in workers'. Moreover, she argues that the use of emotions is regarded as ordinary and expected, as a 'soft skill' as opposed to the 'hard' productive skills of 'managing and enabling change' (Knight, 2014, p 8).

The study

We aim to build on this work by considering probation work as 'emotionful' (Bolton 2000, p 582), an 'emotional arena' (Crawley, 2004a, p 413), or 'emotionally charged arena' (Knight, 2014, p 7). In this chapter, we use the powerful analytic lens (Crawley, 2004b, p 250) of emotional labour to help us understand and unpick much of the emotion management that is required in the relationship-building process. Phillips (2013) states that practitioners find it hard to articulate how they create the relationship; this chapter contributes to our understanding of the role of emotions in this process.

In order to shed light on the way in which effective practice requires the use of emotion, we concentrate on one element of effective practice in SEED, relationship building, and analyse it through the lens of emotional labour. The reasons for focusing on SEED are twofold. First, SEED was an excellent opportunity to implement evidence-based practice with a focus on effectiveness as measured outcomes rather than outputs, as well as an opportunity for implementing practice that was underpinned by theories of desistance (McNeill, 2006). Second, a reintroduction of a slightly revised form of SEED has been mooted by a senior leadership team in the NPS. This, in our view, is a positive development, but we would urge any implementation to take account of the emotional labour aspect of this way of working.

Methodology

Following a pilot study, we conducted semi-structured interviews with probation officers in the NPS in England. This method of data collection was specifically chosen for the rich data it would produce, rather than its generalisability (Denscombe, 2014). A purposive sampling technique was used, and the only criterion was that participants worked in the NPS. Approval for the research was granted by the National Research Committee of the National Offender Management Service, and practitioners were invited take part by responding to an advertisement sent out on our behalf by a research officer in the NPS. We had intended to interview both probation officers (POs) and probation service officers (PSOs), but only POs responded to the call for participants. Thus, the sample was self-selecting. Therefore, there is the potential for skewed data, as those who had something to say would have been more likely to volunteer. However, most of the participants knew very little about the research before the interviews started and wished to volunteer purely out of interest.

The study is geographically bounded as probation workers were recruited for interview from one division of the NPS. In total, 18 POs agreed to be interviewed, and the sample consisted of 12 women and five men. Experience as a qualified PO ranged from six months to 29 years. Participants' ages ranged from 30 to 64, and all except one participant described themselves as white British. The remaining participant described their ethnicity as mixed. We were given access to six local delivery units that employ around 240 POs (MoJ, 2015). Therefore, we interviewed circa 8% of available POs. The majority of participants were 'generic' POs, but we also interviewed three court liaison officers as well as some participants who had specialist roles working with particular clients, such as women or sex offenders. The data were analysed by the three authors using thematic analysis (Braun and Clarke, 2006).

Findings

Before analysing the data, it is interesting and important to note the juxtaposition of the two requirements outlined in SEEDS[1] relating to relationship building. In order to build relationships, SEEDS required practitioners to combine clear boundaries with work to get to know and understand the individual (NOMS, 2011; Rex et al, 2012). These requirements clearly reflect the dual role of probation practitioners, to protect the public and assess the potential risk of clients, as well as to motivate and encourage clients to change. When describing the emotions used to engage in effective probation practice, the majority of practitioners refer to those emotions required to get to know and understand the individual earlier on in the interview. Therefore, we begin by exploring the emotions used in this process, before moving on to the role of emotions in creating clear boundaries.

Work to get to know and understand the client: the importance of empathy

Empathy was the emotion referred to most frequently, with 13 of the 18 participants discussing empathy explicitly, and three referring to it implicitly. This is perhaps unsurprising given the fact that empathy is described as a necessary element of the building relationships aspect of SEEDS and can be found on the engagement skills checklist resource in the *SEED Practitioner Workbook* (NOMS, 2011) under style and motivational interviewing principles. The description of empathy provided by participants, as well as how and why it is used, demonstrates the complexity of this type of emotional labour. Participants who referred to empathy, and indeed any type of emotion, were asked to define it. Participants generally understood empathy to be the ability to put oneself in the position of the client to gain an understanding of them and their situation.

> I think you need to be able to, you know, try and put yourself in their shoes for a little while and, you know, you maybe would react differently but it's about understanding how they react. So I think that's a, you know, a given really for any probation officer, that ability to you know try and, and put yourself in their shoes. (PO19)

Reference was also made to the reasons why empathy was considered to be important. Central to these discussions was the role it plays in developing a good relationship with clients:

> [Empathy is] the main one really isn't it? It's a sense of understanding where they are, how they've come to be where they are and trying to build a relationship. So, I think … you've got to try and get some sort of sense of commonality between yourself and the client to build that relationship and help them move forward. (PO20)

Furthermore, two participants also explicitly referred to the difference between empathy and sympathy. One participant comments that sympathy is not 'constructive', while another elaborates further, referring to sympathy as not allowing the client to 'move forward':

> [Y]ou can express sympathy I suppose if something happens, but we want things to move forward. So we don't want people to look back and almost give them a reason to feel sorry about where they are and that kind of stuff. You know, you just need, we need to understand where they are and help them understand that as well. (PO20)

The importance of assisting clients to 'move forward' is also highlighted by another participant, who describes how she uses empathy as an empowerment tool to assist clients to effect change:

> ... trying to be a bit more, I suppose, empowering for them rather than just, you know, going down to, 'Oh yeah it's terrible isn't it?'... because it doesn't really help them longer term, you know.... I think if people have a very negative outlook on something then it's difficult for them to try and get out of that situation that they're in because, and if then you then end up being in that and saying, 'Oh yeah it is rubbish and it's not your fault and it's all the rest of it.' You know, then it's not going to help them help themselves. (PO12)

This is related to the central value of probation practice – the belief in the capacity for change. Empathy in this context is being used to provide positivity to the client in an attempt to help them develop their assets and thereby shift the focus into their strengths rather than their deficiencies (Kurtz and Linnemann, 2006; Ward and Maruna, 2007). In turn, this can be linked to the importance of optimism and hope that is present in the desistance literature.

Other practitioners described using different techniques for displaying empathy to clients. Arguably, the very definition of empathy provided by probation practitioners suggests the need to use deep acting in order to evoke an empathic response towards the client. Deep acting was first described by Hochschild (1983) and is the concept whereby a person produces an emotion directly (by invoking feelings related to that emotion) or indirectly by producing those emotions through a trained imagination.

> I mean you can never live anybody; no two lives are identical but ... everyone's got some sort of life experience, whatever that may be ... and I think that's how you, you know, you kind of click into those, those feelings and those, your own background to be able to say, 'Well, you know it wasn't always easy for me but, you know, look at, this is how you do it.'... (PO18)

Studies of emotional labour highlight both positive and negative consequences for participants who use deep acting. With respect to the former, studies have found that workers who engage in deep acting feel more personal accomplishment and authenticity than those who do not (Bhowmick and Zubin, 2016). Indeed, for one participant, this type of acting ensures an authenticity, which in turn assists in further building the relationship between themselves and the client:

> Because they've got to feel to some level that you understand what, where they're coming from. You know it's not always easy because they'll say, 'Well you didn't grow up on a council estate in grotty [xxx] and with an alcoholic father who beat you.' Do you know what I mean? But it's just about getting across that even though you haven't necessarily lived their experiences you can try and understand what it was like for them. (PO8)

However, Hochschild (1983) maintains that deep acting may lead to emotional exhaustion as it requires the worker to invoke more of themselves in performing the emotional labour. Additionally, the more deep acting is used, the more the worker may find it difficult to feel the requisite emotion, which in turn leads to burnout (Hochschild, 1983; Van Maanen and Kunda, 1989; Grandey, 2003). Interestingly, there was no clear and discernible link between the use of empathy, deep acting and these negative consequences, but this is not to say that such consequences do not occur, perhaps representing an area for future analysis and research.

Some participants described how they did not find using empathy, and hence deep acting, challenging. However, others highlighted the potential difficulty in connecting with certain clients who were particularly intransigent or who had committed certain offences. For example, one participant said that she was unable to work with people who had been convicted of offences related to animal cruelty. In order to overcome this challenge, some participants described their attempts to concentrate on elements of the client's personality that they could engage with and therefore produce the requisite empathic response indirectly. However, there were a small number of situations where practitioners commented on the fact that even this proved ineffectual:

> And sometimes that has to be a façade because I don't think we can have hope for everybody because some people won't stop offending or don't want to stop offending. We have to be very clear about that, but at the end of the day you've got to manage this person's risk and protect the public and so you have to put that aside and have some

> kind of relationship with them … and that can be a time
> when you're pretending … well I don't like everybody that
> I supervise. (PO7)

This participant describes having to put up a façade, implicitly referring to the fact that they sometimes have to engage in surface acting. Surface acting is where a person does not feel the emotion they are displaying, and, as is the case with deep acting, can lead to negative consequences. Studies have linked surface acting to depression, burnout, low job satisfaction and emotional exhaustion (Erickson and Wharton, 1997; Brotheridge and Grandey, 2002; Bono and Vey, 2004). Such consequences can arguably occur in situations where a worker feels they are not being authentic, or, as Rafaeli and Sutton put it, the worker is 'faking in bad faith' (1987, p 32). However, PO7 acknowledges the importance of this way of performing emotional labour, which can be equated with the need to 'fake in good faith' (Rafaeli and Sutton, 1987, p 32). The motivation for this is explicitly stated by PO7 as being public protection. Therefore, here we see emotion being used as instrumental in achieving organisational goals relating to risk management rather than normative in terms of connecting in a meaningful way with the client. Nevertheless, the aim of building a relationship with the client remains central. Thus, their surface acting is contributing to the goals of the organisation through public protection, while, at the same time, developing a relationship that might, at some point in the future, be used to more normative ends.

In an earlier quote, PO8 refers to the fact that clients sometimes question the probation practitioner's ability to empathise with their situation. In response, five participants refer to the need to self-disclose in order to develop or maintain empathic engagement with clients:

> I mean like if they say, 'You've never used drugs' … you
> might give a comparison or you might, if you didn't want
> to reveal too much about yourself but [if] you wanted to
> reveal you might say, 'Well actually my best friend was a,
> you know, drug addict' or whatever it might be. (PO18)

There remains debate as to the appropriateness of self-disclosure interventions, and particularly self-involving self-disclosures. According to Knight (2012), self-involving self-disclosure involves 'relevant experiences from the clinician's life and circumstances from outside the session'. However, it is clear that PO18 uses this type of self-disclosure as a reactive measure to reinforce the authenticity of empathy displayed by the probation practitioner. In contrast, three participants described self-disclosure as a proactive tool, the aim of which is to aid the creation of an empathic connection with the client:

> I think limited self-disclosure is positive, to let people know that while we can sort of appreciate everything that's going on in their lives; we've been through similar things. (PO2)

> I mean maybe try and relay a situation you've been in where it has been awkward or difficult to do something ... explain to someone, 'This is as difficult for me as it is for you, you know. I know that I do this for a living but this is not easy for me to ask you these questions and expect you to answer them, you know. I have some apprehensions about sitting here and asking you, "Well what are your fantasies? Why did you commit this offence?" You know it can be as difficult for me to ask and to hear what you've got to say as it is for you to thinking about it and verbalise it' ... because I think they then see you on some sort of level footing ... then that makes people maybe not feel so vulnerable and open to attack or challenge, it then becomes more of a constructive conversation. (PO8)

It could be argued that these examples expose the narrowness with which SEEDS engages with empathy where it is primarily with reference to motivational interviewing and reflective listening (Miller and Rollnick, 1991, pp 51–2). Motivational interviewing clearly has benefits in the building and maintaining of relationships between probation practitioners and clients. However, the way in which empathy was described by our participants demonstrates that there are a variety of ways of engaging in empathy, which are not restricted to reflective listening. Instead, they emphasise the importance of sharing of experiences and/or emotions in order to build relationships.

Clear boundaries: honesty and the effective use of authority

In order to build relationships with clients, probation practitioners are also required to create clear boundaries. Participants were less inclined to refer to emotions when discussing this aspect of their work than they were when discussing empathy. However, reference was made by four participants to the need to be honest with clients (see also Phillips, 2013):

… you try to make it clear at the beginning that, you know, these are the rules and that you're trying to help them in any way you can, but it has to be within that, you know, they have to report otherwise you can't do anything can you if they don't actually come in or you don't see them. (PO6)

Participants were mindful of the dual role that they play, and reference was made to the fact that they needed to explain right from the outset the position of the PO in relation to the client. Therefore, while the emotional labour required in order to get to know and understand the client was often described first, there was also reference to the fact that from the beginning it was important to have an honest and transparent relationship in terms of the relationship between the PO and the client.

Nevertheless, emotions did arise during these discussions, primarily where participants described having to use authority in an effective way with clients. While it is acknowledged that the effective use of authority is a separate element of SEEDS, discussion by participants also centres on the effective use of authority in the creation of boundaries in order to build relationships with clients.

However, it is interesting to note that when discussing this aspect of their job, rather than referring to the use of emotions per se, participants described having to be emotionally detached or suppress certain types of emotion:

> I think at the end of the day you sort of go into that risk management mode don't you? So you go away from, you know, I think when I've recalled somebody it's a last, last resort and it's not like I've not spelled out to them that if this happens this will happen. (PO20)

> I do sort of seem to stand back and sort of try and gain a bigger picture rather than be really emotionally connected to an issue at times. So yeah, even in these meetings everyone else is sort of saying, 'Isn't it dreadful?', and I'm thinking, 'It's her choice, sort of thing, and we can do what we can do to support her?', but that's ultimately her choice of how she will lead her life in the next couple of weeks and months. (PO3)

In both of these comments, reference is made to risk and the boundaries, whether explicitly or implicitly referred to, that need to be respected. However, there is a clear difference in the reasons for these participants needing to emotionally detach. PO20 refers to going into risk management mode. The use of the word 'mode' perhaps provides a limited indication of whether deep or surface acting is used. However, it does suggest compartmentalisation in terms of the use of emotion following consideration of this difficult course of action, particularly given the emotional effort made by probation practitioners to build relationships. Additionally, the purposeful way in which PO20 presents the boundary discussed also suggests that effective use of authority requires minimising the potential for an allegation of abuse of power. This is again achieved by detaching from, or suppressing, unwanted emotions.

In contrast, the description by PO3 of the way in which he detaches from the client seems to be more about how he effectively maintains the clear boundaries of the relationship internally rather than it being a demonstration to the client of their position within the relationship. This could be understood as self-care, but it might also be an example of the way in which practitioners have internalised the responsibilisation agenda that has been prevalent in criminal justice policy over the past few decades (Garland, 2001).

Furthermore, there are instances where, in order to ensure that the authority they possess is used effectively, participants said they found it necessary to suppress certain emotions:

> I just kind of check myself at my instance response because I think when somebody, when I do feel disappointed then I think my nature would be to say, 'God, I am so disappointed', you know, 'Why would you do that?' In actual fact, I just check myself and just say, 'OK so this information has come to light. You told me this but this is actually what's happened here.' And try and not get focused, focus at all on how I feel about it. (PO14)

> I were annoyed with him [client] [laughs]. It'd have been really easy for me to just to go, 'Look I'm suspending you from unpaid work and we'll see what the court are going to do about this.'... I don't think I displayed it, I think he, you know he felt, I think that were his last thing to pull out of the hat were, 'This is a vendetta against me', because he'd tried everything else. You know, I think that he could do were [to say], 'This is personal.' I don't think it were anything to do with my emotions, my tone of voice or anything like that. (PO11)

With reference to PO14's description of her need to suppress the disappointment she feels at the way a client has behaved, there is clear movement from surface acting to deep acting and therefore a move from suppression of emotion to a form of emotional detachment. On the other hand, PO11 seems satisfied that using surface acting in order to suppress annoyance at the behaviour of the client is an effective way of ensuring that the boundary remains clear. While it has been suggested earlier that there are potential negative consequences of using surface acting, here we see another example of 'faking in good faith' in order to ensure that the task is completed efficiently (Ashforth and Humphrey, 1993). The task here was to breach the client in a way that would minimise the potential of the client taking the decision personally. Thus, PO11 suppresses annoyance in order to convey to the client a particular image of what it means to be a probation practitioner (Goffman, 1959). This might also be considered as a form of prosocial modelling.

Combining clear boundaries and work to get to know and understand the individual: getting the balance right

In the analysis so far, we have attempted to show, through the lens of emotional labour, how participants engage in emotional labour to get to know and understand clients and create clear boundaries. However, SEEDS guidance expects probation practitioners to combine these two already emotionally complex and difficult requirements. Participants attempted to describe how they achieved this objective:

> I guess the way I see it is I always see probation as two sides.... So I tend to talk about that with people quite explicitly and say, 'Look you know, alright so yeah we're going to work to support you but at the same time if we feel that you know you could cause a, you know, if we think you pose a risk to the public then, then we have to sort of take steps to do something about that.' (PO13)

> [Y]ou're playing two roles aren't you? You're playing the sort of, person who wants to, you know, like in the olden days, advise assist and befriend, sort of the rehabilitative role but you're also playing the like manage the risk to the public role. So you've got, you're wearing two hats and that can be difficult sometimes because that can, you know, lead to a breakdown in relationships, if you do have to breach

somebody or something like that. So like I said from the outset, you need to sort of manage that expectation that this is what I'm here to do. So I suppose, I'm trying to think how to describe it as an emotion or as an emotional display but I suppose it's the good cop, bad cop type thing. (PO20)

These two participants articulate well how emotional labour expectations often demand contrasting emotional displays. Practitioners have to perform at least two roles that are tied to the organisational goals of public protection and rehabilitation. However, inherent in every interaction is a need to prioritise a particular goal, which, based on our analysis above, suggests a need to quickly and spontaneously switch between different display rules. Thus, looking at practice through the lens of emotional labour allows us to see the ways in which the two potentially competing macro-goals of probation (public protection and rehabilitation) manifest at the micro-level of client-facing work. This, we would argue, has the potential to take an emotional toll on probation practitioners as well as requiring considerable emotion management skills. SEEDS asks practitioners to simply 'combine' these two elements of relationship building. This, we would argue, disguises the complexity of the emotional labour required.

Conclusion

As we saw in the literature review, emotions have been marginalised in terms of acknowledging their contribution to effective practice. Arguably, the increasingly managerial approach to probation has led to models of effective practice such as core correctional practice, STICS and SEEDS that have not engaged explicitly with the complexity of the emotional labour required by probation practitioners in building their relationship with clients. This is important because unless we engage with the emotional aspect of practitioners' work with clients, we are restricting ourselves to the 'what' of effective practice rather than the 'how'. We have examined the 'how' through an examination of the way in which people surface act and deep act in probation.

As we have shown, this is a very complex area of probation work and demands considerable emotional management. Participants said that the building of relationships clearly required getting to know and understand the individual. They do this by using empathy in different ways. Of equal importance to practitioners was the creation of clear boundaries. While participants referred less to the active use of emotion in this context, they focused on emotion suppression and detachment. SEEDS requires the combining of these already complex emotional skills, yet the way it is presented belies the difficult and essential nature of this work. Participants described the demand to combine the two elements of relationship building as the need to be two people at once, to have a dual role, to perform two types emotional labour at the same time. This is no mean feat.

We have already highlighted some of the consequences that result from such complex emotional labour. Participants described the way in which they engage in deep and surface acting, both to get to know and understand the client and create clear boundaries. We have already acknowledged that deep and surface acting can result in both positive and negative consequences. With reference to the latter, we need to consider some of the ways in which the negative consequences can be ameliorated.

Emotional labour needs to be made more explicit. This can be achieved through training initiatives such as the new Community Justice Learning programme, as well as through continuous professional development. Furthermore, more generally in probation practice there is the potential for engagement with emotional labour through reflective supervision (a further element of SEEDS). This would go some way to providing the much-needed time and space to develop the emotion management skills required to build relationships with clients.

At a more organisational level, if probation providers are to reintroduce SEEDS (and we think there is great merit for public and private providers in doing so), it is important that the emotional aspect is taken into account. It is important to note that this chapter has only examined one element of SEED – that of relationship building – yet this has shed light on the emotional labour of probation work. Thus, there is scope for more analysis, both in terms of relationship building, as well as more generally across the SEED model. The reintroduction of SEEDS represents an important opportunity to place emotional labour as one of the key pillars of probation work. By showing how probation practitioners perform emotional labour when building relationships, we have demonstrated that emotion is inherent to effective practice. No longer should it be marginalised or dealt with obliquely, but should be recognised as central to the achievement of organisational goals as well as structuring the micro-level interactions between practitioners and their clients.

Note

1   The pilot project, which ran between spring 2011 and spring 2012, was named SEED (Skills for Effective Engagement and Development). SEED

subsequently became known as SEEDS (Skills for Effective Engagement, Development and Supervision) when it was later offered to other probation trusts, which had not formed part of the original pilot.

References

Andrews, D. and Kiessling, J. (1980) 'Program structure and effective correctional practices: a summary of the CaVIC research', in R. Ross and P. Gendreau (eds) *Effective Correctional Treatment*, Toronto: Butterworth.

Ashforth B.E. and Humphrey, R.H. (1993) 'Emotional labor in service roles: the influence of identity', *The Academy of Management Review*, 18(1): 88–115.

Bhowmick, S. and Zubin, M. (2016) 'Emotional labour of policing. Does authenticity play a role?', *International Journal of Police Science & Management*, 18(1): 47–60.

Bolton, S. (2000) 'Who cares? Offering emotion work as a "gift" in the nursing labour process', *Journal of Advanced Nursing*, 32(3): 580–586.

Bono, J.E. and Vey, M.A. (2004) 'Towards understanding emotional management work: a quantitative review of emotional labour research', in N. Ashkanasy and C. Hartel (eds) *Emotions in Organizational Behavior*, Mahwah, NJ: Erlbaum, pp 213–233.

Bonta, J., Rugge, T., Scott, T., Bourgon, G. and Yessine, A.K. (2008) 'Exploring the black box of community supervision', *Journal of Offender Rehabilitation*, 47(3): 248–270.

Braun, V. and Clarke, V. (2006) 'Using thematic analysis in psychology', *Qualitative Research in Psychology*, 3(2): 77–101.

Brotheridge, C. and Grandey. A.A. (2002) 'Emotional labor burnout: comparing two perspectives of "People Work"', *Journal of Vocational Behavor*, 17: 17–39.

Burnett, R. (1996) *Fitting Supervision to Offenders: Assessment and Allocation in the Probation Service*, Home Office Research Study, 153, London: Home Office.

Burnett, R. and McNeill, F. (2005) 'The place of the officer-offender relationship in assisting offenders to desist from crime', *Probation Journal*, 52(3): 221–242

Chapman, T. and Hough, M. (1998) *Evidence-Based Practice: A Review*, London: Home Office.

Crawley, E. (2004a) 'Emotion and performance: prison officers and the presentation of self in prisons', *Punishment & Society*, 6(4): 411–427.

Crawley, E. (2004b) *Doing Prison Work: The Public and Private Lives of Prison Officers*, Cullompton: Willan.

Deering, J. (2011) *Probation Practice and the New Penology: Practitioner Reflections*, Farnham: Ashgate.

Denscombe, M. (2014) *The Good Research Guide: For Small-Scale Social Research Projects*, Maidenhead: Open University Press.

Dowden, C. and Andrews, D.A. (1999) 'What works for female offenders: A meta-analytic review', *Crime & Delinquency*, 45(4): 438–452.

Dowden, C. and Andrews, D. (2004) 'The importance of staff practice in delivering effective correctional treatment: a meta-analytic review of core correctional practice', *International Journal of Offender Therapy and Comparative Criminology*, 48(2): 203–214.

Erickson R.J. and Wharton A. (1997) 'Inauthenticity and depression: assessing the consequences of interactive service work', *Work and Occupations*, 24(2): 188–213.'

Garland, D. (2001) *The Culture of Control: Crime and Social Order in Late Modernity*, Oxford: Clarendon.

Goffman, I. (1959) *The Presentation of the Self in Everyday Life*, New York, NY: Random House.

Grandey, A.A. (2003) 'When "the show must go on": surface acting and deep acting as determinants of emotional exhaustion and peer-rated service delivery', *Academy of Management Journal*, 46(1): 86–91.

Hochschild, A.R. (1983) *The Managed Heart: Commercialization of Human Feeling*, Berkeley, CA: University of California Press.

Home Office (1992) *National Standards for the Supervision of Offenders in the Community*, London: Home Office.

Knight, C. (2012) 'Social workers' attitudes towards and engagement in self-disclosure', *Clinical Social Work Journal*, 40: 297–306.

Knight, C. (2014) *Emotional Literacy in Criminal Justice*, Basingstoke: Palgrave Macmillan.

Kurtz, D. and Linnemann, T. (2006) 'Improving probation through client strengths: evaluating strength based treatments for at risk youth', *Western Criminology Review*, 7(1): 9–19.

Mair, G. (ed) (2004) *What Matters in Probation*, Cullompton: Willan

McNeill, F. (2006) 'A desistance paradigm for offender management', *Criminology and Criminal Justice*, 6(1): 39–62.

McNeill, F. and Weaver, B. (2010) *Changing Lives? Desistance Research and Offender Management*, Glasgow: Scottish Centre for Crime and Justice Research.

Miller, W.R. and Rollnick, S. (1991) *Motivational Interviewing: Preparing People to Change Addictive Behaviour*, New York, NY: Guildford Press.

MoJ (Ministry of Justice) (2013) *Transforming Rehabilitation: A Strategy for Reform*, London: MoJ.

MoJ (2015) *NOMS Workforce Statistics Bulletin*, London: MoJ.

NOMS (National Offender Management Service) (2005) *The NOMS Offender Management Model. Version 1*, London: NOMS.

NOMS (2011) *SEED Practitioner Workbook*, London: NOMS.

Phillips, J. (2013) 'Understanding "the relationship" in English probation practice', in I. Durnescu, and F. McNeill (eds) *Understanding Penal Practice*, Abingdon: Routledge, pp 122–138.

Porporino, F.J. (2010) 'Bringing sense and sensitivity to corrections: from programmes to "fix" offenders to services to support desistance' in J. Brayford, F. Cowe and J. Deering (eds) *What Else Works? Creative Work With Offenders*, Cullompton: Willan, pp 61–85.

Rafaeli, A. and Sutton, R.I. (1987) 'Expression of emotion as part of the work role', *Academy of Management Review*, 12(1): 23–37.

Ranson, S. and Stewart, J. (1994) *Management for the Public Domain: Enabling the Learning Society*, Abingdon: Palgrave.

Raynor, P. and Vanstone, M. (2007) 'Towards a correctional service', in L. Gelsthorpe and R. Morgan (eds) *Handbook of Probation*, Cullompton: Willan, pp 59–89.

Rex, S. (1999) 'Desistance from offending: experiences of probation', *Howard Journal of Crime and Justice*, 38(4): 366–383.

Rex, S. and Hosking, N. (2013) 'A collaborative approach to developing probation practice skills for effective engagement, development and supervision (SEEDS)', *Probation Journal*, 60(3): 332–338.

Rex, S., Ellis, E. and Hosking, N. (2012) 'Developing offender engagement: evaluating probation trust pilots', in E. Bowen and S. Brown (eds) *Advances in Program Evaluation*, Bingley: Emerald Group Publishing, pp 199–209.

Robinson, G. (2003) 'Technicality and indeterminacy in probation practice: a case study', *British Journal of Social Work*, 33(5): 593–610.

Robinson, G. and Ugwudike, P. (2012) 'Investing in "toughness": probation, enforcement and legitimacy', *The Howard Journal of Crime and Justice*, 51(3): 300–316.

Trotter, C. (1996) 'The impact of different supervision practices in community corrections', *Australian and New Zealand Journal of Criminology*, 29(1): 29–46.

Trotter, C. (2012) 'Effective community-based supervision of young offenders' *Trends & Issues in Crime and Criminal Justice*, 448: 1–7.

Ugwudike, P., Raynor, P. and Vanstone, M. (2014) 'The impact of skills in probation work: a reconviction study', *Criminology & Criminal Justice*, 14(2): 235–249.

Van Maanen, J. and Kunda, G. (1989) 'Real feelings: emotional expression and organizational culture', in L.L. Cummings and B.M. Staw (eds) *Research in Organizational Behavior*, Greenwich, CT: JAI Press, pp 43–102.

Ward, T. and Maruna, S. (2007) *Rehabilitation*, Abingdon: Routledge.

THIRTEEN

Staff supervision in youth justice and its relationship to skill development: findings from Australia

Charlene Pereira and Chris Trotter

Introduction

Staff supervision – a forum for critical reflection and learning, or a surveillance tool? Research shows that supervision approaches that predominantly focus on performance management, and fail to balance the supervisory functions of accountability with education and support, limit the space for reflection and skill development (Morrison, 2005; Carroll and Gilbert, 2011). It creates an environment where supervisee practice becomes reactive and mechanistic, maintaining organisational status quo (Weld 2012). While integrated models of staff supervision that encompass task-focused and clinical components are the preferential approach for creating a forum for ongoing professional development, supervisor competencies are not to be overlooked. Process-oriented skills including, but not limited to, role clarification, contracting – including limitations to confidentiality, establishing in partnership the frequency and duration of meetings, and evaluation of the working alliance, together with interpersonal skills including empathy, open and honest communication and the use of challenge, encourage the staff or practitioner being supervised (the supervisee) to foster practice that is evidence-based and promotes client wellbeing and community safety (Davys and Beddoe, 2010; Carroll and Gilbert, 2011). It also contributes to creating a sense of belonging and support for the supervisee, which in turn may increase staff retention and provide for continuity of care for clients (Grant et al, 2012).

This chapter describes the purpose of clinical, professional and managerial supervision, and summarises the key approaches to professional supervision within the helping professions. The chapter then reviews supervisor competencies associated with what works in enhancing practitioner skill development, together with supervisee experiences of what does not work in supervision. Research shows that what works in the direct supervision of offenders parallels what works in staff supervision. The chapter concludes with a brief outline of a study being undertaken in youth justice in Australia, which examines the influence of supervision styles on practitioner skill development and the implementation of evidence-based practice skills.

The findings presented are based on a systematic review approach using the key search terms clinical supervision, professional supervision, staff supervision, corrections, probation, skill development, professional development, decision making and reflective learning. The database search included ProQuest Criminal Justice, SAGE Criminology full text, Taylor and Francis, OVID – Psych Info, Scopus and Google Scholar. The review period spanned 2000- 16. This broad-based review of supervision across several databases was implemented due to the dearth of literature relating to professional supervisory practices with case managers within the criminal justice system and/or working with involuntary clients. Clinical supervision, on the other hand, seems to be closely aligned with psychological practice and is published widely in counselling journals.

The purpose of supervision: clinical, professional and managerial

Clinical supervision

Clinical supervision has historically been associated with psychological practice. It is suggested that Freud initiated 'informal supervision' with a group of doctors training to become psychoanalysts. Clinical supervision within this context involved small group discussions to review and critique treatment practices with patients. This style of supervision was formalised in the 1920s by Max Eitington of the Berlin Institute of Psychoanalysis, who made clinical supervision a formal requirement for individuals undertaking psychoanalytical training (The Bouverie Centre, 2013). In the late 20th century, clinical supervision within the US was officially introduced as a reflective space and supportive tool for professionals other than those engaged in psychological practice, including social work and other helping professions (Carroll, 2007).

With clinical supervision moving away from its psychoanalytical roots and integrating more broadly into the social services, the purpose and application of supervision took on a more educational process, with the 1970s establishing supervision as the 'reflection on practice' aspect of clinical work (Carroll, 2007). Today, irrespective of one's professional training, clinical supervision continues to be viewed as an interaction between the supervisor and supervisee to encourage self-development, enhance skills, competence and confidence, and ensure ethical practice and compliance with professional standards and practice, with the overarching theme of creating 'a structured system of reflection, primarily with the intention of improving practice' (Driscoll, 2000; Spouse and Redfern, 2000; van Ooijen, 2003, cited in Rolfe et al, 2011, p 102). The psychodynamic idea of creating a working alliance is foundational across clinical supervision practices regardless of profession and will be explored further when examining the key competencies associated with creating effective supervision.

Professional supervision

While the terms clinical and professional supervision are used interchangeably within the literature, they are distinctively different from the term managerial supervision. For the purpose of this chapter, professional supervision within youth justice will be defined according to the Australian Association of Social Workers (AASW) Supervision Standards definition, given that case management practices align more closely with social work than psychology. Clinical and professional supervision according to the AASW both share the focus of enhancing professional practice skills and competence in order to ensure quality of service to clients. However, within the professional supervision definition it also acknowledges the importance of the interaction and dialogue between supervisor and supervisee, to create a forum for reflection and learning, and holding one accountable to professional standards, and organisational policies and procedures (AASW, 2014).

Managerial supervision

Line manager supervision is defined as:

> the person to whom the social worker is accountable/ reports to within the organisational structure of the employing organisation. The line manager is responsible for day to day, operational matters. (AASW, 2014, p 13)

Managerial supervision focuses primarily on organisational outcomes and is provided by staff members who often report limited knowledge of skills specific to professional supervisory functions (Davys and

Beddoe, 2010). Morrison and Wonnacott (2010) argue that it is often married with inconsistent induction, training and support in the role of supervisor. The managerial supervisor is responsible for ensuring performance standards are maintained and organisational protocols followed, in addition to completing performance reviews, helping the supervisee with planning and management of their caseload, and reviewing the supervisees' problem-solving and decision-making capacity as an accountability mechanism to manage risk. With the introduction of targets in the public sector, and clients becoming consumers, there has been a shift toward a 'business' model of practice (Weld, 2012). Managerial supervision must also ensure that the supervisee is operating effectively to enable the organisation to meet its required level of productivity, utilise resources efficiently and comply with quality assurance standards (Lawler, 2015). Compared with professional supervision, managerial supervision tends to be more process-driven and corrective, rather than transformative. The supervisory relationship is perfunctory and administration focused (Weld, 2012).

Clinical supervision in the helping professions: key approaches

At its core, professional (and clinical) supervision is concerned with providing a better quality of service to clients by ensuring that ethical and professional practice standards are met and interventions are tailored to the individual needs of the client. For staff working with offenders, this requires case managers to be mindful of evidence-based practices such as the Risk-Need-Responsivity principles to provide a balanced approach to rehabilitation and community safety (Bonta et al, 2013). Supervision is concerned with facilitating the acquisition of practitioner skills to increase competence and confidence, given its association with higher levels of job satisfaction and morale, as well as improved client outcomes (The Bouverie Centre, 2013). It is also posited that supervision may act as a safeguard against practitioner burnout and encourage retention by creating a sense of belonging, encouraging accountability through reflective practice, and fostering the practitioners' professional identity (Tsui, 2005; The Bouverie Centre 2013).

Functional models

The key difference between managerial and professional supervision approaches may be attributed to the way in which the functions of supervision are weighted, and the hierarchical nature of the supervisory relationship where one party (manager) is favoured as the authority and the other (supervisee) the recipient of advice or direction, and disciplinary procedures (The Bouverie Centre 2013). Within the social services, and in particular case management occupations, managerial supervision dominates (Davys and Beddoe, 2010). This style of staff supervision is based on functional approaches that are task-focused and made up of three components – administration (normative), education (formative) and support (restorative) –drawing on the work of Kadushin, Proctor and Morrison (Hawkins and Shohet, 2006), with the administrative function focusing on accountability to policies, protocols, ethics and standards at the forefront (Davys and Beddoe, 2010). Morrison's (2005) task-focused approach to supervision also includes a fourth function – 'mediation' – which is concerned with engaging the individual within the organisation (Morrison and Wonnacott 2010). Morrison's approach is discussed further when exploring the integrated models of supervision.

Studies point to the benefits for supervision approaches to move away from focusing predominantly on performance management, and balance the supervisory functions of accountability with education and support, to facilitate ongoing professional development skills. However, within risk averse environments with high levels of accountability such as youth justice, focus on the educative and support functions, together with attending to the relationship between the practitioner, supervisor and work context, can be overlooked or given less attention. In such circumstances, practitioners may rely more heavily on risk assessment tools at the expense of reflection and professional discretion, with case management practice becoming reactive and mechanistic (Weld, 2012). Parton (2006), Gillingham (2006), and Stanley (2007) suggest that within the child protection sphere this has led to defensive practice where procedural matters dominate. In turn, aspects of practitioners' work, practice or behaviour that need support and attention may be driven underground for fear of reprisals, which could affect careers (Weld, 2012).

Other key approaches to facilitating ongoing professional development of practitioners include the developmental models, integrated models combining clinical and managerial components of supervision, and the current move toward post-modern reflective approaches that are strengths-based and solution-oriented, and foster an experiential learning environment.

Developmental models

The developmental models were most prevalent in the 1980s and are based on the broad premise that supervisees 'follow a predictable and staged path of development' (Davys and Beddoe, 2010, p 31). The role of the supervisor is to attend to each sequential stage of development, ranging from the 'novice' who requires instruction through to the 'expert' autonomous practitioner (Davys and Beddoe, 2010). There are criticisms of developmental approaches for their prescriptive nature and their focus on demonstrated competence, as opposed to the potential development of the supervisee, which may be supported through collaboration. It is suggested that developmental approaches are useful as they encourage the supervisor to: pay attention to the supervisees' level of experience; tailor interventions to the supervisees' stage of development; and work with the supervisees to enhance their level of competence (Davys and Beddoe, 2010).

Integrated models

Integrated models that combine managerial (task-focused) and clinical (skills-based and reflective practice) components have been rated as the preferential approach for social work supervision. A study undertaken by Beddoe (2010) in New Zealand investigated how six social work expert practitioners conduct professional supervision, using semi-structured interviews to explore the impact of 'risk discourse' on their supervisory role. The need for supervisors to pay attention to all three supervision functions (formative, normative and restorative) equally, was noted by the supervisees. These functions can prevent supervisors from blurring managerial and professional goals, and can encourage practitioners to utilise supervision as a reflective process. This finding supports the work of Bradley and Hojer (2009, p 79), which compared supervision practices involving social work case managers in England and Sweden. The case managers were positive about their supervision experience where 'a balance had been struck between the competing aspects' of accountability, education and support.

Tony Morrison's (2005) integrated model of supervision has been widely applied within the social work and case management fields of practice internationally, and in Australia (Morrison and Wonnacott, 2010). Morrison acknowledges that the core tasks of supervision include administration (normative) focusing on monitoring standards and ethical practice; education (formative) focusing on the ongoing professional skill development and resourcing of the practitioner; and support (restorative) focusing on enhancing professional development through reflective practice and attending to the personal relationship between the practitioner and work context. Morrison also claims that task-focused approaches are limited in performance outcome if they do not to take into account the interaction between these functions, or identify the role of the supervisor in facilitating critical analysis of practice. Morrison goes on to suggest that such models need to situate the dynamics of the supervisory process within the wider organisational or inter-agency context and emphasises the need for an integrated model of supervision that has four functions, the additional function being mediation (Morrison and Wonnacott, 2010).

According to Morrison, the supervisor, being in a middle-management position, is often required to adopt the mediator role to balance the needs of the organisation and the needs of the staff member. This integrated model allows the supervisory process to broaden out its focus to the needs and priorities of the four stakeholders: the consumer, the staff members (supervisor and supervisee), the organisation, and inter-agency partners (Morrison and Wonnacott, 2010).

Within the counselling domain, Hawkins and Shohet's (2006) Seven Eyed Model of Supervision and Carroll's (2007) integrative approach also draw attention to the need to consider all stakeholders. This is especially important when inviting supervisees to reflect on, and examine, their relationship with the client, and what influences their assessment and intervention strategies (Carroll and Gilbert, 2011). There is a strong focus on learning through reflective practice, as central to the supervision process, for both the supervisee and supervisor. The supervisor thus assumes a co-exploration role, to help the supervisee develop insight into self and practice. The application of in-session tasks such as role playing alternative interventions and critiquing one's practice skills is encouraged and supported (Davys and Beddoe, 2010; Carroll and Gilbert, 2011). This supervisory style aligns with strengths-based and solution-focused supervision that favours the co-construction of ideas; engages the supervisee in conversations that are supervisee-focused; uses language that is respectful; is non-judgemental of supervisee or clients; is hopeful; entails questions to challenge and stimulate multiple perspectives; and encourages the supervisee to identify what is working well at present, and to take notice of thoughts and feelings in monitoring their progress, with the view to helping the supervisee become their own internal supervisor (Davys and Beddoe, 2010).

In a review of 24 published empirical articles summarising models and concepts used in supervision, findings showed irrespective of the supervisory approach, reflection was often embedded as part of the process. Eighty-two percent of the reviewed articles 'described outcomes consistent with the experiential learning cycle', indicating the centrality of experiential learning to the practice of supervision (Milne et al, 2008, p 181). David Kolb's (1984) experiential learning cycle comprising the four elements 'doing, reflecting, learning, and applying' (Carroll and Gilbert, 2011, p 20), together with the contribution of reflective practice by Donald Schon (1983), who promoted the development of moving the practitioner from 'reflection-on-action' (post the interaction) to 'reflection-in-action' (thinking about what you are doing in the interaction, and what you will do next), not only informs supervisory practices, but is instrumental to all aspects of adult learning (Schon, 1983; Davys and Beddoe, 2010).

In summary, the literature identifies that irrespective of the supervision model adopted, staff supervision is concerned with the key tasks of accountability (adherence to organisational policy, procedures, professional association codes of conduct and ethical guidelines); education (evidence-based practice); and support (fostering ongoing professional development through reflective practice and exploration of the impact of work on personal and professional relationships), with the primary intention of developing an improved service to clients (Davys and Beddoe, 2010). However, the way in which the supervision tasks are prioritised and explored in sessions is dependent on the model used. The functional and developmental models are supervisor-led, while the integrated and reflective/strengths-based approaches adopt a co-exploration role between supervisor and supervisee, modelling a collaborative approach to improving practice. The relationship between the supervisor and supervisee is therefore identified as being of utmost importance, for it is the medium through which supervision objectives are accomplished. Given this correlation, it is important to review supervisor competencies associated with enhancing practitioner skill development.

What works in supervision?

It is asserted that supervisor competencies are instrumental to fostering the process of reflective practice, given that the ability to objectively examine one's beliefs and values, and how it influences actions taken with clients, is difficult to achieve without the professional perspective of another (Rolfe et al, 2011). Supervisor competencies can be separated into two categories: process-oriented skills and interpersonal skills.

Supervisor competencies: process oriented skills. Contracting, role clarification, evaluation, feedback

Process-oriented skills are concerned with establishing the structure and purpose of the supervisory relationship. According to Carroll and Gilbert (2011), contracting or establishing the supervision agreement at the onset of the relationship is essential. The contract clearly stipulates the roles and responsibilities of each party, noting the importance of professional ethics and accountability to clients, employers and professional member bodies. It documents the supervisee's needs in the form of learning goals, and confirms limitations to confidentiality. Practicalities such as frequency, location and duration of sessions is outlined, together with the response to non-attendance and cancellation, the storage of notes and the release of information for supervisory reports (Carroll and Gilbert, 2011; Rolfe et al, 2011; The Bouverie Centre, 2013). Discussion at this stage should also include the supervisor's theoretical orientation, approach to supervision and work experience, to provide the supervisee with an informed understanding of what the supervisor can provide within the space for reflection and learning (Rudland et al, 2010; The Bouverie Centre, 2013). This process is very similar to role clarification skills, which are a key aspect of effective practice with involuntary clients including offender supervision (Trotter, 2013), emphasising again that many of the skills of client supervision reflect the skills of staff supervision.

A study examining supervisory practices with nurses in Iran, completed over a two-year period (2010–12) and comprising semi-structured interviews with 25 participants (10 nurses, nine supervisors, two matrons, and four head nurses) and a review of supervisory notes, supports the importance of contracting. Supervisees suggested that establishing the contract prior to beginning supervision would be beneficial to reach agreement on content and supervision goals. Role clarification inclusive of the responsibilities of supervisor and supervisee was also identified as important. Other skills such as negotiation and the ability to facilitate a collaborative working alliance to assist supervisees with decision making and conflict resolution were identified, and training that encompassed teaching and support for supervisors was recommended given the association between quality of the supervision relationship on the supervision process and staff retention (Dehghani et al, 2016).

Carroll and Gilbert (2011) draw our attention to the need for a scheduled two-way evaluation process to be incorporated into the supervision arrangement to review the working alliance and monitor progress toward the supervisee's professional learning goals (Carroll and Gilbert, 2011; The Bouverie Centre, 2013). When a contract moves from being a two-way agreement between the supervisee and supervisor to a three-way contract involving the organisation, confidentiality boundaries and role clarification must be stipulated clearly and understood by all three parties before supervision begins (Carroll and Gilbert, 2011; The Bouverie Centre, 2013). This may occur when the organisation provides managerial supervision and contracts out clinical supervision to meet the supervisee's clinical practice requirements. Within such arrangements, the clinical supervisor may take on the mediator role identified within Morrison's integrated approach to supervision by advocating on behalf of the supervisee with the organisation, and acting as an accountability mechanism on behalf of the organisation to ensure the supervisee is meeting both professional and program standards (Morrison and Wonnacott, 2010).

According to Carroll and Gilbert (2011, p 41), process-oriented skills are useful for avoiding what they term the 'psychological contract': the implicit agreement between supervisor and supervisee regarding co-creating a safe and facilitative environment in which to discuss case practice and receive evaluative feedback. It may also be described as the unspoken expectation one brings to the relationship regarding the supervision process, which, if left unaddressed, may result in disappointment and misunderstanding. It could rupture the supervisory alliance that is pivotal to creating the context for effective supervision. Weld (2012) proposes that the supervisory relationship may influence not only how supervisees perceives the current and subsequent supervision relationships, but also how they perceive the organisation and other relationships within the workplace.

Supervisor competencies: interpersonal skills

Several interpersonal skills have been associated with influencing the success of supervisory relationships and interventions. These supervisory skills have been mostly adapted from the counselling literature and include the supervisor conveying positive regard, active listening and paraphrasing (Davys and Beddoe, 2010). According to Smythe and colleagues (2009), this cluster of interpersonal skills sets the foundation for engagement and acknowledges the supervisee as being central to the process. Weld (2012) further notes that the supervisor, as the main tool for creating a partnership to foster quality reflection and learning, also needs to generate safety and trust by exhibiting congruency through modelling the skill(s) and the behaviour one is asking of the supervisee: demonstrating openness, honesty, being fully present in sessions and using appropriate humour. Humour at the onset of the supervisory relationship may help support openness, increase warmth and build rapport, and contribute to a positive interaction throughout the supervisory relationship by bringing attention to, and balancing out, the personal and professional elements of the relationship. In addition, Weld (2012) draws attention to the use of empathy in the supervision dialogue as a means of acknowledging that the supervisee is being heard.

Open and closed questions: reframing

Other skills identified within the literature include the use of questioning and reframing. Open question enquiry aligns closely with the reflective learning model of supervision. It requires the supervisor to demonstrate curiosity and allow the supervisee the space and time to enhance work practice through insight and understanding, thus supporting problem solving. Closed questions, by contrast, help clarify information. The skill reframing provides the supervisee with an alternative framework from which to view the issue inclusive of the client's perspective (Davys and Beddoe, 2010). Again, what works in staff supervision reflects what works in the direct supervision of offenders and other involuntary clients, where relationship skills have been consistently identified as core skills in effective practice (see Trotter, 2013, for a review).

Problem solving

Problem solving is the process of working through details of a problem to reach a solution following a set of prescribed steps (Campbell, 2006). According to Trotter (2015, p 126), these steps include: surveying of problems; collaborative decision making regarding the prioritisation of problems; detailed exploration of the problem or problems to be worked on; goal setting; contracting; the development of strategies and tasks; and an ongoing review of progress toward the desired goal. There is support for the effectiveness of problem-solving processes and application of skills in staff supervision. A study by Harkness and Hensley (1991) investigated social work supervision and client outcomes in a community mental health centre comprising one supervisor, six staff members (four psychologists and two social workers), and 161 clients with clinical depression. They found scheduled one-to-one client-focused supervision sessions requiring the supervisee to use basic communication, problem-solving and relational skills in client sessions, as opposed to a mixed-focus supervision arrangement incorporating administration, training and clinical consultation delivered in a team meeting, produced a 10% improvement in client satisfaction with goal attainment, a 20% improvement in client satisfaction with worker helpfulness and a 30% improvement in satisfaction with the partnership between client and worker.

Silence

The use of silence in supervision has been found to encourage the supervisee to engage in reflective practice via the internal processing of information (Davys and Beddoe, 2010). Supervisors guided by the developmental approach described earlier may incorporate the skill of silence more readily with introvert supervisees to allow them the time required to determine their responses. A study exploring silence in supervision confirms the benefits for introverted learners. Farmer (1988, pp 34–5) found that when supervisors paused for approximately three to five seconds after a supervisee spoke, there was an increase in 'contributions made by quiet supervisees; in confidence demonstrated by fewer inflected responses; in speculative thinking; and in the use of questions'.

Challenge

While the abovementioned skills promote support and a safe and trusting working alliance, in order to facilitate the development of a reflective practitioner, the skill – challenge – must also be incorporated. Again, this is consistent with the research on effective offender supervision (Trotter et al, 2016). Challenge is concerned with helping supervisees identify their 'blind spots' by inviting discussion on their assumptions; and/or by raising uncomfortable issues that have emerged in practice in order to identify and implement strategies to improve practice.

Davys and Beddoe (2010) suggest that challenge with feedback is central to professional development. Feedback needs to be a two-way process that occurs on a regular basis and should be delivered with respect, honesty and the opportunity for discussion to assist learning. It is the role of the supervisor to clarify the expectations of feedback, and how it will be delivered (verbal/written). The supervisor should also ensure that feedback is specific and balanced regarding what is working, and what could be done differently by both supervisor and supervisee, to foster a shared responsibility for learning and improvement (Davys and Beddoe, 2010; Carroll and Gilbert, 2011).

Observation

Observation is one of many skills supervisors use in the feedback process. Observation in session usually takes the form of the supervisor tuning into, and taking note of, the supervisees' choice of words, feelings, thoughts, mood and actions when discussing their work. It may also involve reviews of case notes, listening to audio-taped sessions, or, where permitted, viewing direct client work. The purpose of observation is to help support the supervisee make a shift in thinking and/or behaviour, and to improve practice skills. This is facilitated through the supervisor asking a question, making a statement or suggestion to generate insight into what was happening for the supervisee on a personal and professional level, and, where required, developing a plan of action for improvement (Weld, 2012).

Depending on the supervisee's level of reflective practice, the supervisor may need to draw on a range of techniques to facilitate this process. This may include: motivational interviewing: a goal-oriented, person-centred approach for eliciting behaviour change with supervisees who need help to explore and resolve ambivalence; a solution-focused approach of identifying exceptions for the supervisee who is feeling stuck or disempowered; a narrative approach of externalising the issue; and/or a cognitive-behavioural approach of setting tasks to foster self-directed learning and promote active problem solving (Davys and Beddoe, 2010; Weld, 2012).

Self-disclosure

Self-disclosure is a skill taught, applied within the psychology and counselling profession for the betterment of the client. The literature shows that by sharing information based on practice experience, or sharing thoughts and feelings regarding the supervisory relationship, in addition to self-disclosing mistakes, the supervisor can strengthen the supervisory relationship and address some of the power imbalances that may exist (Davys and Beddoe, 2010). According to Weld (2012), self-disclosure may also contribute to normalising supervisees' experiences and help transform supervision into a space where supervisees do not feel shame or judged in relation to their practice, but feel supported to express vulnerability. A study by Lizzio and colleagues (2009) of supervisees' perceptions of supervision processes and outcomes with psychology graduate supervisees supports self-disclosure as a skill that can increase the level of trust between supervisor and supervisee, and in turn supervisee openness, allowing for an authentic learning relationship to be established.

The foregoing description of interpersonal and process-oriented skills identified within the literature highlights the complexity of the supervisor role and reinforces the importance of having skilled supervisors to foster practice that is evidence-based, accountable, innovative and creative in its approach to promoting client wellbeing and community safety, as well as eliciting a sense of belonging and support among supervisees; this, in turn, increases staff retention and provides for continuity of care for clients (Grant et al, 2012).

Parallel process: client supervision and staff supervision

Reference was made earlier to the parallels between client supervision and staff supervision. This is supported by Christensen and colleagues (2008), who propose that there are parallels between the skills contributing to effective staff supervisor–supervisee interaction and effective case manager–client interaction. These skills include: establishing a relationship based on trust and respect; exploring in partnership potential strategies to problems; observing competency; providing constructive feedback; keeping tasks concrete, specific and documented; and mentoring staff as they apply new skills and knowledge. Research on work with offenders also supports the view of Christensen and colleagues (2008).

Taxman and colleagues (2004) and Bonta and colleagues (2008) suggest that when workers employ process-oriented skills – including communicating the objectives of the interview (role clarification); summarising themes from the previous session; modelling the desired behaviour and providing constructive feedback including reinforcement of prosocial behaviours (prosocial modelling and reinforcement); collaboratively exploring problems and setting goals (problem solving); and assigning out-of-session tasks – in collaboration with interpersonal (relationship) skills including empathy, openness, encouragement and humour, the client will be willing to listen and follow advice of the probation officer, increasing their involvement in the interview process. Studies such as the supervision skills study conducted in the Jersey Probation Service in the United Kingdom (Raynor and Vanstone, 2015), and those undertaken in Australia within adult community corrections and NSW Youth Justice (Trotter and Evans, 2012; Trotter,

2015), confirm that prosocial approaches encompassing process-oriented and interpersonal skills (role clarification, prosocial modelling and reinforcement, problem-solving and relationship) contribute to improved client outcomes including reduction in recidivism rates.

With the movement toward evidence-based practices with offenders, workers in some jurisdictions are now required to take on the role of 'change agents'. This adds a therapeutic component to the traditional case management role, and requires worker competency in the application of core effective practice skills associated with improved client outcomes (Bourgon, 2013). The way in which these skills and knowledge are learned and embedded in practice comes into question. How influential is training? How important is staff supervision? Does one outweigh the other?

In 2005, the Corrections Research Division of Public Safety in Canada started to develop the Strategic Training Initiative in Community Supervision (STICS) model to increase probation officers' adherence to the Risk-Need-Responsivity (RNR) principles. It was hypothesised that this would lead to lower recidivism rates. The STICS model consisted of a training curriculum that focused on the practitioner's role in building a rapport, establishing a collaborative working alliance, and applying cognitive-behavioural techniques associated with reductions in offending behaviour (including problem-solving, decision making, consequential thinking and victim awareness) in order to help clients replace procriminal attitudes with prosocial attitudes. In addition to training, officers engaged in ongoing clinical support by way of regular monthly meetings to review and discuss practice skills, participate in refresher courses and receive specific feedback of their skills and techniques as demonstrated on the audio-taped officer–client supervision sessions submitted to the research trainers (Bourgon et al, 2010; Bonta et al, 2013).

The results showed that officers trained in the STICS model focused more on the criminogenic needs of their clients. This includes the characteristics, problems, or issues of an individual that directly relate to their likelihood of reoffending. They were also more likely to apply cognitive-behavioural techniques to address criminogenic needs, and more likely to follow the RNR principles concerned with developing an intervention that matches the level of service to level of risk to reoffend, identify treatment goals according to criminogenic needs, and tailor intervention to the client's level of motivation, strengths and abilities. After two years, the reconviction rate of clients under the supervision of trained officers was 25% compared with 39.5% for those of non-trained officers. An examination of the recidivism rates of clients under the supervision of workers who also participated in the monthly clinical supervision meetings and refresher courses, revealed that the rate reduced further to 19% (Bourgon et al, 2010; Bonta et al 2013). Greater participation in clinical supervision was associated with enhanced skills and more appropriate discussions one year after training, confirming the importance of ongoing clinical supervision and support post-training to align officer behaviour with the 'what works' practice principles in the long term.

According to Bourgon and colleagues (2010), their research findings echo the findings recorded by Walters and colleagues (2005), who undertook a systematic review of 17 studies examining transfer processes on staff skills. Ongoing supervision, together with consultation and feedback post training, was identified as necessary for long-term skills benefit. Lowenkamp and colleagues (2012) are in agreement regarding the benefits of post-training support to foster skill development. In their study investigating how coaching can assist probation officers with the adoption and application of newly acquired practice model skills, the majority of officers (72%) of the 185 participants comprising 90 county probation officers and 95 federal probation officers indicated that coaching increased their likelihood of using skills compared with training alone. A high percentage of officers (93% county and 83% federal) also reported that the coaching arrangement provided the opportunity to ask questions and express concerns about the skills they could not express within training, and provided them with a better understanding of how they could use the skills with clients and as part of their job (88% county and 92% federal).

As already noted, the interpersonal and process-oriented skills associated with generating the context for effective supervision apply across supervisor–supervisee and practitioner–client relationships. There is not enough scope within this chapter for an in-depth review of organisational culture or the influence of professional orientation on the way in which supervision is perceived, delivered and experienced. However, several key challenges to the delivery and receipt of staff supervision that maximises learning and reflective practice from the supervisees' perspective are presented in the next section.

What doesn't work in supervision?

Performance-based supervision

One of the key challenges for supervisees identified by Bradley and colleagues (2010) in their review of supervision practices in England,

South Africa and Sweden is the dominant focus on administration and performance issues as a result of organisational pressures to focus on targets and compliance, limiting space for reflection (Maidment and Beddoe, 2012; Manthorpe et al, 2015). This message was echoed in the Grant and McNeill (2014) study with Scottish criminal justice social workers who felt that the organisation's quest to meet key performance indicators created a tension between front-line staff and management resulting in a negative impact on the delivery of quality supervision, and a resistance by practitioners to what they perceived as technocratic management styles. Practitioners attributed quality of supervision more to the relational processes whereby the supervisor demonstrated congruency, positive regard and active listening, and less to quantifiable aspects of practice, other than measuring case outcomes in terms of progress. Beddoe's (2010) study in New Zealand with six qualified social work supervisors with a minimum of five years' experience explored the impact of 'risk discourse', and reinforced the assertion that the process, therefore the establishment of a contract that clearly stipulated the working relationship inclusive of limitations to confidentiality, roles and responsibilities of each party, and frequency of sessions more so than content, allows for good supervision.

Revell and Burton (2015) purport that when supervision is heavily weighted toward performance management and evaluation, supervisees are less likely to disclose their inability to meet practice demands, or share feelings regarding the impact of the work on their wellbeing due to a fear of being judged as incompetent, or perceived negatively by their manager and organisation. Clouder and Sellars (2004) agree, suggesting that supervisees often sanitise issues within such supervisory environments to avoid addressing certain issues and to present themselves in the best light. In return, supervisors may adopt an optimistic outlook regarding supervisee capacity and focus discussion on tangible issues the supervisor is able to address. Rudland and colleagues (2010) note that it is important for supervisors to engage in the continual appraisal of the supervisees' developmental stage and learning needs to minimise a 'blanket approach' to supervision, or one in which the supervisor becomes overly confident with the practitioner's level of competence, which can jeopardise professional development opportunities.

Wong and Lee (2015) identify the importance of striking a balance between performance management and support to promote ongoing practitioner development and competence. This is particularly important in order to alleviate social work supervisors' sense of being 'caught in the middle' when the organisational focus on outcomes compete with supervisor values of empowering and supporting staff. The study conducted by Hair (2013), comprising a mixed-methods web survey of supervisee needs, with 636 social workers employed across a broad spectrum of social work practice settings in Ontario Canada, support existing findings. Ninety-six percent of participants identified the need for supervision to promote knowledge and skill development, and emotional support. With respect to evaluation and performance, 28% of the participants confirmed that the presence of performance appraisals can make it difficult to raise practice issues in supervision. However, it was noted that establishing a relationship based on trust, with ground rules for supervision, could help eliminate the vulnerability associated with the inclusion of this administrative task concerned with evaluating practice against key performance indicators.

Lack of supervisor preparation and training

According to O'Donoghue (2012), supervision may be viewed as a rite of passage, as opposed to a professional development opportunity requiring a specialised set of skills, for staff within organisations that enter supervisory roles as part of an 'acting up' post with little preparation. Inadvertently, supervisors draw on their experiences of supervision, be it positive or negative, to guide their practice rather than engaging in assessed supervision training and education to facilitate reflective practice. Morrison (2005) suggests the lack of training is often based on the presumption that a competent practitioner will be a competent supervisor, and is often left to their own devices with little, if any, support to cultivate this new professional identity and responsibility.

According to Egan and colleagues (2015) and Rudland and colleagues (2010), the lack of training may lead to an exercise of power and control, reinforcing supervision as a process for accountability and monitoring. It can also position the supervisor as the 'expert' rather than a role model demonstrating reflection and self-evaluation. The need for supervisor training was reinforced in the study by Hair (2013), in which 88% of participants identified not only the need for training, but also the benefit of participating in refresher workshops, together with supervision of the supervisor, in order to provide effective professional supervision. Grant and McNeill (2014), in a study that used the Appreciative Inquiry model (a strengths-based approach to engage stakeholders in self-determined change) to reveal how Scottish criminal justice social workers conceptualise and construct meanings of quality in their daily practice with offenders, also identified the need for training. Participants reported relying on informal peer supervision and advice from more experienced colleagues to help guide their practice with clients, due to the lack of adequate supervisor experience, knowledge and skills required to provide meaningful support and guidance.

Other challenges identified from the supervisee perspective include lack of choice in the selection of supervisor, limited supervisor accountability, time restraints, and difficulties with access to supervision and the feedback process.

Allocation of supervisor

An Australian study comprising semi-structured interviews with 42 rural allied health professionals in Queensland and exploring perspectives on supervision arrangements, including perceived usefulness, effect on practice and barriers, found supervisor and supervisee fit to be of critical importance. Supervisory relationships found to be ineffective were often attributed to a poor match between supervisee and supervisor (Ducat et al, 2016). Similar findings were reported by O'Donoghue (2012) in a New Zealand study exploring the experiences of 16 social work practitioners as supervisees, and in particular how their supervision histories influenced their development and behaviour as a supervisee. Results showed that the participants actively disengaged from supervision when their expectations of the interactional process were not met, and they had limited choice regarding supervision, or selection of the supervisor. This was most notable within managerial supervision relationships (O'Donoghue, 2012). Egan's (2012) study of the practice of social work supervision involved a national online survey of 675 social workers across Australia who were employed in statutory, non-statutory, health and counselling occupations in 2007. The study found that over 80% of participants were supervised, with two thirds engaged in managerial supervision. Participants receiving managerial supervision were not afforded choice in the selection of their supervisor. Beddoe (2010) suggests that the inclusion of external clinical supervision, provided by an accredited professional supervisor engaged either by the organisation or the practitioner, who has some influence in relation to professional accountability, but no authority within the organisation, may prove beneficial in addressing the gap of 'no choice' within managerial supervision. Several benefits of external supervisory arrangements are noted, namely matching on professional and theoretical orientation;

greater sense of freedom to express frustrations with the organisation without fear of negative consequence; and a stronger focus on clinical practice and professional development (Beddoe, 2010).

Time and access to supervision

In a study of social work supervision with 675 social workers across Australia employed in statutory, non-statutory, health and counselling occupations, almost 40% of participants reported having difficulty accessing supervision predominantly due to time issues (Egan 2012). Rudland and colleagues (2010) and Ducat and colleagues (2016) suggest that where the culture of an organisation does not appreciate the importance of supervision, the allocation of resources and time required to support the process may be limited. Participants in Ducat and colleagues' (2016) study reported supervision arrangements that did not progress, and found that those that had been prevented from being initiated were in direct response to organisational drivers such as management support, supervision policies and procedures not being in place. Other factors affecting time and access related to geographical location. For rural staff, there was a greater reliance on technology-based supervision sessions utilising video-conferencing, Skype or telephone that did not always accommodate the type of supervision support required, such as direct observation. Sometimes, due to technical difficulties, supervision was interrupted. Other factors limiting supervisees' access to support were supervisee or supervisor time management skills that failed to prioritise supervision, and employment arrangements (for example, part-time working).

Limited supervisor accountability and feedback

In the study conducted by Hair (2013), participants identified the need for greater levels of supervisor accountability. Participants proposed a two-way performance evaluation process to provide supervisees the opportunity to challenge and/or support supervisors' judgement, contributing to a working alliance built on transparency and trust. With regard to the feedback process, Rudland and colleagues (2010) point to the importance of building in a cycle of continual feedback. This process incorporates the expected measures of performance and strategies for improvement, enables the supervisee to receive feedback on what is working well, and encourages supervisees' to generate their needs and identify options for improvement when dealing with underperformance issues. Practitioners working with offenders in the aforementioned study by Grant and McNeill (2014) concur, reporting that little recognition is received for good practice. A more balanced approach to feedback is warranted.

Need for future research

The literature concerning best practice with young offenders has predominantly focused on the skills used in worker–client interactions and its influence on client outcomes. Little attention has been paid to the influence of professional supervision on worker skill development and the implementation of evidence-based practice skills. One study working toward addressing this gap is being undertaken by one of the current authors, Charlene Pereira. Her PhD project is exploring the relationship between the style of professional supervision and the development and implementation of core effective practice skills by practitioners working with offenders. The project is connected to the overarching Youth Justice Division of the Queensland Department of Justice and Attorney General project in Australia. The Queensland project promotes the use of evidence-based practice (EBP) skills including role clarification, prosocial modelling, problem solving and relationship skills among youth justice workers across the state, with a view to reducing recidivism rates of young offenders under supervision. The project comprises the collection and analysis of audio recordings of youth justice worker–client interviews before and after training in EBP skills, to assess the extent to which the training programme has led to changed client supervision practices.

The PhD project involves audio recordings of client–worker supervision sessions, semi-structured interviews with supervisees and focus groups with supervisors. Interviews with youth justice case managers (supervisees) are concerned with identifying the components of the professional supervision framework found to be most helpful in contributing to their professional development, and in helping them implement the EBP skills with young offenders. The interviews also explore the influence of supervision on professional identity and sense of purpose; level of reflective practice; attitude toward, and engagement in, professional development activities; promotion of a collaborative approach to practice; and overall career satisfaction. Focus groups with the practice leaders (supervisors) explore similar themes, including their experience as a supervisor, professional development needs and overall career satisfaction, in addition to identifying the supervision framework that guides their practice with staff and the components of the framework they find most effective in supporting staff with the integration of the EBP skills with young offenders and in supporting staff members ongoing professional development. Data collection is scheduled to commence in late 2017.

Conclusion

Literature regarding the relationship between supervision and practitioner skill development, while limited, demonstrates the relational and structural skills associated with effective client supervision parallel effective staff supervision. Research findings confirm that further investigation into the relationship between the style of supervision and its influence on practitioner skill development warrants strong attention within criminal justice settings to address the tension between transformative aspirations of case managers taking on the role of 'change agents' requiring competency in the application of evidence-based practice skills, and the bureaucratic constraints reinforcing a compliance culture limiting the use of supervision for reflective practice and obstructing the much-needed shift in practitioner and supervisor perspectives of supervision towards skill development rather than just performance management.

References

AASW (Australian Association of Social Workers) (2014) AASW Supervision Standards, Canberra: AASW.

Beddoe, L. (2010) 'Surveillance or reflection: professional supervision in "the risk society"', British Journal of Social Work, 40(4): 1279–1296.

Bolin, R. and Applegate, B. (2016) 'Adultification in juvenile corrections: examining the orientations of juvenile and adult probation and parole officers', American Journal of Criminal Justice, 41(2): 321–339.

Bonta, J., Bourgon, G., Rugge, T., Gress, C. and Gutierrez, L. (2013) 'Taking the leap: from pilot project to wide-scale implementation of the Strategic Training Initiative in Community Supervision (STICS)', Justice Research and Policy, 15(1): 1–18.

Bonta, J., Rugge, T., Scott, T., Bourgon, G. and Yessine, A. (2008) 'Exploring the black box of community supervision', Journal of Offender Rehabilitation, 47(3): 248–270.

Bourgon, G. (2013) 'The demands on probation officers in the evolution of evidence-based practice: the forgotten foot soldier of community corrections', Federal Probation, 77(2): 2–21.

Bourgon, G., Bonta, J., Rugge, T. and Gutierrez, L. (2010) 'Technology transfer: the importance of ongoing clinical supervision in translating "what works" to everyday community supervision', in F. McNeill, P. Raynor and C. Trotter (eds) *Offender Supervision: New Directions in Theory, Research and Practice*, Cullompton: Willan, pp 91–112.

Bouverie Centre, The (Whittle, T., Rycroft, P., Wills, M., Weir, S., and Rottem, N.) (2013) *Clinical Supervision Guidelines for the Victorian Alcohol and Other Drugs and Community Managed Mental Health Sectors*, Melbourne: La Trobe University.

Bradley, G. and Hojer, S. (2009) 'Supervision reviewed: reflections on two different social work models in England and Sweden', *European Journal of Social Work*, 12(1): 71–85.

Bradley, G., Engelbrecht, L. and Hojer, S. (2010) 'Supervision: a force for change? Three stories told', *International Social Work*, 53(6): 773–790.

Campbell, J. (2006) *Essentials of Clinical Supervision*, Hoboken, NJ: John Wiley & Sons.

Carroll, M. (2007) 'One more time: what is supervision?', *Psychotherapy in Australia*, 13(3): 34–40.

Carroll, M. and Gilbert, M. (2011) *On Being a Supervisee: Creating Learning Partnerships* (2nd edn), Kew, Victoria: PsychOz Publications.

Christensen, D., Todahl, J. and Barrett, W. (2008) *Solution-Based Casework: An Introduction to Clinical and Case Management Skills in Casework Practice*, New York: Aldine Transaction.

Clouder, L. and Sellars, J. (2004) 'Reflective practice and clinical supervision: an interprofessional perspective', *Journal of Advanced Nursing*, 46(3): 262–269.

Davys, A. and Beddoe, L. (2010) *Best Practice in Professional Supervision: A Guide for the Helping Professions*, London, Jessica Kingsley.

Dehghani, K., Nasiriani, K. and Salimi, T. (2016) 'Requirements for nurse supervisor training: a qualitative content analysis', *Iranian Journal of Nursing and Midwifery Research*, 21(1): 63–70.

Driscoll, J. (2000) *Practicising Clinical Supervision*, London: Balliere Tindall.

Ducat, W., Martin, P., Kumar, S., Burge, V. and Abernathy, L. (2016) 'Oceans apart, yet connected: findings from a qualitative study on professional supervision in rural and remote allied health services', *Australian Journal of Rural Health*, 24(1): 29–35.

Egan, R. (2012) 'Australian social work supervision practice in 2007', *Australian Social Work*, 65(2): 171–184.

Egan, R., Maidment, J. and Connolly, M. (2015) 'Who is watching whom? Surveillance in Australian social work supervision', *British Journal of Social Work Advance Access*, pp 1–19.

Farmer, S. (1988) 'Communication competence in clinical education/supervision: critical notes', *The Clinical Supervisor*, 6(2): 29–46.

Gillingham, P. (2006) 'Risk assessment in child protection: problem rather than solution', *Australian Social Work*, 59(1): 86–98.

Grant, S. and McNeil, F. (2014) 'What matters in practice? Understanding "quality" in the routine supervision of offenders in Scotland', *British Journal of Social Work Advance Access*, pp 1–18.

Grant, J., Schofield, M. and Crawford, S. (2012) 'Managing difficulties in supervision: supervisors' perspectives', *Journal of Counseling Psychology*, 59(4): 528–541.

Hair, H. (2013) 'The purpose and duration of supervision, and the training and discipline of supervisors: what social workers say they need to provide effective services', *British Journal of Social Work*, 43(8): 1562–1588.

Harkness, D. and Hensley, H. (1991) 'Changing the focus of social work supervision: effects on client satisfaction and generalised contentment', *Social Work*, 36(6): 506–512.

Hawkins, P. and Shohet, R. (2006) *Supervision in the Helping Professions*, Maidenhead: Open University Press.

Kolb, D. (1984) *Experiential learning: Experience as the source of learning and development*, Englewood Cliffs, NJ: Prentice Hall.

Lawler, J. (2015) 'Motivation and meaning: the role of supervision', *Practice: Social Work in Action*, 27(4): 265–275.

Lizzio, A., Wilson, K. and Que, J. (2009) 'Relationship dimensions in the professional supervision of psychology graduates: supervisee perceptions of processes and outcomes', *Studies in Continuing Education*, 31(2): 127–140.

Lowenkamp, M., Robinson, C., Koutsenok, I., Lowenkamp, C. and Pearl, N. (2012) 'The importance of coaching: a brief survey of probation officers', *Federal Probation*, 76(2): 36–40.

Maidment, J. and Beddoe, L. (2012) 'Is social work supervision in "good heart"? A critical commentary', *Australian Social Work*, 65(2): 163–170.

Manthorpe, J., Moriarty, J., Hussein, S., Stevens, M. and Endellion, S. (2015) 'Content and purpose of supervision in social work practice in England: views of newly qualified social workers, managers and directors', *British Journal of Social Work*, 45(1): 52–68.

Milne, D., Aylott, H., Fitzpatrick, H. and Ellis, M. (2008) 'How does clinical supervision work? Using a "best evidence synthesis" approach to construct a basic model of supervision', *The Clinical Supervisor*, 27(2): 170–190.

Morrison, T. (2005) *Staff supervision in Social Care: Making a Sifference for Staff and Service Users* (3rd edn), Brighton: Pavilion.

Morrison, T. and Wonnacott, J. (2010) *Supervision: Now or Never. Reclaiming Reflective Supervision in Social Work*, Leeds: Children's Workforce Development Council.

O'Donoghue, K. (2012) 'Windows on the supervisee experience: an exploration of supervisees' supervision histories', *Australian Social Work*, 65(2): 214–231.

van Ooijen, E. (2003) Clinical Supervision Made Easy, Edinburgh: Churchill Livingstone.

Parton, N. (2006) *Safeguarding Children: Early Intervention and Surveillance in a Late Modern Society*, Basingstoke, Palgrave Macmillan.

Raynor, P. and Vanstone, M. (2015) 'Moving away from social work and half way back again: new research on skills in probation', *British Journal of Social Work*, 46(4): 1131–1147.

Revell, L. and Burton, V. (2015) 'Supervision and dynamics of collusion: a rule of optimism?', *British Journal of Social Work Advance Access*, pp 1–15.

Rolfe, G., Jasper, M. and Freshwater, D. (2011) *Critical Reflection in Practice: Generating Knowledge for Care* (2nd edn), Basingstoke: Palgrave Macmillan.

Rudland, J., Bagg, W., Child, S., de Beer, W., Hazell, W., Poole, P., Sheehan, D. and Wilkinson, T. (2010) 'Maximising learning through effective supervision', *New Zealand Medical Journal*, 123(1309): 117–125.

Schon, D. (1983) *The Reflective Practitioner: How Professionals Think in Action*, New York, NY: Basic Books.

Smythe, E.A., MacCulloch, T. and Charmley, R. (2009) 'Professional supervision: trusting the wisdom that "comes"', *British Journal of Guidance and Counselling*, 37(1): 17–25.

Spouse, J. and Redfern, L. (eds) (2000) *Successful Supervision in Health Care Practice*, Oxford: Blackwell Science.

Stanley, T. (2007) 'Risky work: child protection practice', *Social Policy Journal of New Zealand*, 30 (March): 163–177.

Taxman, F., Shepardson, E. and Byrne, J. (2004) '"Tools of the trade": a guide to incorporating science into practice', Washington, DC: National Institute of Corrections.

Trotter, C. (2013) 'Reducing recidivism through probation supervision: what we know and don't know from four decades of research', *Federal Probation*, 77(2): 43–48.

Trotter, C. (2015) *Working with Involuntary Clients: A Guide to Practice* (3rd edn), Crows Nest, NSW: Allen and Unwin.

Trotter, C. and Evans, P. (2012) 'An analysis of supervision skills in youth probation', *Australian and New Zealand Journal of Criminology*, 45(2): 255–273.

Trotter, C., Evans, P. and Baidawi, S.H. (2016) 'The effectiveness of challenging skills in work with young offenders', *International Journal of Offender Therapy and Comparative Criminology*, epub, pp 1–16.

Tsui, M.S. (2005) *Social Work Supervision: Contexts and Concepts*, Thousand Oaks, CA: Sage Publications.

Walters, S., Matson, S., Baer, J. and Ziedonis, D. (2005) Effectiveness of workshop training for psychosocial addiction treatments: A systematic review, *Journal of Substance Abuse Treatment*, 29(4): pp 283–293.

Weld, N. (2012) *A Practical Guide to Transformative Supervision for the Helping Professions. Amplifying Insight*, London: Jessica Kingsley.

Wong, P. and Lee, A. (2015) 'Dual roles of social work supervisors: strain and strengths as managers and clinical supervisors', *China Journal of Social Work*, 8(2): 164–181.

Part 3:
Evidence-based practice
with diverse groups

FOURTEEN

Evidence-based skills in Welsh youth justice settings

Pamela Ugwudike and Gemma Morgan

Introduction

There is a dearth of theoretical and empirical knowledge of the skills youth justice practitioners in England and Wales employ during the one-to-one supervision of young people undertaking court orders, and in their interactions with young people involved in the youth justice system in other capacities. Consequently, although efforts have been made to assess and improve the quality of one-one to supervision skills in adult criminal justice settings (see, for example, Rex and Hosking, 2013; Sorsby et al, 2013), not much is known about the quality of front-line youth justice practice. This chapter presents the findings of process evaluations which sought *inter alia* to explore the under-researched subject-matter of supervision skills or the skills practitioners employ during one-to-one supervision in youth justice contexts. Three Statutory Orders Teams (SOTs) in Wales[1] were evaluated, and the evaluation tool employed was the CPAI-2010, which is an empirically validated tool for assessing criminal justice services to ascertain whether the services employ evidence-based skills and practices (Gendreau et al, 2010). CPAI-2010 domains and items derive from studies of effective practices (Latessa et al, 2002). Interventions that have attained high scores on earlier versions of the CPAI have been found to produce reductions in rates of recidivism (Lowenkamp and Latessa, 2004; Lowenkamp et al, 2006; Latessa et al, 2013).

In the current chapter, we focus on sections G and H of the CPAI-2010. Both domains comprise measures of research-based supervision skills known as core correctional practices (CCPs). The domains assess how well services implement the broad range of evidence-based CCPs. By focusing on these domains, the current evaluations follow the model set by other studies that have explored the use of CCPs in other jurisdictions (see, for example, Dowden and Andrews, 2004; Bonta et al, 2008; Robinson et al, 2012; Raynor et al, 2014; Ugwudike et al,

2014; Chadwick et al, 2015) and youth justice settings (Trotter, 2013; Trotter et al, 2015). These studies have observed supervision sessions and some have interviewed practitioners to assess the use of the CCPs. The studies have found that the CCPs are associated with reductions in rates of reoffending and levels of assessed risk.

Assessing the application of CCPs using the CPAI enables researchers to identify and share with services the changes they should introduce to embed evidence-based supervision skills in practice. Indeed, it has been argued that the CPAI represents one of several emerging modes of knowledge transfer that can help bridge the gulf that exists between research and practice by enabling the effective transfer of knowledge about evidence-based practices to real-world settings (Taxman and Belenko, 2011). Studies have shown that practitioners who participate in CPAI evaluations believe that the evaluations are very informative, and evaluations provide useful insights into how best to identify and implement effective skills and practices: 'Feedback from CPAI users has often been positive because just going through the exercise is a tremendous learning experience for agencies …' (Andrews and Bonta, 2010, p 404).

Echoing this, Smith (2013, p 82) remarks that the CPAI-2010 'provides practitioners with the tools needed to implement evidence-based services'. It follows that the process evaluations reported here can help address the lacuna created by the paucity of theoretical and empirical insights on the nature and quality of one-to-one supervision in youth justice settings. In doing so, the evaluation can bridge gaps between research and practice.

Youth justice practice

Very limited research exists on the precise application of one-to-one supervision skills in youth justice contexts. There is an abundance of practice guides on case management, how to implement National Standards, and Key Elements of Effective Practice.[2] But there is limited existing research on what one-to-one youth justice supervision practice looks like in England and Wales. Consequently, not much is known about the precise skills youth justice practitioners should employ to animate the approaches set out in the guides.

The dearth of theoretical and empirical knowledge of the content of youth justice practice was acknowledged in 2008, in a report by Mason and Prior (2008). The report emerged from a review of effective techniques for engaging young people who had offended or were at risk of offending. A key objective of the review, which was commissioned by the Youth Justice Board, was to produce a source document on effective techniques for engaging young people in the justice system. It was envisaged that the document would supplement the Youth Justice Board's guidance on effective practice. In the report, the authors noted the paucity of research on practice skills for engaging young people involved in the youth justice system. They acknowledged the large body of evidence that currently exists on the characteristics of effective interventions including cognitive-behavioural interventions, but decried the paucity of insights on practice skills and techniques that can be used to implement the interventions effectively.

Reflecting on this paucity, Mason and Prior (2008) stated that the existing evidence does not 'tell us about the techniques or lessons for practice when applying interventions' (p 10). In other words, the studies, though insightful, do not illuminate the skills and techniques practitioners should employ to work with young people to build relationships and encourage them to make requisite changes.

Following Mason and Prior's (2008) wide-ranging review of the effective practice literature, the Youth Justice Board commissioned an Ipsos MORI (2010) survey of the techniques practitioners employ to engage young people in youth justice services. It was noted that the survey was 'a first step' towards studying engagement techniques (2010, p 4). The survey generated the views of practitioners on effective engagement techniques, and obstacles to successful engagement. Young people's views were also solicited using questions that assessed their experiences of participating in service delivery. Four-hundred-and-twenty-one practitioners within 66 YOTs in ten regions across England and Wales participated in the survey. Interviews were conducted with 47 practitioners and 78 young people. Reinforcing earlier findings (see, for example, Mason and Prior, 2008), the findings noted the lack of research on youth justice practice skills and indicated that practitioners could not generally define 'engagement' or how it might manifest in practice.

Another review of effective practice with young people in England and Wales, which was commissioned by the Ministry of Justice, drew largely on the international research evidence, mainly from the United States, and attributed the limited knowledge regarding the definition of engagement to the lack of robust research on frontline youth justice practice in England and Wales (Adler et al, 2016). The findings of the review relating to practice skills largely mirrored the earlier findings recorded by Mason and Prior (2008) and Ipsos MORI (2010). Thus, in terms of practice skills that can motivate desired change, the review found that quite unlike punitive practice skills, therapeutic effective skills tended to be more productive. Examples identified were multimodal interventions including advocacy and brokerage practices, and taking into account the wider familial and social contexts of the young person. Motivational interviewing techniques and effective communication skills based on 'mutual understanding, respect and fairness' were also identified as key practice skills. In addition, helping young people build the social and other skills that are useful for prosocial problem solving (using cognitive-behavioural approaches including cognitive skills building) were associated with reductions in reoffending. Indeed, equipping practitioners with skills required for delivering cognitive-behavioural approaches is a key element of the Youth Justice Board's strategy for achieving best outcomes for young people and strategy (Searle, 2015).

Although the reviews cited here point to the efficacy of certain interventions and skills, what is lacking is empirical knowledge of the extent to which the skills are applied effectively, if at all, during supervision. It is important to study the content or 'black box' of supervision (Bonta et al, 2008) to ascertain whether skills that are supported by a large body of research evidence are being deployed. This can help identify and bridge gaps between research and practice. It can, as such, improve the quality of practice and outcomes. Exploring supervision practice skills can also improve our understanding of the conditions (including the organisational arrangements) that affect the application of evidence-based skills.

Studying supervision to bridge gaps between research and practice

Sections G and H of the CPAI-2010 contain items that are used to assess the skills services employ and to also assess whether services apply the evidence-based skills known as core correctional practices (CCPs) (see Table 14.1). As noted earlier, CCPs are practice skills that, according to the international research evidence, are associated with positive outcomes such as engagement, participation and reductions in reoffending rates (Andrews and Kiessling, 1980; Dowden and Andrews, 2004; Lipsey, 2009; Trotter and Evans, 2012; Trotter, 2013; Raynor et al, 2014; Trotter et al, 2015). One of the CCPs – relationship practices – constitutes the relationship principle. It comprises several dimensions of effective interpersonal and relationship-building skills that foster good supervision relationships. The remaining CCPs listed in Table 14.1 underpin the structuring principle, and they are useful for helping service users develop prosocial skills for avoiding or responding to situations that could trigger offending behaviour.

The skills are change-focused and they affect what service users learn during interactions with practitioners and the quality of the influence the practitioners exert on them. Structuring skills are: prosocial modelling; effective reinforcements and disapproval; prosocial skills building; problem solving; cognitive restructuring; advocacy and brokerage practices; effective use of authority; and the structuring elements of motivational interviewing (Bonta and Andrews, 2017).

It could be argued that, as Table 14.1 demonstrates, some of the structuring CCPs comprise relationship-building components. For example, being encouraging, reliable and respectful are useful relationship-building dimensions of the CCP 'effective use of authority'. Equally, showing empathy is a relationship-building dimension of motivational interviewing.

The CCPs are associated with reductions in attrition, greater service-user engagement and reductions in reoffending rates (Dowden and Andrews, 2004; Lipsey, 2009; Trotter and Evans, 2012; Trotter, 2013; Raynor et al, 2014; Trotter et al, 2015). As Latessa and colleagues (2013) note: 'These CCPs have been validated on more than 700 individual adult and juvenile programs by correlating scores with offender recidivism' (p 12). They were first introduced by Andrews and Kiessling (1980), but were expanded by Gendreau and Andrews (1989) in an earlier version of the CPAI, and Table 14.1 sets out the expanded version. Section G of the CPAI-2010 assesses the use of all the CCPs listed in Table 14.1, apart from inter-agency communication/use of community resources, which is assessed using Section H of the CPAI-2010. Most of the CCPs listed in Table 14.1 are implicitly enshrined in the current youth justice skills and knowledge matrix published by the Youth Justice Board (2013), which states that the skills should be used to assess staff professional development and training needs. The skills have also been retained in the latest matrix (Youth Justice Board, 2016).

To our knowledge, no other study has explored the use of these skills in youth justice settings in England and Wales, but studies conducted in other jurisdictions have found that the evidence-based CCPs are not consistently used in practice. Dowden and Andrews (2004) found that the CCPs were 'rarely' used in the programmes or interventions included in their meta-analysis. They found that the use of CCPs was present in only 16% of the studies that explored interventions that had case manager involvement, and they concluded that: 'The majority of the programs that incorporated elements of CCP were associated with substantially higher mean effect sizes than programs that did not' (p 210). Dowden and Andrews (2004) also found that, of the few

Table 14.1: Core correctional practices (CCPs)

Core correctional practices	Examples
Prosocial modelling	Modelling prosocial attitudes and behaviour using child-friendly role plays to encourage young people to learn new behaviours. Employing coping models to vividly demonstrate to young people the prosocial strategies that can be used to cope with problematic situations.
Effective reinforcement	Using positive reinforcements such as praise and rewards to reinforce a specific prosocial behaviour, rather than using punitive measures. Offering clearly described reinforcements and more support immediately after the young person demonstrates the desired behaviour. Encouraging the young person to reflect on reasons for reinforcements and long-term benefits of the desired behaviour.
Effective disapproval	Challenging a specific antisocial attitude or behaviour by showing disapproval but not being judgemental or accusatory. Showing disapproval in a non-blaming way immediately after negative behaviour/speech and explaining reasons for disapproval. Modelling prosocial alternatives and encouraging the young person to reflect on reasons why the behaviour is unacceptable and the long-term consequences of such behaviour. Stopping disapproval once the behaviour is corrected and approving the young person's effort to change the behaviour.
Problem solving	Working with young people to help them learn problem-solving or social skills for dealing with various issues or situations that place them at risk of offending. It involves identifying problems that affect behaviour, identifying and evaluating goals and solutions, and designing, implementing and evaluating a clear plan of action (without criticising the young person at any stage). Useful for helping young people realise that they have the skills to identify their goals and address problems. This can give them a sense of personal strength, control and self-determination, all of which are considered key dimensions of desistance (see, for example, Maruna and LeBel, 2010; McNeill, 2006).
Prosocial skills building (using structured procedures)	Part of the process of helping young people learn problem-solving skills working collaboratively with the young person to identify and practise new prosocial skills. This involves defining the skill clearly to the young person, modelling the skill, using role to encourage the young person to practise the skills in several scenarios including scenarios that become increasingly difficult for the young person to deal with in a prosocial manner. This helps the young person acquire prosocial skills for responding to problematic situations. Feedback and recommendations for improvement should also be offered.

(continued)

Table 14.1: Core correctional practices (CCPs) (continued)

Core correctional practices	Examples
Effective use of authority	Focusing on the young person's behaviour rather than the young person, providing clear guidelines, using a normal voice rather than an intimidating or raised voice, clarifying roles and maintaining an adequate balance between the caring and controlling dimensions of practice, being encouraging, being reliable and action-orientated, being respectful even when compliance issues arise, rewarding and praising compliance.
Cognitive restructuring	Encouraging the young person to identify and describe situations that trigger risky thoughts, feelings, beliefs and attitudes that could give rise to offending behaviour. Encouraging the young person to learn the skills required for replacing these with rational, prosocial alternatives. Providing opportunities for the young person to practise the skills they are learning.
Relationship practices	Being optimistic that the young person can achieve positive change; showing respect, empathy, warmth, enthusiasm, flexibility and commitment to providing help and support; being solution-focused; showing maturity; showing ability to use role plays to model prosocial behaviour; focusing on solutions not problems; being non-judgemental. Good working relationships are considered vital for desistance.
Motivational interviewing	Client-centred practice involving a good supervision relationship that engages the young person, eliciting motivation to change by using evocative and other questioning styles to develop discrepancies between the young person's current and desired states, using questioning rather than confrontational techniques to counter resistance, helping the young person develop self-efficacy, and showing empathy.
Inter-agency communication/use of community resources	Offering advocacy and brokerage services by facilitating access to social welfare services that can help address substance misuse-related problems, socioeconomic problems such as educational, housing and employment-related difficulties, and other related issues.
	(See Andrews and Kiessling, 1980; Miller and Rollnick, 2012; Dowden and Andrews, 2004; Lipsey, 2009; Gendreau et al, 2010)

programmes that did use CCP dimensions, most achieved substantial reductions in recidivism compared with programmes that did not use the CCPs, particularly if the CCPs were used alongside Risk-Need-Responsivity principles (see also Robinson et al, 2012). Recent studies also show that service users supervised by practitioners who apply the CCPs during routine supervision tend to achieve reduced rates of reconviction in adult supervision contexts (Bonta et al, 2008; Raynor et al, 2014; Chadwick et al, 2015;) and youth justice settings (Trotter 2013, 2015).

The study

This chapter presents the findings of process evaluations conducted in three youth justice services. The key objectives of the evaluations were:

- to use sections G and H of the CPAI-2010 (which comprises validated measures of the CCPs) to assess the extent to which youth justice services deploy CCPs, which as noted earlier, are evidence-based skills that can promote service user participation and long-term positive change;
- to assess if sections G and H of the CPAI-2010 will highlight differences between three youth offending services in Wales in terms of the skills they employ;
- to explore the suitability of using the CPAI-2010 (which was developed in Canada) to assess skills and practices in English and Welsh youth justice settings.

The foregoing aims are consistent with the Youth Justice Board's (2015, p 5) commissioning priorities and intention to 'make known and promote good practice in the operation of the youth justice system and the provision of youth justice services'.

Methodology

As already noted, the process evaluations were conducted using the CPAI-2010. This chapter focuses on the findings relating to sections G and H of the CPAI, which as noted earlier, comprise indicators of evidence-based CCPs.

Sample

Three SOTs participated in the process evaluations. As noted earlier, SOTs supervise young people who are serving court-imposed statutory orders and the SOTs form part of the Youth Offending Teams (YOTs), which were created by the Crime and Disorder Act of 1998 with the following remit:

- preventing offending and reoffending by young people; and

- providing 'youth justice services' via multi–agency YOT teams.

YOTs are statutorily required to comprise at least one social worker, one police officer, one probation officer, one health worker and one education worker (Crime and Disorder Act 1998). Some YOTs identify themselves as youth offending services, while others use the title youth justice services, or youth offending and prevention services. The participating SOTs were, at the time of the initial process evaluations (from November 2014 to April 2015), supervising young people who presented mainly with problems relating to substance misuse, violent behaviour, sex offending, poor family relationships and antisocial attitudes.

Phases of the study

The study was conducted in three phases.

Phase 1

Phase 1 involved scoring section G of the CPAI (which assesses the use of CCPs). Structured observations of sessions between participating staff and service users were conducted to score the section, which comprises items that assess whether a specific CCP dimension is present. Each observation lasted an average of one hour.

Phase 2

In contrast, phase 2 of the study involved using section H to conduct structured interviews with participating teams to assess whether they employ skills and practices required for effective communication with, and referrals to, relevant social welfare agencies. The objective of referrals should be to facilitate service users' access to social institutions and services, such as educational, employment, training, housing, substance misuse, healthcare and other services.

Table 14.2: Number of staff interviewed and sessions observed

	Number of staff interviewed	Number of sessions observed
SOT1	8	8
SOT2	9	8
SOT3	9	11
Total	26	27

Scoring both sections of the CPAI-2010 involved selecting 'Yes', 'No' or 'NA.' A score of 'Yes' indicated that the requisite skill is present; a score of 'No' indicated the opposite; and a score of 'NA' indicated that the skill or practice was not applicable. To calculate how an agency performed in each section the CPAI, the assessor added the number of items that were scored as 'Yes' in that section. The assessor then converted the total into a percentage of the number of applicable items in that section. For example, the number of 'Yes' scores SOT1 attained in section G was 18 and the total number of applicable items in that section was 45. Therefore, the overall score was 18/45 = 40%. Scores were allocated according to the classification set out in Table 14.3.

Table 14.3: Classifying CPAI-2010 scores

Classification	Score (%)
Very satisfactory	70+
Satisfactory	50–69
Unsatisfactory	Below 50

Phase 3

In the third phase, the evaluations focused on assessing the issue of what one of us has conceptualised as evaluation responsivity.[3] This relates to the suitability of applying the CPAI-2010, which was developed in a different jurisdiction, in English and Welsh contexts. It is important to recognise that aspects of an evaluation tool developed in one jurisdiction might not be directly relevant or responsive to the policy and practice arrangements in another jurisdiction. Jurisdictional differences mean that evaluation tools may have to be adapted or rendered locally relevant to ensure that meaningful evaluations are conducted.

To assess evaluation responsivity, semi-structured interviews were conducted with 26 staff in the participating teams (see Table 14.2). The data generated were analysed using thematic analysis to identify common themes and summarise the themes regarding the tool's suitability. We envisaged that the themes would be useful for assessing how best to adapt the tool to suit local youth justice contexts in Wales.

Methodological limitations

There are several limitations associated with utilising the CPAI-2010 in England and Wales. As mentioned earlier, the evaluation tool employed was developed in a different jurisdiction (Canada). As such, proper attention should be paid to evaluation responsivity. Another methodological issue relates to the generalisability of findings. Three SOTs within three YOTs in Wales participated in the evaluations. They were not randomly selected, so the generalisability of findings is limited. Furthermore, only one accredited assessor conducted the evaluations, and this poses implications for the reliability of findings.

However, the assessor had undertaken rigorous training on the CPAI-2010 to achieve accreditation. This accreditation facility may have alleviated problems of subjectivity and bias (Durlak and DuPre, 2008). There was also a facility known as a confidence rating (CR), which was used to indicate how confident the assessor was that a score of 'Yes' or 'No' awarded in respect of an item of the CPAI was reliable. The CR is rated from 1–5, and a CR of 4–5 indicates that the assessor is very confident in the score, perhaps because he/she has seen documentary evidence or observed the relevant practice consistently. By contrast, an average CR of anything less than 3 indicates that the assessor is not sure of the reliability of a score. The CR may have improved the reliability of scores.

Findings

As Figure 14.1 indicates, the three SOTs attained 'unsatisfactory' scores (below 50%) in section G.

Table 14.4 shows that the confidence rating was high, indicating a high level of confidence in the reliability of the scores awarded (using section G).

Figure 14.1: Section G – Core Correctional Practices

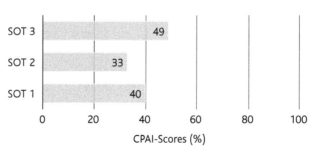

CPAI-Scores (%)

Table 14.4: Section G: confidence rating

	SOT1	SOT2	SOT3
Confidence rating	5	4	5

Table 14.5 sets out the mean scores the three SOTs attained compared with the applicable section G scores. It suggests that the CPAI-2010 revealed some differences (albeit slight differences) between the SOTs in their use of skills.

The table demonstrates that SOT2 was the lowest scoring SOT, and that all three SOTs applied more relationship-related skills than the skills embodied in the structuring principle. The SOTs also attained high scores for effective use of authority. During observations of supervision sessions, there was evidence that the practitioners in all three SOTs were employing the dimensions of effective use of authority that improve the quality of the relationship between the practitioner and the young person. For example, staff were giving encouraging messages to motivate the young people, and they were also being respectful (see Table 14.1 for examples of effective use of authority). However, the observations found very few examples of the structuring dimensions of that CCP (effective use of authority). Thus, skills such as providing 'direct and specific' guidelines, and reinforcing desired attitudes and behaviours, were not being employed consistently.

Table 14.5 also reveals that all three SOTs attained lower scores for the remaining CCPs, and these were the CCPs underpinning the structuring principle (Bonta and Andrews, 2017). The CCPs in question were prosocial modelling, problem solving, cognitive

Table 14.5: Section G: mean scores for the staff observed in each of the three SOTs

CPAI items (section G: CCPs)	Possible scores	SOT1	SOT2	SOT3
Prosocial modelling	4	0.71	0.5	0.72
Effective reinforcement	4	1.8	1.2	1.4
Effective disapproval	4	0.57	0.25	0.36
Problem solving	6	1.2	0.75	2.9
Prosocial skills building	5	0	0	0
Effective use of authority	10	6.8	5.3	7.6
Cognitive self-change	5	1.5	1.5	1.8
Relationship practices	7	5.8	5.8	6.5
Total	45	18.38	15.3	21.28

restructuring and the structuring elements of motivational interviewing.

Unlike section G, section H, which examines how well agencies work in an inter-agency or multiagency capacity, was a high scoring area for the three SOTs. They achieved the highest scores attainable in that section and a classification of 'very satisfactory'. Five items were assessed by the section: 'brokerage' and 'advocacy' (see Table 14.1 for a description), 'communication' (maintaining effective interagency communication), 'coordination' (maintaining effective interagency coordination) and 'links' (providing information about available services). Table 14.6 demonstrates that the average confidence rating was high, indicating that there was a high level of confidence in the reliability of section H scores.

Table 14.6: Section H: confidence rating

	SOT1	SOT2	SOT3
Confidence rating	5	4.6	4.6

Semi-structured interviews

The semi-structured interviews conducted to assess evaluation responsivity revealed two key themes that were conceptualised as:

• utility of CPAI-2010 evaluations;
• implications of jurisdictional differences.

Utility of CPAI-2010 evaluations

As other studies cited earlier have found, staff participating in the current study believed that a CPAI-2010 evaluation could potentially bridge gaps between research and practice:

> From my perspective if we can learn something from it [the CPAI-2010 evaluation], I'm all for it. As a service, we can never stand still. We need to evolve and change and keep up with the latest research. (Senior practitioner 1)

The youth offending service managers quoted as follows reinforced this view:

I found the [CPAI-2010] report very useful. A lot of the time things confirm your suspicions but you can't just act on your suspicions you need to know for definite. And to have someone come in from the outside taking a look at us and from a different perspective as well.... So yeah I think it is useful, there's plenty of recommendations there that we will want to pursue. And I think perhaps for me the most pressing one is the need for staff to have a base level in training of cognitive-behavioural work, because we have such a mix of different skills sets. That will be one as a priority I would like to take forward. (YOT manager 2)

Some of the stuff that you shared in the feedback has been positive and we were able to share that with staff and just doing stuff like that is motivational. (YOT manager 3)

These two YOT managers describe the benefits of CPAI evaluations, alluding to its utility for developing effective practice.

Implications of jurisdictional differences

Some SOT practitioners and managers expressed concerns about aspects of the CPAI's terminology. An example is the term 'criminogenic'. For some, the term was not cognisant of the holistic and welfarist ideals of Welsh youth justice practice:

The language needs to be adapted, that's probably the easiest thing. I guess the second part is where do we use it in our system? Do we just use it to look at a single programme or does it need to be adapted to take into account our holistic approach and to recognize that we have welfare responsibilities as well? It focuses just on the criminogenic really. It has to be adopted to recognise that our role is slightly wider. (YOT manager 1)

Some practitioners also ascribed negative connotations to the term 'satisfactory' which features in the CPAI's scoring protocol. The term is used to describe the overall performance of services that attain a CPAI score of 50%–69% (see Table 14.1):

Satisfactory sounds terrible, it sounds like you are not satisfactory at all. (Practitioner 9)

In this extract, a participating practitioner reports that the term 'satisfactory' does not sufficiently capture the quality of work youth justice practitioners do with children.

> I'm surprised that 70% plus is 'very satisfactory' I thought it would have been higher. (Practitioner 11)

Some of the participating practitioners felt that classifications more complimentary than 'satisfactory' and 'very satisfactory' would accurately describe the quality of work done to attain the accompanying scores. However, a youth justice manager questioned the merit of this position:

> If people can't look at a score and can't say 'that's not so good' 'that's good' then there's something wrong. I don't have a problem with the scoring. (YOT Manager 2)

It is worth noting that the feedback offered by some of the participating practitioners stemmed mainly from misinterpretations, sometimes triggered by jurisdictional differences. The feedback did not reflect the quality of the CPAI as a reliable evaluation tool. Rather, it highlighted the importance of developing a tool that is more suited to policy and practice arrangements within a given jurisdiction.

Overall performance

The evaluations found several areas of very good practice. The SOTs performed well in the section G items that assessed relationship-related practices, indicating that staff were committed to building good working relationships with young people. As already noted, studies show that good relationships can motivate participation and engagement of young people during supervision and could also contribute to desistance (Burnett, 2004; Barry, 2010; Gray, 2013).

However, it is also acknowledged that building relationships is a crucial but not the sole dimension of effective supervision practice. For instance, McNeill (2014), writing from a desistance perspective, argues that interventions should target not only social capital (developing relationships and networks that generate opportunities). They should *also* target human capital (developing offenders' personal capacities and skills). Equally, the Good Lives model of rehabilitation draws attention to the importance of helping service users acquire the tools (the secondary goods – prosocial skills and competencies) they need to achieve the good life (primary goods – life goal or outcomes such as wellbeing, happiness and so on.) to which they aspire (Ward and Fortune, 2013).

Other studies have revealed the tendency to emphasise relationship building alongside practices and activities that are not necessarily change-focused. For example, the Ipsos MORI (2010) survey, cited earlier, found that practitioners laudably built good relationships with young people and focused on activities that were equally commendable but not necessarily change-focused. Key examples were horse riding and cooking. It was noted in the survey that: 'Many of these activities, while beneficial and fun for the young person, did not, other than reducing time available to commit offences, directly address their offending behaviour' (Ipsos MORI, 2010, pp 7–8; see also Mason and Prior, 2008).

Similarly, the current evaluations revealed that in all three SOTs, the evidence-based skills that 'directly address offending behaviour', which are also the skills that inhere in the structuring principle, were not employed consistently (during the period of the observations). This finding reinforces the findings of other studies that have explored supervision skills in other jurisdictions. For example, Bonta and colleagues' (2008) evaluation of audio-recorded supervision sessions involving 62 practitioners and 154 adult and young service users undertaking community-based orders found that prosocial modelling was used in only 3% or the session while cognitive-behavioural approaches were employed in less than 25% of the sessions.

Prosocial modelling and role-play activities that provide opportunities for young people to practise the skills they are learning are practice skills that are significantly linked to reductions in reoffending (Trotter et al, 2015); however, they were not employed consistently by the practitioners who were observed as part of the current study. In the Ipsos MORI (2010) survey, some practitioners noted the importance of giving young people opportunities to practise what they were learning so the new skills could become entrenched and easily replicable. The practitioners suggested that although some young people understood what they were learning from their caseworker about how to change their behaviour, they were necessarily able to implement the key skills effectively:

> I supervise one young person at the moment who is actually amazing in her levels of communication and understanding. And she's brilliant in terms of telling you all about the victim and why victims suffer in society and why her victim

particularly suffered and why she offends, what she sees as the reasons. But actually she still is really quite a high-risk, complex, challenging young person and it's being able to implement all the things that she's saying that she needs help with. (YOT 1, interview 1, caseworker)

Thus, giving young people opportunities to practise the new skills they are learning during interventions is vital. The international research literature also indicates that other skills (underpinning the structuring principle) are not consistently applied in practice. For example, in their meta-analysis of studies that explored the use of practice skills, Dowden and Andrews (2004) noted that challenging or 'showing effective disapproval' was the least observed skill. Yet, studies in adult criminal justice settings, and youth justice contexts, show that employing the technique pays significant dividends (Trotter and Evans, 2012; Trotter, 2013; Trotter et al, 2015), and has been linked to reductions in reconviction rates when employed alongside other CCPs (Dowden and Andrews, 2004; Raynor et al, 2014; Trotter et al, 2015). In addition, there is evidence that when applied independently, this approach can encourage service-user engagement and reductions in reconviction rates (Trotter et al, 2015).

The current evaluations also found that the SOTs performed very well in section H, which measures the quality of inter-agency collaboration to widen young people's access to relevant social welfare and other services. This could in part be attributable to the nature of YOTs as multi-agency services. Their statutory constitution necessitates inter-agency communication and collaboration with social work services, probation, police, educational services, healthcare and other services. The desistance literature emphasises that access to these social institutions and services can aid the desistance process (see, for example, Farrall 2002; Farrall et al, 2014). The desistance literature also suggests that brokerage and advocacy services that link young people (and their families) to these services is indeed preferred by young people to surveillance-focused strategies or efforts to address offending behaviour without consideration of wider social issues that affect their lives (Barry, 2013). Providing access to relevant services can empower young people to participate in civic life as full and active citizens.

Factors that potentially impede the use of structuring skills

Studies reveal that evaluating interventions and providing adequate staff training on evidence-based approaches can help enhance programme integrity because they encourage staff to adopt evidence-based skills and practices (Alexander et al, 2013; Bonta et al, 2011; Landenberger and Lipsey, 2005; Robinson et al, 2012; Sorsby et al, 2013). As already noted, staff who participate in CPAI evaluations find the evaluations useful for identifying effective practices and reflecting on how to align their work with the relevant evidence base (Andrews and Bonta, 2010; Smith, 2013).

However, the findings of the current evaluation point to the need for staff training on how to deploy skills that have been shown by a large body of research to reduce reoffending and support desistance. The few reviews of youth justice practice also draw attention to the need for adequate training (Mason and Prior, 2008; Ipsos MORI, 2010; Adler et al, 2016). The Ipsos MORI (2010) survey found 'few formal training opportunities within the YOTs' and it was noted that:

> Given the importance of the worker in delivering successful interventions and engaging young people effectively, it is clear that staff need training to equip them with the skills they need. Many practitioners felt that they brought training and experience from previous roles into their current work. (p 38)

A participant in the Ipsos MORI survey stated that 'I've been qualified seven years, I don't think I've been ever given any training on how to engage, deal with people that are particularly challenging ...' (Ipsos MORI, 2010, p 38). Similarly, Mason and Prior (2008, p 48) noted in their review of the effective practice literature that 'on the basis of the themes developed throughout this review, we also suggest training in case management practice.... Practitioners need to have, or have access to ... training'.

Equally, the review by Adler and colleagues suggested that:

> Training, particularly around specific techniques for engagement and intervention was highlighted by practitioners. Although engagement can be largely dependent on the relationship between the worker and young person, equipping practitioners with knowledge about relevant guidance, techniques, training and tools can facilitate and encourage best practice. (2016, pp 8–9)

Training programmes such as the Strategic Training Initiative in Community Supervision (STICS) developed by Canadian researchers for adult supervision practitioners represent an example of a validated training model that can embed insights form research evidence in practice (Bonta et al, 2011). Evaluations of the STICS programme have found that the reconviction rates of service users supervised by STICS-trained staff tend to be lower than the reconviction rates of service users supervised by untrained staff.[4]

Added to training deficits, there are other factors that could impede the use of skills such as the CCPs which can be time-intensive.[5] Key examples include heavy caseloads, lack of organisational harmony, staff shortages, inadequate administrative support and constant policy changes (Clarke et al, 2004; Raynor, 2004; Ipsos MORI, 2010). The Youth Justice Board has sustained significant funding cuts (Youth Justice Board, 2015) in recent years. This could reduce staffing levels, increase caseloads and adversely affect training and general availability of resources. A potential upshot of these developments is that they could limit the ability of staff to understand and apply evidence-based supervision skills. Building relationships, effective use of authority, and using the skills that constitute the structuring principle – for example, using role plays to teach service users how to apply the skills they are learning – are all time-intensive practices. These practices might be difficult to accomplish in the midst of an unfavourable policy climate of budget cuts, limited staff resources, heavy caseloads, and other problematic policy and practice arrangements.

Evaluation responsivity: transferability of the CPAI-2010 evaluation methodology to English and Welsh jurisdictions

Most of the participating staff acknowledged the utility of the CPAI-2010 as a tool that can enrich practitioners' knowledge of evidence-based skills and practices. But the participants' concerns about some of the CPAI's terminologies reflected the importance of taking into account jurisdictional differences when applying in one jurisdiction a tool developed in another jurisdiction. For example, some of the participants ascribed punitive connotations to the term 'criminogenic' and also 'correctional', which features in the title of the inventory. They believed that the terms were inconsistent with policy priorities in England and Wales. In both areas, youth justice policy appears to promote an inclusionary approach that prioritises the wellbeing of young people, rather than a punitive approach. Key priorities include promoting young people's wellbeing and diverting them away from the system (Youth Justice Board, 2015). In Wales specifically, there is a policy focus on the children's rights enshrined in the United

Nations Convention on the Rights of the Child (Youth Justice Board and Welsh Government, 2014). Furthermore, in Wales, although youth justice policy is not fully devolved, youth justice services work collaboratively with devolved statutory sectors such as the educational, social service, healthcare and housing sectors. The services also operate within the context of a rights-based, social justice-focused national policy agenda. An evaluation tool that is cognisant of these policy and practice priorities is likely to be more relevant for assessing practices in Welsh youth justice settings.

Another factor that undermines the transferability of the CPAI to English and Welsh contexts is the absence of domains that assess the use of diversionary delabelling strategies. Examples include protocols for liaising with key services (such as the Police Service) to divert young people from the system, and recommending alternatives to custody (Youth Justice Board and Welsh Government 2014). These strategies can reduce the exposure of young people to the harmful stigmatising impact of criminal justice labelling and intervention (McAra and McVie, 2010). As noted in Chapter One, it has been established that youth offending is transitory, given that most people desist from crime as they approach maturation and attain certain turning points; they may, for example, get married (Thorpe et al, 1980; Rutherford, 1986).[6] But early contact with the criminal justice system can lead to increased offending and other negative outcomes (McAra and McVie, 2010). Therefore, an evaluation tool that incorporates measures of how practitioners adapt practices to accommodate these insights from the desistance literature is more useful for evaluating youth justice services in England and Wales.

Conclusion

The CPAI-2010 evaluations addressed a typically overlooked aspect of youth justice practice in England and Wales: the supervision skills employed by practitioners. Studies reveal that evaluating interventions and providing adequate staff training in evidence-based approaches can help enhance the processes and outcomes of service delivery because they alert staff to evidence-based skills and practices (Landenberger and Lipsey, 2005; Bonta et al, 2011; Robinson et al, 2012; Alexander et al, 2013; Sorsby et al, 2013). As already noted, staff who participate in CPAI evaluations find the evaluations useful for identifying effective skills and practices and reflecting on how to align their work with the relevant evidence base (Andrews and Bonta, 2010; Smith, 2013).

Across the three SOTs evaluated, training on how to employ the structuring CCPs could enhance the use of these skills. But there is evidence that staff have limited access to such training. Large-scale reviews of effective youth justice practice have noted that access to training on evidence-based practices such as cognitive-behavioural approaches is very limited (Mason and Prior, 2008; Ipsos MORI, 2010; Adler et al, 2016).

Our evaluations are also exploring other aspects of practice, for example, assessment practice. In addition, we are studying the organisational factors that impair the use of evidence-based skills and practices. Future research could explore the ways in which the use of evidence-based skills in England and Welsh youth justice settings correlate with outcomes such as substantive compliance in the form of engagement with supervision processes and goals, and long-term outcomes, for example, reductions in reconviction rates. Such impact or outcome evaluations usefully demonstrate the possible effects of interventions. But studies (such as the current study) that evaluate the processes through which the interventions are implemented (process evaluations) are more useful for illuminating contextual issues that affect outcomes, and a key example is the quality of practice skills.

Acknowledgement

We express our thanks to the Youth Justice Board in Wales (YJB Cymru) who funded this study. We are also grateful to the youth justice practitioners and managers, and the young people who participated in the study and were so generous with their time.

Notes

[1] SOTs supervise young people who are serving court-imposed statutory orders and the teams are located within Youth Offending Teams (YOTs), which are multiagency teams responsible for delivering youth justice services in England and Wales. YOTs should comprise a social worker, a police officer, a probation officer, a health worker and an education worker (Crime and Disorder Act 1998).

[2] Youth Justice Resource Hub, https://yjresourcehub.uk

[3] Symposium on Innovative Approaches to Evaluating Practices in the Justice System funded by the ESRC/Wales Doctoral College, www. swansea.ac.uk/law/news/collegetohostsymposiumoninnovativeapproaches toevaluatingpracticesinthejusticesystem.php

4   See also Chapters Seven to Nine of this volume for more detailed analysis of the STICS model and information about other training programmes that have drawn on the STICS model.

5   Building relationships, effective use of authority, and using the skills that constitute the structuring principle, for example, using role plays to give service users opportunities to apply the skills they are learning, are all time-intensive practices. These practices might be difficult to accomplish in the midst of an unfavourable policy climate of budget cuts, limited staff resources, heavy caseloads and other problematic developments in youth justice policy.

6   The precise mechanisms that bring about such desistance is contested (compare, for example, Farrall, 2005 and Sampson and Laub, 2005).

References

Adler, J.R., Edwards, S.K., Scally, M., Gill, D., Puniskis, M.J., Gekoski, A. and Horvath, M.A.H. (2016) *What Works in Managing Young People Who Offend? A Summary of the International Evidence*, Ministry of Justice Analytical Series, available at www.gov.uk/government/uploads/system/uploads/attachment_data/file/498493/what-works-in-managing-young-people-who-offend.pdf.

Alexander, A., Lowenkamp, C. and Robinson, C.R. (2013) 'A tale of two innovations: motivational interviewing and core correctional practices in US probation', in P. Ugwudike and P. Raynor (eds) *What Works in Offender Compliance: International Perspectives and Evidence-Based Practice*, Basingstoke: Palgrave Macmillan.

Andrews, D.A. and Bonta, J. (2010) *The Psychology of Criminal Conduct* (5th edn), Boston: Anderson Publishing.

Andrews, D.A. and Kiessling, J.J. (1980) 'Program structure and effective correctional practices: a summary of the CaVIC research', in R.R. Ross and P. Gendreau (eds) *Effective Correctional Treatment*, Toronto: Butterworth, pp 441–463.

Barry, M. (2010) 'Youth transitions: from offending to desistance', *Journal of Youth Studies*, 13(1): 121–136

Barry, M. (2013) 'Promoting desistance among young people' in W. Taylor, R. Earle, and R. Hester. (eds) *Youth Justice Handbook: Theory, Policy and Practice*, Abingdon: Routledge.

Bonta, J. and Andrews, D.A. (2017) *The Psychology of Criminal Conduct* (6th edn), New York, NY: Routledge.

Bonta, J., Rugge, T., Scott, T.L., Bourgon, G., and Yessine, A.K. (2008) 'Exploring the black box of community supervision', *Journal of Offender Rehabilitation*, 47(3): 248–270.

Bonta, J., Bourgon, G., Rugge, T., Scott, T.L., Yessine, A.K., Gutierrez, L. and Li, J. (2011) 'An experimental demonstration of training probation officers in evidence-based community supervision', *Criminal Justice and Behavior*, 38(11): 1127–1148.

Burnett, R. (2004) 'One-to-one ways of promoting desistance: in search of an evidence-base', in R. Burnett and C. Roberts (eds) *What Works in Probation and Youth Justice: Developing Evidence-Based Practice*, Cullompton: Willan.

Chadwick, N., Dewolf, A. and Serin, R. (2015) 'Effectively training community supervision officers: a meta-analytic review of the impact on offender outcome', *Criminal Justice and Behavior*, 42(10): 977–989.

Clarke, A., Simmonds, R. and Wydell, S. (2004) *Delivering Cognitive Skills Programmes in Prison: A Qualitative Study*, Home Office Finding No. 242, Research Development and Statistics Directorate, London: Home Office.

Dowden, C. and Andrews, D.A. (2004) 'The importance of staff practice in delivering effective correctional treatment: a meta-analytic review of the literature', *International Journal of Offender Therapy and Comparative Criminology*, 48(2): 203–214.

Durlak, J.A. and DuPre, E.P. (2008) 'Implementation matters: a review of research on the influence of implementation on program outcomes and the factors affecting implementation', *American Journal of Community Psychology*, 41(3–4): 327–350.

Farrall, S. (2002) *Rethinking What Works with Offenders: Probation, Social Context and Desistance From Crime*, Cullompton: Willan.

Farrall, S. (2005) 'On the existential aspects of desistance from crime, *Symbolic Interaction*, 28(3): 367–386.

Farrall, S., Hunter, B., Sharpe, G. and Calverley, A. (2014) *Criminal Careers in Transition: The Social Context of Desistance from Crime*, Oxford: Oxford University Press.

Gendreau. P. and Andrews, D.A. (1989) *Correctional Programme Assessment Inventory*, New Brunswick: University of New Brunswick.

Gendreau, P. Andrews, D.A. and Theriault, Y. (2010) *Correctional Program Assessment Inventory – 2010*, Saint John: University of New Brunswick.

Gray, P. (2013) *Report of Research on Youth Offending Team Partnership and Social Context of Youth Crime*, Plymouth: Plymouth University.

Ipsos MORI (2010) *A Review of Techniques for Effective Engagement and Participation Research Study Conducted for the Youth Justice Board for England and Wales*, London: Youth Justice Board.

Landenberger, N.A. and Lipsey, M.W. (2005) 'The positive effects of cognitive-behavioral programs for offenders: a meta-analysis of factors associated with effective treatment', *Journal of Experimental Criminology*, 1(4): 451–476.

Latessa, E.J., Cullen, F.T. and Gendreau, P. (2002) 'Beyond correctional quackery – professionalism and the possibility of effective treatment', *Federal Probation*, 66(2): 43–49.

Latessa, E.J., Smith, P., Schweitzer, M. and Labrecque, R.M. (2013) *Evaluation of The Effective Practices in Community Supervision Model (EPICS) In Ohio*, Cincinatti, OH: University of Cincinatti, www.uc.edu/content/dam/uc/ccjr/docs/reports/Final%20OCJS%20Report%202.22.13.pdf.

Lipsey, M. (2009) 'The primary factors that characterize effective interventions with juvenile offenders: a meta-analytic overview'. *Victims and Offenders*, 4(4): 124–147.

Lowenkamp, C.T. and Latessa, E.J. (2004) *Understanding the Risk principle: How and Why Correctional Interventions can Harm Low-Risk Offenders*, Technical Report, Topics in Community Corrections 2004, Washington, DC: US Department of Justice, National Institute of Corrections.

Lowenkamp, C.T., Latessa, E.J. and Smith, P. (2006) 'Does correctional program quality really matter? The impact of adhering to the principles of effective intervention', *Criminology & Public Policy*, 5(3): 575–594.

Maruna, S. and LeBel, T.P. (2010) 'The desistance paradigm in correctional practice: from programs to lives', in F. McNeill, P. Raynor and C. Trotter (eds) *Offender Supervision: New Directions in Theory, Research and Practice*, Abingdon: Routledge.

Mason, P. and Prior, D. (2008) *Keeping Young People Engaged: Source Document*, London: Youth Justice Board.

McAra, L. and McVie, S. (2010) 'Youth crime and justice: key messages from the Edinburgh study of youth transitions and crime', *Criminology & Criminal Justice*, 10(2): 179–209.

McNeill, F. (2006) 'A desistance paradigm for offender management', *Criminology and Criminal Justice*, 6(1): 39–62.

McNeill, F. (2014) 'Changing lives, changing work: social work and criminal justice', in I. Durnescu and F. McNeill (eds) *Understanding Penal Practice*, Abingdon: Routledge, pp 167–178.

Miller, W.R. and Rollnick, S. (2012) *Motivational Interviewing: Helping People Change*, New York, NY: Guilford Press.

Raynor, P. (2004) 'The probation service "Pathfinders": finding the path and losing the way?', *Criminal Justice*, 4(3): 309–325.

Raynor, P., Ugwudike, P. and Vanstone, M. (2014) 'The impact of skills in probation work: a reconviction study', *Criminology & Criminal Justice*, 14(2): 235–249.

Rex, S. and Hosking, N. (2013) 'A collaborative approach to developing probation practice: skills for effective engagement, development and supervision (SEEDS)', *Probation Journal*, 60(3): 332–338.

Robinson, C.R., Lowenkamp, C.T., Holsinger, A.M., VanBenschoten, S., Alexander, M. and Oleson, J.C. (2012) 'A random study of Staff Trained at Reducing Re-arrest (STARR): using core correctional practices in probation interactions', *Journal of Crime and Justice*, 35(2): 167–188.

Rutherford, A. (1986) *Growing Out of Crime*, Harmondsworth: Penguin.

Sadlier, G. (2010) *Evaluation of the Impact of the HM Prison Service Enhanced Thinking Skills Programme on Reoffending Outcomes of the Surveying Prisoner Crime Reduction (SPCR) Sample*, Ministry of Justice Research Series 19/10, London: Ministry of Justice.

Sampson, R.J and. Laub, J.H. (2005) 'A life-course view of the development of crime', *Annals of the American Academy of Political and Social Science*, 602(1): 12–45.

Searle R. (2015) 'Workforce development strategy for the youth justice system 2015–2018', available at https://yjresourcehub.uk/yjb.../57_2 71bc826323864f8e9ae1b6cca6cde4f.html (accessed December 2016).

Smith, P. (2013) 'The psychology of criminal conduct', in F.T. Cullen and P. Wilcox (eds) *The Oxford Handbook of Criminological Theory*, Oxford: Oxford University Press, pp 69–88.

Sorsby, A., Shapland, J., Farrall, S., McNeill, F., Priede, C. and Robinson, G. (2013) *Probation Staff Views of the Skills for Effective Engagement Development (SEED) Project*, Centre for Criminological Research Occasional Paper No 4, Sheffield: University of Sheffield, available at www.sheffield.ac.uk/polopoly_fs/1.293093!/file/ probation-staff-views-seed.pdf (accessed 27 February 2017).

Taxman, F.S.,and Belenko, S. (2011) *Implementing evidence-based practices in community corrections and addiction treatment*. New York, NY: Springer.

Thorpe, D.H., Smith, D., Green, C.J. and Paley, J. (1980) *Out of Care*, London: Allen & Unwin.

Trotter, C. (2013) 'Effective supervision of young offenders', in P. Ugwudike and P. Raynor (eds) *What Works in Offender Compliance: International Perspectives and Evidence-Based Practice*, Basingstoke: Palgrave Macmillan, pp 227–241.

Trotter, C. and Evans, P. (2012) 'Analysis of supervision skills in youth probation', *Australian and New Zealand Journal of Criminology*, 45(2): 255–273.

Trotter, C., Evans, P. and Baidawi, S. (2015) 'Effectiveness of challenging skills in work with young offenders', *International Journal of Offender Therapy and Comparative Criminal Justice*, 61(4): 397–412.

Ugwudike, P. Raynor, P. and Vanstone, M. (2014) 'Supervision skills and practices: the Jersey Study', in I. Durnescu and F. McNeill (eds) *Understanding Penal Practice*, Abingdon: Routledge.

Ward, T. and Fortune, C. (2013) 'The Good Lives model: aligning risk reduction with promoting offenders' personal goals', *European Journal of Probation*, 5(2): 29–46.

Youth Justice Board (2013) 'YJ skills and knowledge matrix + NOS signposting', available at http://webarchive.nationalarchives.gov.uk/20140715125548/http://www.justice.gov.uk/downloads/youth-justice/workforce-development/yj-skills-matrix.pdf.

Youth Justice Board (2015) 'Youth Justice Board for England and Wales Strategic Plan 2015–18', available at www.gov.uk/government/uploads/system/uploads/attachment_data/file/469954/YJB_Strategic_Plan_2015-18.pdf.

Youth Justice Board (2016) 'Youth justice skills and knowledge matrix + NOS signposting', available at https://yjresourcehub.uk/yjb-training-and-develpment/yjb-workforce-development-publications/item/20-yj-skills-and-knowledge-matrix.html.

Youth Justice Board/Welsh Government (2014) 'Children and young people first', available at www.gov.uk/government/uploads/system/uploads/attachment_data/file/374572/Youth_Justice_Strategy_English.PDF.

FIFTEEN

The impact of training and coaching on the development of practice skills in youth justice: findings from Australia

Chris Trotter

Introduction

A number of studies have found that the skills and practices of probation and parole officers, and others who supervise offenders in the community, have an impact on the recidivism rates of offenders under supervision. Studies in Australia, Canada, the United Kingdom and the United States have found that when probation officers use particular supervision skills, offenders under their supervision have recidivism rates as much as 60% lower than offenders supervised by workers who do not use these skills (Trotter, 2013). The impact applies to both reoffending and compliance with conditions.

The argument presented in the literature is not that correctional interventions always work, but that appropriate forms of intervention can be effective. In a review of meta-analysis of treatment effectiveness, Andrews and Bonta (2006, p 329) argued that appropriate treatment led to reductions in recidivism of 'a little more than 50 percent from that found in comparison conditions'.

Effective practice skills

My review of studies on the effectiveness of offender supervision (Trotter, 2013) found that the studies identified similar supervision skills as being effective. These include role clarification, prosocial modelling and reinforcement, problem solving, cognitive-behavioural techniques and relationship factors. These skills are generally more effective when used with medium- to high-risk offenders (Trotter, 2013).

Role clarification

Work with offenders involves what Ronald Rooney (2009) and Jones and Alcabes (1993) refer to as client socialisation, or what others have referred to as role clarification (Trotter, 2015). One aspect of role clarification involves helping the client to accept that the worker can help with the client's problems even though the worker has a social control role. Other aspects of role clarification involve exploring the client's expectations, helping the client to understand what is negotiable, the limits of confidentiality and the nature of the worker's authority. Some research has been undertaken on this issue in mental health (Videka-Sherman, 1988) and in child protection (Trotter, 2004). Less work has been done in corrections settings, although several studies (for a review, see Trotter, 2013) found that role clarification skills were part of a group of skills that related to reduced reoffending by probationers.

Prosocial modelling and reinforcement

Prosocial modelling and reinforcement have been shown to be effective in a number of studies, including studies focused on community supervision in adult and juvenile settings (Andrews et al, 1979; Trotter, 1990, 1996, 2013; Bourgeon et al, 2010). It is included as one of the core components of effective probation supervision in meta-analysis and other reviews of studies on probation supervision (Dowden and Andrews, 2004; Trotter, 2013). There is support for probation officers modelling prosocial behaviours, for positively reinforcing clients' prosocial behaviours and for challenging clients' procriminal behaviours. The meta-analysis by Dowden and Andrews (2004) found a correlation with an effect size of 0.34 for effective modelling, .24 for effective reinforcement and 0.17 for effective disapproval.

Problem solving

Effective interventions in corrections address the issues that have led offenders to become offenders, often referred to as criminogenic needs (Andrews and Bonta, 2006). Criminogenic needs may include employment, family relationships, drug use, peer group associations, housing, finances or procriminal attitudes. A number of studies also suggest that working collaboratively with offenders and focusing on the issues or problems that the offenders themselves identify as problematic leads to lower recidivism (McNeill and Whyte, 2007; Trotter, 1996,

2013). There is also support for problem solving approaches whereby workers canvass a wide range of client issues, reach agreement on problems to be addressed, set goals and develop strategies to achieve those goals (Andrews and Bonta 2006; Dowden and Andrews, 2004; Trotter, 1996, 2013). Dowden and Andrews point to a correlation with effect size of 0.29 for problem solving in their meta-analysis of core correctional practice.

Cognitive-behavioural techniques

Cognitive-behavioural interventions, which help offenders address thinking patterns that relate to crime, are often targeted towards groups of offenders, rather than individuals. Nevertheless, these interventions may also be used in one-to-one supervision in probation. The Dowden and Andrews (2004) meta-analysis of core practices indicates an effect size of 0.37 for structured learning that involves cognitive-behavioural interventions, the highest effect size of any of the variables.

Relationship factors

Dowden and Andrews (2004) also identified the client–worker relationship as one of the elements of core correctional practice in their meta-analysis. Relationship skills are also referred to in other reviews (for example, Gendreau et al, 1996; Trotter, 2006, 2013; Bonta et al, 2008; Bourgeon et al, 2010). It is argued that probation officers should have relationships with clients that are characterised by empathy, openness, warmth, humour, enthusiasm, appropriate self-disclosure and a positive view about the clients' capacity to change. Dowden and Andrews (2004) in their meta-analysis indicate a correlation with effect size of 0.25 for relationship factors.

Developing skills across organisations

Most of the studies undertaken on effective practice skills have focused on relatively small samples rather than considering the development of skills across the whole organisation. There is evidence to suggest, however, that evidence-based practice skills are not used routinely in probation and parole supervision (Taxman and Sachwald, 2010), and that probation and parole supervision may have little overall impact (Hyatt and Barnes, 2014).

In recent years, there has been considerable interest in how the use of evidence-based practice skills can be developed across organisations (for example, Bonta et al, 2013; Latessa et al, 2016), and some work has examined the extent to which these skills can be learnt by probation officers through training and coaching. The limited amount of research in this area suggests that while some probation officers may have a natural pre-disposition towards the use of effective practice skills, training and coaching may increase the level of skills of most probation officers (Trotter, 2013; Castle et al, 2016). On the other hand, it is argued that the successful implementation of evidence-based practice skills requires more than training and coaching; it should involve a broad systemic approach that addresses barriers such as agency culture, supervisors' attitudes, buy-in from staff and organisational leadership.

There is a need for studies that examine attempts to implement evidence-based practices across organisations and the extent to which these actually change the practices of workers. The study described in this chapter aims to help fill this gap by examining a project undertaken in youth justice that aimed to increase the skill levels of probation officers through training and coaching.

The study

The aim of the study is to examine the extent to which the skills of youth justice workers are enhanced by training, coaching and other support mechanisms offered in an Australian Department of Youth Justice. The project also examines which skills were developed most following the intervention. Are workers developing role clarification skills as opposed to cognitive-behavioural techniques, for example?

Methodology

The design of the study is a before/after comparison using quantitative methods (Bachman and Schutt, 2007). The procedure is as follows:

1. A series of two-day training courses on effective practice skills were offered to all youth justice workers and staff supervisors.
2. Participants in the training courses brought along an audio tape of an interview they had recently conducted with a youth justice client. (Client consent was gained at the time of recording for the tape to be used for research purposes, consistent with Monash University ethics.)
3. Participants in the training were invited to be involved in the research project.

4. The audio tapes were coded for skills using a coding form developed for this purpose in previous research (Trotter, 2012; Trotter and Evans, 2012).

5. Following training, youth offices were regularly coached by senior staff by analysing and coding audio tapes of interviews, followed by feedback to workers about their use of the skills. This involved group and/or individual supervision. The workers also received the usual routine supervision with senior staff.

6. Researchers coded for skills evident in the pre-training audio tapes and tapes recorded following training. The data were then analysed to determine changes in use of skills between the pre-training tapes and the post-training tapes.

The coding manual

As mentioned, the audio tapes were coded using a coding manual developed for a previous project (Trotter and Evans, 2012) in consultation with others doing similar work, in particular James Bonta and colleagues in Canada and Peter Raynor and colleagues in the UK (Bonta et al, 2011; Raynor et al, 2014).

The coding manual is divided into 15 sections including: set-up of the interview; structure of the interview; role clarification; needs analysis; problem solving; developing strategies; relapse prevention/cognitive-behavioural techniques; prosocial modelling and reinforcement; nature of the relationship; empathy; confrontation; termination; use of referral/community resources; non-verbal cues; and incidental conversations. Each of the 15 sections contains a number of items that can be rated on a five-point scale. For example, the problem-solving section included: problem survey and identifying criminogenic needs; problem ranking; problem exploration; setting goals; time frame; review; developing a contract; developing strategies; ongoing monitoring; and time spent conducting problem solving. For the skill to be rated highly, it needed to be implemented in a way that was consistent with the research about good practice referred to in the literature review.

The coding manual demonstrated high levels of reliability in earlier research (Trotter, 2012). For example, the correlation on the overall global skill score between first and second coders was 0.741 (sig 0.000), for time spent discussing role clarification it was 0.548 (sig 0.006), for time spent on problem solving it was 0.626 (sig 0.002), and for prosocial modelling it was 0.561 (sig 0.005).

Analysis

Thirty-eight tapes, 19 pre-training and 19 post-training tapes, were coded and entered into the Statistical Package for the Social Sciences (SPSS) and analysed to determine the overall use of skills and the use of the individual skills. The use of skills was compared using comparisons of means in order to examine the differences between skill scores on the pre- and post-training tapes. The tapes were supplied by 21 workers, with each worker providing between one and three tapes. In only 19 cases did the worker provide both before and after tapes. The relatively small number of workers who supplied both before and after tapes is discussed in the limitations section later in the chapter.

Findings

Overall use of skills

The researchers used the following scale to code an overall ten-point global score on the use of the effective practice skills:

1. The worker did not utilise any of the effective practice principles.
3. The worker used minimal effective practice skills, almost unintentionally.
5. The interview showed some use of the effective practice principles.
7. The worker used several of the effective practice principles in a deliberate manner.
10. The worker deliberately used the effective practice principles in an efficient and successful manner.

Table 15.1 shows that the global score on the 19 post-training tapes was significantly higher than the global score on the 19 pre-training tapes. The workers went from minimal use of the skills to some use of the skills (3–4 on the ten-point scale).

Table 15.1: Global score out of 10

Pre- or post-training	Mean	N	Standard deviation
Pre	2.8947	19	1.14962
Post	4.1579	19	1.83373
Total	3.5263	38	1.63966

p = 0.015

Table 15.2 shows that clients were also generally more engaged in the post-training interviews (although this does not quite reach statistical significance).

Table 15.2: Was client engaged overall (out of 10)?

Pre- or post-training	Mean	N	Standard deviation
Pre	3.1579	19	1.70825
Post	4.1579	19	2.36322
Total	3.6579	38	2.09602

Use of individual skills

The use of individual skills was also coded using the following scale regarding the extent to which the skill was used during the interview that was coded:

1. None
2. Not much
3. Some of the time
4. Quite often
5. A lot

Role clarification

The amount of time discussing role clarification was significantly greater in the post-interview tapes, as shown in Table 15.3.

The individual role clarification skills were also coded before and after the training. Table 15.4 shows that there was a significant increase in the skill of discussing the nature of the worker's authority and in discussions about the worker's dual role as helper/investigator. On each of the other role clarification skills there was a non-significant increase in the score given by the coder with the exception of discussions about confidentiality.

Table 15.3: Time spent discussing role clarification

Pre- or post-training	Mean	N	Standard deviation
Pre	1.3684	19	0.49559
Post	2.2632	19	1.04574
Total	1.8158	38	0.92577

p = 0.002

Table 15.4: Role clarification skills

Pre- or post-training		Confidentiality	Nature of authority	Helping orientation of worker	Purpose of workers interventions	Dual role as helper/ investigator
Pre	Mean	1.4211	1.0000*	1.2105	2.3158	1.00*
	N	19	19	19	19	19
	Standard deviation	1.26121	0.00000	0.71328	1.52944	0.000
Post	Mean	1.4211	2.0526*	1.8421	3.2105	2.05*
	N	19	19	19	19	19
	Standard deviation	1.26121	1.80966	1.67542	1.96013	1.810
Total	Mean	1.4211	1.5263	1.5263	2.7632	1.53
	N	38	38	38	38	38
	Standard deviation	1.24405	1.37028	1.30977	1.79239	1.370

Note:$*p < 0.05$.

There was generally more use of prosocial modelling skill, as shown in Table 15.5. The differences did not, however, reach statistical significance.

Table 15.5: Time spent using prosocial modelling

Pre- or post-training	Mean	N	Standard deviation
Pre	2.1579	19	0.60214
Post	2.2632	19	0.80568
Total	2.2105	38	0.70358

The use of the individual components of prosocial modelling were also greater following the training, although again this was not at significant levels, as shown in Table 15.6.

More time was also spent using relationship skills, as shown in Table 15.7. This was outside the conventional 0.05 level of significance, but within the 0.10 level, which may be considered acceptable when the direction of the relationship is predicted (Weinbach and Grinnell, 2010).

Table 15.6: Prosocial modelling and reinforcement

Pre- or post- training		Identifying pro-social actions	Rewarding pro-social actions	Challenging pro-criminal actions	Modeling desirable behaviours
Pre	Mean	2.2632	2.1579	1.7895	1.1053
	N	19	19	19	19
	Standard deviation	1.32674	1.42451	0.97633	0.45883
Post	Mean	2.6842	2.4211	1.8947	1.2778
	N	19	19	19	18
	Standard deviation	1.49267	1.64370	1.10024	0.95828
Total	Mean	2.4737	2.2895	1.8421	1.1892
	N	38	38	38	37
	Standard deviation	1.40918	1.52294	1.02736	0.73929

Table 15.7: Time spent using relationship skills

Pre- or post-training	Mean	N	Standard deviation
Pre	2.4444	18	0.70479
Post	2.9474	19	0.91127
Total	2.7027	37	0.84541

$p = 0.070$

Report

There was also more use of some, but not all, of the individual relationship skills, as shown in Table 15.8. This is within the 0.10 level of significance.

Problem solving

The coders found no examples in pre-training tapes of using problem-solving skills. A low level of problem-solving skills was evident in the post-training tapes, as shown in Table 15.9.

There was also no use of the individual problem solving skills in the pre-training tapes and minimal use in the post-training tapes. Nevertheless, there were increases in the use of problem survey, problem exploration, and developing strategies, which were within the 0.10 level of significance, as shown in Table 15.10.

Youth workers also received some training in cognitive-behavioural techniques; however, the evidence of use of cognitive-behavioural techniques in the interviews was relatively low, with no significant increases following training.

Table 15.8: Use of relationship skills

Pre- or post- training		Open and honest	Non-blaming	Optimistic	Enthusiastic	Articulate client/family's feelings
Pre	Mean	3.2632*	4.3684	2.7368	2.5789	2.2105
	N	19	19	19	19	19
	Standard deviation	1.40800	1.30002	1.19453	1.30451	1.47494
Post	Mean	4.3158*	4.8947	2.5263	2.2222	2.5263
	N	19	19	19	18	19
	Standard deviation	0.88523	0.45883	1.54087	1.51679	1.34860
Total	Mean	3.7895	4.6316	2.6316	2.4054	2.3684
	N	38	38	38	37	38
	Standard deviation	1.27678	0.99786	1.36404	1.40356	1.40311

Note: * p < 0.10.

Table 15.9: Time spent conducting problem solving

Pre- or post-training	Mean	N	Standard deviation
Pre	1.0000	19	0.00000
Post	1.4211	19	0.90159
Total	1.2105	38	0.66405

Table 15.10: Problem-solving skills

Pre- or post- training		Problem survey	Problem ranking	Problem exploration	Setting goals	Developing strategies
Pre	Mean	1.0000*	1.0000	1.0000*	1.0000	1.0000*
	N	19	19	19	19	19
	Standard deviation	0.00000	0.00000	0.00000	0.00000	0.00000
Post	Mean	1.6316*	1.2105	1.6842*	1.4211	1.5263*
	N	19	19	19	19	19
	Standard deviation	1.49854	0.91766	1.49267	1.26121	1.30675
Total	Mean	1.3158	1.1053	1.3421	1.2105	1.2632
	N	38	38	38	38	38
	Standard deviation	1.09311	0.64889	1.09733	0.90518	0.94966

Note: * p > 0.10.

Table 15.11: Cognitive skills

Pre- or post-training		Cognitive coping skills	Managing lapses	Time spent discussing relapse prevention	Examining high-risk situations
Pre	Mean	1.6842	1.5789	1.8947	1.4737
	N	19	19	19	19
	Standard deviation	1.41628	1.38707	1.37011	1.26352
Post	Mean	1.6667	2.0000	2.0526	1.8889
	N	18	18	19	18
	Standard deviation	1.37199	1.57181	1.39338	1.56765
Total	Mean	1.6757	1.7838	1.9737	1.6757
	N	37	37	38	37
	Standard deviation	1.37546	1.47451	1.36534	1.41527

Content of interviews

It is evident from the coding of the interviews that there was a low level of use of skills. While there were some significant increases in the scores following training, even after training, the overall global score and individual scores on role clarification, problem solving and cognitive skills remained low. The mean global score was 5.7 using the same coding scale in previous research in youth justice (Trotter, 2012).

Given that the skills were used infrequently, the question may be raised as to what the workers were doing in the interviews. The coders provided brief descriptions of the content of each interview and it was apparent from the descriptions that many of the interviews were focused on doing reports, completing assessments, writing case plans or working through CHART modules (workbooks focusing on issues such as finding work or reducing drug use). Working through CHART workbooks was coded as problem solving only if they were used as part of a problem-solving framework and following identification of issues and setting goals with the client.

The workers seemed therefore to have little time to use the practice skills in interviews because they were often involved in other tasks. The following selected qualitative comments from the coders provide some insight into the contents of the interviews.

> Interview was 14 minutes. Session focused on reviewing information collated in a previous session for an assessment report. Worker discussed and asked questions of the young

person with respect to the assessment domains and provided a summary of young person's strengths.

Interview was 14 minutes. Worker identified that the session would focus on working through the CHART (workbook) module concerned with employment.

Interview was 18 minutes. Client was in custody. Worker had an established working relationship with the client. This session was focused on collecting information for the case plan.

Interview was 22 minutes. The session focused on gathering information to complete an assessment report. Client was in custody. Worker focused on asking questions and did not always engage client in discussion, to explore issues raised by the client.

Interview was 22 minutes. Purpose of interview was not identified by worker. Young person set the agenda. The session focused on educational course and social security payments.

Interview was 28 minutes. Session focused on working through the CHART relapse prevention module. Worker engaged the client well with the use of several examples to help him understand the content and make linkages to his life. Worker was warm, enthusiastic and friendly in her interactions.

Interview was 37 minutes. Session focused on working through the CHART module concerned with self-talk. Worker engages the young person by using examples to help the young person understand the content. Worker paraphrases and challenges the client throughout the session.

Interview was 38 minutes. Worker identified purpose of session is completing the Healthy Relationships module of CHART and provided an explanation of what the module entails. Session was conducted in a collaborative manner demonstrating a good working alliance with the young person.

Interview was 42 minutes. Client was in custody. Session focused on getting ready to leave custody and identifying what would be beneficial for the young person to assist with this transition.

Interview was 43 minutes. Young person was present in person at the YJ [youth justice] office, while his mother was participating via telephone. Purpose of session was to conduct a formal warning with regards to attendance with supervision and community service; and to conduct a final probation meeting. Given the focus of the session, the worker was limited in her applications of skills.

Interview was 5 minutes. Session focused on discussing progress with community work and what is required of client with respect to remaining hours left on his court order.

Interview was approximately 30 minutes. Client was in custody. Purpose of the session was to collect information for a risk assessment. YJ worker was focused on collating the information with little demonstration of the effective supervision skills.

Session is held in the car while transporting young person to an animal shelter. Focus of session is on helping young person find volunteer work and exploring job readiness. Majority of questions used by the worker are closed, and in response the young person provides limited information. Young person's level of engagement is low.

Total duration of interview was 28 minutes. Recording of interview was divided into four parts. Session focused on working through an anxiety and drug module. Client sounded engaged in the sessions with the YJ worker. This was demonstrated by the client responding to questions; and where the client was unsure of the question asked of him, he would seek out clarification.

YJ worker was friendly in her interaction with the young person. She explained the purpose of the session and reviewed the young person's understanding of confidentiality as discussed in the previous interview. Overall limited application of skills, due to YJ worker's focus on information gathering.

Conclusion

The examination of the before and after tapes suggests that the training and coaching offered to youth justice workers in the study made a difference to the use of skills. However, while there were significant increases in skills following training, the use of the skills was relatively low even after training. These findings are consistent with previous studies in a number of jurisdictions that suggest that workers make minimal use of effective practice skills (Bonta et al, 2008; Trotter and Evans, 2012) and that training may have an increase the use of skills (Trotter 1996, 2013; Robinson et al, 2011).

In relation to the individual skills, the workers were strongest on relationship skills, particularly in terms of being open and non-blaming. The scores on the use of role clarification skills were low at the pre-training stage, with only discussions about the purpose of the workers' interventions reaching a score of 2 out of 5. The scores on role clarification were higher following training; however, the skills were still used minimally, with only discussions about the purpose of the intervention coded as being used some of the time. The use of prosocial skills remained at 'not much', with minimal increase after training. Similarly, problem-solving skills and cognitive skills were used minimally before and only slightly more following training.

The comments from the coders suggest that one of the reasons for the minimal use of worker skills as they have been defined in this study is that workers tended to be involved in other tasks such as assessments, reports, CHART modules and case plans. This left little time for their use of skills.

This study has limitations. It does not examine recidivism. An examination of recidivism would show both the relationship between the programme and use of the skills, and the impact of the skills on offenders. While this may be the ultimate desired outcome in any correctional setting, as outlined in the literature review as many as eight studies have already shown that evidence-based practice relates to reduced recidivism (Trotter, 2013).

The sample is small and was also dependent on volunteers. Nevertheless, the numbers were large enough to show statistically significant differences between before and after tapes.

Another potential limitation of the study is that staff are likely to record their best interviews and the level of skills displayed may not therefore be reflective of their general practice. Similarly, resistant staff may have poor skills and may not agree to being involved in the research, thereby suggesting a higher level of skills than is actually present across organisations. Given the relatively low use of skills, this may not be the case in this study. In any case, the main aim of the study was to examine the impact of the training and coaching; these should have an effect, regardless of the extent to which good interviews are chosen.

A final potential criticism is that successful implementation of any policy or practice is heavily dependent on organisational culture, management and staff involvement. This study does not capture these factors. In some ways, this is a fair criticism, and there is evidence that these factors apply in corrections settings (Taxman and Sachwald, 2010). Further research might examine these factors in more detail.

Despite these limitations, the results do suggest that the training had an impact on the skills of the youth officers who participated in the study. There was, however, little if any problem solving evident in the tapes. In other words, even after training there was little evidence of youth officers working collaboratively with young people to address the issues relating to their offending. The comments by the coders suggest that the interviews were characterised by other tasks, involving assessments, court reports or CHART, rather than working collaboratively through clients' problems.

On the other hand, while the workers may have shown minimal use of problem-solving skills, they were relatively strong on relationship skills, particularly the skill of non-blaming, which proved to be strongly related to positive outcomes in our previous youth justice study (Trotter, 2012). The interviews were also often taken up with CHART modules, which are broadly based on cognitive-behavioural theory and techniques. Further research would be needed to understand the effectiveness of the CHART modules, particularly as they interact with other skills.

Further research might also consider the impact of alternative methods to develop workers' skills, including the style and duration of training, coaching methods, the nature of staff supervision, leadership issues and organisational culture. What this study does suggest is that if organisations wish to increase the use of practice skills by staff, consideration should be given to how they can do this given the other demands placed on their time.

References

Andrews, D.A. and Bonta, J. (2006) *The Psychology of Criminal Conduct*, Cincinnati, OH: Anderson.

Andrews, D.A., Keissling, J.J., Russell, R.J. and Grant, B.A. (1979) *Volunteers and the One-to-One Supervision of Adult Probationers*, Ontario: Ministry of Correctional Services, Toronto.

Bachman, R. and Schutt, R., (2007) *The practice of research in criminology and criminal justice*, Thousand Oaks, CA: Sage Publications.

Bonta, J., Bourgon, G. and Rugge, T. (2013) 'Taking the leap: from pilot project to wide-scale implementation of the Strategic Training Initiative in Community Supervision (STICS)', *Justice Research and Policy*, 15(1): 1–35.

Bourgon, G., Bonta, J., Rugge, T. and Gutierrez, L. (2010) 'Technology transfer: the importance of ongoing clinical supervision in translating what works to everyday community supervision', in F. McNeill, P. Raynor and C. Trotter (eds) *Offender Supervision: New Directions for Theory, Research and Practice*, Cullompton: Willan.

Bonta, J., Rugge, T., Scott, T., Bougon, G. and Yessine, A. (2008) 'Exploring the black box of community supervision', *Journal of Offender Rehabilitation*, 47(3): 248–270.

Bonta, J., Bourgon, G., Rugge, T., Scott, T.-L., Yessine, A.K., Gutierrez, L., and Li, J. (2011) 'Community supervision: an experimental demonstration of training probation officers in evidence-based practice', *Criminal Justice and Behavior*, 38(11): 1127–1148.

Castle, R., Hayes, D. and Lavely, T. (2016) 'Ready, set, coach: How to effectively implement core correctional practices in community supervision', APPA (American Probation and Parole Association) 41st Annual Training Institute Workshop, Cleveland, OH, 29 August.

Dowden, C. and Andrews, D.A. (2004) 'The importance of staff practice in delivering effective correctional treatment: a meta-analytic review of the literature', *International Journal of Offender Therapy and Comparative Criminology*, 48(2): 203–14.

Gendreau, P., Little, T. and Goggin, C. (1996) 'A meta-analysis of the predictors of adult offender recidivism: What works', *Criminology*, 34(4): 575–608.

Hyatt, J. and Barnes, G. (2014) 'An experimental evaluation of the impact of intensive supervision on the recidivism of high-risk probationers', *Journal of Offender Rehabilitation*, 47(3): 248–270.

Jones, J.A. and Alcabes, A. (1993) *Client Socialisation: The Achilles Heel of the Helping Professions*, Westport, CT: Auburn House.

Latessa, E., Sleyo, J. and Schweitzer, M. (2016) 'Researchers in the real world: evidence-based practices, implementation barriers and lessons learned', *Offender Programs Report*, 19(5): 65–69.

McNeill, F. and Whyte, B. (2007) *Reducing Offending Social Work and Community Justice in Scotland*, Cullompton: Willan.

Raynor, P., Ugwudike, P. and Vanstone, M. (2014) 'The impact of skills in probation work: a reconviction study', *Criminology & Criminal Justice*, 14(2): 235–249.

Robinson, C., Van Benschoten, S., Alexander, M. and Lowenkamp, C. (2011) 'A random (almost) study of Staff Training Aimed at Reducing Re-arrest (STARR): reducing recidivism through intentional design', *Federal Probation*, 75(2): 57–63.

Rooney, R. (ed) (2009) *Strategies for Work with Involuntary Clients* (2nd edn), New York, NY: Columbia University Press.

Taxman, F.S., and Sachwald, J. (2010) 'Managing chaos: Techniques to improve the quality of supervision', in F. McNeill, P. Raynor and C. Trotter (eds) *Offender Supervision: New Directions in Theory, Research and Practice*, Cullompton: Willan.

Trotter, C (1996) 'The impact of different supervision practices in community corrections', *Australian and New Zealand Journal of Criminology*, 29(1): 29–46.

Trotter, C. (2004) *Helping Abused Children and their Families: Towards an Evidence-Based Model*, New South Wales: Allen and Unwin.

Trotter, C. (2006) *Working with involuntary Clients: A Guide to Practice*, 2nd edn, London: Sage.

Trotter, C. (2012) 'Effective supervision of young offenders', *Trends and Issues in Criminal Justice*, 448: 1–8.

Trotter, C. (2013) 'Reducing recidivism through probation supervision: what we know and don't know from four decades of research', *Federal Probation*, 77(2): 43–46.

Trotter, C. (2015) *Working with Involuntary Clients* (3rd edn), Sydney: Allen & Unwin.

Trotter, C. and Evans, P. (2012) 'Analysis of Supervision Skills in Juvenile Justice', *Australian and New Zealand Journal of Criminology*, 45(2): 255–273.

Videka Sherman, L. (1988) 'Meta-analysis of research on social work practice in mental health', *Social Work*, 33(4): 323–338.

Weinbach, R. and Grinnell, R. (2010) *Statistics for Social Workers*, New York, NY: Longman.

SIXTEEN

Can the recruitment of ex-offenders enhance offender engagement? An assessment of the London Probation Trust's engagement worker role

Nigel Hosking and John Rico

Introduction

Research studies have long established that the most effective strategy for reducing reoffending is to demonstrate a quality level of offender engagement by relating effectively to service users, and using evidence-based supervision skills. The research literature also suggests that in order to 'relate' to service users, practitioners need to exhibit empathy, mutual respect, and an appreciation for the life, perspectives, and needs that the service user experiences (see, for example, Dowden and Andrews, 2004; Raynor et al, 2014; Bonta and Andrews, 2017; Chapters Six to Eleven, and Fourteen, Fifteen and Seventeen of this volume describe these skills in detail). However, it is not always easy for practitioners – often forced to play the role of disciplinarian and authority figure – to connect with service users in a way that allows for this relationship to develop; the balance between trusted confidante, and enforcer and disciplinarian is a difficult one to achieve.

With this in mind, in 2013 the London Probation Trust (LPT) developed the role of engagement worker in order to provide practitioners with another resource to be used in their attempts to establish successful working relationships with service users. The engagement workers are former users of the probation service themselves – a life experience that may enable them to successfully engage current service users in a way that practitioners are not always able to do. In addition to supporting individuals to change, the experience of being an engagement worker may contribute to the engagement workers' own desistance.

Following a year of the engagement worker experiment, the project was evaluated by the LPT research analyst, John Rico (LPT is now the London Community Rehabilitation Company [CRC]). This chapter explores the question 'Who works?' (Durnescu et al, 2014) and asks whether employing ex-offenders in this way can enhance engagement, improve outcomes and provide a substantive value that is both tangible and unique.

Employing ex-service users

Unfortunately, there is little research regarding the employment of ex-service users directly in probation departments or other criminal justice organisations. Instead, the underlying research base for engagement workers mostly derives from studies surrounding the effectiveness of peer mentoring programmes, which also often make use of former service users (see, for example, Maguire et al, 2010; Fletcher and Batty, 2012).

Within the CRC, the engagement worker's role is different from that of a mentor; mentors typically work intensely with individuals over extended periods of time, whereas individual engagement is only one aspect of the engagement worker's role (engagement workers also perform group inductions, for example), and the individual engagement they perform is just as likely to be a one-off experience as a protracted engagement.

However, for the purposes of finding relevant research literature, the role of peer mentor is the closest approximation; having a shared experience (in this instance, prison or probation and criminal convictions) serves as the basis for developing a relationship. Peer mentoring differs from traditional mentoring in that peer mentors tend to be of the same age, ethnicity, experience, or some other relevant demographic qualifier; traditional mentors tend to be older more experienced individuals who assist those younger and less experienced than themselves.

Fletcher and Batty's (2012) paper summarised many of the prominent research findings relating to peer mentoring and the positive outcomes peer mentoring can offer:

- Boyce and colleagues (2009) concluded that offenders were more likely to seek help from peers rather than figures within positions of authority.
- Cook and colleagues (2008) reported that inmates who were on the path to rehabilitation, and were provided with proper training,

were more likely to be viewed as authentic and were more likely to 'demonstrate understanding' than hired treatment staff.

- Huggins (2010) found that peers provided offenders with 'successful role models', by serving as an actual example of someone, from a shared background, who had managed to turn their life around; this provided a substantively different model for rehabilitation than a paid staff worker from a different background explaining the need for one to turn one's life around.
- A 2003 study from the United Nations Office on Drugs and Crime found that offenders were more likely to both accept and act on information when it was presented by a figure with whom they could identify. This same study also found that peers were more effective at communicating, as they could communicate within the specific context of a particular culture that was understood by both mentor and mentee (but was not always understood in an authentic way by paid authority figures).

However, the research literature also identifies the risks of peer mentoring programmes, with multiple studies articulating the difficulties inherent in developing a quality mentor programme.

Again, referencing Fletcher and Batty (2012):

- Boyce and colleagues (2009) discovered that selection criteria often necessarily restricted the pool of suitable offenders, with many younger offenders lacking the emotional maturity to serve as peer mentors.
- Scott and colleagues (2004) found that many mentor programmes had high rates of turnover, with mentors finding it difficult to commit the time and dedication needed to become successful; this is a finding, of course, that will be readily apparent to anyone who has managed a mentor programme before.
- Foster (2011) identified that many mentor programmes had routine issues with mentors maintaining appropriate boundaries and maintaining professional confidentiality.

While there is research literature to suggest that pairing present service users with peer mentors may produce beneficial outcomes, it is unclear whether one of these outcomes will be a reduction in reoffending. As a 2014 Ministry of Justice report on the government's Transforming Rehabilitation reforms explained: 'Of those that have been evaluated, some mentoring programmes have demonstrated a positive impact on reoffending, but not all. The effectiveness of mentoring is therefore mixed/promising' (p 38). Fletcher and Batty (2012) found that serving as a peer mentor increased the mentors' self-confidence, provided a route back to employment, and left peer mentors feeling empowered and responsible, thereby decreasing the chance of reoffending.

For the CRC and its engagement worker programme, this research literature provides important guidance: namely, there are definite benefits to such programmes if implemented well. For example, great care needs to be taken to ensure the recruitment of high-quality mentors, the provision of a high level of managerial support, and sufficient training on how to maintain professional boundaries.

The study

In 2011, User Voice (an ex-offender-led charity) was commissioned by the LPT to develop Service User Councils (SUCs) across the organisation. SUCs are committees made up of current service users, which enable these service users to organise collectively and express their views on how probation services should be delivered. One of the ideas emanating from the councils was for LPT to hire ex-offenders directly as engagement workers; the idea was subsequently endorsed by the LPT chief executive officer, Heather Munro.

Although the LPT was in some internal turmoil as a result of the Transforming Rehabilitation reforms (see Chapter Four in this volume), the Equality and Communities Engagement Team, working with User Voice, began implementing the role. The process started by recruiting from an existing bank of volunteers within User Voice. Additionally, a training induction was developed, the role was communicated to probation staff, and finally, the new workers were deployed throughout the organisation. The first engagement workers were recruited in September 2013. Their main role was to support probation practitioners in order to improve service-user engagement and outcomes, particularly with 'hard-to-reach' service users. Secondary roles were to support the running of the local SUCs, acting as a link between staff and council members, and to provide a viewpoint on new developments within London Probation Trust.

It should be stated that the introduction of this role was considered a learning exercise by the organisation, as employing former service users was new territory. Furthermore, it was understood from the outset that it was inevitable that certain conflicts would occur. Indeed, there was initially some tension among some probation staff regarding the placement of engagement workers. Practitioners were worried about losing their jobs and there was some nervousness that the engagement worker programme was a pilot initiative with eventual aims to replace them. Other staff members were simply bothered by the idea of working professionally alongside a former service user and concerned about whether or not there were any risk implications involved with their employment.

Fortunately, as the engagement workers took their positions and began working effectively, most staff members quickly warmed to them and began to appreciate the role. However, in a small number of cases things did not go well in the early stages. In these cases, the initial response to the engagement worker role was less positive, with some staff finding that their initial concerns about the role not working were reinforced. Many of those staff members who were initially suspicious of the role subsequently revised their opinion after the placement of a more effective engagement worker. Staff opinions were an important part of the evaluation exercise, described in more detail later in this chapter.

Methodology of project evaluation

Engagement worker focus groups

There were two engagement worker focus groups, one of which had five participants and the other seven. Focus group participants were asked to write down on a piece of paper three things that worked well and three things that did not work well. The papers were collected and reviewed as a group, mapping the themes on a marker board, and drawing connections as they emerged.

The benefits of utilising this model of focus group is that it only asks open-ended questions, which allow participants to prioritise the importance of the issues they know to be relevant. It also focuses equally on what works well and what needs improvement, so the focus groups tend to be more constructive and positive, rather than simply forums for offering complaints.

Follow-up conversations were held with a number of engagement workers following on from the focus groups over both email and telephone.

Stakeholder interviews

Individual phone interviews were conducted with a total of 53 individuals:

- 31 offender managers (OMs) (consisting of probation officers and probation service officers);
- 4 assistant chief officers (ACOs);
- 12 senior probation officers (SPOs);
- four practice development officers (PDOs);
- the engagement workers' programme manager;
- the manager at User Voice.

Interviewees (apart from the engagement workers' programme manager and the manager at User Voice) were asked the same standard questions in addition to follow-up questions, which were based on the initial responses provided. The interviews were kept short (usually only 10–15 minutes) to limit the demands on the interviewees' time.

The service-user survey

Five question surveys were delivered to the engagement workers and they were asked to pass on the questionnaires to the service users with whom they regularly worked, and who were willing to participate, regardless of whether the engagement workers anticipated that the service users would provide a positive or a negative response. The questionnaires came with pre-addressed envelopes and service users were asked to complete them anonymously in the reception area without the involvement of engagement workers or other staff. Once completed, service users were expected to seal the questionnaire in the envelope provided and hand it to the receptionist, who then placed it in the outgoing mail bag so it could be forwarded to the research department. In total, 21 surveys were returned.

The results may have suffered from 'sampling bias', whereby the sample was not representative of the larger group but instead biased towards a particular outcome. In this instance, all 21 survey respondents provided positive responses, and while it is possible that they all legitimately held positive views about the programme, it is also possible that the engagement workers gave the surveys to service users they knew would respond positively. Alternatively, it is possible that the service users who were willing to complete the survey were those who appreciated the engagement worker's role.[1] Consequently, the results of the service-user survey should be considered within the context of understanding that a broader distribution of the survey to additional service users might have resulted in less positive results. However, the comments provided within an open text box, and the replies to a question that asked about preferences between users' engagement worker and offender manager (OM), indicate that the survey responses received were generally accurate. These results are described in more detail in the 'Findings' section. An audit was also performed of 30 pre-existing engagement workers' referral forms, in order to determine the information already made available within these forms.

Case studies

As the work of engagement workers is not typically included on Delius (the CRC case management system), the engagement workers themselves were asked to send summary case reports, which were read in parallel with Delius case notes. From these two sources, case studies emerged summarising the details of each case and providing narrative explanation for the reasons why a particular case study was relevant. The evaluation was written with the assistance of two contract workers (Harriet Fearn and Anna Wilkinson). Additional interviews were conducted by Professor Anthony Goodman of Middlesex University.

Findings

The stakeholder interviews

The initial 51 stakeholder interviews comprised a series of standard questions that were put to each participant.[2] In this section, the results of these standardised questions are quantified and the results discussed. (The themes discovered throughout the course of the interviews are discussed in the next section.)

Q1: How satisfied are you with the engagement worker role? Out of 51 stakeholders interviewed, 27 reported being satisfied with the engagement worker role, while 14 were unsatisfied, and 10 had mixed views. Those reporting mixed views tended to be staff members who had two experiences with engagement workers: a bad experience with the first worker, and a good experience with the replacement worker (who typically had only been in their new post for a short time). Consequently, if the question had been framed differently – to ask, 'How satisfied are you with your most recent engagement workers?' – it is likely that the satisfaction rate would have been higher.

It is worth noting that the survey respondents tended to have strongly held positions. Consider that a majority of all interviewees reported – entirely unprompted – that their engagement worker was 'excellent'; this means that a majority of those who were satisfied felt that way strongly, and would more likely have chosen a more intense qualifier than 'satisfaction', which can simply denote a slightly positive view. 'Excellent' was the term used most frequently as a descriptor.

Q2: Either from anecdotal reports you've received from your colleagues, or your own observations, how well do engagement workers engage with service users?

Perhaps a more relevant finding to consider for those seeking affirmation that the role works is that 42 of the 51 interviewed stakeholders reported that they believed engagement workers did a good job in trying to engage service users. One implication of this figure is that there is a significant proportion of stakeholders who, while they are not satisfied overall with the engagement worker role (perhaps being dissatisfied with its implementation), nonetheless believe that the core function of the role – offender engagement – is performed well.

Q3: Do you believe that having the shared experience of offending allows engagement workers to make a connection that would not be possible with offender managers (OMs)?

Thirty-four interviewed stakeholders reported that they believed the shared history of offending allowed most engagement workers to engage service users more easily than most OMs would be able to.

In light of the responses to the first three questions, some negative views should be noted:

- Eight interviewed stakeholders believed that engagement workers did a good job engaging service users, but that this was not due to their shared prison experience.
- Nine interviewed stakeholders were unsatisfied with the role and believed that engagement workers did not engage service users well.

Q4: Have you experienced or noticed any instances of inappropriate behaviour on the part of engagement workers?

Twelve survey respondents reported that they had personally experienced or were aware of engagement workers engaging in poor workplace habits. Additionally, 16 stakeholders stated that they had personally experienced or were aware of conflicts with engagement workers around the issue of maintaining professional boundaries.

Q5: Is your engagement worker well utilised by staff?

There were an equal number of positive and negative responses to this question, with half of the respondents reporting that they believed their engagement worker was very busy and half believing that their engagement worker was under-used and could handle additional work.

This issue is relevant, as perceptions of being busy were shown to have an impact on how satisfaction was viewed. Engagement workers who were not perceived as being busy tended to be the subject of more negative views, as OMs believed they could have been 'doing more for certain cases'. Conversely, less was expected of engagement workers who were perceived to be very busy, and OMs were more grateful and satisfied for small efforts when they perceived themselves to be in competition with others for the engagement worker's time.

Frequently, though, perceptions of how busy people are have little to do with reality; it is quite possible that engagement workers who were perceived as not being very busy actually had a large workload that simply was not visible to OMs. This could have been because they were often out of the office accompanying service users to the Jobcentre, Citizens Advice Centre, court and so on – all time-consuming tasks that may not have been noticed or appreciated by OMs. One of the inherent problems with the engagement worker programme was attempting to quantify time spent and levels of productivity.

Q6: How are the engagement workers perceived by colleagues?

A healthy 42 stakeholders reported that engagement workers were perceived as regular colleagues by probation staff, and that there were no reports of problems such as engagement workers being isolated or treated differently from other staff members.

Key findings from stakeholder interviews

The bulk of the evaluation related to the 51 interviews with the different stakeholders (ACOs, SPOs, OMs and PDOs). Some of the recurring themes that emerged in the interviews are identified as follows.

Overall satisfaction with engagement workers

Stakeholders were largely satisfied with the role. As one probation officer stated, "In my opinion, it is helpful for staff to see that people can change, and can progress." Or as an ACO commented, "I think he is able to engage better because of his shared experiences." Many answered this first question asked of them by saying, "They're excellent! I wish I had more than one!" This suggests that one of the major aims of the pilot has been successfully achieved: a majority of probation staff (53%) appreciated the employment of ex-service users because of their ability to engage current service users. However, staff satisfaction was not limited to offender engagement. Staff seemed most appreciative about engagement workers' ability to work in the field on time-intensive tasks such as home visits, signing up service users for benefits, visiting the housing office, or taking service users shopping for groceries or other errands.

These, of course, are not tasks that have to be done by a former service user, but could be done by any support worker. Indeed, in the past, they would often have been done by probation officers themselves. However, both engagement workers and OMs acknowledged that these tasks enabled engagement workers to engage service users and build relationships. Interviewed stakeholders also widely praised engagement workers who were running group induction sessions for service users undertaking new community orders, stating that the sessions were very successful. Finally, stakeholders commended the attempts made by engagement workers to contact service users who had disengaged from probation. Interviewed stakeholders were able to recount a number of instances where engagement workers were able to convince service users to re-engage, even if the re-engagement was not always long-lived. This suggests a possible role for engagement workers in improving compliance and perhaps avoiding unnecessary breaches, but further research is needed to confirm this.

Concerns about cultural capital

Another recurring theme in the stakeholder focus groups was that as a group, the engagement workers had deficits in their cultural capital in relation to the workplace. (Cultural capital is defined here as the unspoken knowledge regarding appropriate behaviour at work, or simply put, 'how we do things around here'). While this was not a majority opinion – indeed, the majority opinion was that engagement workers did not have deficits – observing or being aware that the engagement workers had deficits was mentioned in 24% of the interviews. Specifically mentioned were the following issues:

- Some engagement workers did not take notes during meetings to write down actions.

- Some were not proficient in diary or time management.
- Some did not use proper email etiquette or spell check.
- Some used inappropriate vocabulary when giving a presentation. (As one SPO stated, "He arranged to give a presentation to a cohort of SPOs. Everyone was very impressed, but his terminology wasn't very PC and he was getting some worried looks.")
- One SPO commented that a particular engagement worker did not have the best writing skills and that, "Unfortunately, like it or not, a lot of people are going to look at their writing and then infer their level of competency in a lot of other areas based on this one example, that may not be particularly relevant to their skills in other areas."

As one SPO stated, "We have to remember that some things we take for granted, like working in an office, are very new to them." This was affirmed by the engagement workers' programme manager, although he also reiterated that, in part, the purpose of the role was to provide former service users with professional employment opportunities to assist in their own journey of desistance. This frames the role of engagement workers as a training opportunity that could equip engagement workers with experience and the cultural capital they would require for future employment outside of probation. Indeed, Fletcher and Batty's (2012) study, cited previously, found that the largest beneficiary of peer mentor programmes were the mentors themselves. It should also be noted that the Equalities Department had already scheduled additional training events as part of the overall long-term training strategy for engagement workers.

Tension with probation staff

While there was not a single interviewee who confessed to still feeling uncomfortable working with engagement workers, a number of interviewees did articulate a tension in roles of the OMs and the engagement workers. Specifically, this tension related to the idea that engagement workers were 'better' at offender engagement than OMs. As one SPO suggested, "Some OMs might feel engagement is the job of the POs and that the engagement workers might be treading on their toes."

Some OMs felt that their years of training, experience and professionalism were being diminished, and that they were being pushed – in some areas – to utilise engagement workers when they felt more than capable of doing the work themselves.

It should be noted that ACOs were given clear instructions to fully integrate the engagement workers into their areas, and were instructed on how to communicate the role to staff, which is to say that staff should have been reminded that the engagement worker role was not in competition with OMs. The perceived role conflict with engagement workers often seemed to reflect the level of ACO support. Those ACOs who supported the position experienced little or no tension between the roles; those who did not support the role were more likely to feel that there was role conflict.

Findings from the service-user survey

Although only a limited number of service-user respondents completed the questionnaires, the outcomes of the survey were very clear. For the first two questions, each of the service users surveyed reported that they appreciated the role their engagement worker performed and that their engagement worker was able to connect with them in a way probation staff could not.

Perhaps the most interesting question was the one that was purposefully provocative in an attempt to ascertain whether service users preferred engagement workers to OMs. While a quarter agreed with this statement, stating they would prefer to meet with engagement workers, most reported being neutral on the subject and not feeling strongly one way or another. However, within the framing of this question, any response that was not in agreement should be considered an acknowledgement by service users that the OM role retained its value even when compared with that of engagement workers.

The last question was open-ended, asking respondents to explain why they appreciated their engagement worker. The responses to this question demonstrated that the shared experience of having been under probation supervision was valuable to service users and that engagement workers were making a definite impact:

> The thing I like about him is I can relate easier.

> Because they've been through what I went through.

> The main thing for me is the fact that I can relate with my engagement worker. I feel like he understands me because we're both coming from the same background. It really eases the mind to know that I am not being judged.

They understand the situation I am in so they are more considerate with me.

Relates to me, communicates with me, makes me feel that I can turn my life around.

Personally, I feel these guys are the right guys for the job and that I can relate to them.

Findings from the engagement worker focus groups

Perhaps the most important finding from the focus groups was that engagement workers self-assessed themselves as performing high-quality work. As one engagement worker stated, "I know I've done some damn good work!" Or, as another stated, "I have too many success stories to count!" It was also widely agreed in both focus groups that their experience with prison or probation gave them an edge in successfully engaging service users compared with probation officers. One engagement worker stated: "I see a guy sit down, I immediately know that he's in a gang, I've been with offender managers who were clueless and didn't pick up on it." Or as another stated:

> A lot of service users I deal with feel that some OMs look down on them and judge them as a criminal rather than dealing with them as an individual and with some respect. As an ex-service user, I know how it feels to be on the other side and they don't get that vibe with us and it does help to engage them and to hopefully make them see that probation isn't so bad and there are people who want to help you change your life and giving them the knowledge to know it can be done.

While having confidence in their own work is definitely positive, it also becomes apparent how existing workplace tension could develop regarding which group – OMs or engagement workers – is better at working with service users.

Information sharing

Engagement workers provided mixed feedback with regard to information sharing. Some reported that they were routinely kept in the loop about new case updates by OMs regarding cases that had been referred to them. Others stated that they never received any updates. There was also mixed feedback regarding engagement workers receiving sufficient information with referrals before the start of engagement with a service user. Whether they received relevant information, such as offence, risk and other pertinent details, depended on which OM they were working with at the time. Information sharing was also problematic when engagement workers felt that their contribution to certain cases, and their notes regarding their meeting, had not been formally entered into the case file, thus making it appear as if their contribution were invisible, as it would not show up on Delius records.

Tension with probation staff

Perhaps the single most personal and sensitive theme to emerge within the focus groups was the perceived conflict regarding having a former (or current) service user working alongside probation staff. The two focus groups were relatively evenly split regarding those who felt somewhat isolated within their office, and those who felt entirely welcomed and integrated into the office. Within these two 'sides' there were graduated degrees of perception, as some engagement workers reported usually feeling comfortable and only feeling the stigma of being a former service user on specific occasions. Taking both focus groups together, there were a range of viewpoints, with some engagement workers feeling entirely comfortable, others feeling largely uncomfortable, while others had mixed feelings.

A specific concern was being identified as a 'former service user' while attending probation functions or when there was a visiting VIP, a title that engagement workers felt ignored their professional experience, training and skills, and reduced them to a stereotype. As one engagement worker stated: "Day to day, I'm respected, I know my co-workers appreciate me, then the probation chief or some visitor comes to the office and I'm suddenly introduced as 'the offender'. It's embarrassing."

Additionally, engagement workers were split regarding the degree of individual integration they experienced in probation offices. While most of the engagement workers seemed to have been fully and comfortably integrated into their offices, four reported not being invited to team meetings, having their desk separated from the rest of staff, not receiving routine supervision, and/or being treated differently from other staff members; this difference in treatment was a source of considerable role dissatisfaction.

Training

In both focus groups, engagement workers were frustrated with the lack of professional development and training opportunities available to their role. Many of the courses they wanted to take were restricted to OMs only. Engagement workers expressed a strong desire for continuous professional development regarding offender engagement.

Differential workloads

In both focus groups, members were divided between those who were working at capacity and were extremely busy and those who were struggling to find work.

In areas where they were fairly busy, engagement workers reported that their supervising SPOs had helped promote them internally within the office, and that they had been able to attend team meetings, and work side by side with probation staff so they could increase their profile in the office. Conversely, those engagement workers who struggled to find work also reported being somewhat isolated within the office (desk segregated from other probation staff, forced to stay in reception area, or not invited to participate in team meetings).

Managing expectations

In both focus groups, it was mentioned that sometimes the engagement worker role had been 'built up too much', meaning that sometimes OMs had an unrealistic expectation about workers' abilities. As one engagement workers stated, "Just because I'm good at engaging doesn't mean that I'm always going to be successful. There are still going to be people that don't want to work with probation, regardless of whether they're talking to me or their probation officer." This feeling was substantiated by at least two OMs in the individual interviews; one reported being disappointed in the ability of the engagement worker after they had been "... built up to have this awesome ability to engage service users".

Job satisfaction

Almost all the focus group participants reported enjoying their jobs, though there were a number of issues that threatened to destroy their future satisfaction should nothing change. Indeed, half of the participants in both groups raised their hand when asked if they were already contemplating looking for new work. Finally, half of the focus group participants stated they would be interested in someday being a PSO or a PO, but they were all unclear whether this was possible given their past convictions. As one engagement worker stated, "I wouldn't mind staying here if I knew there was some role for me to move to, if there was the possibility to advance."

Conclusion

Although the evaluation primarily examined the role itself, not the project delivery of the role, it appears that the delivery of the role was largely successful. The role was a new one for the organisation; the project required taking a number of risks, and it was attempted at what was perhaps the most inopportune moment of the past five years because of the government's plans to transform the probation service (Ministry of Justice, 2013). Nevertheless, given the popularity of the role and the success of the workers, it appears that the introduction of the role can be regarded as a generally positive development. The engagement worker role was valued within the organisation by both probation staff (stakeholders) and service users. The evaluation also found that engagement workers were often – but not always – able to make connections with service users based on their prior offending history, and that this connection could have helped facilitate substantive change in service users, although the change may not always have been reported as lasting or permanent. Unfortunately, the degree and scope of the change could not be easily defined, as the study did not aim to measure change directly

Although skill and experience levels varied among the engagement workers, it was evident within the case studies that many of the workers were proficient, skilled and experienced in offender management (contrary to the perceptions of some probation staff who assumed they were novices). The majority of probation staff recognised this proficiency and believed that engagement workers were, as a group, skilled in their job. The study did not include any specific assessment of skills, but the positive views of other practitioners are an important indicator.

It is difficult to determine whether the engagement worker programme represented good value for money, but when measured against the cost of running it, there does seem to be a definite need for support workers who are able to accompany service users into the field to assist with housing issues, benefits claims and other time-intensive tasks. This was one of the most beneficial aspects of the programme, in the view of OMs. Consequently, the evaluation concluded that the added value provided by the engagement workers, while taking on the role of support worker, provided sufficient evidence for the continued employment of former service users in the probation service. If support workers are needed, it makes sense to employ those who have a better chance of making a connection.

Postscript

During the early part of 2016, the method used by the Ministry of Justice to measure the amount of work being undertaken by the CRCs, and the money to be paid to them, resulted in the London CRC receiving less money. This, in turn, led to a review of resourcing levels across the organisation. One consequence of this review was that the engagement worker role was discontinued. While this was disappointing, on a positive note, eight out of the 11 engagement workers were redeployed and three of those eight were successful in applying for PSO posts, which was effectively a promotion, and something that the project manager had been working towards with regard to long-term career progression. Unfortunately, three of the engagement workers were later made redundant. While the engagement worker project may have been relatively short-lived, it arguably demonstrated that ex-offenders can make an effective contribution to probation work, and can adapt sufficiently to the culture of probation to progress to positions of greater responsibility.

Notes

[1] Ideally, another member of staff such as the receptionist would have delivered the survey to the service users. Unfortunately, as only a small percentage of the overall service-user population would need to fill out the survey, and given the difficulties that have occurred in the past with getting receptionists to deliver surveys to selected populations, it was determined that the only feasible model of delivery was through the engagement workers, even though there was a risk to survey integrity.

[2] The total number of interviews performed was 53, but in their interviews Daniel Hutt and Nigel Hosking were not asked the same questions as other interviewees, and thus the number of available surveys was reduced to 51.

References

Bonta, J. and Andrews, D.A. (2017) *The Psychology of Criminal Conduct* (6th edn), New York, NY: Routledge.

Boyce, I., Hunter. G. and Hough, M. (2009) *St Giles Trust Peer Advice Project: An Evaluation*, London: St Giles Trust.

Cook, J., McClure, S., Koutsenok, I. and Scot, L. (2008) 'The implementation of inmate mentor programs in the correctional treatment system as an innovative approach', *Journal of Teaching in the Addictions*, 7(2): 123–132.

Dowden, C. and Andrews, D. (2004) 'The importance of staff practice in delivering effective correctional treatment: a meta-analytic review of core correctional practice', *International Journal of Offender Therapy and Comparative Criminology*, 48(2): 203–214.

Durnescu, I., Grigoras, V., Lazar, F. and Witec, S. (2014) 'Who works in the probation service of Romania?', in F. McNeill and I. Durnescu (eds) *Understanding Penal Practice*, Abingdon: Routledge.

Fletcher, D. and Batty, E. (2012) *Offender Peer Interventions: What do we Know?*, Sheffield: Centre for Regional Economic and Social Research, Sheffield Hallam University, available at www.shu.ac.uk/ research/cresr/sites/shu.ac.uk/files/offender-peer-interventions.pdf.

Foster, J. (2011) *Peer Support in Prison Health Care: An Investigation into the Listening Scheme in One Adult Male Prison*, London: University of Greenwich.

Huggins, R. (2010) *Mentoring for Progression: Prison Mentoring Project. Assessing Strengths, Outcomes and Roll-Out Potential*, Oxford: Oxford Brookes University.

Maguire, M., Holloway, K., Liddle, M., Gordon, F., Gray, P., Smith, A. and Wright, S. (2010) 'Evaluation of the Transitional Support Scheme (TSS): Final report to the Welsh Assembly Government', available at http://wccsj.ac.uk/images/docs/tss-report-en.pdf.

Ministry of Justice (2013) *Transforming Rehabilitation: A Strategy for Reform*, Cm 8619, London: Ministry of Justice.

Ministry of Justice (2014) *Transforming Rehabiltiation: A Summary of Evidence on Reducing Reoffending* (2nd edn), London: Ministry of Justice.

Raynor, P., Ugwudike, P. and Vanstone, M. (2014) 'The impact of skills in probation work: a reconviction study', *Criminology and Criminal Justice*, 14(2): 235–249.

Scott, D.P., Hzarzke, A.J., Mizwa, M.B., Pugh, M. and Ross, M.W. (2004) 'Evaluation of an HIV peer education program in Texas prisons', *Journal of Corrective Health*, 10(2): 151–173.

United Nations Office on Drugs and Crime (2003) *Peer to Peer: Using Peer Strategies in Drug Abuse Prevention*, New York, NY: United Nations.

SEVENTEEN

Collaborative family work in youth justice

Chris Trotter

Introduction

The study described in this chapter involves the delivery of collaborative family work by youth justice workers in New South Wales (NSW), Australia, to young people and their families as part of a statutory youth justice service. The chapter first outlines the literature that supports the value of working in the community with the families of young offenders. It then outlines the family model used by the youth justice workers, the mechanisms used by the region to support the programme and the reflections of clients and workers regarding the intervention. The primary objective of the chapter is to provide information about the implementation of family work for the benefit of youth justice services (or other service providers) that might be interested in developing similar programmes in the future.

Family relationships, youth offending and risk

Family relationships are clearly a factor in the development of delinquent and criminal behaviour. This can be explained through a number of criminological theories, including learning theory, labelling theory and social control theory. Children and young people may be socialised into prosocial or criminal behaviour by a process of reinforcement and through the personal models to whom they are exposed (Burke, 2001).

There is also evidence that family relationships are a factor not just in the development of offending, but also in reoffending. Family factors are a key factor in risk of reoffending prediction instruments for young people. For example, the Youth Level of Service/Case Management Inventory (YLS/CMI) (Andrews and Bonta, 2003) identifies family and relationships, including parent–child relationships, as one of eight key criminogenic needs. The authors argue that addressing criminogenic needs leads to reduced reoffending. Furthermore,

Trotter and Evans (2012) found that family issues were one of the most commonly discussed in youth justice supervision sessions.

There is also evidence that work with families of young offenders can be effective in improving family relationships and reducing reoffending. Lipsey and Cullen (2007) considered four different meta-analyses on the effectiveness of family interventions for young offenders and found an average reduction in recidivism compared with comparison studies of between 20% and 52%. A meta-analysis by Dowden and Andrews (2003) of the effectiveness of 38 family interventions in corrections found that these interventions were effective, although this was only when they were based on effective practice principles, that is, including a focus on medium- to high-risk offenders and on factors related to the offending behaviour. The study also found that the effective interventions were based on cognitive-behavioural and social learning approaches, including 'modelling, graduated practice, rehearsal, role playing, reinforcement, resource provision, and detailed verbal guidance and explanations' (Dowden and Andrews, 2003, p 2).

The importance of delivering interventions as they are intended is further emphasised in a study by Sexton and Turner (2010), who found a reduction in recidivism of young offenders offered functional family therapy (a systems cognitive-behavioural approach), compared with young offenders offered probation alone. They found the benefits were only present if the family workers adhered to the functional family therapy model.

There is also some research support for the collaborative family work model (Trotter, 2013) discussed in this chapter. Previous research has found high levels of worker and family member satisfaction with collaborative family work interventions offered to child protection and juvenile justice clients. Further positive outcomes from the NSW juvenile justice study in terms of take-up rates, completion rates, client and worker satisfaction with the model, and reduced problems are provided in Trotter (2017).

The study

The project was undertaken in the western region of New South Wales in Australia, a region that includes rural and remote parts of NSW. Juvenile justice staff in the region provide supervision to young people placed on court orders such as probation and supervision orders or on parole following release from detention centres. While work with families is a part of the work of juvenile justice staff, structured work with family groups is not routinely offered.

The director and staff in the western region agreed to undertake a pilot project that involved offering a series of six to 10 structured family work sessions to young people and their families. A two-day practical training course in collaborative family work was offered to youth justice staff in the region. A group of staff from a non-government welfare organisation was also involved in the training, with a view to those staff co-working with juvenile justice staff and with client families who were involved with both agencies. The training course was repeated on a regular basis as new staff were appointed and regular updates to the training were also offered. Staff were then asked to offer family work to suitable young people and their families. The family work is known as ANTS within the region. ANTS is an acronym for Act Together Now Strong and honey ants are also commonly represented in indigenous art. For this reason, it was felt that the term ANTS might help to engage indigenous families.

In total, 72 young people and their families were assessed as suitable and were offered family work. For 31 young people and their families, however, the family work did not go ahead, for the most part because the family members did not wish it to. On some occasions, they agreed but then changed their mind.

Forty-one young people and their families thus accepted the offer and undertook at least one family work session. Thirty-one families completed the family sessions with an average number of 6.5 sessions over 8.9 weeks. Completion was defined as having worked through the model over at least four and up to 10 sessions and the workers and the family members agreeing that the work had been completed. The 10 families who did not complete the work undertook an average of 2.7 sessions.

The families who began but did not complete the family work provided various reasons for non-completion. Five of the families did not continue because the families or the young person moved to live outside the western region during the period of the family work. The remaining five discontinued because, for various reasons, one or more of the family members did not wish to continue. Of the 10 families who did not complete, four completed four or more sessions, but discontinued even though the workers felt that the intervention was not complete.

Following the family work, whether it was completed or not, research officers contacted family members and workers to interview them regarding their experiences with the intervention. In total, 63 family members from 27 families responded to a series of questions about the experience of the family work when followed up two months after the family work finished. Fifty-nine of the family members interviewed had completed the family work intervention. Sixty-three workers were also interviewed about their experiences with the model.

Ethics

Family members were given an explanatory statement by a research officer and asked to provide informed consent to be involved in the research. The project was approved by the Monash University Ethics Committee and by the NSW Juvenile Justice Research Unit. The programme itself raises some ethical issues, given that it is the young people rather than their families who have offended and been placed under supervision. There is not space to address this issue in any detail here, suffice to say that care was taken to ensure that family members understood that their participation was entirely voluntary and that they could withdraw from the family work (or the research) at any time.

The collaborative family work model

The implementation of the model in the youth justice project comprised initial preparation, followed by home-based work sessions involving co-facilitators.

Preparation

Prior to beginning work with the family group (any two family members), the worker discussed with the family members the nature of the family work and what was expected of the family members. These discussions were then followed up in the first session.

Home-based work sessions

The family work sessions were held in most cases in the family home. Often this involved long-distance travel by the workers, sometimes over several hours, to reach remote communities. Home-based sessions have advantages and disadvantages. Certainly, family members are more likely to participate when the sessions are at home; they often feel more comfortable in this environment and feel a greater sense of control over the intervention.

Co-facilitators

Two facilitators were involved in each family session. As mentioned earlier, sometimes youth justice workers worked with a worker from a voluntary agency. The aim in using two workers is both educational and supportive, and also addresses some of the safety issues related to home visiting.

Commonly the two workers would alternate roles. One worker would lead the discussion on a particular issue free from interruptions from the other worker. At the completion of the segment of work, lasting perhaps 10 minutes or so, the second worker, who had been taking notes, would summarise the content of the discussion with a particular focus on reflecting the views of each participant. This would be done with the assistance of a notepad or large piece of paper placed on the wall in the room in which the work is taking place. On some occasions a more experienced worker would take the lead throughout the sessions. As the workers became more comfortable with each other, they often varied these methods and developed less formal ways of working together.

The presence of two workers provided an opportunity for the workers to learn from each other and to improve their skills by giving feedback about the way they conducted the sessions. Two workers often also allowed for continuity of contact between a primary worker and a client family. Sometimes a worker might feel that their client, a young person on a probation order, for example, would benefit from family work, but would not feel sufficiently confident or skilled to undertake the family work themselves. In this situation, the worker might involve a second worker with confidence and expertise in working with families. By involving a second person, the primary worker would offer the family work as a separate but complementary process to the ongoing work they were doing with the young person. The worker would then continue to see the young person on an individual basis between family work sessions. The individual work aimed to support the family work, but generally did not focus on issues being addressed in the ANTS sessions. In a small number of cases, the primary worker was not involved in the family work, but continued to work with the young person on an individual basis. In these cases, the primary worker would discuss issues with the family workers between sessions (assuming the young person and family members agreed to this).

Training, supervision and debriefing

All staff involved in delivering the family work undertook a two-day training course in collaborative family work. This involved explanations, demonstrations and role-play practice in each of the steps of the model. Half-day booster sessions were also offered to some staff.

Prior to each family beginning the work, a planning session was held with the workers, senior staff in the region, supervisors and an expert with knowledge of the model. The regional director also participated in many of these sessions. In these sessions, the suitability for family work of the young person and their family was discussed (although no families were declined for family work at this stage). The workers were also offered suggestions regarding how to conduct the first session. Following the first session, a debriefing panel was convened to review the session and to provide suggestions for the conduct of the next session. Debriefing panels were then convened following all subsequent family work sessions. The debriefing involved the workers presenting what they had done in the session, which steps of the model they had covered, how the family had responded to the various discussions and activities and what they planned to do in the next session.

The debriefing followed similar principles to working with the families, being non-blaming, supportive and strengths-focused, and was used in addition to the usual supervision offered in the region. It frequently focused on keeping the workers on track in terms of implementing the model.

Prosocial modelling

One distinctive feature of the collaborative family work model is the concept of prosocial modelling and reinforcement. The workers were encouraged through training and coaching to make use of prosocial skills (Trotter, 2013). This involves modelling prosocial values such as reliability and fairness, and reinforcing clients' prosocial comments and actions such as attending school or accepting responsibility for offences. The process of modelling and reinforcement also includes respectful and exploratory challenging by the workers when clients make antisocial comments or display antisocial behaviour (Trotter et al, 2016).

Rating scales

The workers also made use of family functioning rating scales and problem rating scales. The value of these scales has been highlighted in research by Miller and colleagues (2006) that found that clients' perceived improvement between sessions is an important predictor for adherence and treatment outcome. Also clients' retention rates increased significantly if they had the opportunity to voice their perception of progress between sessions on a regular basis and in a systematic way.

Rating scales were completed in each session by the family members in order to give a sense of the extent to which the family members were progressing in relation to general family functioning and in relation to specific problems that had been identified.

The model

Workers and family members worked though the following steps. The workers used the acronym RIDGES to remind them of the six steps.

1. **R**ole and ground rules
2. **I**dentify problems
3. **D**ecide what to work on first
4. **G**oals
5. **E**xplore problems
6. **S**trategies to solve problems

Ground rules and role clarification

Initially, workers review with family members what is involved in the sessions, including the way they will be conducted and how the model works. Copies of the family work outline are taken by the worker and displayed where the family work takes place (most commonly in the family home). This process is undertaken as part of the preparation for the work but reviewed at the commencement of the first session to ensure that family members have a good understanding of the process.

The workers then discuss with family members how the sessions will be conducted. For example, they discuss issues such as what happens in the sessions; who will know about what goes on in the sessions; whether this information will be discussed with others; what will happen if disclosures are made about child abuse or further offences; whether information from the sessions will be included in court reports; whether individual family members will have discussions with the facilitators between sessions; and whether these discussions will be confidential. For the most part, these issues are determined collaboratively by the family members, although in some cases they are determined by the workers, for example with regard to disclosure of child abuse or further offences.

Family members are then asked to identify specific ground rules for conduct of the sessions. The workers write these on large sheets of paper and put them on a wall in the room. Examples of ground rules include the following: sessions will be for 45 minutes once a week; abusive language will not be accepted; TVs and phones will be turned off; family members may leave the session temporarily if they are feeling distressed; the content of sessions will not be discussed with anyone outside of the sessions; family members will all speak positively to each other.

Identify problems

Each family member is asked to describe issues that concern them or things they would like to change. The workers prompt the family members so that a full picture of the problem is presented (for example, they might ask clients how they are getting on at school, who their friends are, whether they have enough money, how they get on with other family members). The worker then lists the problems of each family member on a whiteboard or on a large piece of paper that can be displayed on a wall in the family home.

The workers encourage family members to express problems in non-blaming terms and often reframe problems for the client. A 12-year-old boy might say that his biggest problem is his sister: 'She goes out whenever she likes and teases me all the time.' This might be reframed in the following terms: 'It upsets me that my mother does not have fair rules about what my sister is allowed to do and what I am allowed to do. I feel like they are ganging up on me.'

The worker then tries to identify common family problems. For example, concern about different expectations for family members might be a common issue. Failure to listen to each other might also be a common concern.

Decide what to work on first

The next stage of the process involves attempting to reach agreement with the family members as to which problems are to be worked on in the short and long term. In making a decision about which problems to address, workers take into account issues such as the family members' wishes (if they vary between family members, they may work on more than one problem); whether the problem is solvable

360

(for example, a problem with pocket money is more solvable than a problem with a parent who is not involved and has no interest in the family); legal requirements (for example, in a case where a young person is to be expelled from school); and whether problems relate to offending (for example, mixing with a procriminal peer group).

Goals

The next step involves setting clear and specific goals that are agreed on by the worker and the clients and are directly related to the problem or problems to be addressed. An example might be: 'For Amy and Mrs L to reach agreement on whether Amy should continue to see her boyfriend and if so how often and where she should see him. This goal to be achieved by week 7.' Other examples include: developing communication between a father and son when all communication has ceased; coming to an agreement between a mother and daughter regarding the amount of freedom the young person should be allowed; or reuniting a young person living away from home with her family.

Explore problems in more detail

The next stage involves a detailed exploration of the problem with family members in order to get a clear picture of the nature and degree of the problem and what has been done to address it previously. It is important that this is done thoroughly so that realistic strategies to address the problem can be developed. Questions asked of family members during this process might include: What is the history of the problem? When does it occur? How did it begin? What has the family done to address the problem previously? Have these things helped or hindered? Are there occasions when the problem is not present?

Strategies to solve problems

Strategies or tasks are then be developed by the worker and family members to address the goals. Strategies may be carried out in the family work sessions, for example, role play, teaching listening skills, helping family members to acknowledge what other family members are saying, brainstorming solutions or expressing problems in a non-blaming way. Strategies for family members might include engaging in mutually enjoyable activities, spending specified time together, a mother visiting a school, or a child coming home early in return for the mother giving more pocket money. The worker might also have strategies or tasks, such as approaching a social security department.

Written summaries

As the family work progresses, it is important to regularly revise what has been done and where the family is in relation to the steps in the model. This involves the use of written summaries of ground rules, problems, goals and strategies. These are commonly displayed on large sheets of paper in the room where the family work takes place. In the final session, a review of what has been achieved is undertaken and strategies put in place to maintain any gains that have been made. As the literacy levels of family members may vary, workers use accessible language in the written summaries and read them out to family members.

Timing

The first meeting is usually devoted to clarifying roles and developing ground rules. The second meeting is usually devoted to identifying issues for family members and it is usually not until the third or fourth meeting that workers and clients begin to develop tasks to address family members' goals and problems.

Facilitative strategies

While workers are strongly encouraged to work systematically through the six steps, the model also allows for some flexibility. It allows, for example, for facilitative strategies that do not relate to specific goals but may be used because workers feel that they want to give the family members some concrete things to do. These tasks may occur in the session or at home at other times, and may involve, for example, commenting on what family members like about each other or writing up ground rules. Strengths cards are often used – these involve family members selecting cards with words that describe positive aspects of other family members – for example, kind, thoughtful, funny, generous, loving, honest or helpful.[1]

The sample

The NSW youth justice service has approximately 1,700 young people under supervision, with over half of the custodial population being indigenous (New South Wales Bureau of Crime, Statistics and Research, 2015). The western region of NSW is one of four regions in the state, and includes predominantly rural and remote communities. Each of the 41 young people involved in the family work was on an order for a criminal offence ranging from serious assault to property offences. The region purposely targeted medium-to high-risk young people for the family work based on the YLS/CMI (Hoge and Andrews, 2003). The average age of the young people at the time of commencing the family work was 15.26, and 36% had previous experience of custody. Twenty of 40 clients (50%) identified as indigenous (in one case the ethnicity was unclear).

The average number of participants in the sessions was 5.1, comprising two workers and 3.1 family members. The family members included 41 young persons or primary clients, 34 mothers, 12 fathers, 12 brothers, seven grandmothers, six sisters, three stepmothers, two family friends and one stepfather.

The juvenile justice workers in NSW at the time could be employed as juvenile justice officers or as juvenile justice counsellors. While juvenile justice officers often did not have tertiary qualifications, they commonly had experience and training in juvenile justice work. Juvenile justice counsellors, on the other hand, were required to have tertiary qualifications and adopted a greater counselling role. The family work was delivered to the 41 families in pairs, by 42 juvenile justice officers, eight juvenile justice counsellors, 18 case managers from a local non-governmental organisation and two workers from Justice Health, a government organisation that delivers health services in the region. Twenty percent of the workers identified as aboriginal. Sixty-one percent of the workers were female and 39% male.

Family problems

Prior to each family intervention, the referring workers completed a screening tool with information about the family and the young person. This was gathered from files and from the family members and the young person. Multiple issues and problems were identified: for 61% of the young people, alcohol or drug issues were evident; 26% had an intellectual disability; 56% had violence involved in their offending; 28% had a history of self-harm; 88% had negative (or criminal) peers; 32% had a mental health issue; 42% had domestic violence in the family; 32% had unstable accommodation; 34% had a health problem and 10% were also clients of child protection.

These were complex and troubled families. The nature of the family issues was also described through comments on the screening forms. Some examples are as follows:

> Two younger brothers have ADHD [Attention Deficit Hyperactivity Disorder], the stepfather has alcohol misuse issues and mum has serious mental health issues.... The young person's best friend has a serious criminal history.

> Father suicided. Brother drowned 10 years ago. Neighbour murdered last year. Disabled aunt passed away, Grandmother died soon after.

> There are grief and loss issues within family relating to a stillborn child.

> There are issues around police harassment in a small town.

> There is a long history of the young person running away from home.

> Mum has previously lived with DV [domestic violence] and tends to avoid issues and admitted to not setting boundaries with her son.

> The client lives with dad who is reported to binge drink and then direct the young person not to get along with mum's new partner.

> Mother has an apprehended violence order (a court order which requires someone to stay away from another person) out against the young person due to reported intimidation at home.

> Young person has been diagnosed with Asperger's [Asperger syndrome] and has difficulties with anxiety.

> Mother disclosed client has assaulted her previously.

Thematic analysis of the qualitative comments

Family members and workers were interviewed in person approximately two months after completion or discontinuation of the family work. They were asked a number of specific questions and given opportunities to expand on their responses and to make general comments about the family work. The interviews were then analysed to determine the frequency of particular comments and common themes. This involved using a method of grouping the responses according to the questions and the use of open coding (Rubin and Babbie, 2005). There was a high degree of consistency in the comments made by workers and family members. The comments were overwhelmingly positive.

Findings

The data indicate that workers and family members found the development of ground rules for the sessions to be particularly helpful; that they found the length of the intervention to be suitable; that they liked the work being undertaken in the family home; that they liked the straightforward and easy-to-follow nature of the family work model; that they felt that the use of rating scales provided valuable feedback; and that they enjoyed the strengths-based activities. The workers felt that they improved their skills as a result of the family work experience and the debriefing that accompanied it.

Which aspects of the model were most helpful?

Family members and workers commented on the individual strengths of the model, and many also commented on how the model worked as a whole. Many workers and family members felt that a strength of the model was working through all the steps, as the following comments show:

> All of it. You can't miss a step. You need to keep it together. You always have to bring it back to the model.

> I cannot separate the aspects of the model as they are all part of the same model and they all go hand in hand.

Nevertheless, when asked to comment on which aspects of the family sessions they found most helpful, of the 39 family members who responded to this question, 21 said that clarifying roles and setting ground rules was the most helpful aspect of the work. Five found problem exploration helpful, four found problem ranking most helpful, three home tasks, and one goal setting.

> The group rules were a constant reminder to the family during and after ANTS. The group rules became the family rules.

365

> The family still have the group rules and the poster has been displayed on the fridge [since the family work finished].

> Anything visual worked well. We had a token for a talking stick and visual group rules. The foundation worked well. It was comfortable policing the rules. They were initially talking all over the top of each other and strong blaming. It was going to derail if we were not careful.

The workers gave similar responses. Forty-five of the 52 workers who responded to this question identified role clarification and ground rules as the most helpful aspect of the work.

> Everyone got to put down rules – mostly the rules around 'wait for others to stop talking and listen, don't judge'.

> Everyone had their own time to speak – the 'talking boomerang' – whoever had it got to speak.

> The family are clear about their boundaries and they have ownership as they develop the ground rules.

> Ground rules enabled the young person and mother to review and reflect on their expectations.

One worker commented on the value of allowing each family member to speak:

> The family work provided a wonderful opportunity for the 12 year old to have a voice and attention. Talking about the impact on the young person of having been locked up was very powerful for her because she had been dismissed.... Reframing and using non-blaming language was a light-bulb moment for dad and the young person. She got a voice and it empowered her without being put down.

Other workers and clients found other aspects of the work to be the most helpful:

> I think problem exploration and goal setting are the mainstays of the programme. The participants have control

over both these aspects which gives them ownership to move forward.

You need for the family to identify the problem in order to work on their goal. Their goal was for the young person to seek employment and he got work. Determining the goal also helped sort out a lot of their other issues. Mum was upset that Bradley wasn't achieving and was greatly relieved when he got a job.

Duration of the family work

The family work was limited to six to 10 sessions over six to 12 weeks. The average length of a session was around about 45 minutes. Seventy-four percent of the workers who responded to this question felt that the duration of the work was about right, with 21% saying it was a bit short and 5% that it was a bit long. The workers often felt that the brief intervention encouraged the family members to learn how to get on better and the use the skills they had learnt without becoming dependent on the workers. Clients made similar comments. One client commented:

> Everything is fine ... two months taught us a lot in that time for example not to give up ... to deal with our problems and how to deal with them correctly.

A worker commented:

> I have done a number of family sessions now and it is best to stop when the problem is worked out. If you continue then you find more problems and you have to continue to fix them and then they don't learn the strategies they rely on the worker.

However, one family member was concerned that the young person was advantaged by the follow up, which was only available to clients of Juvenile Justice:

> Some follow-up would be good. The young person still sees the facilitator (probation officer) weekly but there is nothing for the rest of the family. I would have liked the

family work to continue for another couple of weeks to practise the strategies.

Access to family work services

A number of workers and clients commented that they had not been able to access, or they had been turned away from, family work services in the past. One worker commented:

> A lot of families are similar where communication is yelling or screaming – they had been turned away again and again from services.

Home visits

A number of workers and clients commented on the benefits of providing the service in the family home, including in remote communities where families receive few services.

> We fitted in with their schedule. We had to travel and didn't get home until about 9pm. They really appreciated the commitment that we put into their family.

> I am pushing for better trained people to come out to those communities. I found the experience of my co-facilitator beneficial to me. She had a counselling background which was helpful.

Easy-to-follow model

Clients were asked if they could understand the model. Of the 45 who answered this question, all said that they could understand the model, although two clients were initially uncertain about it:

> The worker explained it all before we started.

> I was sceptical beforehand but that changed when we started.

The workers provided similar responses:

The family tended to wander and the model kept them on task and we ensured that they knew we were there to facilitate and not tell them what to do.

Rating scales

Many workers and clients commented on the value of the rating scales:

Each week we would ask how the person felt in the last week with their family and review what has changed and was it for the better or worse.

It gave us (workers) an understanding of what the family saw as important or how they would rate issues, which would be very different to how we would rate the problem. It was also a good conversation starter to ask why they used a '3' and why it differed from the previous week.

Strengths-based activities

Many of the workers and family members commented favourably on the strengths-based activities:

The young person and his siblings enjoyed the strength based activities. They enjoyed hearing what they thought of each other and what the family strengths were.

When we (the workers) introduced the strengths cards it was a turning point for both of the family members as for the first time they heard each other say positive things about each other.

Skill development and debriefing

A number of workers commented that they felt a sense of achievement in completing the family work intervention:

It's a real achievement to finish the model, however it is never easy going. The young person's positive feedback made it all worthwhile – with YP [young person] maturing over the sessions and creating more positive connections with the worker and his mother. The young person also began to bridge gap with his grandparents (who were impacted on by his crime).

A number of workers commented on the value of the debriefing panel that reviewed each session and helped with planning the next session; they also felt that the family work and the debriefing helped to improve their skills.

> The manager was extremely supportive and complimentary with the work we had done. I learnt so much undertaking this programme as a worker – analysis and reflection of my professionalism as a practitioner. I felt extremely privileged undertaking this work with the family.

One worker, however, felt that the problems presented by the family were beyond the scope of the family work, particularly those issues relating to previously undisclosed child abuse.

> A number of significant family issues and traumas presented during the programme that were beyond the scope of both the programme and the facilitator's skills/qualifications and these have been referred for ongoing follow up/support.

Family recruitment

A number of workers commented on the need to put more effort into recruiting families for the family work.

> It is hard to find families to participate. It is hard because small towns talk and that could be why families don't want to be involved. It is hard to go into a family that you know quite well.

Conclusion

This chapter has outlined a practical model for working with families in youth justice, and has shown that it is possible to implement family work interventions as a routine part of practice in a youth justice service. It has also shown that workers and family members find the experience to be rewarding and effective in helping family members with their problems.

In particular, workers and family members found the development of ground rules for the sessions to be helpful in showing family members how better to communicate with each other; they found the length of the intervention to be suitable; they liked the fact that the work was generally undertaken in the family home; they liked the straightforward and easy-to-follow nature of the collaborative family work model; they felt that the use of rating scales provided valuable feedback on progress of families; and they enjoyed the strengths-based activities. Moreover, the workers felt that they improved their skills as a result of the family work experience and the debriefing that accompanied it.

This study has limitations. It has not at this stage been able to follow up reoffending rates by the young people (we are waiting for a two-year follow-up period to elapse), which is perhaps the key effectiveness measure of a programme such as this. While the study does point to the feasibility of providing family work services in a statutory youth justice probation service, it should be acknowledged that the project has been carried out as a pilot study with enthusiastic support from regional managers. Similar support and commitment would no doubt be needed for the service to be provided elsewhere. Nevertheless, it is clear from this study that one of the most important needs of young offenders can be addressed within the routine confines of a statutory youth justice service.

Note

[1] See https://innovativeresources.org/resources/card-sets/strength-cards/

References

Andrews, D. and Bonta, J. (2003) *The Psychology of Criminal Conduct*, Cincinnati, OH: Anderson.

Burke, R. (2001) *Criminological Theory*, Cullompton: Willan.

Dowden, C. and Andrews, D.A. (2003) 'Does family intervention work for delinquents? Results of a meta-analysis', *Canadian Journal of Criminology and Criminal Justice*, 45(3): 327–342.

Hoge, R.D. and Andrews, D.A. (2003) *Youth Level of Service/Case Management Inventory (YLS/CMI) User's Manual*, Toronto: Multi-Health Systems.

Lipsey, M. and Cullen, F. (2007) 'The effectiveness of correctional rehabilitation: a review of systematic reviews', *Annual Review of Law and Social Science*, 3: 297–320.

Miller, S., Duncan, B., Brown, J., Sorrell, R. and Chalk, M. (2006) 'Using formal client feedback to improve retention and outcome: making ongoing real time assessment feasible', *Journal of Brief Therapy*, 5(1): 5–22.

New South Wales Bureau of Crime, Statistics and Research (2015) New South Wales Custody Statistics, available at bocsar.nsw.gov.au/documents/custody/nswcustodystatisticsmar2015.pdf (accessed September 2017).

Rubin, A. and Babbie, E. (2005) *Research Methods for Social Work*, 6th edn, Belmont CA: Thompson Brooks/Cole.

Sexton, T. and Turner, C.W. (2010) 'The effectiveness of functional family therapy for youth with behavioural problems in a community practice setting', *Journal of Family Psychology*, 24(3): 339–348.

Trotter, C. (2013) *Collaborative Family Work: A Practical Model for Working with Families in the Human Services*, Sydney: Allen & Unwin.

Trotter, C. (2017) 'Working with families in youth justice,' *Probation Journal*, 64(2): 94–107.

Trotter, C. and Evans, P. (2012) 'Analysis of supervision skills in juvenile justice', *Australian and New Zealand Journal of Criminology*, 45(2): 255–273.

Trotter, C.J., Evans, P. and Baidawi, S.H. (2016) 'The effectiveness of challenging skills in work with young offenders', *International Journal of Offender Therapy and Comparative Criminology*, epub: 1–16.

EIGHTEEN

Resisting effective approaches for BAME offenders in England and Wales: the triumph of inertia

Patrick Williams and Pauline Durrance

Introduction

Over a decade ago, we co-authored an article that made a plea for the use of empowerment programmes on the grounds that the evidence available to date, limited though it was, suggested their relevance to Black, Asian and minority ethnic (BAME) people on probation (Durrance and Williams, 2003). Comparing different models of change, we questioned whether the cognitive-behavioural theory base intrinsic to Home Office Pathfinder Programmes[1] was likely to be the best way to reduce offending behaviour among BAME individuals. Occurring in the aftermath of the Macpherson report, which identified institutional racism within the criminal justice system (CJS) of England and Wales (Macpherson, 1999), we were concerned at the superficial adaptation of Pathfinder projects based on cognitive-behavioural theory to 'fit' particular offender populations and questioned the logic that such approaches would have an appreciable impact on the structural and social problems experienced by BAME people.

In 2001, under the auspices of the Effective Practice Initiative, there were four intervention programmes specifically designed for BAME offenders subject to community disposals or post-release supervision (Durrance and Williams, 2003). Today, there are none. This dearth of specific interventions for BAME offenders can be read in a number of ways. It could result from a lack of evidence that specifically designed programmes were successful. Another explanation could be that research exploring the link between people's experience of racism and offending have been inconclusive. Taken together this has tended to result in a consensus that Black and Asian offenders do not have sufficiently different criminogenic needs to warrant separate provision (Walmsley and Stephens, 2006). An alternative interpretation, however, is the continued resistance to exploring the use of empowerment approaches that acknowledge the lived experience of many BAME individuals in British society.[2]

Within this chapter, we aim to excavate the 'triumph of inertia' (Players, 2013) wherein the contemporary probation service[3] neglects to recognise and respond to the specific needs of BAME people under supervision. To this end, we revisit the central arguments of the earlier article in order to assess whether the intervening years have seen any change in the experience of BAME individuals both within our society and the CJS, or added anything to our understanding of how best to work with BAME individuals. Alongside this, we explore the barriers that may impede the implementation of innovative practices that could improve outcomes for criminalised BAME people. Finally, we offer a number of key principles derived from evaluations of interventions in Toronto, Canada that demonstrate that interventions that are cognisant of the lived realities of racialisation and structural inequality for BAME people can be effective in improving the lives of people subject to community disposals and reducing recidivism.

Our central argument in 2003 was that in order to respond to the offending behaviour of BAME people there was a need to broaden the agenda around 'what works' for black and Asian people. This necessitated a shift away from individualised, behaviourist assumptions of criminogenic factors associated with the onset of offending behaviour towards a desistance approach that focused on the future rather than the past and acknowledged the personal, social and economic realities of a significant proportion of the BAME population of England and Wales. Central to this would be an acknowledgement of the impact of racism(s) both within the CJS and wider society on the process of criminalisation and people's ability to move on from offending.

The contemporary context

Has the position of BAME individuals within society and the CJS improved since the 2003 paper? Recent evidence suggests that for many people it has not. An Equality and Human Rights Commission (EHRC) report paints a picture of the multidimensionality of inequalities within society and the way this is likely to affect the opportunities available to some BAME individuals (EHRC, 2016). BAME children are twice as likely to live in poverty than White people (EHRC, 2016, p 29) and more likely to live in overcrowded households (EHRC, 2016, p 27). The picture, however, is complex.

Black children and those of mixed White/Black Caribbean parentage are particularly likely to be excluded from school (EHRC, 2016, p 27), a factor likely to seriously limit future opportunities. A recent report, however, highlights the significant improvements in the grades achieved by Chinese, Indian, Black African and Bangladeshi students over the past two decades; overall, they are now out performing White British children. In comparison, Black Caribbean and Pakistani students continue to perform relatively poorly. The report writer attributes these differences in attainment to variations in the support structures available to students from different ethnic groups regardless of overall poverty (Shah, 2016).

In some spheres, differences in opportunities appear to be getting worse. Whereas between 2010 and 2015 the number of long-term unemployed young White people decreased by 2%, the number of long-term unemployed Black young people increased by 49% (EHRC, 2016). Even when in employment, disparities continue: Black workers with degrees earn on average 23% less than their White counterparts (EHRC, 2016). Although there are variations in the extent to which each factor affects different ethnic groups, one thing becomes clear: being born into a web of interacting disadvantages is likely to limit the social capital available to many individuals from BAME backgrounds. By social capital, we mean those 'connections among individuals – social networks and the norms of reciprocity and trustworthiness that arise from them' (Putnam, 2000, p 19).

Within the CJS, data from the most recent publication of *Statistics on Race and the Criminal Justice System* (MoJ, 2015) reconfirms that the percentage of the prison population who come from BAME backgrounds is approximately twice that of the general population, although overall figures disguise considerable variations between different ethnic groups (Black or mixed race individuals are particularly over-represented, those from Asian backgrounds considerably less so). The percentage of prisoners who are Muslim has risen from 7.7% in 2002 to 14.7% in 2012: this needs to be set against 2011 census figures, which showed 4.2% of the population of England and Wales over the age of 15 years identifying as Muslim (NOMS, 2016, p 7). Similarly, a recent report produced by the Ministry of Justice shows a large reduction (81%) in the number of children entering the youth justice system, with admissions to young offender institutions also significantly reducing (MoJ, 2016, p 3). Set against these reductions, the report expresses concerns at 'the continued over-representation in the youth justice system of BAME young people' (MOJ, 2016, p 12.)

Not only are the chances of being stopped and searched by the police five times greater if you are Black than if you are White (EHRC, 2016), but trends in the use of section 60 of the Police and Criminal Evidence Act 1984 show that its disproportionate use against BAME people is increasing. This power enables the police to undertake 'suspicionless' (Bowling, 2014) stop and searches of individuals where 'police believe there is a possibility or potential of serious violence, that a person is carrying a dangerous weapon or offensive weapon'. In 2007/08, just over a quarter (28%) of all section 60 stops were recorded as being carried out on BAME people, with 65% conducted on White people. By 2010/11, this situation was reversed, with 64% of section 60 stops involving BAME people against 31% for White people. It is important to note that such figures do not reflect actual rates of offending behaviour, but emanate from the monitoring function of CJS agencies: consequently, the report clearly states that 'no causative links can be drawn from these summary statistics' (MoJ 2015, p 7, Williams and Clarke, forthcoming).

Given this situation, it is not surprising that in February 2016, the then prime minister David Cameron felt the need to ask 'difficult' questions about whether the CJS treats people differently based on race and commissioned the Lammy Review to ascertain why BAME individuals are over-represented within the criminal justice system of England and Wales and seemingly suffer worse outcomes than others. The Lammy Review currently in progress now sits alongside the ongoing Young Review set up with the aim of 'improving outcomes for young Black and/or Muslim men in the Criminal Justice System' (Clinks, 2014, p 1). Their very existence only serves to highlight the disconnect between a political acknowledgement of CJS 'discrimination' and the dearth of National Probation Service (NPS) or community rehabilitation company (CRC) programmes of intervention that specifically focus on the 'needs' of BAME people.

Theoretical models of social disadvantage and criminality

Criminological explanations of the relationship between race and crime have been derived from both 'left' and 'right' realist approaches. These suggest that BAME individuals offend more because they are concentrated within areas where poverty, disadvantage and unemployment, all factors known to be related to offending, are rife (Lea and Young, 1984). The sense of powerlessness, frustration and rage incurred at being locked into a 'cycle of deprivation' results in the adoption of pathological and criminogenic sub-cultural values that, by definition, place members of certain communities outside normative boundaries and accepted social norms and are deemed conducive to offending behaviour. For these theories to hold, however, it has to be demonstrated that disadvantage and criminality are not only contiguous but causal.

Psychosocial explanations of the relationship between disadvantage and criminality stress the importance of skill acquisition, and argue that patterns of socialisation and poor education can lead to cognitive and behavioural deficits and dysfunctional social skills (McGuire, 1995). If these can be corrected and different ways of thinking taught, the individual may stop offending. Interventions based on these explanations have a tendency to decontextualise the lived experience of offenders and locate responsibility for change firmly with the individual.

An unfortunate byproduct of these conceptualisations is a tendency to perceive all members of specific ethnic groups as adhering to those 'alternative cultural values' deemed conducive to offending behaviour. This can lead to assumptions being made, often erroneously, about an individual's motivations and propensities simply because they belong to certain ethnic or religious groupings. Disadvantage, especially when combined with discrimination, not only limits access to opportunity but can also affect self-image if these negative beliefs become internalised (Robinson, 1995). It is not surprising, therefore, to find dispiriting accounts of how all-pervading negative stereotyping affects young BAME offenders' levels of motivation and feeds into their feelings of disaffection, alienation and hopelessness about the future (Clinks, 2014). While we acknowledge that such ideas have long been accepted within probation practice, little attention is paid to how disproportionality affects an individual's sense of group identity and of (non-)conforming to stereotypes of that group. If negative concepts of self and identity are not to be perpetuated, it is crucial that interventions designed for BAME people move away from stereotypical criminal constructs (Williams, 2013).

Common to these theoretical approaches, and contrary to research evidence, lies the assumption that the over-representation of BAME individuals within the CJS does actually reflect higher levels of criminality than those among the White majority. As such, they fail to fully consider alternative contributory factors that stem from within the CJS itself, the possibility that BAME people may have a greater chance of being criminalised than White people or that they may find it more difficult to move on from offending as the criminal justice interventions to which they are subjected do not correspond with or address their specific needs (Wright and Williams, 2015).

The ascendancy of risk, racialisation and their relevance to discriminatory practice

There exists a disjuncture between the political concerns around the persistence of discriminatory practices within the CJS and a lack of statutory responses to ameliorating the impact of discrimination for BAME people. In 1999, the Macpherson Report into the death of Stephen Lawrence identified institutional racism as a feature of the CJS of England and Wales (Macpherson, 1999). It detected within the 'processes, attitudes and behaviours ... racist stereotyping' that served to discriminate against minority ethnic people and resulted in a lower quality of service provision (Macpherson, 1999, section 6, p 34). Yet, as discussed earlier, the figures on the current use of section 60 stop and search and continued over-representation of BAME people in the youth justice system suggest that little may have changed, and, in some situations, may even have intensified. We feel here a need to focus on the impact of those contemporary features of CJS practice, and in particular the ever-increasing emphasis and stress on risk management to 'protect the public', and how these can contribute to discriminatory practices and experiences for BAME offenders.

The recent reconfiguration of the probation service in England and Wales has been driven by 'risk' with 'high-risk' offenders being supervised by the NPS while those deemed as presenting a lower risk of harm are supervised by CRCs (MoJ, 2013). The antecedents and constructions of risk has been a critical feature of probation practice since the implementation of the Effective Practice Initiative in the mid- to late 1990s (Chapman and Hough, 1998). Newly emerging practice principles posited that risk of reoffending (and harm) would be appreciably reduced if probation practice targeted 'criminogenic needs', that is, those deemed to be directly related to offending (Bonta and Andrews, 2010). Probation interventions were to be tailored to the individual through 'responsivity', that is, by being delivered in a way that not only matched the learning styles of the offender but was also sensitive to issues around gender, culture, religion and levels of motivation (Bonta and Andrews, 2007).

In the case of Black and Asian offenders, an acknowledgement of the persistence of racism(s) and the concentration of BAME people within the socioeconomic margins of British society led to the Home Office piloting Pathfinder models for Black and Asian offenders in 2001 (Calverley et al, 2004; Stephens et al, 2004). This arguably reflected an ongoing organisational aspiration to foster desistance from offending through targeting the wider socioeconomic needs associated with poverty and inequality, which many believed to be related to offending behaviour. By 2004, however, the Black and Asian Pathfinder initiative, beset from the start by implementation problems, had come to an abrupt end (Walmsley and Stephens, 2006). It proved relatively difficult to recruit, train and retain suitable staff, and, for those who were recruited, it was not always possible to provide appropriate treatment management. The number of offenders being referred to the programmes also fell short of that required to fully test out the different models. It was argued that language issues, a lack of input around Asian culture and problems around the availability of management information and data were compounded by a lack of consistency in implementation across the different sites (Stephens et al, 2004). While it is difficult to ascertain the precise factors that signalled the premature ending of the Pathfinder programme, it is significant that the Home Office was subject to restructure that resulted in a number of research programmes being abandoned. However, more tellingly, Lord Ouseley notes that by 2004/05, 'the government felt that they had discharged their responsibilities for implementing the measures arising from the Macpherson report …and wanted to demolish the CRE [Commission for Race Equality]' (Bourne, 2015). The result was a significant shift away from approaches that espoused empowerment to redress racialised inequalities and criminalisation toward strategies that concentrated resources on the 'risks' posed by particular communities, groups and individuals. Such a shift towards a 'culture of control' (Garland, 2001) was further characterised by the emergence of 'law and order' rhetoric conceptualised around a public and media ordained need to contain and manage 'risk' to 'protect the public'. Marking the 'new penology', as espoused by Feeley and Simon (1992), criminal justice practice was reconfigured to prioritise the maintenance of an efficient and cost-effective CJS through which risky populations could be identified, assessed, regulated and managed.

This saw the genesis of multi-agency protection panels for those offenders who posed 'high risk' of harm, the piloting of electronic and satellite tracking and the monitoring of sex offenders. Yet, specifically in relation to BAME offenders, there emerged the 'gun and gang units' in Manchester, London, Birmingham, Liverpool and Nottingham, the selective and disproportionate use of stop and search powers, and 'collective punishments' through the re-evocation of joint enterprise as a means of arresting perceived levels of youth violence. More recently, we have witnessed the emergence of the government's Prevent strategy as a powerful device intended to address concerns around those young people deemed to be 'at risk' of radicalisation and extremism. Comprising one component of the government's larger counter-terrorism policy (known as CONTEST), Prevent focuses specifically on preventing individuals either from becoming terrorists or supporting terrorism. This involves 'challenging extremist (and non-violent) ideas that are also part of a terrorist ideology. Prevent will also mean intervening to try to stop people moving from extremist groups or extremism into terrorist-related activity' (HM Government, 2011a, p 24).

Why do these strategies disproportionately affect BAME individuals, particularly young people? Crucially, the London and Manchester gang units specifically targeted Black communities and individuals who it was argued were involved in 'gangs' and serious violence (HM Government, 2011b; HM Government, 2015). As a result, in 2013, 89% of police-identified 'gang members' in Manchester were recorded as belonging to a BAME group, with 80% of 'gang members' in London similarly identified as belonging to a BAME group (Bridges, 2015). As will be discussed, whether advertent or not, the implication was that the perpetuation of violent offending and gang membership were related, and thus mediated as a Black issue. The need to 'end gangs and youth violence' (HM Government, 2011b) required the strict policing of potential gang members who, given this conceptualisation, were constructed as Black (Bullock and Tilley, 2002; Alexander, 2008). Within this context, then, the shifts in the use of section 60 stop and search described earlier are better understood as a government reaction to the construction of BAME people and, in particular, young Black men as predisposed to gang-enabled offending behaviour including serious violence.

In relation to radicalisation, Kundnani (2015) questions the link between holding extremist views and the perpetration of violent offences, arguing that many people who hold extremist views never commit violent offences and those who commit 'extremist' violence do not always hold extremist views. Yet this belief not only underpins the Prevent agenda but has been used to support the prosecution of individuals found in possession of 'extremist' material even though they have no intention of acting on it. As 'extremism' is defined in terms of opposition to British values, individuals questioning these values leave themselves open to scrutiny and, potentially, to being referred to a 'de-radicalisation' project (Kundnani, 2015).

The parallels between these gang and radicalisation discourses are striking. Both involve individuals from highly visible groups, visible either because of colour, religious affiliation or both. Both involve the surveillance of large numbers of individuals who may or, far more likely, may not subsequently be involved in violent crime or terrorist activity. The large numbers stem from acknowledged difficulties in ascertaining degrees of involvement, and in differentiating between who is 'hard core', who is on the fringes of involvement and who is 'associated' with but not involved in any offending behaviour (Pitts, 2014; Kundnani, 2015). Unsurprisingly, the high levels of surveillance on those who 'may' be involved and hence constructed as risky is guaranteed to fall disproportionately on BAME individuals and, potentially, increase their criminalisation. Moreover, as resources follow the direction of perceived risk, it is not surprising that government funding has been allocated to interventions structured around gangs and radicalisation, which further serves police and CJ strategies to target those racialised communities (Williams, 2015; Kundnani, 2015).

Paradoxically, however, studies have demonstrated that BAME offenders have significantly lower criminogenic risks and crime-prone attitudes than their White counterparts (Calverley et al, 2004; Raynor and Lewis, 2006). More worryingly, and as previously indicated, evidence that contradicts the link between gangs and serious youth violence has, until very recently, been ignored. In Manchester, Black individuals made up 81% of the gang cohort but only 6% of the parallel serious youth offending cohort, while in London the corresponding figures were 72% and 27% respectively (Williams and Clarke, forthcoming). Despite these disjunctures between racialised assumptions and reality, the gang label has been repeatedly used to legitimise the imposition of collective punishments for BAME people who are deemed to be gang-involved, gang-associated or even those 'at risk' of gang violence. This has, on occasion, resulted in long prison sentences for offences committed by 'associates' (Williams and Clarke, forthcoming).

A final mechanism whereby the ascendency of risk has 'hardwired' racialised discrimination into criminal justice practice is through the algorithms of risk assessment tools. The Offender Group Reconviction Score (OGRS) is one such tool used within the offender management process to provide an 'objective' indication of the likelihood of future offending behaviour on the basis of seven key variables. These include 'age at first contact with the police' and 'age at first conviction' (Fitzpatrick and Williams, 2016), thus reflecting police activity, which, as we have demonstrated, is likely to fall disproportionately on BAME people. By removing the context, history and needs of those subject to assessment, the use of such tools can disproportionately (re)present BAME people as endowed with criminogenic tendencies and again as a risk to be managed.

Unsurprisingly, therefore, studies have found that many BAME people with experience of the CJS feel a sense of implicit prejudice in their treatment. Calverley and colleagues (2004) found that BAME people reported 'unfair treatment', particularly with reference to their experience of the police, courts, sentencing and the prison service. In extreme cases, BAME people have expressed a fatalistic sense of hopelessness in terms of the mediated representations of their group and the extent to which they are able to change their lives or reach their potential. This was found to be common among young men between the ages of 18 to 23 who are currently serving prison sentences (Durrance and Williams, 2003; Clinks 2014). Equally, Crewe and colleagues (2015) found that Black prisoners serving lengthy joint enterprise prison sentences were particularly likely to feel that their sentences lacked moral legitimacy, due to 'an absence of procedural fairness' in the prosecution of their cases.

In light of this, there emerges a picture of continued racialised criminal stereotyping and bias toward BAME people through the contemporary constructs of the 'gang', extremism and radicalisation, which have, arguably, inflated the (imagined) risk posed by particular groups and, in turn, legitimises punitive criminal justice interventions. Moreover, the ascendency of risk has transcended the previously held rehabilitative ideals and assumptions of the NPS (and CRCs) curtailing the practitioner's capacity and resolve to respond to the wider social problems experienced and endured by BAME people. It is conceivable that concerns around illegitimacy that stem from procedural unfairness and feelings of hopelessness may undermine attempts to build productive working relationships between criminal justice practitioners and BAME people subject to probation.

Principles of effective interventions: lessons from Toronto

Understanding the predicaments of young black and Muslim men is not a question of making excuses for criminal behaviour and the devastating effect it has on communities and society as a whole – indeed, the necessity for offenders to face up to the havoc wreaked by their crimes against people and property is a challenge for the offender population in general. The point is actually the inverse: in order to continue to reduce the number of crimes committed, we have to find better ways of ensuring that the drivers that contribute to repeated patterns of offending behaviour are reduced. (Baroness Young, cited in Clinks, 2014, p 5)

Ultimately, the purpose of criminal justice interventions is to inhibit recidivism. 'Rehabilitation has been defined as the process whereby offenders are afforded the opportunity to be full member of society, with the rights and responsibilities that this entails. For some, this will mean the restoration of a former state. For others, it will mean the receipt of services, the acquisition of skills and the establishment of rank rights and responsibilities previously denied' (Lewis, 2005, p 123). Further:

> ... both citizen and state have duties [and] citizens are more likely to comply with the law if the demand that they do so is experienced as legitimate. States attain this legitimacy by the proper performance of their obligations towards [all] citizens, including the maintenance of adequate conditions of life so that the expectation of law-abiding behaviour becomes reasonable and fair. (Lewis, 2005, p 123)

Research into an intervention programme delivered in Toronto, Canada that builds on this concept of rehabilitation delineates practice principles that, we believe, demonstrate the mechanisms whereby fostering a more positive self-regard can feed into attitude and value shifts and prosocial behaviours, and, ultimately, reaffirm self-identity as a citizen. These principles are developing knowledge of self; acknowledging racialisation; responding to 'needs', not risk; being paid to change; and developing community-based interventions (Wright and Williams, 2015).

This initiative – the Youth Justice Education Programme (YJEP) – is a culturally specific service for African Canadian adults in conflict with the law, funded by the Ministry of the Attorney General and administered by the African Canadian Legal Clinic (ACLC). Its ultimate goal is to empower young African Canadians by providing them with culturally relevant, holistic and anti-oppressive educational programmes and referral services. In order to foster opportunities for positive development, growth and change, this youth-led initiative requires participant attendance every day throughout its three-year duration. The ACLC assert it is crucial to 'work with high-risk offenders for no less than three years, because that's the time we feel you need to change people's behaviour, attitudes, their thinking' (Margaret Parsons, cited in Wright and Williams, 2015, p 20).

From the outset, it is notable that the YJEP did not describe participants as 'offenders', but embraced the more prosocial language of 'youth' and 'youth justice worker' (YJW). By way of programme structure, the first of the three phases involves YJEP 'hiring' the young people, who then receive education and training using an African-centred, anti-oppression and anti-racism framework. The aim here is to build a common understanding of cultural self-awareness, legal rights and advocacy and to develop those life skills (assets) likely to facilitate a shift towards desistance. During the second phase, YJWs collaboratively develop training modules that embrace those cultural and emotional considerations required to support other young people who have been involved with the CJS. The third and final phase involves programme participants using their newly developed skills to conduct outreach work with mainstream organisations.

Developing a 'knowledge of self'

Empowerment models acknowledge that experiencing explicit and implicit racism are criminogenic factors for BAME people (Powis and Walmsley, 2002) and use a critical historical and contemporary approach to explore BAME cultural definitions and the role of people of African, Black British and Caribbean descent. Individuals are encouraged to explore how they see themselves, where they feel their views come from both within the context of the family and wider society. Such explorations are a precursor to negotiating questions around what sort of person they would like to be and how they might move forward within the context of the society within which they live (Wright and Williams, 2015, p 16). Situated within the contemporary Canadian context, such approaches focus on African Canadian heritage, culture and significantly, a commitment to community, focusing on the 'we' not the 'I' (Wright and Williams, 2015). Developed alongside a recognition of the prosocial accomplishment and cultural contributions of BAME people, such approaches serve to motivate young people and build confidence through the provision of positive images which challenge and contradict popular racialised stereotypes and affirm to the young person their rightful place within society.

Acknowledging racialisation

Acknowledging racialisation/racism, as being of historical and contemporary relevance to the experience of minority ethnic communities in England and Wales, is an important component of exploring a knowledge of self. Yet, still, few statutory interventions take into account the relevance of racialised representations and how such discourses intersect with processes of criminalisation. Importantly, the YJEP programme accompanies young people on a journey of self-exploration that locates the individual within the context of their social environment without making assumptions about which specific factors will be most relevant for any particular individual. This recognises that while BAME offenders may have common racialising experiences, they are a very heterogeneous group. Interventions then should acknowledge the societal structures within which offending behaviour occurs alongside the interplay of racism(s) and discrimination in the everyday experiences of the individual.

Examining the self within the context of social circumstances not only helps individuals consider the impact of racialisation on their (in)ability to access social capital such as meaningful employment and educational opportunities, but also offers potential for developing an appreciation of the ways in which racialisation as encountered has curtailed their access to legitimate opportunities. Within the UK context, one reason underlying poor referral to group work programmes designed specifically for BAME offenders is a denial by staff (and some offenders) of the role racism plays within people's everyday lives. Yet, in our earlier research (Durrance and Williams, 2003), when participants were interviewed at the end of the empowerment programme, they reported having been exposed to conceptualisations of their world that were entirely new to them. They had not, until that time, been aware of the extent to which negative views held by wider society had limited their structured opportunities within economically poor and marginalised communities (Durrance and Williams, 2003). It is noteworthy that Harries (2014) recognises the conspicuous silence of racism within processes of policy and practice making, arguing that since the watershed of institutionalised racism in 1999, we have now entered a moment of deracialisation that inhibits young BAME people's claims, discussions and articulations of their experiences of racialisation. Consequently, the predominance of individualised explanations of offending behaviour serves to conceal the role racism(s) can play in processes of criminalisation serving to legitimise the prioritisation of offender and risk management.

Responding to needs, not risk

Facilitating desistance as theorised by Ward and Maruna (2007) argues that building on individuals' skills and strengths provides the best means of moving them on from offending. By focusing on approach goals, individuals have to think about where they want to be and formulate realistic plans for achieving their goals. An integral part of this process is taking into account structural and personal constraints, assessing existing skills and abilities and (re)defining others that may need to be developed. For example, people subject to supervision may be asked to consider how skills used for criminal ends might be utilised to achieve more prosocial aims. This process of reframing experience works at several levels. Practically, it looks at how skills can be used differently but, it can also contribute to building self-confidence and foster changes in self-image as people begin to see the possibilities for becoming a different sort of person.

Within the Canadian context, there is a clear acknowledgement of how interactions with the CJS, and prison in particular, 'strips the individual of their assets' and impedes their ability to negotiate their environment(s) on release from custody. The YJW referred to within the YJEP programme had committed a range of serious offences. Despite this, by adopting an empowering positive, practical and forward-looking desistance model, the project signals faith in participants' ability to change; this is a powerful message in itself. Ward and Maruna's (2007) Good Lives model provides a structured way of helping individuals define their own values and priorities and explore the societal factors that need to be taken into account when forging a way forward. In contrast, by focusing on the past and on deficits, risk models tend to be inherently negative. They imply that the individual is either not prepared to change or does not have the capacity for change: neither is an engaging message. More worryingly, prioritising the control and management of 'risks' is likely to work against (re) settlement and (re)integration, as measures such as curfews, exclusion orders, surveillance and monitoring restrict still further already limited opportunities. Paradoxically these short-term control measures may actually increase long-term risks, as individuals are excluded from the community assets and resources that may facilitate improvement on the basis that their past behaviour makes them too risky (Williams, 2015).

The attribution of police-ascribed 'risky' status through the imposition of racialised criminal labels (such as gang-involved, extremist, radicalised and terrorist) affirms to BAME people who have been in prison or on probation their status as 'other'. They become marked as 'failed citizens', as one of 'them' as opposed to one of 'us' (Anderson, 2013). Conversely, a needs-based approach enables the allocation of resources to (re)build assets and, more importantly, to tackle the socioeconomic hardship and realities experienced by many criminalised BAME people. This process is inevitably client-centred, as strengths and needs will be specific to the individual in the same way as were factors precipitating offending. Nevertheless, to suggest that the needs of all BAME offenders are the same arguably constitutes another form of oppression. It is also important to say that a concentration on needs does not ignore the issue of risk, as some of the needs identified during this process may mean helping the individual to avoid situations that may involve risk to themselves and/or others.

Results by payment, not payment by results

A controversial aspect of the Canadian intervention project is that participants are paid a salary of C\$30,000 per annum for their role as 'youth justice workers' (Williams, 2015, p 19). While 'paying offenders to change' will always be met with concern, such an approach constitutes, on one level, an attempt to move offenders on from the *pre-contemplative* state that many find themselves in when faced with the hardships of poverty, social inequality and their differential treatment within the CJS (Prochaska and Di Clemente, 1982). A prerequisite for engaging individuals in any programme is moving them on from the pre-contemplative stage, which is characterised by a lack of any intention to change in the foreseeable future. (For a fuller discussion of the Stages of Change model, see Prochaska et al, 1992.) Another argument for paying offenders to change is that the costs of interventions, prison 'accommodation' and 'social security' payments mean that criminalised people already constitute a significant cost (Wright and Williams, 2015). Criminalised people who receive financial support to work no longer represent a 'tax burden' but become contributors to the tax base. From this position, participants on the YJEP programme are legitimate 'employees', afforded healthcare benefits and paid holidays in the same way as non-criminalised employees.

Moreover, having an income, maybe for the first time, has a practical benefit, in that it removes pressing worries about accommodation and subsistence. But it also lays the foundations for developing 'financial literacy', which can be difficult if you have never had a legitimate income. Participants on the programme are required to open bank accounts, keep and manage budgets and regularly discuss expenditure. Again, the impact of the intervention is multi-layered. It develops skills, helps people develop the self-discipline necessary to hold down paid employment and signals a fundamental change of citizen status; the person is now an 'employee', with all the rights and responsibilities that entails. The intervention, therefore, fosters an environment within which the individual is required to take on the various facets of a whole new way of life. While we acknowledge the potential conflicts in paying offenders to change, there already exist examples of such practices within the UK context, specifically the use of 'personalisation' where financial 'budgets' and 'resources' are made available to facilitate the development of bespoke interventions for people subject to community disposals and interventions (Fox and Albertson, 2011; Fox et al, 2014).

Delivery by non-statutory agencies

> It comes back to the individual probation officer, their level of cultural sensitivity or cultural competence to say, I see what I have in front of me, where do I need to refer them? For me, it's an acknowledgement that racism exists in society. That acknowledgment is not always there. So, if you can't acknowledge that, how can you move beyond? [S]o for Black, Brown or Asian people, if you don't understand that [they're] pissed off or angry about racism, how you gonna give anger management programme when we haven't dealt with the substantial issue, which in my mind a lot of things can flow from? (Correctional officer, cited in Wright and Williams, 2015, p 20)

The term BAME embraces a diverse group of people with different cultural, ethnic and religious backgrounds. While offender managers should be sensitive to cultural differences, it is unrealistic to expect individual offender managers within statutory agencies to have the cultural knowledge and understanding that may be used to help to move all individuals on from offending. Prior to the introduction of Pathfinder Programmes, London Probation had developed and run a number of Black Self Development Groups which reflected empowerment principles. Whilst completion rates were generally excellent, concerns were raised about how well these groups served offenders from Asian backgrounds: given that Black staff running the groups tended to be drawn from similar ethnic backgrounds to Black participants it was felt that they may be more aware of their relevant issues (Durrance et al, 2001). Equally, existing programmes are still likely to be built on research and evaluation studies involving non-BAME groups reflecting the bulk of the client group, but these may not be reflective of the lived reality of BAME offenders.

In order to circumvent these difficulties, it may be preferable to use non-statutory organisations and charities to deliver interventions. The value of client-centred, community-based projects and those that recognise the importance of identity and family is well established (Carrington and Denney, 1981; Ahmed et al, 1998). Given the need to rehabilitate individuals within society, the best way of ensuring that different needs are addressed is to use pre-existing community groups as these are the ones likely to be most sensitive to variations in culture between the different groups that identify as 'Black'. The community is then seen as representing a pool of expertise and as a resource for reintegration rather than as being culturally criminogenic and part of the problem; religion is seen as a potential way out of offending rather than being viewed as a factor potentially driving it. This reinforces the concept of rehabilitation as a two-way process, whereby offenders need to (re)join a 'community' prepared to accept them. For example, imams, in addition to helping offenders rethink their behaviour, can work with communities, promoting forgiveness as an Islamic concept and breaking down negative feelings about prisoners (Clinks, 2014, p 42). When voluntary, community and faith groups have a role in controlling the quality of complaints procedures, the resulting improved transparency enhances the subjective experience of BAME prisoners, as decisions are perceived as more legitimate. Despite this, community groups have reported difficulties in getting prison staff to accept any such role (Clinks, 2014, p 35–36).

Within statutory agencies, practitioners are inevitably driven by the priorities and obligations of offender management and, given the ethnicity of the majority of their caseloads, are required to undertake essentially Eurocentric accredited group work interventions. Within the YJEP context, it was argued that there was a 'lack of commitment' from senior management to respond to the reality of racism and discrimination in the CJS (Wright and Williams, 2015). Clearly, organisations working outside of the political and practice constraints faced by NPS and CRCs may find it easier to engage in non-discriminatory and empowering ways of developing the non-criminal identity of criminalised BAME people.

Conclusion

As Baroness Young, quoted earlier, suggests, the interests of criminalised young Black and Muslim men and those of the wider society are not necessarily in conflict (Clinks, 2014, p 5). As the ongoing Canadian project illustrates, programmes designed to have an impact simultaneously at psychological wellbeing and practical levels and that acknowledge the need for input from both the individual and the larger society can start to bring about enduring change (Wortley and Owusu-Bempah, 2013). In line with desistance thinking, an interim evaluation completed six months into the Canadian Youth Justice Education Programme yields mixed results: a significant reduction in both self-reported offending, in particular violent offending, and in victimisation and attitude change have been observed. Most importantly, while the numbers undertaking it are small, to date, all the young people recruited to the programme are still involved and report finding it useful (Wortley and Owusu-Bempah, 2013.) We can think of no reason why similar programmes would not bring about comparable results if introduced in England and Wales.

The implementation of similar empowerment models, if more limited in scope, has hitherto been resisted in the UK because of perennial questions around programme effectiveness. Arguably, however, if criminal justice interventions were driven by evidence of effectiveness, the prison system would have been disbanded decades ago. As research and evaluation officers within the probation service, we collectively accrued over 25 years' experience evaluating probation programmes, interventions and practices. Involved in the 'what works?' debate, we observed the 'empirical haggling' around 'what counts?' as research evidence (Chitty and Harper, 2005). We believe that the more nuanced research question 'what helps?' is likely to be more productive than 'what works?' in helping build successful interventions (Ward and Maruna 2007). This more inclusive approach acknowledges the value of factors that move someone towards a particular goal, even when they do not manage to actually reach it, and fits well with the desistance literature, which stresses that giving up (on) offending is a process rather than an event (Maruna, 2001).

Contact with the CJS, alongside the social harms of reduced opportunities, emerge as powerful criminogenic 'needs' that are not acknowledged or addressed by criminal justice interventions for BAME people. A re-engagement with racism(s) would present a valuable starting point through which to understand the persistence of racialised disproportionality inherent in criminal justice practice (Phillips, 2011). Yet in 2014, the commissioning intentions that informed the tendering process for CRCs required bidders to demonstrate their commitment to 'diversity' by adhering (only) to the protected characteristics of 'gender, disability and age' (MoJ, 2014, p 11). The exclusion of 'race and ethnicity' and 'religion and belief' within the contemporary context is somewhat unbelievable. Clearly, statutory responses to BAME people subject to community supervision remain in a pre-contemplative state, illustrative of a historical and contemporary resistance to change.

Notes

[1] Pathfinder Programmes were introduced as part of the Effective Practice Initiative current in the early 2000s. This aimed to build an evidence base which could inform practice in both the prison and probation services.

[2] Throughout this chapter, BAME refers to people of Black, Asian or minority ethnic descent. While contested, this system of classification emerges from the omnibus categories employed within the 2011 census and corresponds with the race and ethnicity monitoring categories used across the criminal justice system of England and Wales. However, at times the chapter will refer to Black and Asian offenders, again adopting the terminology employed by the Home Office throughout its Pathfinder programme in 2001. While we recognise and are concerned at the potential for the reader to simplistically attribute a homogeniety to those captured within the BAME groupings, by way of consistency and with reference to published documents we retain the classifications captured therein. However, where information relates to a specific ethnic group, we specify that group.

[3] In 2015, the probation service was subject to a significant restructure, which saw the service reorganised into two agencies. The National Probation Service is responsible for the management and supervision of 'high-risk' offenders, and community rehabilitation companies, a framework of private, voluntary and community sector, and public organisations, are now responsible for the supervision of low- to medium-risk offenders.

References

Ahmed, S.H., Webster, R. and Cheston, L. (1998) 'Bengali young men on supervision in Tower Hamlets', *Probation Journal*, 45(2): 78–81.

Alexander, C. (2008) *(Re)thinking 'Gangs'*, London: Runnymede Trust, available at www.blackeducation.info/upload/docs/RethinkingGangs-2008.pdf (accessed 3 September 2012).

Anderson, B. (2013) *Us and Them: The Dangerous Politics of Immigration Control*, Oxford: Oxford University Press.

Bonta, J. and Andrews, D.A. (2007) *Risk-Need-Responsivity Model for Offender Assessment and Rehabilitation*, Ottowa: Public Safety Canada.

Bonta, J. and Andrews D.A. (2010) 'Viewing offender assessment and rehabilitation through the lens of the Risk-Needs-Responsivity model', in F. McNeill, P. Raynor and C. Trotter (eds) *Offender Supervision: New Directions in Theory, Research and Practice*, Cullompton: Willan, pp 19-40.

Bourne, J. (2015) 'The Race Relations Act 1965 – blessing or curse?', www.irr.org.uk/news/the-race-relations-act-1965-blessing-or-curse (accessed 9 March 2016).

Bowling, B. (2014) *There is Much Still to do on Stop and Search*, London: Centre for Crime and Justice Studies, available at www.crimeandjustice.org.uk/resources/there-much-still-do-stop-and-search (accessed 1 March 2017).

Bridges, L. (2015) *The Met Gang Matrix: Institutional Racism in Action*, London: Institute of Race Relations, available at www.irr.org.uk/news/the-met-gangs-matrix-institutional-racism-in-action.

Bullock, K. and Tilley, N. (2002) *Shootings, Gangs and Violent Incidents in Manchester: Developing a Crime Reduction Strategy*, Crime Reduction Research Series Paper 13, London: Home Office.

Calverley, D., Cole, B., Kaur, G., Lewis, S., Raynor, P., Sadeghi, S., Smith, D., Vanstone, M. and Wardak, A. (2004) *Black and Asian Offenders on Probation*, Research Study 277, London: Home Office.

Carrington, B. and Denney, D. (1981) 'Young Rastafarians and the probation service', *Probation Journal*, 28(1): 111–17.

Chapman, T. and Hough, M. (1998) *Evidence Based Practice: A Guide to Effective Practice*, London: HM Inspectorate of Probation.

Chitty, C. and Harper, G. (2005) *The Impact of Corrections on Re-offending: A Review of 'What Works'*, Home Office Research Study 291, London: Home Office.

Clinks (2014) *The Young Review: Improving Outcomes for Young Black and Muslim Men in the Criminal Justice System*, London: Barrow Cadbury Trust, available at www.youngreview.org.uk (accessed 1 March 2017).

Crewe, B., Liebling, A., Padfield, N. and Virgo, G. (2015) 'Joint enterprise: the implications of an unfair and unclear law', *Criminal Law Review*, 4: 252–269.

Durrance, P. and Williams, P. (2003) 'Broadening the agenda around what works for black and Asian offenders', *Probation Journal*, 50(3): 211–224.

Durrance, P., Hignett, C., Merone, L. and Asamoah, A. (2001) *The Greenwich and Lewisham Self-Development and Educational Attainment Group: Evaluation Report*, London: London Probation Area.

EHRC (Equality and Human Rights Commission) (2016) *Healing a Divided Britain*, London: EHRC.

Feeley, M. and Simon, J. (1992) 'The new penology: emerging strategy of corrections and its implications', *Criminology*, 30(4): 449–474.

Fitzpatrick, C. and Williams, P. (2016) 'The neglected needs of care leavers in the criminal justice system: practitioners' perspectives and the persistence of problem (corporate) parenting', *Criminology & Criminal Justice*, doi: 10.1177/1748895816659324.

Fox, C. and Albertson, A. (2011) 'Payment by results and social impact bonds in the criminal justice sector: new challenges for the concept of evidence-based policy?', *Criminology & Criminal Justice*, 11(5): 395–413.

Fox, C., Fox, A. and Marsh, C. (2014) *Personalisation in the Criminal Justice System: What is the Potential?*, Policy Briefing, Criminal Justice Alliance, available at http://criminaljusticealliance.org/wp-content/uploads/2015/02/Personalisation_in_the_CJS.pdf (accessed 1 March 2017).

Garland, D. (2001) *The Culture of Control*, Oxford: Oxford University Press.

Harries, B. (2014) 'We need to talk about race', *Sociology*, 48(6): 1107–1122.

HM Government (2011a) *Prevent* Strategy, Cm 8092, London: The Stationery Office.

HM Government (2011b) *Ending Gang and Youth Violence: A Cross Government Report Including Further Evidence and Good Practice Case Studies*, Cm 8211, London: The Stationery Office.

HM Government (2015) *Ending Gangs and Youth Violence Programme: Annual Report 2014/15*, London: The Stationery Office.

Howarth, C. (2002) 'Identity in whose eyes? The role of representations in identity construction', *Journal of the Theory of Social Behaviour*, 32(2): 145–162.

Kundnani, A. (2015) *A Decade Lost: Rethinking radicalisation and extremism*, London: Claystone, available at www.claystone.org.uk/wp-content/uploads/2015/01/Claystone-rethinking-radicalisation.pdf (accessed 3 March 2017).

Lea, J. and Young, J. (1984) *What is to be Done about Law and Order?*, Harmondsworth: Penguin.

Lewis, S. (2005) 'Rehabilitation: headline or footnote in the new penal policy?', *Probation Journal*, 52(2): 119–135.

Macpherson, W. (1999) *The Stephen Lawrence Inquiry*, Cm 4262-I, London: HMSO. www.gov.uk/government/uploads/system/uploads/attachment_data/file/277111/4262.pdf (accessed 1 March 2017).

Maruna, S. (2001) *Making Good: How Ex-Convicts Reform and Rebuild Their Lives*, Washington, DC: American Psychological Association.

McGuire, J. (1995) (ed) *What Works: Reducing Re-offending. Guidelines from Research and Practice*, New York, NY: John Wiley & Sons.

MoJ (Ministry of Justice) (2013) *Transforming Rehabilitation: A Strategy for Reform*, Cm 8619, London: MoJ.

MoJ (2014) *NOMS Commissioning Intentions 2014*, London: MoJ, available at http://www.justice.gov.uk/downloads/about/noms/commissioning-intentions-2014.pdf (accessed 1 March 2017).

MoJ (2015) *Statistics on Race and the Criminal Justice System 2014: A Ministry of Justice Publication under Section 95 of the Criminal Justice Act 1991*, London: MoJ.

MoJ (2016) *Review of the Youth Justice System: An Interim Report of Emerging Findings*, London: MoJ.

NOMS (National Offender Management Service) (2016) *Offender Equalities Annual Report*, London: MoJ.

Phillips, C. (2011) 'Institutional racism and ethnic inequalities: an expanded multilevel framework', *Journal of Social Policy*, 40(1), 173–192.

Pitts, J. (2014) 'Who dunnit? Gangs, joint enterprise, bad character and duress', *Youth & Policy*, 113: 48–59.

Players, E. (2013) 'Women in the criminal justice system: the triumph of inertia', *Criminology & Criminal Justice*, doi: 10.1177/1748895813495218.

Powis, B. and Walmsley, R.K. (2002) *Programmes for Black and Asian offenders on Probation: Lessons for Developing Practice*, Home Office Research Study 250, London: Home Office.

Prochaska, J.O. and Di Clemente, C.C. (1982) 'Transtheoretical therapy: towards a more integrative model of change', *Psychotherapy Theory, Research and Practice*, 19(3): 276–288.

Prochaska, J.O., DiClemente, C.C. and Norcross, J.C. (1992) 'In search of how people change: applications to addictive behaviours', *American Psychologist*, 47: 1102–1104.

Putnam, R.D. (2000) *Bowling Alone: The Collapse and Revival of American Community*, New York, NY: Simon & Schuster.

Raynor, P. and Lewis, S. (2006) 'Black and Asian men on probation: who are they and what are their criminogenic needs?', in S. Lewis, P. Raynor, D. Smith and A. Wardak (eds) *Race and Probation*, Cullompton: Willan, pp 61–80.

Robinson, L. (1995) *Psychology for Social Workers: Black Perspective*, London: Routledge.

Shah, S. (2016) 'Against the odds: ethnic minority students are excelling at school', available at www2.le.ac.uk/offices/press/think-leicester/education/2016/against-the-odds-ethnic-minority-students-are-excelling-at-school (accessed 1 March 2017).

Stephens, K., Coombs, J. and Debdin, M. (2004) *Black and Asian Offenders Pathfinder: Implementation Report*, Home Office Development and Practice Report 24, London: Home Office.

Walmsley, R.K. and Stephens, K. (2006) 'What works with Black and minority ethnic offenders: solutions in search of a problem', in S. Lewis, P. Raynor, D. Smith and A. Wardak (eds) *Race and Probation*, Cullompton: Willan, pp 164–180.

Ward, T. and Maruna, S. (2007) *Rehabilitation: Beyond the Risk Paradigm*, Abingdon: Routledge.

Williams, P. (2013) *Evaluation of the Yes You Can Programme*, Unpublished report, Manchester: Greater Manchester Probation Trust.

Williams, P. (2015) 'Criminalising the Other: Challenging the race and crime nexus', *Race and Class*, 56(3): 18–35.

Williams, P. and Clarke, B. (2016) *Dangerous Associations: Joint Enterprise, Gangs and Racism*, London: Centre for Crime and Justice Studies, available at www.crimeandjustice.org.uk/sites/crimeandjustice.org.uk/files/Dangerous%20assocations%20Joint%20Enterprise%20gangs%20and%20racism.pdf (accessed 1 March 2017).

Williams, P. and Clarke, B. (forthcoming) 'Disrupting the "single story": Collective punishments, myth-making and the criminalisation of racialised communities' in S. Poynting, M. Bhatia and W. Tufail (eds) *Racism, Crime and Media*, London: Palgrave.

Wortley, S. and Owusu-Bempah. A. (2013) *The African Canadian Legal Clinic's Youth Justice Education Program: Interim Evaluation Report*, Toronto: University of Toronto.

Wright, W. and Williams, P. (2015) *Developing Appropriate Interventions for Young Black Offenders: Identifying Effective Practice Principles from Toronto, Canada*, Manchester: Rhodes Foundation Scholarship Trust.

NINETEEN

The ambiguity of therapeutic justice and women offenders in England and Wales

Jill Annison, Tim Auburn, Daniel Gilling
and Gisella Hanley Santos

Introduction

This chapter explores issues relating to rehabilitation and desistance with regard to women offenders, drawing on empirical data from a two-year research project that investigated the operation of different elements of a Community Justice Court in a city in the south-west of England.[1] In particular, analysis is applied here in respect of the interactions with, and the situations of, some of the women offenders who appeared in the court during the period of the study (2012–24). This Community Justice Court, sitting once a week within a local Magistrates' Court complex, was created in 2007 to deal with low-level offences and included the option of pre-sentence referrals to problem-solving meetings (see MoJ, 2014a).[2] Within these sessions, defendants could be further assessed and could discuss their personal problems, so they could be offered support and signposted to relevant agencies and services in the community; this contact was intended especially for those defendants who did not reach the threshold of intervention from statutory agencies (see Auburn et al, 2016).

This review focuses specifically on the application of therapeutic jurisprudence within the community court proceedings in relation to women offenders. This approach could be seen to align with the view espoused by Birgden (2004, p 285) that this 'is a legal theory that can usefully address the responsivity principle in offender rehabilitation', seeing 'the law itself – legal rules, procedures, and the roles of legal actors – as potential therapeutic agents'. Such a focus on responsivity emphasises the importance of ensuring that interventions are tailored to the specific circumstances of each individual, endeavouring to be more effective than a 'one-size-fits-all' approach. In terms of criminal justice policy and practice in England and Wales, this innovative development thus appeared to fit well with the entreaty from the renowned Corston Report (Corsten, 2007, p 79) for a 'distinct, radically different, visibly-led, strategic, proportionate, holistic, women–centred, integrated approach' for women offenders.

The model applied in this setting envisioned that the offences that came before the court would be situated within the context of local social problems. In addition to the problem-solving meetings (Wolf, 2007), it was planned that the court would adopt a community justice approach, a term that 'denotes a vision of justice practices with particular concern for the way crime and justice affect community life' (Karp and Clear, 2000, p 324). However, while this remained a general principle, over time connections between the magistrates and the local communities and community groups diminished, not least because the geographical area that the court served was extended, thus loosening the direct contacts within the immediate vicinity.

Notwithstanding the shift in terms of its community focus, the court model continued its emphasis on developing proactive, rehabilitative responses to defendants, which, for the women offenders, could take into account the potential for gender-sensitive provision (see Rumgay, 2000). Thus, this amalgamation of these different ways of 'doing justice' (Donoghue, 2014) could be seen to be engaging with Corston's interest in specialist courts and alternative approaches for women offenders in England and Wales (Corston, 2007, p 54). This is an aspect that has seemed under-developed and under-researched since the publication of the Corston Report (although for a more recent development, see Moynihan, 2016).

The study

The findings reviewed within this chapter draw on detailed observational data collected over a three-month period when members of the research team sat in court for every case, noting down on a template form the exchanges that took place in the community court proceedings and any other factors (such as the demeanour of the defendant, whether they were represented by a solicitor, any family or friends present and so on). This rich collection of data was subsequently entered onto an electronic database, which facilitated a thematic analysis of issues across the whole dataset and, more specifically here, in relation to these women offenders (Braun and Clark, 2012). The data were also cross-checked against information from other sources, such as court, police and probation records. This enabled triangulation of the details (Bryman, 2016), but even so, it needs to be acknowledged that there was sometimes a lack of reliability in the data (this has been noted as relevant in relation to any individual cases that follow).

In summary, the court's main remit was to take cases where the charges related to relatively low-level offences and where it was anticipated that the defendants would plead guilty. Over the period of the research project, most cases heard in this court were for drug or alcohol-related offences, including theft offences that were often related to drug or alcohol problems.[3] Within this setting, the community court and its mode of therapeutic justice was characterised as providing an opportunity for diversion, particularly given the oft-repeated phrase that 'people are here to help you' (see Moore, 2011), and the emphasis of the staff from the voluntary sector court support and advisory agency being on 'early intervention, identifying and addressing issues before they become entrenched' (Whitehead, 2013, p 1).

However, in practice, the court found itself buffeted by the top-down directive to apply simple, speedy and summary justice (Crown Prosecution Service, 2008; Morgan, 2008), with a much larger through-flow of cases than met the stated criteria. In effect, the foregrounding of these centrally directed efficiency measures had taken precedence over the criteria for this specialised community court, prioritising the continuous running of cases throughout the whole court complex over the more time-consuming and individualised approach intended within a therapeutic justice setting (see Wexler, 2001). While such operational constraints were only occasionally made explicit with the community court, these conflicting tensions became apparent in the wider range of cases being listed for hearing in this setting than would have been anticipated, and meant that any gaps in hearings (for instance, for problem-solving meetings to take place) were potentially seen as disruptive to the overall effective use of court time (Jones, 2012).

Methodology

Within the three-month observation period, 286 cases were listed, with 249 cases being processed through the court; only 146 (approximately 60%) matched the original profile of cases that were anticipated. The gendered breakdown of these 146 cases was 117 men and 29 women.[4]

The application of a gendered perspective in relation to the female defendants within the research study seemed particularly valuable in terms of its potential contribution to policy and practice, especially given the oft-cited quote from the Corston Report (Corsten, 2007, p 2) that 'women have been marginalised within a [criminal justice] system largely designed by men for men for far too long'. In this respect, the new approach of this Community Justice Court seemed to provide an opportunity for a more individualised, 'different way of doing things' with regard to women defendants, also taking on board Corston's suggestion that 'sentencers themselves could play a greater part' (Corston, 2007, p 54).

However, as the research progressed, it became apparent that many of the women defendants appearing in the community court, while apparently 'low level' in terms of their current offence, were in fact already embedded in the criminal justice system, particularly in terms of already being known to probation (either on current community orders or prison licences, or having recently completed – or breached – such sentences). This aspect was unexpected and was thus investigated as a specific strand of the research, leading to the critique that now follows.

The chapter turns to focus on 10 cases drawn from the three-month observation period, all of which proceeded to sentence on the day they were listed. These were also the cases where detailed and cross-referenced data were obtained from across the different sources, confirming the details of the women's current offence(s); their previous convictions; their age; information from the police and probation records; information from probation risk assessments; and finally, the sentence passed in relation to the offence being heard in the community court. All of the defendants in these cases had experienced contact with the police, the courts and probation before and it was thus of particular interest to review their experiences within this different type of court, not least to examine how therapeutic justice was applied and whether it facilitated any potential pathways out of (re)offending.

Focus on the women defendant case studies: initial overview

In order to investigate the application of therapeutic justice within this local community court, a case study approach in relation to the 10 female defendants is utilised within the review that follows. This draws on the observational data from the three-month intensive period and also includes factual data drawn from the range of contemporaneous sources from across the various criminal justice agencies: police records (Police National Computer); court records; information from the problem-solving assessment (if this took place) or otherwise from the third sector agency case notes (if available); and details from probation records. Access to these data had involved considerable negotiation, including formalised data-sharing agreements, and the extraction and collation of data by research team members from diverse IT systems.

The assemblage of such information is a unique contribution to research findings in this area. It supplies a comprehensive and in-depth set of contextual information, which underpins the qualitative data obtained from the contemporaneous court observations. Altogether this has provided rich descriptive data and has enabled a critical theoretical 'lens' (Westmarland, 2001) to be turned onto the operation of therapeutic justice with regard to female defendants within this community court setting.

Descriptive information

An overview of the situations of the 10 female defendants under review is provided in Table 19.1. (An explanation of the abbreviations OGRS, OGP and OVP, together with a table outlining the low, medium, high and very high bandings for OGRS 3, OGP and OVP, is given in the associated notes.)

This summary thus confirms the much more complex situation than low-risk, first-time offenders /early entrants into the criminal justice system than might have been anticipated given the court's stated remit, both in terms of the defendants' previous convictions and the risk assessment scores. The relatively wide range of ages also seems noteworthy, indicating a diversity of individuals and personal situations.

Findings

The application of therapeutic justice: operational considerations within the community court setting

An overview of the observational notes from the 10 cases under review with female defendants indicated that while the magistrates endeavoured to humanise the proceedings, the level of actual engagement often remained superficial, not least, as indicated earlier, because of the emphasis on efficiency in processing cases through the overall court complex. Most of the court proceedings started with the Chair of the Bench[5] explaining that this was a Community Justice Court and that there were various agencies that could be called on 'to help us before we proceed to sentence' (observation notes in relation

Table 19.1: Overview of the situations of the 10 female defendants

Defendant*	Offence	Previous convictions	Age	Information from police/probation records†	Information from risk assessments (probation)‡	Sentence
Defendant 1 (research ID 19)	Possession of a controlled drug (Subutex)	Theft/possession of drugs/possession of offensive weapons	39	Contact with probation since 2002; previous community order terminated for failure to comply; short prison sentences	OGRS§: 67 (medium); 81 (high); OGP: 62 (high); 75 (high); OVP: 7 (low); 12 (low). Medium risk of harm to children	Conditional discharge 9 months
Defendant 2 (research ID 41)	Shoplifting (box of wine)	Shoplifting	30	Community order with alcohol treatment programme – revoked due to failure to comply	OGRS: 93(very high); 97 (very high); OGP: 74 (high); 84 (high); OVP: 20 (low); 32 (medium)	Deferred sentence¶
Defendant 3 (research ID 84)	Drunk and disorderly	Assault on police officer	19	Community order – revoked due to failure to comply	OGRS: 44 (low); 62 (medium); OGP: 23 (low); 35 (medium) OVP: 18 (low); 30 (medium)	Fined £65 + victim surcharge £20
Defendant 4 (research ID 85)	Driving without due care and attention	Assault on police constable	25	Generic community order 6 months – completed normally	OGRS: 31 (low); 48 (low)	Conditional discharge 12 months + victim surcharge £15 + 5 penalty points on driving licence

(continued)

Defendant*	Offence	Previous convictions	Age	Information from police/ probation records†	Information from risk assessments (probation)‡	Sentence
Defendant 5 (research ID 114)	Possession of Class C drug (Diazepam)	Attempting to drive while unfit through drink; supplying heroin	39	Community order 12 months; 48 months' prison sentence	OGRS: not available; OGP: 53 (medium); 68 (high); OVP: 5 (low); 9 (low)	Conditional discharge 18 months, victim surcharge £15
Defendant 6 (research ID 123)	Criminal damage	Notifying police with false information (Sexual Offences Act)	21	Community order 12 months – completed normally	OGRS: 74 (medium); 86 (high); OGP: 41 (medium); 56 (medium); OVP: 14 (low); 24 (low)	Conditional discharge
Defendant 7 (research ID 202)	Drunk and disorderly; assault on police × 2	Yes. Specific details unavailable but of a different nature to current offence	36	Detailed information not found on IT systems	Detailed information not found on IT system**	Community order 6 months; curfew 3 months; £100 compensation × 2
Defendant 8 (research ID 220)	Criminal damage	Breach of conditional discharge from earlier offence	39	Detailed information not found on IT systems	Detailed information not found on IT system	Fined £30; victim surcharge £20
Defendant 9 (research ID 261)	Using threatening words; obstructing the police	Breach of conditional discharge from earlier offence	25	Flagged for public protection/ MAPPA [Multi-Agency Public Protection Arrangement] considered	OGRS: 32 (low); 49 (low)	Community order 12 months, including 40 hours' unpaid work; victim surcharge £60
Defendant 10 (research ID 265)	Using threatening words	Violent disorder	20	Generic community order 12 months	OGRS: 10 (low); 18 (low)	Conditional discharge 12 months

(notes to table overleaf)

Notes to Table 19.1:

* This designation was to ensure anonymity and confidentiality, which were key elements of this research.

† This was sometimes because a pre-sentence report had been prepared in the past, not necessarily because the defendant had been subject to a previous community order or prison licence (this seems relevant to the cases of defendant 7 and defendant 8).

‡ The two scores represent 12- and 24-month predictions – see Moore (2015).

§ At the time this research was conducted, OGRS 3 was in operation. This is described as follows: 'The Offender Group Reconviction Scale v. 3 is a static risk predictor, using criminal history and offender demographic data to provide a percentage prediction of proven reoffending' (Howard, 2011, p ii). OGP and OVP are described as follows: 'The OASys General Reoffending Predictor (OGP) and OASys Violence Predictor (OVP) predict the likelihood of nonviolent and violent proven reoffending respectively, by combining information on the offender's static and dynamic risk factors' (Howard, 2011, p i). The following table below indicates the bandings for the scores from these risk assessments (MoJ/NOMS, 2010):

Band	OGRS 3 2-year %	OGP 2-year %	OVP 2-year %
Low	0–49	0–33	0–29
Medium	50–74	34–66	30–59
High	75–89	67–84	60–79
Very high	90–99	85–99	80–99

¶ Further monitoring over the whole period of the research project revealed that this defendant reoffended and then broke bail conditions. She was remanded in custody for the preparation of a pre-sentence report and eventually received a further community order.

** The importance of accurate and timely risk assessment information, in turn feeding into sentence planning and co-ordination with other agencies has been repeatedly noted by reports conducted by HM Inspector of Probation; see for instance, HMIP (2009) and HMIP (2016).

to defendant 6). However, this preamble was sometimes overlooked at the start of proceedings and in any case the physical layout of the court remained the same as the other, more traditional courtrooms within the complex: the magistrates sat at a higher level than the defendant, and the defence solicitor (if there was one) was positioned in between the defendant and the magistrates. The more informal tone that some of the community court magistrates endeavoured to establish therefore often came over awkwardly vis-à-vis the decorum of the court setting and the rigidity of the court layout (see Popovik, 2006; Gilling and Jolley, 2012).

For instance, in the case of defendant 10 (who had been charged with offences of using threatening words and behaviour likely to cause harassment, alarm or distress), after the defendant had pleaded guilty, the Chair of the Bench addressed her, saying, "You have got to learn how to control yourself, this has got to stop. You're ruining your life."

There followed discussion between the legal adviser and the magistrates about outstanding court debts and breach of the community order. After conferring with the other magistrates sitting on the bench, the Chair spoke directly to defendant 10:

> It's one of those occasions where it's up to you. You are getting help [the defendant was already subject to a one-year community sentence]. Up to you whether you take it and get on with your life or go down the slippery slope....

The case then moved to sentencing, when defendant 10 received a 12-month conditional discharge, together with a victim surcharge of £15. The magistrate decided not to order costs because of her limited means (she was on benefits), but then rounded off the case with the following words:

> You've got the opportunity to sort your life out and move on – or come and see us again. And it will all get worse and you'll get sent to prison. It's entirely your choice.

In this way, the magistrate displayed initial concern about defendant 10's situation, but quickly moved onto a message of responsibilisation (Moore and Hirai, 2014). While the implementation of a conditional discharge did not place defendant 10 further up the sentencing tariff (Cavadino et al, 2013), it did hold a 'sting in its tail' insofar as she was now subject to two sentences (the conditional discharge and the community order), both of which were likely to be subject to breach action should she reoffend. Indeed, Hannah-Moffat and Maurutto (2012, p 214) have commented that 'specialized courts clearly exemplify how welfare initiatives are regularly interconnected with punishment and consequently distort the boundaries between welfare and punishment'. Thus, women offenders such as defendant 10 faced the potential of future 'uptariffing'. As Malloch and McIvor have outlined:

> If these penalties are breached, then uptariffing is likely to arise as a result of the perception that they have exhausted the range of non-custodial penalties available to the courts. This suggests that enforcement practices need to be sufficiently flexible if high levels of breach (and resulting imprisonment) are to be avoided. Further, while acknowledging that diverting women from prison is a

central concern, diversion from community supervision for women convicted of minor offences is also important (particularly in relation to mental health issues and poverty) to prevent their unnecessary absorption into the criminal justice system. (Malloch and McIvor, 2013, p 5)

Gender and therapeutic justice coming in and out of focus

In reviewing the operation of the community court and the interactions therein, it is important to acknowledge that, in reaching their decisions, the magistrates were required to take into account the wider sentencing principles that are embedded within the Sentencing Guidelines in England and Wales. As outlined by the Sentencing Council,[6] the aims of sentencing are to:

- **punish the offender** – this can include going to prison, doing unpaid work in the community, obeying a curfew or paying a fine;
- **reduce crime** – by preventing the offender from committing more crime and putting others off from committing similar offences;
- **reform and rehabilitate offenders** – changing an offender's behaviour to prevent future crime, for example, by requiring an offender to have treatment for drug addiction or alcohol abuse;
- **protect the public** – from the offender and from the risk of more crimes being committed, for example, by putting offenders in prison, restricting their activities or subjecting them to supervision by probation;
- **make the offender give something back** – for example, by the payment of compensation or through restorative justice. Restorative justice gives victims the chance to tell offenders about the impact of their crime and get an apology.

The following case involving defendant 9 illustrates some of the tensions that could arise with regard to these disparate aims, in particular those that often seemed most discordant within the community court, namely rehabilitation and punishment.[7] In this instance, a problem-solving meeting was requested with a view to informing the subsequent sentencing decision (Bowen and Whitehead, 2013).

In the initial part of the proceedings, the magistrate enquired into the circumstances of the offences (using threatening words; obstructing the police), and into the alcohol problems experienced by the defendant:

MAGISTRATE: You had a lot to drink.

DEFENDANT 9: Yeah.

MAGISTRATE: Do you often drink that amount of alcohol? Half a bottle of vodka?

DEFENDANT 9: No, it was Miss X's birthday

[Brief dialogue about other matters]

MAGISTRATE: 1 caution and 1 conditional discharge in 6 months.... Do you consider yourself to have a drink problem?

DEFENDANT 9: No, because I don't drink all the time.

MAGISTRATE: Ask [her] to be seen by the problem-solving team and then come back when we have a gap in sentencing and then...

This case subsequently reconvened after the problem-solving meeting and the court support and advisory staff member read out a summary of the defendant's situation in open court. This revealed a much more multifaceted and complicated situation than had been mentioned hitherto, with details of a 'blended' family of five children, three of whom had disabilities. The defendant and her partner were living on benefits and had problems with debts, particularly in relation to council tax. Defendant 9 was experiencing panic attacks and was in contact with her GP and another agency in connection with these difficulties. It was perhaps not surprising that the defendant herself had not disclosed the full extent of the personal and social problems she was experiencing ahead of the problem-solving meeting; she was not represented by a defence solicitor and was taciturn in the public space of the courtroom (Lyons, 2013). At that point the magistrates decided to request a fast-delivery (same-day) report from the probation service; again, further intimate personal and family details were revealed in open court when presented verbally by the probation officer.

Although the magistrates had seemed intent on taking account of the defendant's wider problems in relation to her offending behaviour, the application of therapeutic jurisprudence became increasingly derailed as the case proceeded. First, the manner of reporting back on the assessments conducted by the staff of the court advisory service and by the probation officer meant that personal information was revealed in the formal setting of court room, rather than within a respectful therapeutic environment (Wexler, 2001). Second, there was a lack of integration of the different elements, with little coordination in relation to the assessments (see Casey et al, 2007). An important factor in this respect was that only the third sector court and advisory service was located within the court complex, while all other statutory and voluntary organisations were situated elsewhere; this lack of co-location put constraints on effective liaison and timely collaborative work (Clinks, 2010).

Overall, there seemed to be different paradigms of justice in operation within this one case; in effect, there was an 'identity dilemma' in relation to the court's role in terms of what therapeutic jurisprudence could and should represent (Slobogin, 1995). The shift from one mode to another was indicated most noticeably by the formal tone adopted by the Chair of the Bench in pronouncing the sentence at the end of these proceedings – a community order that included unpaid work (in other words, a sentence incorporating both rehabilitative and punitive elements). The official requirements were briefly outlined, with only a passing reference to the defendant's situation, with the comment from the Chair of the Bench that "[You have] obligations with the children but because they are in school you can work around that."

This response brought the court case to an end in a way that concluded the legal process, but left the defendant with an outcome that decontextualised and seemingly dismissed her personal problems. From a gendered perspective, the assumption that the defendant could comply with her sentence despite her childcare responsibilities also overlooked official policy guidance that 'such work may also be insufficiently flexible to accommodate some women's recurring commitments' (MoJ/NOMS, 2012, p 20). For instance, the magistrates did not enquire about practical support with transport or any local provision of childcare to enable and maintain the defendant's engagement with such a requirement (Gelsthorpe, 2011). Indeed, as Birkett has recently noted:

> While official documents, policy statements and legislative developments continue to argue for the need to consider women offenders differently, this philosophy sits uncomfortably for many magistrates who believe that judicial office holders must remain gender-neutral. (Birkett, 2016, p 509)

Challenges posed by the interactional nature of a therapeutic approach

Over the course of the observational period, it was noticed that many of the lay magistrates,[8] while asking the women defendants in front of them about personal and social problems, showed a reluctance to incorporate into the proceedings any in-depth exploration of significant issues. It seemed that while some of the magistrates brought with them relevant knowledge, experience and training from their wider personal and professional backgrounds, the training afforded to them for this role was very limited,[9] thus overlooking the importance of knowledge of, commitment to, and enactment of 'key components, guiding principles, strategies, responses, models, approaches, blueprints and tool kits' (Hora, 2011, p 7).

The case of defendant 6 reveals such a process where compassion was expressed by the magistrates but was not incorporated into a 'hands-on approach to solving problems' (Wexler and Winick, 2003, p 54). Defendant 6 revealed in open court that she was self-harming; that she had been a carer for a relative who had recently died; that she was not working; and was on benefits due to mental health problems. The defendant described the offence (of criminal damage) as "just out drinking – got a bit stupid". The Chair of the Bench responded as follows:

> We're very concerned about what you said about things going on in your life, things need addressing. [We're making a] strong recommendation to see your doctor. Although we're not going to direct you, the [court support and advice service] team might help, they can make referrals. We can't make you do that today but we strongly recommend [that you do that].

This response indicated recognition on the part of the magistrates of the problems that were related to the offending behaviour of the defendant. However, as noted in relation to some of the other cases, practical reasons again intervened: on this occasion, this was the last case of the day and relevant staff members were unavailable, thus making it impossible to convene a problem-solving meeting. Once again, the logistics of the operation of the court and the integration of the relevant agencies had militated against the implementation of therapeutic justice and a more holistic approach in relation to the court hearing and the matters that arose there.

In addition, although the Chair of the Bench seemed to be endeavouring to be empathetic, the directness of the recommended course of action – closely followed by the sentence of a £30 fine – limited the sense of engagement and a meaningful application of therapeutic justice. Indeed, the main narrative thread seemed to be that the defendant had been invited to construct 'an identity worthy of leniency' (Gathings and Parrotta, 2013, p 668), but only in relation to the sentencing outcome, not in terms of the full application and process of therapeutic justice within the court hearing.

A similar type of scenario also arose in relation to defendant 4. The defendant had been charged with driving without due care and attention, causing damage and failure to stop. On this occasion, there was a defence solicitor and the same 'identity talk strategies' (Gathings and Parrotta, 2013) seemed to arise: the solicitor gave a detailed account of the custody case that was taking place in connection with the defendant's child and the difficulties she was having with her estranged husband since he had been released from prison (including domestic violence and financial problems). The current offence was placed within the context of this background, with her solicitor emphasising that at the time of the offence she was not consciously attempting to evade her responsibilities with regard to reporting the accident.

The comments made by the Chair of the Bench in passing sentence that "[we] shouldn't be doing this as [it] sits outside our guidelines" were particularly interesting. A sentence of a conditional discharge for 12 months, together with penalty points, and a £15 victim surcharge was passed – arguably a lenient decision in the circumstances. In this case (and with defendant 9 above), it seemed that the community court was stepping away from the punitiveness that has characterised much sentencing in relation to repeat female offenders (Prison Reform Trust, 2015) and was engaging in sentencing as 'an imaginative art insofar as it involves imagination and creative ability' (Tombs, 2008, p 84). However, there were limitations: first of all, the magistrates generally had to operate within the relevant sentencing guidelines for the type of offence(s).[10] Second, on an interpersonal level, the procedures, processes and layout of the court often precluded any attempts by the magistrates to try to respond in a more engaged and holistic way to the complex set of issues and problems presented by the defendants – responses that in any case would have required the application of a skill set and level of expertise and knowledge that was not an embedded part of this court's operation (see, for instance, Fook et al, 1997). It is thus interesting to see the recent recommendations that 'magistrates' training needs should be reviewed, with more funding and a Continuing Professional Development scheme' (Neill, 2016).[11]

Conclusion

Revisiting the application of therapeutic justice in relation to women offenders

This chapter has considered some of the research findings from a study that investigated the operation of therapeutic justice within a Community Justice Court in England and Wales, which incorporated a problem-solving element as part of its overall procedures. The review here of the empirical data from the research study conducted in 2012–14 in relation to women offenders has located its analysis within the context of the recommendations of the Corston Report and, in particular, the cautionary words that:

> The majority of female offenders have committed non-violent offences and present little risk to the public. Many present a far greater risk to themselves. They have been recognised as more 'troubled' than 'troublesome'. (Corston, 2007, p 16)

The findings from the research indicated that most of the women defendants who came within the scope of the study committed relatively low level offences, but in the context of a complex constellation of personal and social problems that often involved existing contact with agencies in the criminal justice system. While it is important to acknowledge that the small sample of cases explored here were not 'uptariffed' (see Gelsthorpe and Wright, 2015), there did seem to be a disconnect in the interface between penal and social policy and practices as played out in these individual cases. There was also little evidence of therapeutic interventions that focused on pathways out of crime and towards desistance for these women defendants.

In this respect, the application of therapeutic justice faced difficulties in this setting: the conflicting time and procedural pressures, together with the constraints of the physical layout, posed tensions in relation to any in-depth level of engagement. In practical terms, this meant that the court lacked a clear identity and sense of purpose, aspects that restricted the operationalisation of therapeutic jurisprudence in this setting.

Moreover, the extent of the problems revealed by the female defendants indicated a much more complex situation than might be anticipated by the characterisation of 'low-level' charges. This in turn came up against the multifaceted requirements of the Sentencing Guidelines leading to any rehabilitative elements often being incorporated into a more punitive rhetoric. As Gelsthorpe has written:

> Not only is there evident 'liquidity' in the concepts of 'welfare' and 'punishment', which suggests that they have always been two sides of the same coin insofar as women are concerned, but regulatory powers go well beyond discourses of 'welfare' and 'punishment', with moral tutelage shaping a number of different discourses. (Gelsthorpe, 2010, p 382)

Furthermore, while the defendants' personal and social problems were taken into account in court, this seemed to serve more as a mitigating factor in the sentencing, rather than as an integrated part of the court approach. The findings here therefore seem to lend support to the recent statement by Richard Garside, Directory of the Centre for Crime and Justice Studies:

> Those advocating for a new network of problem-solving courts are doing so with the best of intentions. But we need to be careful that problem-solving courts do not become problem-creating courts. The fact remains that there is little strong evidence that problem-solving courts solve problems, and a fair bit to suggest that they might make the problem worse. There is a strong argument for better health and welfare support for law-breakers with drug, alcohol, housing and other personal problems. This is best delivered through mainstream provision. Using the court process as a bespoke health and welfare service for law-breakers is more likely to be harmful than helpful. (Garside, 2016)

These thoughtful observations need to be considered carefully given the recent renaissance of interest in this area (Bowen et al, 2016), after an apparent loss of momentum at central government level (Bowcott, 2016). While therapeutic justice and problem-solving interventions do offer the potential of an alternative way of 'doing justice', there are challenges given the range of skills and expertise that are required to apply such an approach within a court setting (Ward, 2014). Besides, in relation to female defendants, there are still more significant issues: as Hannah-Moffat (2008, p 214) has cautioned, 'What is even less certain is what gendered responsiveness "in practice" means in terms of how practitioners organise and deliver correctional treatment.' This appeared to be a particular lacuna in the setting under review here, with therapeutic jurisprudence remaining more of an ambiguous aspiration, rather than a reality.

To conclude, the issues arising from the absence of a sound theoretical and organisational framework, together with the lack of full integration of evidence-based practice, placed constraints on the operationalisation of therapeutic jurisprudence in this setting. This had implications for the experience of the women defendants in the cases explored here, particularly in relation to integrating rehabilitative interventions. These limitations seemed to be epitomised by the heartfelt response from a female defendant (from the wider study) about her attempted yet frustrated attempts at desistance (Wright, 2015) when she said: "Well, I'm going to not get in any more trouble; I'll really try not to. I can't think that I'm never going to get into trouble again, but I am trying not to."

Notes

[1] Research project funded by the Economic and Social Research Council, Grant ES/JO10235/1. This study incorporated four 'work packages': to assess how and to what extent the Community Justice Court affected recidivism, reoffending and other measures associated with desistance from crime; to gain an in-depth understanding of the processes and criteria by which community court cases were selected for problem-solving intervention and how these problem-solving interventions were perceived and understood by those with a stake in the court procedures; to analyse the social organisation of problem-solving meetings, in particular how professional and third sector organisation participants collaborated, in what ways the offenders themselves were involved in the meetings and how the mode of participation affected offenders' commitment to the meeting decisions or recommendations; and to assess the impact that the CJC had on public confidence in the court processes and to understand how it achieved this objective.

[2] This Community Justice Court never took on board the option of subsequently reviewing the progress of offenders on a community sentence as provided for in the Criminal Justice Act 2003 (see section 178 of the legislation, available at www.legislation.gov.uk/ukpga/2003/44/pdfs/ukpga_20030044_en.pdf.

[3] It should be noted that policy changes since this time have resulted in an increase of out-of-court disposals carried out by the police in relation to such offences (see, for instance, MoJ, 2014b).

4   Over the two-year period of the research study, the gender balance of the defendants appearing in the Community Justice Court was approximately 80% men to 20% women. This situation is approximately in alignment with the information summarised in the government document *Statistics on Women and the Criminal Justice System 2013: A Ministry of Justice Publication under Section 95 of the Criminal Justice Act 1991* (MoJ/National Statistics, 2014).

5   There were usually three magistrates sitting at any one time, with two women and a man, or one woman and two men. The Chair of the Bench was sometimes a man, sometimes a woman. Their gender is not identified here in order to ensure anonymity.

6   See: https://www.sentencingcouncil.org.uk/

7   A hardening of political rhetoric at this time meant that all community sentences were expected to include 'some form of punishment, such as a fine, unpaid work, curfew or exclusion from certain areas' (MoJ, 2012). In October 2012, Chris Grayling, the then Secretary of State for Justice, announced that 'We're today putting punishment back into community sentencing. This is about sending a clear message to offenders and the public that if you commit a crime, you can expect to be punished properly'; see www.gov.uk/government/news/community-sentences-to-deliver-proper-punishment.

8   The community court cases were usually heard by lay magistrates, but occasionally such cases were listed to be heard by a district judge.

9   See: https://www.gov.uk/become-magistrate/can-you-be-a-magistrate

10 See: https://www.sentencingcouncil.org.uk/

11 Magistrates need to be able to devote 'at least 13 days, or 26 half-days, a year' (information from 'Become a magistrate', available at www.gov.uk/become-magistrate/can-you-be-a-magistrate). There was therefore a tension in terms of logistical planning insofar as all courts needed to have a bench of magistrates for all sittings (usually three magistrates). This posed administrative problems in terms of accommodating individual preferences with regard to available dates to undertake such duties, alongside particular requests to sit on the community court bench. However, it is important to note that the magistrates who were particularly engaged with the Community Justice Court approach did acknowledge the advantage of sitting regularly in this setting to maintain and develop relevant competences.

References

Auburn, T., Smart, C., Hanley Santos, G., Annison, J. and Gilling, D. (2016) 'Discovering mental ill health: "problem solving" in an English Magistrates' Court', in M. O'Reilly and J.N. Lester (eds) *The Palgrave Handbook of Adult Mental Health*, Basingstoke: Palgrave Macmillan, pp 633–652.

Birgden, A. (2004) 'Therapeutic jurisprudence and responsivity: finding the will and the way in offender rehabilitation', *Psychology, Crime & Law*, 10(3): 283–295.

Birkett, G. (2016) '"We have no awareness of what they actually do": magistrates' knowledge of and confidence in community sentences for women offenders in England and Wales', *Criminology & Criminal Justice*, 16(4): 497–512.

Bowcott, O. (2016) 'US-style problem solving courts plan losing momentum, says legal charity', *The Guardian*, Society section, 12 October.

Bowen, P. and Whitehead, S. (2013) *Better Courts: Cutting Crime Through Court Innovation*, London: New Economics Foundation.

Bowen, P. and 35 other signatories (2016) 'Innovative courts', Letter in *The Times*, 12th October, p 28.

Braun, V. and Clarke, V. (2012) 'Thematic analysis', in H. Cooper (ed) *APA Handbook of Research Methods in Psychology: Vol 2. Research Designs*, Washington, DC: American Psychological Association, pp 57–91.

Bryman, A. (2016) *Social Research Methods*, Oxford: Oxford University Press.

Casey, P.M., Rottman, D.B. and Bromage, C.G. (2007) Problem-solving justice toolkit, National Centre for State Courts, available at www.ndcrc.org/content/problem-solving-justice-toolkit.

Cavadino, M., Dignan, J. and Mair, G. (2013) *The Penal System: An Introduction*, London: Sage Publications.

Clinks (2010) 'Big judges and community justice courts', Members' briefing, available at www.clinks.org/sites/default/files/Members%20 Briefing%20-%20Big%20Judges%20project.pdf.

Corston, J. (2007) *The Corston Report: A Report by Baroness Jean Corston of a Review of Women with Particular Vulnerabilities in the Criminal Justice System*, London: Home Office.

Crown Prosecution Service (2008) 'Improving performance in the Magistrates' Courts', Annual Report and Resource Accounts 2008–2009, available at www.cps.gov.uk/publications/reports/2008/ performance_magistrates_court.html.

Donoghue, J. (2014) *Transforming Criminal Justice? Problem-Solving and Court Specialisation*, Abingdon: Routledge.

Fook, J., Ryan, M. and Hawkins, L. (1997) 'Towards a theory of social work expertise', *British Journal of Social Work*, 27(3): 399–417.

Garside, R. (2016) 'Caution needed over problem-solving courts', Statement released by Centre for Crime and Justice Studies, 13 October, available at www.crimeandjustice.org.uk/news/caution-needed-over-problem-solving-courts.

Gathings, M.J. and Parrotta, K. (2013) 'The use of gendered narratives in the courtroom: constructing an identity worthy of leniency', *Journal of Contemporary Ethnography*, 42(6): 668–689.

Gelsthorpe, L. (2010) 'Women, crime and control', *Criminology & Criminal Justice*, 10(4): 375–386.

Gelsthorpe, L. (2011) 'Working with women offenders in the community', in R. Sheehan, G. McIvor and C. Trotter (eds) *Working with Women Offenders in the Community*, Abingdon: Willan, pp 127–150.

Gelsthorpe, L. and Wright, S. (2015) 'The context: women as lawbreakers', in J. Annison, J. Brayford and J. Deering (eds) *Women and Criminal Justice: From the Corston Report to Transforming Rehabilitation*, Bristol: Policy Press, pp 39–58.

Gilling, D. and Jolley, M. (2012) 'A case study of an English community court', *British Journal of Community Justice*, 10(2): 55–69.

Hannah-Moffat, K. (2008) 'Re-imagining gendered penalities: the myth of gender responsivity', in P. Carlen (ed) *Imaginary Penalities*, Cullompton: Willan, pp 193–217.

Hannah-Moffat, K. and Maurutto, P. (2012) 'Shifting and targeted forms of penal governance: bail, punishment and specialized courts', *Theoretical Criminology*, 16(2): 201–219.

HMIP (Her Majesty's Inspectorate of Probation) (2009) *Risk of Harm Inspection Report: A Stalled Journey. An Inquiry into the Management of Offenders' Risk of Harm to Others by London Probation in: Greenwich & Lewisham; Hackney & Tower Hamlets; Merton, Sutton & Wandsworth; and Brent, Barnet & Enfield*, London: HMIP.

HMIP (2016) *Transitions Arrangements: A Follow-up Inspection*, London: HMIP.

Hora, P.F. (2011) 'Courting new solutions using problem-solving justice: key components, guiding principles, strategies, responses, models, approaches, blueprints and tool kits', *Chapman Journal of Criminal Justice*, 2(1): 7–52.

Howard, P. (2011) *Hazards of Different Types of Reoffending*, Ministry of Justice Research Series 3/11, London: Ministry of Justice.

Jones, M.D. (2012) 'Mainstreaming therapeutic jurisprudence into the traditional courts: suggestions for judges and practitioners', *Phoenix Law Review*, 5(4): 753–775.

Karp, D.R. and Clear, T.R. (2000) 'Community justice: a conceptual framework', in C.M. Friel (ed) *Boundary Changes in Criminal Justice Organizations, Vol. 2*, Washington, DC: United States Department of Justice, Office of Justice Programs, National Institute of Justice, pp 323–368.

Lyons, T. (2013) 'Judges as therapists and therapists as judges: the collision of judicial and therapeutic roles in drug treatment courts', *Contemporary Justice Review: Issues in Criminal, Social and Restorative Justice*, 16(4): 412–424.

Malloch, M. and McIvor, G. (2013) 'Women, punishment and social justice', in M. Malloch and G. McIvor (eds) *Women, Punishment and Social Justice: Human Rights and Penal Practices*, Abingdon: Routledge, pp 3–12.

MoJ (Ministry of Justice) (2012) 'Community sentences to deliver proper punishment', Press release, available at www.gov.uk/government/news/community-sentences-to-deliver-proper-punishment.

MoJ (2014a) *Justice Data Lab Re-offending Analysis: Community Justice Court at Plymouth Magistrates' Court*, London: Ministry of Justice.

MoJ (2014b) *Out of Court disposals Consultation Response*, London: HM Government/College of Policing.

MoJ/National Statistics (2014) *Statistics on Women and the Criminal Justice System 2013: A Ministry of Justice Publication under Section 95 of the Criminal Justice Act 1991*, available at www.gov.uk/government/uploads/system/uploads/attachment_data/file/380090/women-cjs-2013.pdf.

MoJ/NOMS (National Offender Management Service) (2010) *O-DEAT [OASys Data Evaluation and Analysis Team] Data Post-OASys Release 4.3.1 (End of August 2009): Explanatory Notes*, London: Ministry of Justice.

MoJ/NOMS (2012) *A Distinct Approach: A Guide to Working with Women Offenders*, London: NOMS Women and Equalities Group.

Moore, D. (2011) 'The benevolent watch: therapeutic surveillance in drug treatment court', *Theoretical Criminology*, 15(3): 255–268.

Moore, D. and Hirai, H. (2014) 'Outcasts, performers and true believers: responsibilized subjects of criminal justice', *Theoretical Criminology*, 18(1): 5–19.

Moore, R. (2015) (ed) *A Compendium of Research and Analysis on the Offender Assessment System (OASys) 2009–2013*, Ministry of Justice Analytical Series, London: NOMS.

Morgan, R. (2008) *Summary Justice: Fast – But Fair?*, London: Centre for Crime and Justice.

Moynihan, K. (2016) 'Problem-solving court: Manchester & Salford Magistrates' Court', Paper presented at the Confederation of European Probation Conference on 'Alternatives to Detention', Bucharest, Romania, 6–7 October.

Neill, B. (2016) 'Government must develop over-arching strategy for magistracy', News release accompanying Justice Select Committee Report *The Role of the Magistracy*, available at www.parliament.uk/business/committees/committees-a-z/commons-select/justice-committee/news-parliament-20151/role-of-the-magistracy-report-published-16-17.

Popovic, J. (2006) 'Court process and therapeutic jurisprudence: have we thrown the baby out with the bathwater?' *eLaw Journal*, 1(Special Series): 60–77.

Prison Reform Trust (2015) 'Why focus on reducing women's imprisonment?', Prison Reform Trust briefing, available at www.prisonreformtrust.org.uk/Portals/0/Documents/why%20focus%20on%20reducing%20women's%20imprisonment%20BL.pdf.

Rumgay, J. (2000) 'Policies of neglect: female offenders and the probation service', in H. Kemshall and R. Littlechild (eds) *User Involvement and Participation in Social Care: Research Informing Practice*, London: Jessica Kingsley, pp 193-213, extract in G. Mair and J. Rumgay (eds) (2014) *Probation: Key Readings*, London: Routledge, pp 389–394.

Slobogin, C. (1995) 'Therapeutic jurisprudence: five dilemmas to ponder', *Psychology, Public Policy and Law*, 1(1): 193–219.

Tombs, J. (2008) 'Telling sentencing stories', in P. Carlen (ed) *Imaginary Penalities*, Cullompton: Willan, pp 84–112.

Ward, J. (2014) *Are Problem-Solving Courts the Way Forward for Justice?*, Howard League What is Justice? Working Papers 2/2014, London: The Howard League for Penal Reform.

Westmarland, N. (2001) 'The quantitative/qualitative debate and feminist research: a subjective view of objectivity', *Forum: Qualitative Social Research*, available at www.qualitative-research.net/index.php/fqs/article/view/974.

Wexler, D.B. (2001) 'Robes and rehabilitation: how judges can help offenders "make good"', *Court Review*, Spring: 18–23.

Wexler, D.B. and Winick, B.J. (2003) 'Putting therapeutic jurisprudence to work', *ABA Journal*, May: 54–57.

Whitehead, S. (2013) *Better Courts Case-Study: Plymouth Community Advice and Support Service*, London: New Economics Foundation.

Wolf, R.V. (2007) *Principles of Problem-Solving Justice*, New York, NY: Center for Court Innovation.

Wright, S. (2015) '"Persistent" and "prolific" offending across the life-course as experienced by woman: chronic recidivism and frustrated desistance', Unpublished PhD Thesis, University of Surrey.

TWENTY

Conclusion

Pamela Ugwudike, Jill Annison and Peter Raynor

Developing and promoting evidence-based skills in criminal justice

In our introductory chapter, we highlighted the vibrant forum for research and collaborative engagement provided by the Collaboration of Researchers for the Effective Development of Offender Supervision (CREDOS) network over the past 10 years. Of note has been the interaction between academics, policymakers and practitioners. There have also been opportunities for dialogue and debate from different theoretical and practice perspectives, and the dissemination of research findings on an international scale.

Thus, working collaboratively or in their relative international and subject domains, CREDOS members have, over the years, developed and disseminated theoretical and empirical knowledge of effective supervision skills for supporting rehabilitation and desistance. The current volume is a tangible realisation of this collaborative exercise: it has adopted a broad international focus, and its three sections comprise rigorous and insightful contributions, and demonstrate the broad significance of effective practice skills in the field of criminal justice and associated settings.

Implementing evidence-based skills: policy developments and organisational issues

The chapters in the first section of the book acknowledge the impact of wider policy and organisational contexts on the implementation of effective practice skills. In this respect, Chapters Two and Three by Maurice Vanstone and Peter Raynor respectively, indicate that the application of evidence-based skills in England and Wales has not been a straightforward incremental process, not least because of the often unrealistic expectations of politicians and short time scales that are imposed (see Colebatch, 2009).

The subsequent chapters in Part 1 also draw attention to the external and internal turbulence that can affect criminal justice agencies or organisations. Thus, in Chapter Four, Lol Burke, Matthew Millings and Gwen Robinson explore the rapid changes that have occurred in England and Wales, and the threats the changes pose to the realisation of evidence-based practice in criminal justice settings.

Burke and colleagues note that the Transforming Rehabilitation (TR) agenda (Ministry of Justice, 2013) which is predicated on a 'Payment by Results' approach whereby services will be funded on the basis of the quantifiable outcomes they produce, could extend the commercialisation agenda of criminal justice policy. This agenda could overshadow practices that are not amenable to quantification. Examples of these practices include using evidence-based skills to engage service users and support their efforts to address difficulties and obstacles to long-term positive change. Business imperatives of maximising value for money might encourage services to focus instead on quantifiable practices (for example, improving rates of court breach). Such practices do not necessarily contribute to rehabilitation or desistance. Further, as Burke and colleagues note in their chapter, under the TR agenda, competition between service providers for limited government funding could engender fragmentary and inconsistent service delivery as the providers become insular and more interested in maximising their share of the market and protecting their commercial interests.

Burke and colleagues conclude that the success of the TR agenda (if success equates to rehabilitation and desistance) would in part depend on the ability of Community Rehabilitation Companies (CRCs) to extend their focus beyond commercial interests to facilitating effective practice by employing skilled practitioners who can successfully engage service users and encourage long-term change. Lol Burke and colleagues also emphasise the need for adequate staff training, including the enhancement of staff members' emotional skills.

Echoing the point about developing staff's emotional skills amid challenging policy transformations, Andrew Fowler and colleagues argue in Chapter Twelve that limited attention has been paid to the ways in which staff's emotions contribute to effective practice. Later in this chapter, we shall have more to say about Fowler and colleagues' conceptualisation of emotional labour as a key practice skill. Meanwhile, another contribution, which provides a contextual account of the wider policy and organisational-level factors that affect the implementation of practice skills, is Chapter Four by Danielle and colleagues. Offering a US perspective, the chapter considers organisational pressures that affect agencies in the US. It draws on a study that was conducted in probation settings within two states to demonstrate that managers, charged with interpreting policy developments and monitoring staff compliance, can undermine the effective implementation of evidence-based policies.

By focusing on the impact of managerial culture, the chapter provides an insightful analysis of a key but often neglected factor that can affect the quality and outcomes of penal supervision practice. Rudes and colleagues point to the reticence with which some managers implement evidence-based policies, often with limited effort, to highlight the links between the evidence-based policies and set goals. This reticence, the authors argue, might stem from the managers' belief that evidence-based policies do not necessarily contribute to effective practice and can impinge on already limited time and financial resources.

In sum, the chapters in Part 1 of the book enhance our understanding of the contexts in which supervision skills are deployed. They draw attention to wider policy and organisational challenges that may affect implementation.

International research on evidence-based skills

Part 2 of the book also touches on policy-related and organisational issues that affect the implementation of evidence-based supervision skills. But the chapters in this section focus on the skills themselves, their implementation, and the models of rehabilitation that underpin them. Together, the chapters present illuminating international perspectives from Australia, North America (Canada and the US), and Europe (England and Wales, Spain, Belgium and Romania).

A critical analysis of key rehabilitation models

The section starts with a chapter by Martine Herzog-Evans, which critically reviews key models of rehabilitation, namely the Risk-Need-Responsivity (RNR) model (Bonta and Andrews, 2017), desistance model (Maruna, 2001) and Good Lives model of desistance (Ward and Maruna, 2007; Ward and Fortune, 2013). Herzog-Evans calls for an integrative model that encompasses key elements of the three models and other complementary models rooted in legal principles and ethics. In the chapter, Herzog-Evans provides an incisive account of the theoretical and empirical modifications that should be introduced to expand the contours of the existing models, particularly the RNR model, in order to develop the integrative model. According to Herzog-Evans, a key area for modification is the issue of non-programmatic factors. The factors are: staff and offender characteristics; the quality of interactions between both parties; caseload levels; frequency of contact; the degree to which interventions are clearly defined; and the supervision or programme setting.

Herzog-Evans argues that these were excluded from the RNR model largely because they lacked sufficient theoretical and empirical validation. In Herzog-Evans' view, they should be evaluated alongside other relevant factors. Insights from the evaluations should then inform the development of the proposed integrative model of rehabilitation.

Evidence-based skills: content and implementation

In her critique of key models of rehabilitation, Herzog-Evans also provides a detailed account of evidence-based skills associated with some of the models (particularly the RNR model which has a substantial evidence-base). Herzog-Evans describes how knowledge of the skills has evolved in line with insights from research and acknowledges their increasing relevance as tools for effective supervision practice. Several chapters in this volume provide empirical accounts of real-world applications of the skills and identify key challenges that circumscribe effective implementation.

The evidence-based skills are known as core correctional practices (CCPs). First identified by Andrews and Kiessling (1980), CCPs, as James Bonta, Guy Bourgon and Tanya Rugge (Chapter Nine) rightly observe, initially comprised five dimensions: positive relationship with the client; effective use of authority; prosocial modelling and reinforcement; problem solving; and the effective use of community resources. The skills have since been expanded by other researchers to include cognitive restructuring and motivational interviewing techniques (see Chapters Six, Eleven and Fourteen of this volume, and Gendreau and Andrews, 1989). Nevertheless, there is substantial international evidence that the skills are associated with positive outcomes such as service-user engagement and reductions in reconviction rates (Raynor et al, 2014; Chadwick et al, 2015; Trotter, 2006). The skills can thus support rehabilitation. As noted in the introductory chapter, the skills also comprise key elements that desistance scholars identify as vital for secondary desistance.

As already noted, several chapters in the current text present the findings of studies that explored the application of these skills in real-world supervision practice. These comprise Chapter Seven by Ester Blay and Johan Boxstaens, which focuses on insights from Spain and Belgium; Chapter Eight by Ioan Durnescu, which is based on research from Romania; and Chapter Fourteen by Pamela Ugwudike and Gemma Morgan, which presents findings from Welsh youth justice. Collectively, these chapters indicate that the skills are not applied frequently and consistently. This echoes the findings of earlier studies (see, for example, Dowden and Andrews, 2004) which, as we shall see, have prompted researchers and others to develop staff training models. A key objective of the models is to equip frontline staff with CCPs and other evidence-based skills and practices. It is to the issue of staff training processes and challenges that we now turn.

Translating evidence-based skills into one-to-one supervision practice: key staff training models

Alongside the chapters that explore the implementation of evidence-based skills, other chapters in Part 2 emphasise the importance of training staff to equip them with these skills. The chapters present compelling research evidence that identify staff development as a *sine qua non* of effective practice. Reinforcing this in Chapter Nine, James Bonta and colleagues rightly observe that the impetus for training models that equip staff with CCPs stemmed from insights from meta-analytic studies indicating that programmes based on the RNR model were not producing anticipated reductions in recidivism rates (Bonta et al, 2008). A meta-analytic study of supervision practice by Dowden and Andrews (2004) also found that evidence-based CCPs were linked to reductions in recidivism but were not being applied frequently.

In Chapter Nine, Bonta and colleagues describe the creation and evaluation of one of the first staff training models that emerged to facilitate the process of translating evidence-based skills into practice. The model, known as the Strategic Training Initiative in Community Supervision (STICS), built on Trotter's (1996) earlier work in Australia and was developed by researchers based in Canada. The STICS model trains practitioners in RNR principles, with emphasis on identifying and addressing criminogenic needs, and employing cognitive-behavioural approaches (see also, Bonta and Andrews, 2017). Alongside these, staff also receive training on the CCPs.

Bonta and colleagues' description of the 2011 evaluation of STICS is very informative; the evaluation found that STICS training led to changes in the behaviour of the probation officers towards their clients. Subsequent evaluations of the training model are in progress, but the emerging results are promising; unlike untrained staff, STICS-trained staff tend to use evidence-based skills and practices. In Chapter Nine,

Bonta and colleagues rightly note that the STICS model has been replicated internationally, and the Skills for Effective Engagement and Development (SEED) model, which is the subject of Chapter Ten by Angela Sorsby, Joanna Shapland and Ioan Durnescu, is an example.

The SEED training model was introduced in some probation areas in England and Wales to equip staff with the skills required for building good supervision relationships and engaging service users during one-to-one supervision practice (Rex and Hosking, 2013). The model was informed by RNR principles and the CCPs. In Chapter Ten, Sorsby and colleagues set out the processes of delivering SEED training in England and Romania, and reveal that staff found the training valuable but identified limited time, caseload issues, limited office space, and other impediments. Some of the participating service users also provided positive feedback on the quality of supervision. In addition, there was evidence that SEED-trained practitioners in England applied more SEED skills (such as the CCPs) compared with their untrained counterparts.

These and other findings point to the benefits of training staff in evidence-based skills. Evaluations of staff training models such as STICS and SEEDS have yielded promising results, and reveal that staff and service users believe that they can enhance the quality of supervision. Furthermore, robust impact evaluation of the STICS model has found that it encourages the application of evidence-based skills and is associated with reductions in recidivism.

Added to the STICs and SEEDS models, other training models have emerged, notably Staff Training Aimed at Reducing Re-arrest (STARR), Effective Practices in Community Supervision (EPICS), Proactive Community Supervision (PCS) and Skills for Offender Assessment and Responsivity in New Goals (SOARING2). In Chapter Eleven, Heather Toronjo and Faye S. Taxman critique these models and argue that while STARR and EPICS draw explicitly on the CCPs, PCS and SOARING2 embody the 'sprit' rather than the terminologies of the CCPs. They also argue that research is required to assess the comparative efficacy of the models.

Supervising and supporting staff to implement evidence-based skills and practices

The remaining chapters in Part 2 move away from the focus on evidence-based staff skills and their implementation. These chapters emphasise instead the value of supporting front-line staff. They argue that attention should also be paid to the utility of emotional skills

426

and the need for staff development and supervision processes that recognise the emotional resources staff invest in the often challenging work they do. In Chapter Twelve, Andrew Fowler, Jake Phillips and Chalen Westaby suggest that building relationships with service users requires a degree of empathy, but effective relationship building also involves creating boundaries, and this requires the use of quite different emotions. Indeed, Fowler and colleagues argue that emotion suppression and detachment are required for creating clear boundaries. They conceptualise these and other complex emotional dimensions of practice as emotional labour, and argue that it is a form of effective practice that deserves similar levels policy, theoretical and empirical attention accorded to other practice skills such as the aforementioned CCPs.

Clinical and other forms of staff supervision that can support staff members' efforts to navigate the emotional labour of probation work are the foci of Chapter Thirteen (by Charlene Pereira and Chris Trotter). In a chapter that illuminates another neglected aspect of practice – the skills required for supervising and supporting staff effectively – Pereira and Trotter argue that unlike performance management strategies and surveillance-focused staff supervision practices, the relationship and other skills associated with effective service-user supervision are also useful for effective staff supervision. They argue that these skills improve staff retention, staff skills and contribute to effective practice with service users.

The international reach of the chapters in this section provides an unparalleled corpus of emerging research on specific practice skills that are theoretically informed *and* empirically linked to positive outcomes such as reduced recidivism. Furthermore, they provide knowledge of effective skills and practices that apply in both adult criminal justice and youth justice settings, and within public and private sector service delivery contexts. While the various locations are situated within different legislative and policy frameworks, the insights provided with regard to effective criminal justice skills offer theoretically informed examples of practice in action that transcend the local settings. In short, the objective of the chapters in this section is to inform policy and evidence-based practice across multidisciplinary contexts.

Effective practice with diverse groups

In Part 3, the focus turns to a consideration of evidence-based approaches in a way that acknowledges the diversity of those who come into the orbit of the criminal justice systems and practitioners in these different settings. The importance of developing inclusive practice is a crucial element of the emerging range of skills and research base that are explored and interrogated within these chapters.

Implementing evidence-based skills in youth justice settings

The scope for implementing evidence-based skills in the field of youth justice is shown in Chapters Fourteen to Sixteen, which demonstrate the ways in which research and practice can engage in constructive dialogue and development. In Chapter Fourteen, Pamela Ugwudike and Gemma Morgan present the findings of a study that assessed the use of evidence-based CCPs in Welsh youth justice settings. A key finding was that the participating practitioners employed relationship skills. But, as other studies of CCPs have found, the study also found that most of the skills were not being applied routinely.

Chris Trotter acknowledges this recurring finding in Chapter Fifteen, which also focuses on youth justice practice skills. In addition, the chapter extends to youth justice contexts, the themes addressed by the chapters in part 2 that focus on staff training. Thus, Trotter presents the findings of a study that explored the process of training and coaching staff on how to apply evidence-based skills (most of which are incorporated in the CCPs). The study found that training and coaching can significantly increase the rate at which staff apply the skills. There were notable increases in the use of the skills, particularly relationship skills. The study found, however, that despite the significant increases, the use of skills was not sufficiently high and the chapter notes that efforts should be made to address systemic challenges that impede the application of evidence-based skills. Examples provided include agency culture, supervisors' attitudes, buy-in from staff and organisational leadership. As other evaluations of staff skills have found (see for example, Chapter Eight of this volume), time constraints and demands on staff to complete other tasks posed additional challenges.

Co-producing rehabilitation: service-user participation as effective practice

As noted above, the studies of supervision skills reported in Chapters Fourteen and Fifteen found that relationship skills were the most frequently used skills, with Trotter observing that 'the workers [in his study] were strongest on relationship skills' (p 330). Chapter Sixteen, by Nigel Hosking and John Rico, extends the discussion about relationship skills by focusing on a project that explored the relational benefits of employing ex-service users as probation workers. Underpinning the project was the co-productive aim of involving service users in the delivery of one-to-one supervision services.[1] The underlying assumption was that ex-service users were more likely to forge strong relationships with service users, given the ex-service users' previous experience as service users.

In their chapter, Hosking and Rico note that an evaluation of the project found that despite systemic issues including the restructuring of services that accompanied the phasing-in of the TR agenda, the ex-service users' relational role was deemed successful by probation staff and the service users. There was evidence that the ex-service users' previous involvement in offending and probation enhanced their understanding and empathy. These in turn strengthened their ability to forge positive relationships with the service users. The chapter usefully draws attention to the typically overlooked issue of service-user participation in the delivery of services within the justice system and addresses the value of enabling their involvement.

Effective practice with families, ethnic minority groups and women: an exercise in routine marginalisation

While service-user participation in the co-production of service delivery is often marginalised from key debates about effective practice, the benefits of co-productive work with family members have also been ignored. Chapter Seventeen seeks to address this by drawing attention to the importance and benefits of rehabilitative work with family members in youth justice settings. In the chapter, Chris Trotter also describes the skills required for collaborating effectively with this group.

Following on from this, Patrick Williams and Pauline Durrance note in Chapter Eighteen, which focuses on arrangements in England and Wales, that Black, Asian and minority ethnic (BAME) service users are also another typically overlooked group. There is a paucity of theoretical and empirical knowledge of the skills required for engaging this group and working with them to achieve long-term positive change. Williams and Durrance observe that in 2001, bespoke cognitive-behavioural programmes were developed for BAME people as part of the Effective Practice Initiative that introduced the 'what works'/RNR model in England and Wales. However, these programmes no longer exist, and Williams and Durrance decry the current state of affairs. They argue that programmes or interventions that empower BAME people who are subject to penal supervision, whilst recognising their adverse experiences of racialisation and structural inequality, can help improve their lives.

Another group that is often marginalised from studies of effective practice is women (Annison et al, 2015), and Chapter Nineteen seeks to address this gap. In this chapter, Jill Annison and colleagues present the findings of a study that explored the role of the courts in enhancing the responsivity of penal interventions. The chapter focused on a community court that was established to provide therapeutic justice by tailoring sentences to suit the individual needs of female defendants. As Bonta and Andrews (2017) and others note, adapting interventions to the individual attributes of service users such as their gender, culture and cognitive ability, is a key dimension of the specific responsivity principle of effective practice.

Annison and colleagues' study found that similar to penal supervision contexts, in court settings, operational issues can militate against efforts to achieve specific responsivity. Examples of these issues include demands for expedited outcomes (in this case, 'simple, speedy and summary justice') and pressures to deal with a larger volume of cases than anticipated. These are largely linked to performance and efficiency-related imperatives and can undermine efforts to deliver tailored services. By studying how the courts might apply the specific responsivity principle, Annison and colleagues move beyond the tendency to focus on the responsivity issues that pertain to penal supervision contexts.

In sum, most of the chapters in this text point to 'real-world' challenges and constraints that affect effective practice in diverse settings. In England and Wales, for instance, there is particular concern that the ideological and economic restrictions of the neoliberal TR project (Burke and Collett, 2016) will override the application of evidence-based skills in relation to diverse groups. That said, the different chapters indicate that positive developments can, and do, take place. The chapters provide rich insights by bringing together international research on evidence-based skills and effective one-to-one practice in penal supervision settings.

Indeed, the contributors to this edited collection have demonstrated the rigour of their research in their respective areas and the direct application of their findings to policy and practice. An overview of this volume thus reveals an in-depth, rigorous and intellectually critical engagement with:

- the development, application and evaluation of evidence-based skills in criminal justice settings;

- the importance of the wider organisational contexts and the crucial need to identify and overcome constraints that impede the operationalisation of research-informed skills and practices;
- the crucial link between these skills and positive outcomes, particularly those that support pathways towards desistance and reductions in reoffending;
- the constructive implementation of training, staff development and evaluation as a way of bridging gaps between practice and research.

Furthermore, the international reach of the contributors makes the findings within the various chapters of significance for policymakers, managers, practitioners, academics and researchers working in different jurisdictions and across a wide range of settings. The connections that have come about via the CREDOS network have thus supported a vibrant interchange of knowledge, research and practice applications. It is hoped that this edited book will contribute to the development and implementation of effective practice in the present, and facilitate and extend such collaborative and comparative work in the future.

Note

[1] See Weaver (2014) and Ugwudike (2016) for detailed accounts of the benefits of co-production and user participation.

References

Andrews, D. and Kiessling, J. (1980) 'Program structure and effective correctional practices: a summary of the CaVIC research', in R. Ross and P. Gendreau (eds) *Effective Correctional Treatment*, Toronto: Butterworth, pp 441–463.

Annison, J., Brayford, J. and Deering, J. (eds) (2015) *Women and Criminal Justice: From the Corston Report to Transforming Rehabilitation*, Bristol: Policy Press.

Bonta, J. and Andrews, D. (2017) *The Psychology of Criminal Conduct* (6th edn), Abingdon: Routledge.

Bonta, J., Rugge, T., Scott, T., Bourgon, G. and Yessine, A.K. (2008) 'Exploring the black box of community supervision', *Journal of Offender Rehabilitation*, 47(3): 248–270.

Burke, L. and Collett, S. (2016) 'Transforming Rehabilitation: organizational bifurcation and the end of probation as we knew it?', *Probation Journal*, 63(2): 120–135.

Chadwick, N., DeWolf, A. and Serin, R. (2015). 'Effectively training community supervision officers: a meta-analytic review of the impact on offender outcome', *Criminal Justice and Behavior*, 42(10): 977–989.

Colebatch, H.K. (2009) *Policy* (3rd edn), Maidenhead: Open University Press.

Dowden, C. and Andrews, D. (2004) 'The importance of staff practice in delivering effective correctional treatment: a meta-analytic review of core correctional practice', *International Journal of Offender Therapy and Comparative Criminology*, 48(2): 203–214.

Gendreau. P. and Andrews, D.A. (1989) *The Correctional Program Assessment Inventory*, New Brunswick: University of New Brunswick.

Maruna, S. (2001) *Making Good: How Ex-Convicts Reform and Rebuild their Lives*, Washington, DC: American Psychological Association Books.

Ministry of Justice (2013) *Transforming Rehabilitation: A Strategy for Reform*, London: The Stationery Office.

Raynor, P., Ugwudike, P. and Vanstone, M. (2014) 'The impact of skills in probation work: a reconviction study', *Criminology & Criminal Justice*, 14(2): 235–249.

Rex, S. and Hosking, N. (2013) 'A collaborative approach to developing probation practice: Skills for Effective Engagement, Development and Supervision (SEEDS)', *Probation Journal*, 60(3): 332–338.

Trotter, C. (1996) 'The impact of different supervision practices in community corrections', *Australian and New Zealand Journal of Criminology*, 29(1): 29–46.

Trotter, C. (2006) *Working with Involuntary Clients: A Guide to Practice* (2nd edn), London: Sage Publications.

Ugwudike, P. (2016) 'The dynamics of service user participation and compliance in community justice settings', *The Howard Journal of Crime and Justice*, 55(4): 455–477.

Ward, T. and Fortune, C. (2013) 'The Good Lives model: aligning risk reduction with promoting offenders' personal goals', *European Journal of Probation*, 5(2): 29–46.

Ward, T. and Maruna, S. (2007) *Rehabilitation: Key Ideas in Criminology*, Abingdon: Routledge.

Weaver, B. (2014) 'Co-producing desistance: who works to support desistance?', in I. Durnescu and F. McNeill (eds) (2014) *Understanding Penal Practice*, Abingdon: Routledge, pp 193–205.

Index

References to tables and figures are shown in *italics*

Q

qualitative research 37–8

R

radicalisation 379–81
Radzinowicz, L. 41–2
Rafaeli, A. 252
Raynor, P. 27, 140, 212
Reasoning and Rehabilitation
   programme 44–5
Rees, J. 72–3
reflective practice 204, 269–70
reinforcement 218–20, 229, *236*, *296*,
   302, 318
relationships with service users, initial
   phase 127–50
   and dual professional role 131–2,
      143, 146, *147*
   findings of study 138–50
   importance of 130, 132–3
   and Klockars' theory 130–3, 146
   and legal mandate 128, 129
   and mechanisms for effective
      supervision 132
   methodology 127–8, 137–8
   nature of 128–30
   skills of 138–43, *144–5*
   the study 133–7
   synthetic officers 131–2, 143, 146,
      147
   in therapeutic context 128–9
   two study sites compared 148–9
   as working alliance 129–30, 132–3,
      138–47
resilience 29–30
respect 140, *144*, *147*, *165*
responsivity 110–12, *114–16*
Revell, L. 279
Rex, S. 208, 246
Risk-Need-Responsivity (RNR)
   99–117
   and cognitive behavioural treatment
      (CBT) 102–3
   core correctional practice (CCP)
      106–8, *107*, *114*, *115*
   criticisms of 99–105
   and desistance theory 103, 105–7
   and diversity issues 105
   effectiveness of 170, 217
   and Good Lives model 100–8
   integrative model 109–16, *113–16*,
      423–4
   non-programmatic factors 100,
      109–10
   and offender agency and motivation
      103–5

principles of 99, 169–70
   and problem solving 108
   response to critics 105–9
   responsivity 110–12, *114–16*
   training need 171
   see also supervision skills
risk/needs assessment *see* needs
   assessment
RNR model *see* Risk-Need-
   Responsivity (RNR)
Robinson, C.R. 27
Robinson, G. 59, 60, 64, 67, 68, 70,
   208–9, 244
Rogers, C.L. 128
role clarification *107*, *165*, 231, *236*,
   271, 318, 323–4, *323–4*
Rolfe, G. 265
Romania *see* desistance-related skills;
   SEEDs programme
Rooney, R. 318
Rudes, D.S. 80
Rudland, J. 279, 280, 282

S

Sachwald, J. 29, 222–3
Samstag, L.W. 128
Schon, D. 21, 270
Scott, D.P. 337
SDT (self-determination theory) 103
secondary desistance 3–5
SEEDS programme 46, 180, 193–214,
   243–58
   aim of 194–5, 246
   background to 193–4
   and compliance 208–9, 212–13
   and creating boundaries 253–7
   emotional labour 246, 248–58
   and empathy 248–53
   evaluation of 195
   findings of studies 199–213, *199–
      200*, *203*, 248–58
   methodologies 196–9, 247–8
   and policy transfer 210–11
   popularity of in Romania 209–10
   positive aspects of 199–201
   practitioners' views of 198–9
   problems with 201–2
   studies of 195–6, 247
   study sites 196
   supervisees' views of 204–8, 212
   and working together 202–4, *203*
self-determination theory (SDT) 103
self-disclosure *165*, 252–3, 275–6
Sellars, J. 279
Sentencing Guidelines (England &
   Wales) 406
Serin, R. 105

third sector organisations, and
Transforming Rehabilitation 70–3
Tombs, J. 410
training *see* staff development; staff
development models
Transforming Rehabilitation and
constructive practice 57–74
aim of study 58
artistic or technical 59–64
collaborative or instrumental 70–3
and competition 69, 70, 422
concerns about reforms 59, 60–4,
65–6, 67–8, 69, 70–1
constructive practice definition 57,
59
and contractual culture 68–9, 72–3
creative or procedural 64–70
findings of study 59–73
future legacy of 73–4
methodology 58–9
and organisational restructuring 65–6
Payment by Results (PbR) 72–3
and privatisation 50, 62–3, 422
and splitting of the Probation Trust
61–3
Trotter, C. 28, 45, 106, *107*, 132, 171,
246, 273, 354
Truax, C.B. 18
Trump, Donald 51
trust, creating 142–3, *145*
Turley, C. 202
Turner, C.W. 354

U

Ugwudike, P. 4, 212, 245
Ulmer, J.T. 80
understanding, demonstrating 142,
145, 147, 165
see also empathy
United Nations Office on Drugs and
Crime 337
USA
Cambridge Somerville Youth Study
40
EPICS 180, 181, 230–3, *236–7*,
236–8
and post-truth politics 51
Proactive Community Supervision
(PCS) 222–5
and social work evaluations 41
STARR programme 27, 30, 46,
180–1, 228–30, 236–8, *236–7*
see also organisational contexts and
evidence-based reforms
User Voice 338

V

Vanstone, M. 21, 27, 64, 140
Vogelvang, B. 29–30
voluntary organisations, and
Transforming Rehabilitation 70–3

W

Wales *see* Black, Asian and minority
ethnic people (BAME); staff
development; Transforming
Rehabilitation and constructive
practice; women offenders; youth
justice, use of evidence-based skills
Walsh, J. 105
Walters, S. 278
Wanamaker, K. 186–7
Ward, T. 102, 386
Warr, M. 158
Weld, N. 272–3, 275
White, A. 58
Whitehead, P. 19, 20–1, 30
Whitehead, S 399
Whyte, B. 158
Wilkins, L.T. 42
Williams, P. 381, 383, 384, 385, 388
women offenders 397–413, 430
challenges of therapeutic approach
408–12
Community Justice Courts 397–9
findings of study 401–13
methodology 399–401, *402–4*
and operational considerations 401,
404–6
and RNR model 105
and sentencing principles 406–8,
410, 412
and STICS 186–7
the study 398–9
Wong, P. 279
Wonnacott, J. 266
Wootton, B. 41
Work Programme 73
working alliances 129–30, 132–3,
138–47
skills of 138–43, *144–5, 147*
Wormith, J.S. 106
Worrall, A. 58, 59
Wright, W. 383, 384, 388

Y

Young, Baroness 382–3
Young Review 376